Philad<sup></sup> Dec<sup>r</sup>: 13. 1753

...ved your fav<sup>d</sup>. of the 5<sup>th</sup> Inst<sup>t</sup>.
...our kind Congratulations .
...e time since, and sent you
...bound Books; the Parcel was
...Care of M<sup>r</sup> Theyvesandt at
...don it is not yet got to hand.
...Truth give you a good Acc<sup>t</sup>
...cellent Pieces of yours; but where.
...had, the best Work comes to the
...wish the enclos'd were better
...me. — I know nothing
...mention having never seen

# The Founding Fathers

B. FRANKLIN L.L.D. F.R.S. PRESIDENT OF PENNSYLVANIA, & LATE MINISTER OF THE UNITED STATES OF AMERICA AT THE COURT OF FRANCE. HIS EXCELLENCY

C.W. Peale pinxit et Fecit 1787

*The Founding Fathers*

# BENJAMIN FRANKLIN

*A Biography in His Own Words*

Edited by
THOMAS FLEMING

With an Introduction by
WHITFIELD J. BELL, Jr.
Librarian, American Philosophical Society

JOAN PATERSON KERR
Picture Editor

Published by NEWSWEEK, New York
Distributed by HARPER & ROW, PUBLISHERS, INC.

*Benjamin Franklin, A Biography in His Own Words,*
has been produced by the Newsweek Book Division:

Joseph L. Gardner, Editor

Janet Czarnetzki, Art Director

S. Arthur Dembner, Publisher

This book is based on Volumes 1-15 of *The Papers of Benjamin Franklin,*
edited by Leonard W. Labaree (Vols. 1-14) and William B. Willcox (Vol. 15)
and published by Yale University Press.
The texts of documents to be published in forthcoming volumes
of this edition have been supplied by Mr. Willcox, and permission to reproduce
exerpts from these documents has been obtained from their owners.

For information address Harper & Row, Publishers, Inc.,
10 East 53rd Street, New York, N.Y. 10022.
Published simultaneously in Canada by Fitzhenry & Whiteside Limited, Toronto.

ISBN: 06-011286-7
Library of Congress Catalog Card Number 72-75999
Copyright © 1972 by Newsweek, Inc.
ENDPAPERS: FRANKLIN TO SAMUEL JOHNSON, DEC. 13, 1753; PRIVATE COLLECTION

# Contents

# Introduction

*by Whitfield J. Bell, Jr.*
*Librarian, American Philosophical Society*

In a memorable passage in his famous *Autobiography* Benjamin Franklin tells how he learned to write good English prose. With only two years of formal schooling, he read every book he could find, including works of polemic divinity from his father's collection. An odd volume of *The Spectator* falling into his hands, he was so delighted with it that he took its style for a model. He would outline the major points, then rewrite the essay from the outline; mix up the heads of topics and then reorganize them and compose the essay afresh; and at every stage compare his version with the original. To improve his vocabulary, Franklin tried his hand at ballad-making, cast prose into verse and verse into prose. "Extreamly ambitious" to become "a tolerable English writer," he took every opportunity to practice the art. His surviving commonplace book and drafts of other writings show how carefully he composed even personal letters and routine business correspondence. He was determined that everything he wrote should meet his standards—that it be smooth, clear, and short; in other words, agreeable to the ear, understanding, and patience. That he succeeded in his aim many readers gladly testified. "America has sent us many good things," the Scottish historian and philosopher David Hume told him, "Gold, Silver, Sugar, Tobacco, Indigo, &c.: but you are the first Philosopher, and indeed the first Great Man of Letters for whom we are beholden to her."

From the time when—as a sixteen-year-old apprentice—he had slipped the first Silence Dogood essay under his brother's printing office door, Franklin's skill with a pen was generally recognized. Most of the clubs, societies, and other bodies to which he belonged made him their secretary (and his willingness to discharge the secretary's duties was one of the reasons those groups succeeded). He drafted letters and petitions, wrote notices for the papers, composed bylaws and histories, and was called on for memorial and ceremonial inscriptions. For the Pennsylvania Hospital, for example, Franklin drafted the original petition to the Assembly, the managers' memorial to the Proprietors, the hospital's appeal to the public for financial support, and the regulations for the election of officers. He wrote the managers' business letters, prepared *Some Account of the Pennsylvania Hospital* in 1754, and when the cornerstone of the first building was ready to be laid, he composed the inscription. Not only did he serve the hospital, the American Philosophical Society, the fire company, and the Masonic lodge as author and editor, but he filled the same role in the Pennsylvania Assembly and the First Continental Congress, and as Minister to France—wherever precise thought, logical argument, and a persuasive tone were especially required. "Prose writing has been of great use to me in the course of my life," he reflected, "and was a principal means of my advancement."

As author and publisher, Franklin addressed his writings to the general public. He wrote to inform, instruct, persuade, or entertain, not to gratify himself. But even his personal letters and private literary exercises won him public recognition and fame. His sister-in-law showed around a letter of condolence he wrote her ("a man is not completely born until he be dead: Why then should we grieve that a new child is born among the immortals?"); friends asked for copies; and thus, passing from hand to hand, the letter gave solace and comfort to many beyond the family circle. A similar reputation was earned by a letter Franklin wrote to an officious clergyman whom he had helped cure in an illness, and who undertook to warn his benefactor against taking pride in his achievement. Franklin reminded the clergyman that "real good Works, Works of Kindness, Charity, Mercy, and Publick Spirit" were a more acceptable Christian service than "Holiday-keeping, Sermon-Reading...or making long Prayers, fill'd with Flatteries and Compliments." The epitaph (page 129) Franklin composed for himself in some Junto exercise also achieved popular fame during his lifetime: it was printed and re-printed, and friends sometimes asked for a copy, which he would write out from memory.

Inevitably, selected letters and papers were collected and published during Franklin's lifetime. His reports of electrical experiments sent to Peter Collinson in London were given by Collinson to a printer; and as Franklin made new experiments, they were published as supplements to the original printing. In 1769, when Franklin was in London as the agent for Pennsylvania, a quarto volume of 496 pages was published, which included both the electrical papers and others of a "philosophical" nature and many of general interest. This edition was revised and enlarged five years later. The Continent was no less eager to read Franklin's writings, especially France, where he already had eager admirers and disciples. One of these, the *philosophe* Barbeu Dubourg in 1773 brought out a French translation of the 1769 edition, with the addition of letters Franklin had sent French savants. Not even the American Revolution put a stop to the growing demand. Franklin assisted his young Whig friend Benjamin Vaughan to publish a volume of his *Political, Miscellaneous and Philosophical Pieces* (London, 1779); and Charles Dilly, the London bookseller, in 1787 issued still another collection of letters and papers. None of these volumes, however, nor all of them together, contained more than a fraction of Franklin's writings—and by 1787 he was generally known to be composing an autobiography, which none of his editors had yet seen. But America's patriarch died in 1790 before the book could be either completed or published.

Franklin bequeathed his books and papers to his grandson William Temple Franklin. Temple divided his inheritance, depositing the bulk of it—including thousands of letters to Franklin—in the care of his friend Dr. George Fox of Champlost near Philadelphia, but taking some three thousand letters and papers to London in 1791. From all sides Temple Franklin was called on promptly to publish a comprehensive edition of his grandfather's writings; but Temple proved to be, in the words of a later Franklin scholar, "a slow coach." More than a quarter of a century passed before his *Memoirs of the Life and Writings of Benjamin Franklin* in three volumes appeared in London in 1817–18.

The manuscripts that Dr. Fox received from Temple descended to his son, Charles Pemberton Fox, who eventually stored them in the stable at Champlost—

from which, from time to time, he extracted samples to give his house guests. In 1831 Professor Jared Sparks of Harvard, in Philadelphia to collect materials for his *Writings of George Washington* and other studies of the Revolutionary period, was conducted to the Champlost stable. Fox allowed Sparks to include many of the letters in his ten-volume *Works of Benjamin Franklin,* which appeared in 1836–40. In the latter year, at Sparks's suggestion, Fox gave the entire collection to the American Philosophical Society.

Among the manuscripts that Temple inherited was an autograph draft of his grandfather's *Autobiography.* Begun in 1771—in the form of a long letter to his son William—then laid aside, it was in Franklin's library when the British occupied Philadelphia in 1777 and requisitioned the house of the archrebel for officers' quarters. In the confusion of the time, the manuscript was thrown out, but rescued from the street by sheerest chance—an old friend of Franklin's saw it lying in a gutter, recognized the handwriting, picked it up, and later returned it to the author. Encouraged by friends who read the manuscript, Franklin resumed writing at Passy in 1784, where he showed portions of it to his French friends, among them M. Le Veillard, mayor of the village. In 1789, in response to his friend's request, Franklin sent Le Veillard a clean copy of the *Autobiography;* he retained the original, on which he continued to work in Philadelphia until within a few months of his death. It took the story forward only as far as Franklin's first mission to England in 1757.

One of Temple Franklin's first acts, after he received his grandfather's legacy, was to ask Le Veillard for the clean copy of the *Autobiography,* in exchange for Franklin's original. Thus, Temple Franklin obtained a fair copy suitable for the printer, while Le Veillard received the working draft of the manuscript with Franklin's last additions and revisions. In 1791 a French translation of Franklin's memoirs appeared, and this was promptly translated into English. At the same time there was published in London, in 1793, a small volume entitled *Works of the late Dr. Benjamin Franklin...together with Essays Humorous, Moral & Literary.* Comprising the *Autobiography,* some letters, bagatelles, and other popular pieces, this work was issued in one edition after another in England, on the Continent, and in America for almost a century after Franklin's death. It fashioned the popular image of Franklin much as Parson Weems's *Life* molded that of Washington; and, like Weems's book, it had a lasting effect on the national character.

The manuscript *Autobiography* that Le Veillard received survived the vicissitudes of the French Revolution, in which Le Veillard was guillotined, and descended to his daughter and her family. Although never willfully concealed, its existence was barely known, and it was almost never seen by any outsider. Not until 1866 was it located and examined. John Bigelow, United States Minister to France, bought the manuscript and in 1868 published for the first time a complete and accurate version of Franklin's own manuscript of the *Autobiography.* This publication, like James Parton's exhaustive *Life and Times of Benjamin Franklin,* published four years earlier, awakened wide popular and scholarly interest in the man.

After his volumes were published, Temple Franklin abandoned the manuscripts he had carried to London, for they were no longer of interest or value to him. About 1840, seventeen years after Temple's death, they were discovered in a London tailor's shop—Temple had lived upstairs, and the tailor, incredibly, had used the papers as patterns for garments he was cutting. They were acquired by "an officer under government," who offered them without success to the British Museum, the British Foreign Office, and several American ministers, until at last the Yankee bookseller in London Henry Stevens of Vermont purchased them in 1851.

In the characteristic spirit of many scholarly booksellers, Stevens made grand plans for the manuscripts, but he was also in debt. He pledged the Franklin papers as collateral, and they disappeared from public sight into a bank vault for nearly thirty years until at last in 1881, after anxious negotiations, they were bought by the United States Government and lodged in the Department of State in Washington. John Bigelow, whose interest in Franklin was unabated after his initial coup of finding the manuscript *Autobiography*, undertook a new edition of Franklin's writings, incorporating material newly acquired in London. The work appeared in ten volumes in 1887–88.

The bicentennial of Franklin's birth in 1906 provided the occasion for yet another edition of Franklin's writings. Albert Henry Smyth, professor of English in Philadelphia's Central High School and the author of several scholarly works on early American literature, undertook the task. Not only could he draw on the great collections of the American Philosophical Society and the Department of State, but, unlike his predecessors, he obtained copies of Franklin's letters in the French Foreign Office and in the possession of descendants and private collectors in the United States, England, and France. The Smyth edition, augmented by I. Minis Hays's *Calendar of the Papers of Benjamin Franklin in the Library of the American Philosophical Society* (1908), was the principal source of authoritative information on Franklin for half a century thereafter.

By 1950, however, the limitations of the Smyth edition and of Hays's *Calendar* were generally recognized. Smyth's volumes contained but a fraction of what was available even in 1906, and Hays's *Calendar* was out of date: in the 1930's and 1940's the American Philosophical Society had acquired several large collections of Franklin's letters. Furthermore, scholars now believed that any edition of collected writings should include letters and papers addressed to the subject. To print only the subject's letters, someone has said, is like listening to one side of a telephone conversation. Besides all this, the existing editions had done little to explicate the text by way of annotation. Clearly what was needed was a new edition of Franklin that should be truly comprehensive and adequately annotated and that should fully meet the canons of twentieth-century scholarship.

That such a scheme was feasible was triumphantly demonstrated in 1950 when the first volume of *The Papers of Thomas Jefferson*, edited by Julian P. Boyd, was published by the Princeton University Press. The Jefferson *Papers* combined financial support, the cooperative efforts of a team of scholars, and modern technology—notably cheap photoduplication—in an imaginative and effective way. In the ensuing few years several scholars privately urged that Franklin's writings should also be published; and Dr. William E. Lingelbach, Librarian of the American Philosophical Society, began to sound out his colleagues and several Franklin scholars on the subject. Before the Society reached a decision, however, there was movement from another quarter.

In the summer of 1952, Bromwell Ault, an alumnus of Yale University, suggested to President A. Whitney Griswold that Yale should undertake an edition like Princeton's Jefferson *Papers.* The proposal was reasonable because Yale had owned since 1936 the magnificent Franklin collection assembled by William Smith Mason—unexcelled in printed works by and about Franklin. From Time Inc., through Henry R. Luce, another Yale alumnus, assurance was obtained of a substantial gift to underwrite the costs. The result was that the two institutions, the American Philosophical Society and Yale, agreed to publish a comprehensive edition of Franklin's writings under their joint auspices. The decision was announced on the anniversary of Franklin's birth in 1954. Meanwhile, Leonard W. Labaree, Farnham professor of history at Yale, had been appointed editor of the new project. During the late winter and spring of 1954 he assembled his staff, and by September of that year work was under way.

The first major task of the new Franklin editors was to locate and copy Franklin's letters in all the places where they were preserved. The American Philosophical Society, the Library of Congress (to which the Department of State's collection had been moved), the Historical Society of Pennsylvania, the University of Pennsylvania, Yale University, and a dozen more institutions accounted for about 85 per cent of the surviving papers; to obtain photocopies of their holdings was not difficult. But the remaining 10 to 15 per cent—some three thousand documents—were, as the search revealed, owned by more than three hundred institutions and private persons. These letters were in one sense the most important, because many were not easily available to scholars and most in fact had never been printed anywhere. In person and by written inquiries the editors searched systematically through libraries and archives where Franklin letters might be expected to be. The Pennsylvania Hospital, which Franklin founded and fostered; the archives of the Pennsylvania Society for Promoting the Abolition of Slavery, which he headed; the Royal Society of London, of which he was a fellow; the Library Company of Philadelphia, which he founded; the Associates of the Late Reverend Dr. Bray, to whom he provided data on the education of Negro children, all yielded manuscripts. Still others were found in such unlikely places as Windsor Castle, the Karl Marx University of Leipzig, and a resort hotel in northern Pennsylvania (which had framed a Franklin letter as a room decoration).

The editors sought out descendants of Franklin—several dozen, although none bore the name of Franklin—who received them cordially, as their parents and grandparents had received Smyth and Sparks, and came away with copies of warmly treasured letters, some of a moving, personal kind. Every owner of a set of autographs of the signers of the Declaration of Independence was solicited for a copy of his Franklin document; and scores of other private collectors were no less willing to cooperate. Perhaps the most unexpected discovery was that of some 150 letters that passed between Franklin, Mrs. Margaret Stevenson, his London landlady, and her daughter Polly, which were owned by descendants of the latter, not twenty minutes from the library of the American Philosophical Society in Philadelphia. All in all, Labaree and his colleagues located and copied some 30,000 manuscripts written by or to Franklin; they represented correspondence with some 4,200 different persons.

When the task of locating was nearly completed—it can never be entirely completed—that of editing began. By checking transcriptions, copy, and proof at every stage against the photocopies, the editors assured a high standard of accuracy; while in their editing they aimed to present Franklin fully and accurately, as his contemporaries saw him. For their annotations, the editors used all the standard works of reference to identify persons and allusions in the text—the dictionaries of national biography, the *Pennsylvania Archives*, for example—and called on some unconventional means as well. Faced with four dated and undated letters from Franklin to his brother John about the latter's bladder complaint, they consulted a urologist, who unhesitatingly diagnosed brother John's trouble and, on the basis of the symptoms described, placed the letters in correct chronological order.

The Benjamin Franklin who has emerged from the volumes thus far published in the new series by the Yale University Press is not remarkably different from the one known through the pages of Temple Franklin, Sparks, Bigelow, and Smyth. Familiar episodes are only drawn in greater detail, and the familiar figure emerges in sharper outline. *The Papers of Benjamin Franklin* have pulled together the story of many single episodes in Franklin's career from many different sources—on American prisoners of war in the Revolution, for example, from the Library of Congress and the American Philosophical Society, the National Maritime Museum at Greenwich, the Public Record Office in London, the Berkshire Record Office in Reading, and the National Library of Scotland. How deeply Franklin was involved in the work of Negro education—to take another example—had not been generally known before; yet no reader is surprised to learn that he was concerned in the matter: this is what one would expect of the man Americans have always known and long admired.

From the published volumes of *The Papers of Benjamin Franklin* and from the much greater mass of papers remaining to be edited, Thomas Fleming has selected and extracted materials for this biography. These selections, explained and annotated by the editor, present Benjamin Franklin largely in his own words. They show him in the many facets of his busy life, public and private; they reveal him in his intense commitment and in his wise reasonableness, moderation, and unfailing good humor.

## EDITORIAL NOTE

Most of the Franklin writings reprinted in this biography have been excerpted from the longer original documents being published in their entirety by Yale University Press. Omissions at the beginning or ending of a document are indicated only if the extract begins or ends in the middle of a sentence; however, omissions within a quoted passage are indicated by ellipses. The original spellings in all cases have been retained; editorial insertions are set within square brackets.

# Chronology of Franklin and His Times

| | | |
|---|---|---|
| Benjamin Franklin born in Boston, January 17 (January 6, Old Style) | 1706 | |
| | 1713 | Treaty of Utrecht ends War of Spanish Succession |
| | 1714 | Reign of George I of England, 1714–27 |
| Apprenticed to brother James | 1718 | |
| First issue of *The New-England Courant* | 1721 | Robert Walpole, British Prime Minister, 1721–42 |
| Silence Dogood letters published | 1722 | |
| Leaves Boston for Philadelphia | 1723 | |
| Sails for England with James Ralph | 1724 | |
| Returns to America | 1726 | |
| Junto organized | 1727 | George II, King of England, 1727–60 |
| *The Pennsylvania Gazette* begins publication | 1729 | |
| Takes Deborah Read as wife, September 1 | 1730 | |
| Library Company of Philadelphia founded; son William Franklin born (?) | 1731 | |
| Compiles first edition of *Poor Richard*; birth of son Francis Folger Franklin | 1732 | |
| | 1733 | Molasses Act; founding of Colony of Georgia |
| | 1735 | John Peter Zenger tried for libel |
| Union Fire Company formed; death of Francis Folger Franklin | 1736 | |
| | 1739 | War of Jenkins' Ear, 1739–42 |
| | 1740 | War of the Austrian Succession, 1740–48 |
| Daughter Sarah Franklin born; American Philosophical Society founded | 1743 | King George's War, American phase of hostilities, 1743–48 |
| "The Speech of Miss Polly Baker" printed; begins experiments with electricity | 1747 | |
| Founds Pennsylvania Hospital; elected to Assembly | 1751 | |
| Experiments with kite during thunderstorm | 1752 | |
| Academy of Philadelphia chartered; description of lightning rod; named joint Deputy Postmaster General with William Hunter of Virginia | 1753 | French expedition sent to occupy Ohio |
| Presents Plan of Union at Albany Congress | 1754 | Americans defeated at Fort Necessity in first action of French and Indian War, 1754–63 |
| Rising dispute between Penns and Quakers | 1755 | Braddock's campaign |
| Leads Philadelphia volunteers to western Pennsylvania; elected to Royal Society | 1756 | Seven Years' War in Europe, 1756–63 |
| Sails to England to negotiate with Proprietors | 1757 | Coalition ministry of Newcastle and Pitt |
| Receives degree from St. Andrews; travels to north of England and Scotland | 1759 | Wolfe defeats Montcalm at Quebec |
| | 1760 | Reign of George III of England, 1760–1820 |
| | 1761 | Ministry of Lord Bute |
| Receives degree from Oxford; returns to America | 1762 | William Franklin named Governor of New Jersey |
| | 1763 | Pontiac's Uprising; march of Paxton Boys; Ministry of George Grenville, 1763–65 |

| | | |
|---|---|---|
| Militia bill; drafts petition for change in government; goes to London as agent for Pennsylvania | 1764 | Sugar Act; committees of correspondence formed to protest taxation without representation; nonimportation |
| | 1765 | Stamp Act; Rockingham ministry, 1765–66 |
| Testifies before House of Commons on Stamp Act | 1766 | Stamp Act repealed; Chatham ministry, 1766–67 |
| Visits France | 1767 | Townshend duties; revival of nonimportation; Grafton ministry, 1767–70 |
| Named agent for Georgia | 1768 | |
| Becomes agent for New Jersey | 1769 | |
| Elected agent for Massachusetts | 1770 | Boston Massacre; Townshend duties repealed; North Ministry, 1770–82 |
| Begins *Autobiography*; tours Ireland | 1771 | |
| Privy Council approves Grand Ohio Company; Hutchinson letters sent to Massachusetts | 1772 | Committees of correspondence reappear |
| Discloses part in publication of Hutchinson correspondence | 1773 | Tea Act passed; Boston Tea Party |
| Hearing before Privy Council; dismissed as postmaster; Deborah Franklin dies | 1774 | Punitive Acts; First Continental Congress; Galloway's plan of union; Louis XVI, King of France, 1774–92 |
| Returns to America; named to Second Continental Congress | 1775 | Battles of Lexington and Concord, Ticonderoga, and Bunker Hill |
| Signs Declaration of Independence; sails to France as commissioner to negotiate alliance | 1776 | British evacuate Boston; Americans retreat from Long Island and New York City; Battle of Trenton; Captain James Cook's third voyage to Pacific, 1776–79 |
| Meets Madame Brillon | 1777 | Battle of Saratoga; Congress agrees to Articles of Confederation |
| Treaties of alliance and commerce with France; arrival of John Adams | 1778 | Lord North's conciliation plan; British evacuate Philadelphia; John Paul Jones's raids in *Ranger* |
| Named minister to French court | 1779 | Spain declares war on Britain; John Jay named minister to Madrid; *Bonhomme Richard* defeats *Serapis* |
| Madame Helvetius rejects marriage | 1780 | Jones sails to America in *Ariel* |
| Offers resignation; appointed to peace commission | 1781 | John Laurens mission; Robert Morris named Superintendent of Finance; Battle of Yorktown |
| Preliminary articles of peace with Britain signed | 1782 | Rockingham ministry, March–July; Shelburne ministry, July–February, 1783 |
| Definitive treaty of peace proclaimed | 1783 | British evacuate New York City |
| | 1784 | John Jay named Secretary for Foreign Affairs |
| Returns to America; chosen President of Pennsylvania Executive Council | 1785 | Adams and Jefferson appointed ministers to Britain and France |
| | 1786 | Shays' Rebellion |
| Attends Constitutional Convention at Philadelphia | 1787 | |
| | 1788 | Constitution ratified; first Federal elections |
| President of Society for Promoting the Abolition of Slavery | 1789 | Washington and Adams inaugurated; first Federal Congress; beginning of French Revolution and institution of National Assembly, 1789–91 |
| Benjamin Franklin dies, April 17 | 1790 | Hamilton's First Report on Public Credit; Jefferson takes office as Secretary of State; Louis XVI accepts constitutional monarchy in France |

## Chapter 1

# Boston Boy

Benjamin Franklin was born on January 17, 1706, in Boston, Massachusetts. The little Colonial seaport on the edge of the British Empire was still struggling to emerge from the seventeenth century, with its religious obsessions and antagonisms. The Salem witch trials were only fourteen years in the past. Although the Church no longer dominated the State, ministers still wielded considerable secular influence, and a man's religious opinions were considered crucial to his standing in society. But business was already becoming at least as important in Boston's life. Some three hundred merchants and investors depended upon the fortunes of the city's fleet. Wharves, distilleries, and mansions were rising at a rapid rate. The population was edging toward ten thousand, and America's first newspaper, the *Newsletter*, had begun publishing in 1704. Boston was a bustling, growing place, with its own highly developed sense of identity. Unlike the other Founding Fathers, who as a group were rather reticent about their early lives, Franklin wrote a great deal about his boyhood in Boston. Most of these recollections are in his famous *Autobiography*, which he wrote in the form of a letter to his son William in the summer of 1771. After discussing the background of the Franklin family in England—they were small tradesmen with a special interest in blacksmithing in the Northamptonshire village of Ecton—Franklin described the father and mother he remembered from his Boston boyhood.

*Autobiography*, 1771

Josiah, my Father, married young, and carried his Wife with three Children unto New England, about 1682. The Conventicles having been forbidden by Law, and frequently disturbed, induced some considerable Men of his Acquaintance to remove to that Country, and he was prevail'd with to accompany them thither, where they expected to enjoy their Mode of Religion with Freedom. By the same Wife he had 4 Children more born there, and

*The Boston of Franklin's birth and boyhood, from a 1722 map*

15

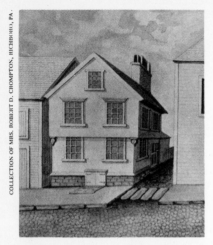

*This water color of the Franklin home on Milk Street is a copy of a sketch made on the spot before fire destroyed the house in 1810.*

by a second Wife ten more, in all 17, of which I remember 13 sitting at one time at his Table, who all grew up to be Men and Women, and married. I was the youngest Son and the youngest Child but two, and was born in Boston, N. England.

My mother the 2d Wife was Abiah Folger, a Daughter of Peter Folger, one of the first Settlers of New England, of whom honourable mention is made by Cotton Mather, in his Church History of that Country, (entitled Magnalia Christi Americana) as a *godly learned Englishman*, if I remember the words rightly. I have heard that he wrote sundry small occasional Pieces, but only one of them was printed which I saw now many Years since. It was written in 1675, in the homespun Verse of that Time and People, and address'd to those then concern'd in the Government there. It was in favour of Liberty of Conscience, and in behalf of the Baptists, Quakers, and other Sectaries, that had been under Persecution; ascribing the Indian Wars and other Distresses, that had befallen the Country to that Persecution, as so many Judgments of God, to punish so heinous an Offence; and exhorting a Repeal of those uncharitable Laws.

Franklin's only comment of his mother was that she had "an excellent Constitution. She suckled all her 10 Children." His father made a far deeper impression on him, as this description of Josiah Franklin reveals.

*Autobiography*, 1771

I think you may like to know Something of his Person and Character. He had an excellent Constitution of Body, was of middle Stature, but well set and very strong. He was ingenious, could draw prettily, was skill'd a little in Music and had a clear pleasing Voice, so that when he play'd Psalm Tunes on his Violin and sung withal as he sometimes did in an Evening after the Business of the Day was over, it was extreamly agreable to hear. He had a mechanical Genius too, and on occasion was very handy in the Use of other Tradesmen's Tools. But his great Excellence lay in a sound Understanding, and solid Judgment in prudential Matters, both in private and publick Affairs. In the latter indeed he was never employed, the numerous Family he had to educate and the straitness of his Circumstances, keeping him close to his Trade, but I remember well his being frequently visited by leading People, who consulted him for his Opinion in Affairs of the Town or of the Church he belong'd to and show'd a good deal of Respect for his Judgment and Advice. He was also much consulted by private Persons about their Affairs when any Difficulty occur'd, and frequently chosen an Arbitrator between contending Parties. At his Table he lik'd to have as often as he could, some sensible Friend or Neighbour, to converse with, and always took care to start some ingenious or useful Topic for Discourse, which might tend to improve the Minds of his Children. By this means he turn'd our Attention to what was good, just, and prudent in the Conduct of Life; and little or no Notice was ever taken of what related to the Victuals on the Table, whether it was well or ill drest, in or out of season, of good or bad flavour, preferable or inferior to this or that other thing of the kind; so that I was bro't up in such a perfect Inattention to those Matters as to be quite Indifferent what kind of Food was set before me.

Franklin learned very early about the need for a thick skin to cope with the rough give-and-take of life in a big family. It was an ideal preparation for the political combat of his later years. This recollection is from an essay he wrote in his old age, commonly known as "The Whistle." Typically, he drew a moral from the experience—most of life's troubles, he later decided, came from "giving too much for the whistle."

Passy [France], November 10 1779

*Illustration of "The Whistle" from Holley's* Life of Franklin

When I was a Child of 7 Years old, my Friends on a Holiday fill'd my little Pocket with Halfpence. I went directly to a Shop where they sold Toys for Children; and being charm'd with the Sound of a Whistle, that I met by the way, in the hands of another Boy, I voluntarily offer'd and gave all my Money for it. When I came home, whistling all over the House, much pleased with my Whistle, but disturbing all the Family, my Brothers, Sisters & Cousins, understanding the Bargain I had made, told me I had given four times as much for it as it was worth, put me in mind what good Things I might have bought with the rest of the Money, & laught at me so much for my Folly that I cry'd with Vexation; and the Reflection gave me more Chagrin than the Whistle gave me Pleasure.

Growing up in a seaport surrounded by water, with numerous ponds and bays, Franklin "learned early to swim well and to manage boats." In a letter to a French friend, Barbeu Dubourg, written in

1773, Franklin recalled some of his aquatic experiments, which foreshadowed, in both their ingenuity and their observation, the scientist of the future.

[London, February–March, 1773]

When a youth, I made two oval pallets, each about ten inches long, and six broad, with a hole for the thumb, in order to retain it fast in the palm of my hand. They much resembled a painter's pallets. In swimming I pushed the edges of these forward, and I struck the water with their flat surfaces as I drew them back. I remember I swam faster by means of these pallets, but they fatigued my wrists. I also fitted to the soles of my feet a kind of sandals, but I was not satisfied with them, because I observed that the stroke is partly given by the inside of the feet and the ancles, and not entirely with the soles of the feet....

I amused myself one day with flying a paper kite; and approaching the bank of a pond, which was near a mile broad, the weather being very warm, I tied the string to a stake, and the kite ascended to a very considerable height above the pond, while I was swimming. In a little time, being desirous of amusing myself with my kite, and enjoying at the same time the pleasure of swimming, I returned; and, loosing from the stake the string with the little stick which was fastened to it, I went again into the water, where I found that lying on my back and holding the stick in my hands, I was drawn along the surface of the water in a very agreeable manner. Having then engaged another boy to carry my clothes round the pond to a place which I pointed out to him on the other side, I began to cross the pond with my kite, which carried me quite over without the least fatigue, and with the greatest pleasure....

*The title page illustration in an 1852 book,* The Works of Benjamin Franklin, *shows the boy innovator swimming with the aid of a kite.*

In the eighteenth century, most sons of tradesmen had their futures decided for them by their fathers at an early age. A boy could learn a trade only by becoming an apprentice and toiling for many years at extremely low wages. At first, Josiah Franklin envisioned a different future for his son Benjamin. But he was also a realistic man.

*Autobiography,* 1771

My elder Brothers were all put Apprentices to different Trades. I was put to the Grammar School at Eight Years of Age, my Father intending to devote me as the Tithe of his Sons to the Service of the Church. My early Readiness in learning to read (which must have been very early, as I do not remember when I could not read) and the Opinion of all his Friends that I should certainly make a

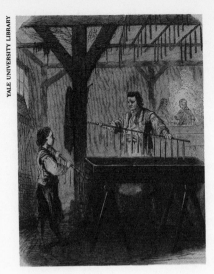

*A French engraving shows Franklin helping his father to make candles.*

good Scholar, encourag'd him in this Purpose of his. My Uncle Benjamin too approv'd of it, and propos'd to give me all his Shorthand Volumes of Sermons I suppose as a Stock to set up with, if I would learn his Character. I continu'd however at the Grammar School not quite one Year, tho' in that time I had risen gradually from the Middle of the Class of that Year to be the Head of it, and farther was remov'd into the next Class above it, in order to go with that into the third at the End of the Year. But my Father in the mean time, from a View of the Expence of a College Education which, having so large a Family, he could not well afford, and the mean Living many so educated were afterwards able to obtain, Reasons that he gave to his Friends in my Hearing, altered his first Intention, took me from the Grammar School, and sent me to a School for Writing and Arithmetic kept by a then famous Man, Mr. Geo. Brownell, very successful in his Profession generally, and that by mild encouraging Methods. Under him I acquired fair Writing pretty soon, but I fail'd in the Arithmetic, and made no Progress in it.

At Ten Years old, I was taken home to assist my Father in his Business, which was that of a Tallow Chandler and Sope-Boiler. A Business he was not bred to, but had assumed on his Arrival in New England and on finding his Dying Trade would not maintain his Family, being in little Request. Accordingly I was employed in cutting Wick for the Candles, filling the Dipping Mold, and the Molds for cast Candles, attending the Shop, going of Errands, &c. I dislik'd the Trade and had a strong Inclination for the Sea; but my Father declar'd against it. . . .

I continu'd thus employ'd in my Father's Business for two Years, that is till I was 12 Years old; and my Brother John, who was bred to that Business having left my Father, married and set up for himself at Rhodeisland, there was all Appearance that I was destin'd to supply his Place and be a Tallow Chandler. But my Dislike to the Trade continuing, my Father was under Apprehensions that if he did not find one for me more agreable, I should break away and get to Sea, as his Son Josiah had done to his great Vexation. He therefore sometimes took me to walk with him, and see Joiners, Bricklayers, Turners, Braziers, &c. at their Work, that he might observe my Inclination, and endeavour to fix it on some Trade or other on Land. . . .

19

From a Child I was fond of Reading, and all the little Money that came into my Hands was ever laid out in Books.... This Bookish Inclination at length determin'd my Father to make me a Printer, tho' he had already one Son, (James) of that Profession. In 1717 my Brother James return'd from England with a Press and Letters to set up his Business in Boston. I lik'd it much better than that of my Father, but still had a Hankering for the Sea. To prevent the apprehended Effect of such an Inclination, my Father was impatient to have me bound to my Brother. I stood out some time, but at last was persuaded and signed the Indentures, when I was yet but 12 Years old. I was to serve as an Apprentice till I was 21 Years of Age, only I was to be allow'd Journeyman's Wages during the last Year. In a little time I made great Proficiency in the Business, and became a useful Hand to my Brother.

The printer's apprentice was soon enjoying the greatest advantage of his trade. He had access to better books than the ones he had read at home, which consisted mostly of polemic works on religion. Inevitably this fondness for words led to Franklin's first experiments as a writer. In this passage he recalled the fate of those experiments, and then moved swiftly into a discussion of how he taught himself to write good prose. Unfortunately, no copies of his two ballads survive.

*Autobiography*, 1771

An Acquaintance with the Apprentices of Booksellers, enabled me sometimes to borrow a small one, which I was careful to return soon and clean. Often I sat up in my Room reading the greatest Part of the Night, when the Book was borrow'd in the Evening and to be return'd early in the Morning lest it should be miss'd or wanted. And after some time an ingenious Tradesman Mr. Matthew Adams who had a pretty Collection of Books, and who frequented our Printing House, took Notice of me, invited me to his Library, and very kindly lent me such Books as I chose to read. I now took a Fancy to Poetry, and made some little Pieces. My Brother, thinking it might turn to account encourag'd me, and put me on composing two occasional Ballads. One was called the *Light House Tragedy*, and contain'd an Account of the drowning of Capt. Worthilake with his Two Daughters; the other was a Sailor Song on the Taking of *Teach* or Blackbeard the Pirate. They were wretched Stuff, in the Grubstreet Ballad Stile, and when they were printed he sent me about the Town to sell them. The first sold wonderfully, the Event being recent, having made a great Noise. This flatter'd my Vanity. But my Father discourag'd me, by ridiculing my Performances, and telling me Verse-makers were generally Beggars; so I escap'd being a Poet, most probably a very bad one. But as Prose Writing has been of great Use to me in the Course of my Life, and was a principal Means of my Advancement, I shall tell you how in such a Situation I acquir'd what little Ability I have in that Way.

There was another Bookish Lad in the Town, John Collins by Name, with whom I was intimately acquainted. We sometimes disputed, and very fond we were of Argument, and very desirous of confuting one another. Which disputacious Turn, by the way, is apt to become a very bad Habit, making People often extreamly disagreable in Company, by the Contradiction that is necessary to bring it into Practice, and thence, besides souring and spoiling the Conversation, is productive of Disgusts and perhaps Enmities where you may have occasion for Friendship. I had caught it by reading my Father's Books of Dispute about Religion. Persons of good Sense, I have since observ'd, seldom fall into it, except Lawyers, University Men, and Men of all Sorts that have been bred at Edinborough. A Question was once some how or other started between Collins and me, of the Propriety of educating the Female Sex in Learning, and their Abilities for Study. He was of Opinion that it was improper; and that they were naturally unequal to it. I took the contrary Side, perhaps a little for Dispute sake. He was naturally more eloquent, had a ready Plenty of Words, and sometimes as I thought bore me down more by his Fluency than by the Strength of his Reasons. As we parted without settling the Point, and were not to see one another again for some time, I sat down to put my Arguments in Writing, which I copied fair and sent to him. He answer'd and I reply'd. Three or four Letters of a Side had pass'd, when my Father happen'd to find my Papers, and read them. Without entring into the Discussion, he took occasion to talk to me about the Manner of my Writing, observ'd that tho' I had the Advantage of my Antagonist in correct Spelling and pointing (which I ow'd to the Printing House) I fell far short in elegance of Expression, in Method and in Perspicuity, of which he convinc'd me by several In-

*An early* Life *of Franklin depicts him reading at night.*

21

stances. I saw the Justice of his Remarks, and thence grew more attentive to the *Manner* in Writing, and determin'd to endeavour at Improvement.

About this time I met with an odd Volume of the Spectator. It was the third. I had never before seen any of them. I bought it, read it over and over, and was much delighted with it. I thought the Writing excellent, and wish'd if possible to imitate it. With that View, I took some of the Papers, and making short Hints of the Sentiment in each Sentence, laid them by a few Days, and then without looking at the Book, try'd to compleat the Papers again, by expressing each hinted Sentiment at length and as fully as it had been express'd before, in any suitable Words, that should come to hand.

Then I compar'd my Spectator with the Original, discover'd some of my Faults and corrected them. But I found I wanted a Stock of Words or a Readiness in recollecting and using them, which I thought I should have acquir'd before that time, if I had gone on making Verses, since the continual Occasion for Words of the same Import but of different Length, to suit the Measure, or of different Sound for the Rhyme, would have laid me under a constant Necessity of searching for Variety, and also have tended to fix that Variety in my Mind, and make me Master of it. Therefore I took some of the Tales and turn'd them into Verse: And after a time, when I had pretty well forgotten the Prose, turn'd them back again. I also sometimes jumbled my Collections of Hints into Confusion, and after some Weeks, endeavour'd to reduce them into the best Order, before I began to form the full Sentences, and compleat the Paper. This was to teach me Method in the Arrangement of Thoughts. By comparing my work afterwards with the original, I discover'd many faults and amended them; but I sometimes had the Pleasure of Fancying that in certain Particulars of small Import, I had been lucky enough to improve the Method or the Language and this encourag'd me to think I might possibly in time come to be a tolerable English Writer, of which I was extreamly ambitious.

Franklin also applied his ingenuity to his daily life. He needed more time to read books and practice his exercises in prose style. He gained some time by "evading as much as I could the common Attendance on publick Worship." And he found additional time by reforming his diet.

*Autobiography,* 1771

When about 16 Years of Age, I happen'd to meet with a Book, written by one Tryon, recommending a Vegetable Diet. I determined to go into it. My Brother being yet unmarried, did not keep House, but boarded himself and his Apprentices in another Family. My refusing to eat Flesh occasioned an Inconveniency, and I was frequently chid for my singularity. I made my self acquainted with Tryon's Manner of preparing some of his Dishes, such as Boiling Potatoes or Rice, making Hasty Pudding, and a few others, and then propos'd to my Brother, that if he would give me Weekly half the Money he paid for my Board I would board my self. He instantly agreed to it, and I presently found that I could save half what he paid me. This was an additional Fund for buying Books: But I had another Advantage in it. My Brother and the rest going from the Printing House to their Meals, I remain'd there alone, and dispatching presently my light Repast, (which often was no more than a Bisket or a Slice of Bread, a Handful of Raisins or a Tart from the Pastry Cook's, and a Glass of Water) had the rest of the Time till their Return, for Study, in which I made the greater Progress from that greater Clearness of Head and quicker Apprehension which usually attend Temperance in Eating and Drinking.

Three years after Benjamin Franklin went to work as an apprentice printer, James Franklin brought out the first issue of *The New-England Courant.* Young Benjamin recalled how "after having work'd in composing the Types and printing off the Sheets I was employ'd to carry the Papers thro' the Streets to the Customers." But the younger Franklin was not satisfied with this laborious side of the newspaper business. He yearned to see some of his own writing in the paper. In this passage from his *Autobiography,* he explained why he felt this way and the method he used to satisfy his desire.

*Autobiography,* 1771

He had some ingenious Men among his Friends who amus'd themselves by writing little Pieces for this Paper, which gain'd it Credit, and made it more in Demand; and these Gentlemen often visited us. Hearing their Conversations, and their Accounts of the Approbation their Papers were receiv'd with, I was excited to try my Hand among them. But being still a Boy, and suspecting that my Brother would object to printing any Thing of mine in his Paper if he knew it to be mine, I contriv'd to disguise my Hand, and writing an anonymous Paper I put it in at Night under the Door of the Printing House. It was found in the Morning and communicated to his Writing Friends when they call'd in as usual. They read it, commented on it in my Hearing, and I had the exquisite Pleasure, of finding it met with their Approbation, and that in their different Guesses at the Author none were named but Men of some Character among us for Learning and Ingenuity.

Young Benjamin signed his contribution to the paper "Silence Dogood," and then proceeded to create a character to go with the name. Silence described herself as the widow of a country minister, who was "an Enemy to Vice, and a Friend to Vertue. . . . A hearty Lover of the Clergy and all good Men, and a mortal Enemy to arbitrary Government and unlimited Power." She also admitted she had "a natural Inclination to observe and reprove the Faults of others, at which I have an excellent Faculty." Fourteen letters over the signature of Silence came from the sixteen-year-old Franklin's pen between April and October of 1722. Perhaps the best of them was the fourth, in which the apprentice printer took revenge for being denied a college education.

Boston, May 14, 1722

Discoursing the other Day at Dinner with my Reverend Boarder, formerly mention'd, (whom for Distinction sake we will call by the name of Clericus,) concerning the Education of Children, I ask'd his Advice about my young Son William, whether or no I had best bestow upon him Academical Learning, or (as our Phrase is) *bring him up at our College*: He perswaded me to do it by all Means, using many weighty Arguments with me, and answering all the Objections that I could form against it; telling me withal, that he did not doubt but that the Lad would take his Learning very well, and not idle away his Time as too many there now-a-days do. These Words of Clericus gave me a Curiosity to inquire a little more strictly into the present Circumstances of that famous Seminary of Learning; but the Information which he gave me, was neither pleasant, nor such as I expected.

As soon as Dinner was over, I took a solitary Walk into my Orchard, still ruminating on Clericus's Discourse with much Consideration, until I came to my usual Place of Retirement under the *Great Apple-Tree*; where having seated my self, and carelessly laid my Head on a verdant Bank, I fell by Degrees into a soft and undisturbed

A *wood engraving from* Pictorial Life of Benjamin Franklin, *1846, shows Franklin as a printer.*

Slumber. My waking Thoughts remained with me in my Sleep, and before I awak'd again, I dreamt the following DREAM.

I fancy'd I was travelling over pleasant and delightful Fields and Meadows, and thro' many small Country Towns and Villages; and as I pass'd along, all Places resounded with the Fame of the Temple of LEARNING: Every Peasant, who had wherewithal, was preparing to send one of his Children at least to this famous Place; and in this Case most of them consulted their own Purses instead of their Childrens Capacities: So that I observed, a great many, yea, the most part of those who were travelling thither, were little better than Dunces and Blockheads. Alas! alas!

At length I entred upon a spacious Plain, in the Midst of which was erected a large and stately Edifice: It was to this that a great Company of Youths from all Parts of the Country were going; so stepping in among the Crowd, I passed on with them, and presently arrived at the Gate.

The Passage was kept by two sturdy Porters named *Riches* and *Poverty,* and the latter obstinately refused to give Entrance to any who had not first gain'd the Favour of the former; so that I observed many who came even to the very Gate, were obliged to travel back again as ignorant as they came, for want of this necessary Qualification. However, as a Spectator I gain'd Admittance, and with the rest entred directly into the Temple.

In the Middle of the great Hall stood a stately and magnificent Throne, which was ascended to by two high and difficult Steps. On the Top of it sat LEARNING in awful State; she was apparelled wholly in Black, and surrounded almost on every Side with innumerable Volumes in all Languages. She seem'd very busily employ'd in writing something on half a Sheet of Paper, and upon Enquiry, I understood she was preparing a Paper, call'd *The New-England Courant.* On her Right Hand sat *English,* with a pleasant smiling Countenance, and handsomely attir'd; and on her left were seated several *Antique Figures* with their Faces vail'd. I was considerably puzzl'd to guess who they were, until one informed me, (who stood beside me,) that those Figures on her left Hand were *Latin, Greek, Hebrew,* &c. and that they were very much reserv'd, and seldom or never unvail'd their Faces here, and then to few or none, tho'

*The lower right-hand column of this
1722 issue of* The New-England
Courant *bears Franklin's signature
above the first appearance of
an article signed "Silence Dogood."*

most of those who have in this Place acquir'd so much
Learning as to distinguish them from *English*, pretended
to an intimate Acquaintance with them. I then enquir'd
of him, what could be the Reason why they continued
vail'd, in this Place especially: He pointed to the Foot
of the Throne, where I saw *Idleness,* attended with
*Ignorance*, and these (he informed me) were they, who
first vail'd them, and still kept them so.

Now I observed, that the whole Tribe who entred into
the Temple with me, began to climb the Throne; but
the Work proving troublesome and difficult to most of
them, they withdrew their Hands from the Plow, and
contented themselves to sit at the Foot, with Madam
*Idleness* and her Maid *Ignorance*, until those who were
assisted by Diligence and a docible Temper, had well
nigh got up the first Step: But the Time drawing nigh
in which they could no way avoid ascending, they were
fain to crave the Assistance of those who had got up
before them, and who, for the Reward perhaps of a
*Pint of Milk*, or a *Piece of Plumb-Cake*, lent the Lubbers
a helping Hand, and sat them in the Eye of the World,
upon a Level with themselves.

The other Step being in the same Manner ascended,
and the usual Ceremonies at an End, every Beetle-
Scull seem'd well satisfy'd with his own Portion of
Learning, tho' perhaps he was *e'en just* as ignorant as
ever. And now the Time of their Departure being come,
they march'd out of Doors to make Room for another
Company, who waited for Entrance: And I, having seen
all that was to be seen, quitted the Hall likewise, and
went to make my Observations on those who were just
gone out before me.

Some I perceiv'd took to Merchandizing, others to
Travelling, some to one Thing, some to another, and some
to Nothing; and many of them from henceforth, for want
of Patrimony, liv'd as poor as Church Mice, being unable to dig, and asham'd to beg, and to live by their
Wits it was impossible. But the most Part of the Crowd
went along a large beaten Path, which led to a Temple
at the further End of the Plain, call'd, *The Temple of
Theology.* The Business of those who were employ'd in
this Temple being laborious and painful, I wonder'd
exceedingly to see so many go towards it; but while I
was pondering this Matter in my Mind, I spy'd *Pecunia*

behind a Curtain, beckoning to them with her Hand, which Sight immediately satisfy'd me for whose Sake it was, that a great Part of them (I will not say all) travel'd that Road. In this Temple I saw nothing worth mentioning, except the ambitious and fraudulent Contrivances of Plagius, who (notwithstanding he had been severely reprehended for such Practices before) was diligently transcribing some eloquent Paragraphs out of Tillotson's *Works*, &c., to embellish his own.

Now I bethought my self in my Sleep, that it was Time to be at Home, and as I fancy'd I was travelling back thither, I reflected in my Mind on the extream Folly of those Parents, who, blind to their Childrens Dulness, and insensible of the Solidity of their Skulls, because they think their Purses can afford it, will needs send them to the Temple of Learning, where, for want of a suitable Genius, they learn little more than how to carry themselves handsomely, and enter a Room genteely, (which might as well be acquir'd at a Dancing-School,) and from whence they return, after Abundance of Trouble and Charge, as great Blockheads as ever, only more proud and self-conceited.

While I was in the midst of these unpleasant Reflections, Clericus (who with a Book in his Hand was walking under the Trees) accidentally awak'd me; to him I related my Dream with all its Particulars, and he, without much Study, presently interpreted it, assuring me, *That it was a lively Representation of* HARVARD COLLEGE, *Etcetera.* I remain, Sir, Your Humble Servant,

SILENCE DOGOOD

The success of Silence Dogood had an unhappy effect on Franklin's relationship with his brother when the secret of the authorship was at last revealed. James Franklin felt that the attention his friends paid to Benjamin made him "too vain," and this soon led to more serious differences.

*Autobiography,* 1771

Tho' a Brother, he considered himself as my Master, and me as his Apprentice; and accordingly expected the same Services from me as he would from another; while I thought he demean'd me too much in some he requir'd of me, who from a Brother expected more Indulgence. Our Disputes were often brought before our Father, and I fancy I was either generally in the right, or else a better Pleader, because the Judgment was generally in my favour: But my Brother was passionate and had often beaten me, which I took extreamly amiss; and thinking my Apprenticeship very tedious, I was continually wishing for some Opportunity of shortening it.

Franklin added in a footnote that he believed his brother's "harsh and tyrannical Treatment" created in him "that Aversion to arbitrary Power that has stuck to me thro' my whole Life." Events "in a manner unexpected" gave him a chance to revolt against his brother's rule and say farewell to Boston at the same time.

*Autobiography*, 1771

One of the Pieces in our News-Paper, on some political Point which I have now forgotten, gave Offence to the Assembly. He was taken up, censur'd and imprison'd for a Month by the Speaker's Warrant, I suppose because he would not discover his Author. I too was taken up and examin'd before the Council; but tho' I did not give them any Satisfaction, they contented themselves with admonishing me, and dismiss'd me; considering me perhaps as an Apprentice who was bound to keep his Master's Secrets. During my Brother's Confinement, which I resented a good deal, notwithstanding our private Differences, I had the Management of the Paper, and I made bold to give our Rulers some Rubs in it, which my Brother took very kindly, while others began to consider me in an unfavourable Light, as a young Genius that had a Turn for Libelling and Satyr. My Brother's Discharge was accompany'd with an Order of the House, (a very odd one) *that James Franklin should no longer print the Paper called the New England Courant.* There was a Consultation held in our Printing House among his Friends what he should do in this Case. Some propos'd to evade the Order by changing the Name of the Paper; but my Brother seeing Inconveniences in that, it was finally concluded on as a better Way, to let it be printed for the future under the Name of *Benjamin Franklin.* And to avoid the Censure of the Assembly that might fall on him, as still printing it by his Apprentice, the Contrivance was, that my old Indenture should be return'd to me with a full Discharge on the Back of it, to be shown on Occasion; but to secure to him the Benefit of my Service I was to sign new Indentures for the Remainder of the Term, which were to be kept private. A very flimsy Scheme it was, but however it was immediately executed, and the Paper went on accordingly under my Name for several Months. At length a fresh Difference arising between my Brother and me, I took upon me to assert my Freedom, presuming that he would not venture to produce the new Indentures. It was not fair in me to take this Advantage, and this I therefore reckon one of the first Errata of my Life: But the Unfairness of it weigh'd little with me, when under the Impressions of Resentment, for the Blows his Passion too often urg'd him to bestow upon me. Tho' he was otherwise not an ill-natur'd Man: Perhaps I was too saucy and provoking.

When he found I would leave him, he took care to prevent my getting Employment in any other Printing-House of the Town, by going round and speaking to every Master, who accordingly refus'd to give me Work. I then thought of going to New York as the nearest Place where there was a Printer: and I was the rather inclin'd to leave Boston, when I reflected that I had already made myself a little obnoxious to the governing Party; and from the arbitrary Proceedings of the Assembly in my Brother's Case it was likely I might if I stay'd soon bring myself into Scrapes; and farther that my indiscrete Disputations about Religion began to make me pointed at with Horror by good People, as an Infidel or Atheist. I determin'd on the Point: but my Father now siding with my Brother, I was sensible that if I attempted to go openly, Means would be used to prevent me. My Friend Collins therefore undertook to manage a little for me. He agreed with the Captain of a New York Sloop for my Passage, under the Notion of my being a young Acquaintance of his that had got a naughty Girl with Child, whose Friends would compel me to marry her, and therefore I could not appear or come away publickly. So I sold some of my Books to raise a little Money, Was taken on board privately, and as we had a fair Wind in three Days I found my self in New York near 300 Miles from home, a Boy of but 17, without the least Recommendation to or Knowledge of any Person in the Place, and with very little Money in my Pocket.

# Chapter 2

# Footloose Journeyman

In 1723, New York was far from the metropolis it would eventually become. In fact, it was little more than a village, smaller than Boston and Philadelphia, on the lower tip of Manhattan Island. Franklin soon found it had nothing to offer him except an opportunity to become a sailor, which no longer interested him.

*Autobiography*, 1771

My Inclinations for the Sea, were by this time worne out, or I might now have gratify'd them. But having a Trade, and supposing my self a pretty good Workman, I offer'd my Service to the Printer of the Place, old Mr. Wm. Bradford, (who had been the first Printer in Pensilvania, but remov'd from thence upon the Quarrel of Geo. Keith). He could give me no Employment, having little to do, and Help enough already: But, says he, my Son at Philadelphia has lately lost his principal Hand, Aquila Rose, by Death. If you go thither I believe he may employ you. Philadelphia was 100 Miles farther. I set out, however, in a Boat for Amboy, leaving my Chest and Things to follow me round by Sea. In crossing the Bay we met with a Squall that tore our rotten Sails to pieces, prevented our getting into the Kill, and drove us upon Long Island. In our Way a drunken Dutchman, who was a Passenger too, fell over board; when he was sinking I reach'd thro' the Water to his shock Pate and drew him up so that we got him in again. His Ducking sober'd him a little, and he went to sleep, taking first out of his Pocket a Book which he desir'd I would dry for him. It prov'd to be my old favourite Author Bunyan's Pilgrim's Progress in Dutch, finely printed on good

Paper with copper Cuts, a Dress better than I had ever seen it wear in its own Language. . . .

When we drew near the Island we found it was at a Place where there could be no Landing, there being a great Surff on the stony Beach. So we dropt Anchor and swung round towards the Shore. Some People came down to the Water Edge and hallow'd to us, as we did to them. But the Wind was so high and the Surff so loud, that we could not hear so as to understand each other. There were Canoes on the Shore, and we made Signs and hallow'd that they should fetch us, but they either did not understand us, or thought it impracticable. So they went away, and Night coming on, we had no Remedy but to wait till the Wind should abate, and in the mean time the Boatman and I concluded to sleep if we could, and so crouded into the Scuttle with the Dutchman who was still wet, and the Spray beating over the Head of our Boat, leak'd thro' to us, so that we were soon almost as wet as he. In this Manner we lay all Night with very little Rest. But the Wind abating the next Day, we made a Shift to reach Amboy before Night, having been 30 Hours on the Water without Victuals, or any Drink but a Bottle of filthy Rum: The Water we sail'd on being salt.

In the Evening I found my self very feverish, and went in to Bed. But having read somewhere that cold Water drank plentifully was good for a Fever, I follow'd the Prescription, sweat plentifully most of the Night, my Fever left me, and in the Morning crossing the Ferry, I proceeded on my Journey, on foot, having 50 miles to Burlington, where I was told I should find Boats that would carry me the rest of the Way to Philadelphia.

It rain'd very hard all the Day, I was thoroughly soak'd and by Noon a good deal tir'd, so I stopt at a poor Inn, where I staid all Night, beginning now to wish I had never left home. I cut so miserable a Figure too, that I found by the Questions ask'd me I was suspected to be some runaway Servant, and in danger of being taken up on that Suspicion. However I proceeded the next Day, and got in the Evening to an Inn within 8 or 10 Miles of Burlington, kept by one Dr. Brown.

Dr. Brown was an itinerant physician who had wandered around most of the countries of Europe. He was an atheist and the young freethinker Franklin got along very well with him. After trudging from his inn to the Delaware, Franklin caught a boat that missed the city in the darkness, and he thus spent another night on the water. Not until nine on Sunday morning did he land at the Market Street wharf. His entry into the city where he was to find fame and wealth was anything but prepossessing.

*Autobiography,* 1771

I was in my Working Dress, my best Cloaths being to come round by Sea. I was dirty from my Journey; my Pockets were stuff'd out with Shirts and Stockings; I knew no Soul, nor where to look for Lodging. I was fatigu'd with Travelling, Rowing and Want of Rest. I was very hungry, and my whole Stock of Cash consisted of a Dutch Dollar and about a Shilling in Copper. The latter I gave the People of the Boat for my Passage, who at first refus'd it on Account of my Rowing; but I insisted on their taking it, a Man being sometimes more generous when he has but a little Money than when he has plenty, perhaps thro' Fear of being thought to have but little.

Then I walk'd up the Street, gazing about, till near the Market House I met a Boy with Bread. I had made many a Meal on Bread, and inquiring where he got it, I went immediately to the Baker's he directed me to in second Street; and ask'd for Bisket, intending such as we had in Boston, but they it seems were not made in Philadelphia, then I ask'd for a threepenny Loaf, and was told they had none such: so not considering or knowing the Difference of Money and the greater Cheapness nor the Names of his Bread, I bad him give me three penny worth of any sort. He gave me accordingly three great Puffy Rolls. I was surpriz'd at the Quantity, but took it, and having no room in my Pockets, walk'd off, with a Roll under each Arm, and eating the other. Thus I went up Market Street as far as fourth Street, passing by the Door of Mr. Read, my future Wife's Father, when she standing at the Door saw me, and thought I made as I certainly did a most awkward ridiculous Appearance. Then I turn'd and went down Chestnut Street and part of Walnut Street, eating my Roll all the Way, and coming round found my self again at Market Street Wharff, near the Boat I came in, to which I went for a Draught of the River Water, and being fill'd with one of my Rolls, gave the other two to a Woman and her Child that came down the River in the Boat with us and were waiting to go farther. Thus refresh'd I walk'd again up the Street,

*Two nineteenth-century books on Franklin's life show him passing by Miss Read's door and giving away his rolls to a woman at the wharf.*

An *illustrated* Autobiography *from 1849 included numerous "designs" by J. G. Chapman, such as Franklin asleep in meeting.*

which by this time had many clean dress'd People in it who were all walking the same Way; I join'd them, and thereby was led into the great Meeting House of the Quakers near the Market. I sat down among them, and after looking round a while and hearing nothing said, being very drowzy thro' Labour and want of Rest the preceding Night, I fell fast asleep, and continu'd so till the Meeting broke up, when one was kind enough to rouse me. This was therefore the first House I was in or slept in, in Philadelphia.

Walking again down towards the River, and looking in the Faces of People, I met a young Quaker Man whose Countenance I lik'd, and accosting him requested he would tell me where a Stranger could get Lodging. We were then near the Sign of the Three Mariners. Here, says he, is one Place that entertains Strangers, but it is not a reputable House; if thee wilt walk with me, I'll show thee a better. He brought me to the Crooked Billet in Water-Street. Here I got a Dinner. And while I was eating it, several sly Questions were ask'd me, as it seem'd to be suspected from my youth and Appearance, that I might be some Runaway. After Dinner my Sleepiness return'd: and being shown to a Bed, I lay down without undressing, and slept till Six in the Evening; was call'd to Supper; went to Bed again very early and slept soundly till the next Morning.

Philadelphia did not offer Franklin much in the way of work—there were but two printers in the place. But he was fortunate to find employment with one.

*Autobiography*, 1771

I made my self as tidy as I could and went to Andrew Bradford the Printer's. I found in the Shop the old Man his Father, whom I had seen at New York, and who travelling on horse back had got to Philadelphia before me. He introduc'd me to his Son, who receiv'd me civilly, gave me a Breakfast, but told me he did not at present want a Hand, being lately supply'd with one. But there was another Printer in town lately set up, one Keimer, who perhaps might employ me; if not, I would be welcome to lodge at his House, and he would give me a little Work to do now and then till fuller Business should offer.

The old Gentleman said, he would go with me to the new Printer: And when we found him, Neighbour, says

Bradford, I have brought to see you a young Man of your Business, perhaps you may want such a One. He ask'd me a few Questions, put a Composing Stick in my Hand to see how I work'd, and then said he would employ me soon, tho' he had just then nothing for me to do....

Keimer's Printing House I found, consisted of an old shatter'd Press, and one small worn-out Fount of English, which he was then using himself, composing in it an Elegy on Aquila Rose before-mentioned, an ingenious young Man of excellent Character much respected in the Town, Clerk of the Assembly, and a pretty Poet. Keimer made Verses, too, but very indifferently. He could not be said to write them, for his Manner was to compose them in the Types directly out of his Head; so there being no Copy, but one Pair of Cases, and the Elegy likely to require all the Letter, no one could help him. I endeavour'd to put his Press (which he had not yet us'd, and of which he understood nothing) into Order fit to be work'd with; and promising to come and print off his Elegy as soon as he should have got it ready, I return'd to Bradford's who gave me a little Job to do for the present, and there I lodged and dieted. A few Days after Keimer sent for me to print off the Elegy. And now he had got another Pair of Cases, and a Pamphlet to reprint, on which he set me to work.

These two Printers I found poorly qualified for their Business. Bradford had not been bred to it, and was very illiterate; and Keimer tho' something of a Scholar, was a mere Compositor, knowing nothing of Presswork. He had been one of the French Prophets and could act their enthusiastic Agitations. At this time he did not profess any particular Religion, but something of all on occasion; was very ignorant of the World, and had, as I afterwards found, a good deal of the Knave in his Composition. He did not like my Lodging at Bradford's while I work'd with him. He had a House indeed, but without Furniture, so he could not lodge me: But he got me a Lodging at Mr. Read's before-mentioned, who was the Owner of his House. And my Chest and Clothes being come by this time, I made rather a more respectable Appearance in the Eyes of Miss Read, than I had done when she first happen'd to see me eating my Roll in the Street.

I began now to have some Acquaintance among the young People of the Town, that were Lovers of Reading

*Franklin courting Deborah Read*

with whom I spent my Evenings very pleasantly and gaining Money by my Industry and Frugality, I lived very agreably, forgetting Boston as much as I could, and not desiring that any there should know where I resided, except my Friend Collins who was in my Secret, and kept it when I wrote to him. At length an Incident happened that sent me back again much sooner than I had intended.

Franklin's brother-in-law Robert Homes, husband of his sister Mary, was captain of a sloop that traded between Boston and Delaware. Homes heard that young Ben was in Philadelphia and wrote him a letter, urging him to come home. Franklin wrote him a stiff reply, making it clear that there was not much hope of his returning to Boston, or finding reconciliation there. Homes showed the letter to Sir William Keith, Governor of Pennsylvania, who happened to be visiting "the Lower Counties," as Delaware was then called. Apparently Homes hoped that the Governor would force or persuade Ben to return to his family. Instead, young Franklin's well-written letter set off a totally unexpected chain reaction.

*Autobiography*, 1771

The Governor read it, and seem'd surpriz'd when he was told my Age. He said I appear'd a young Man of promising Parts, and therefore should be encouraged: The Printers at Philadelphia were wretched ones, and if I would set up there, he made no doubt I should succeed; for his Part, he would procure me the publick Business, and do me every other Service in his Power. This my Brother-in-Law afterwards told me in Boston. But I knew as yet nothing of it; when one Day Keimer and I being at Work together near the Window, we saw the Governor and another Gentleman (which prov'd to be Col. French, of New Castle) finely dress'd, come directly across the Street to our House, and heard them at the Door. Keimer ran down immediately, thinking it a Visit to him. But the Governor enquir'd for me, came up, and with a Condescension and Politeness I had been quite unus'd to, made me many Compliments, desired to be acquainted with me, blam'd me kindly for not having made my self known to him when I first came to the Place, and would have me away with him to the Tavern where he was going with Col. French to taste as he said some excellent Madeira. I was not a little surpriz'd, and Keimer star'd like a Pig poison'd. I went however with the Governor and Col. French, to a Tavern the Corner of Third Street, and over the Madeira he propos'd my Setting up my

*Governor Keith and Colonel French pay a visit to Franklin at Keimer's.*

*Sir William Keith*

Business, laid before me the Probabilities of Success, and both he and Col. French assur'd me I should have their Interest and Influence in procuring the Publick Business of both Governments. On my doubting whether my Father would assist me in it, Sir William said he would give me a Letter to him, in which he would state the Advantages, and he did not doubt of prevailing with him. So it was concluded I should return to Boston in the first Vessel with the Governor's Letter recommending me to my Father. In the mean time the Intention was to be kept secret, and I went on working with Keimer as usual, the Governor sending for me now and then to dine with him, a very great Honour I thought it, and conversing with me in the most affable, familiar, and friendly manner imaginable.

Toward the end of April, 1724, young Ben returned to Boston with a letter from Governor Keith to Josiah Franklin, "saying many flattering things of me . . . and strongly recommending the Project of my setting up at Philadelphia, as a Thing that must make my Fortune." Although his father and mother greeted Ben affectionately, Josiah Franklin was not especially impressed with Governor Keith's letter.

*Autobiography*, 1771

When Capt. Homes returning, he show'd it to him, ask'd if he knew Keith, and what kind of a Man he was: Adding his Opinion that he must be of small Discretion, to think of setting a Boy up in Business who wanted yet 3 Years of being at Man's Estate. Homes said what he could in favour of the Project; but my Father was clear in the Impropriety of it; and at last gave a flat Denial to it. Then he wrote a civil Letter to Sir William thanking him for the Patronage he had so kindly offered me, but declining to assist me as yet in Setting up, I being in his Opinion too young to be trusted with the Management of a Business so important, and for which the Preparation must be so expensive. . . .

My Father, tho' he did not approve Sir William's Proposition was yet pleas'd that I had been able to obtain so advantageous a Character from a Person of such Note where I had resided, and that I had been so industrious and careful as to equip my self so handsomely in so short a time: therefore seeing no Prospect of an Accommodation between my Brother and me, he gave his Consent to my Returning again to Philadelphia, advis'd me to behave respectfully to the People there, endeavour to obtain the general Esteem, and avoid lampooning and libelling to which he thought I had too much Inclination; telling me, that by steady Industry and a prudent Parsimony, I might save enough by the time I was One and Twenty to set me up, and that if I came near the Matter he would help me out with the rest. This was all I could obtain, except some small Gifts as Tokens of his and my Mother's Love, when I embark'd again for New-York, now with their Approbation and their Blessing.

Franklin's best friend in Boston, John Collins, decided to return to Philadelphia with him. He went overland to New York, while Ben took a sloop that put in at Newport, Rhode Island, enabling him to visit his brother John, who had been living there for some years. Samuel Vernon, a merchant friend of John's, asked Franklin to collect some thirty-five pounds due to him in Pennsylvania, and gave him an order for that sum. This was the usual way that merchants collected debts in other Colonies. In New York, Franklin found his friend Collins had become a very different person from the young man he had known in Boston.

*Autobiography*, 1771

We had been intimate from Children, and had read the same Books together. But he had the Advantage of more time for reading, and Studying and a wonderful Genius for Mathematical Learning in which he far outstript me. While I liv'd in Boston most of my Hours of Leisure for Conversation were spent with him, and he continu'd a sober as well as an industrious Lad; was much respected for his Learning by several of the Clergy and other Gentlemen, and seem'd to promise making a good Figure in Life: but during my Absence he had acquir'd a Habit of Sotting with Brandy; and I found by his own Account and what I heard from others, that he had been drunk every day since his Arrival at New York, and behav'd very oddly. He had gam'd too and lost his Money, so that I was oblig'd to discharge his Lodgings, and defray his Expences to and at Philadelphia: Which prov'd extreamly inconvenient to me. The then Governor of N York, Burnet, Son of Bishop Burnet hearing from the Captain that a young Man, one of his Passengers, had a great many Books, desired he would bring me to see him. I waited upon him accordingly, and should have taken Collins with me but that he was not sober. The Governor treated me with great Civility, show'd me his

Library, which was a very large one, and we had a good deal of Conversation about Books and Authors. This was the second Governor who had done me the Honour to take Notice of me, which to a poor Boy like me was very pleasing.

We proceeded to Philadelphia. I received on the Way Vernon's Money, without which we could hardly have finish'd our Journey. Collins wish'd to be employ'd in some Counting House; but whether they discover'd his Dramming by his Breath, or by his Behaviour, tho' he had some Recommendations, he met with no Success in any Application, and continu'd Lodging and Boarding at the same House with me and at my Expence. Knowing I had that Money of Vernon's he was continually borrowing of me, still promising Repayment as soon as he should be in Business. At length he had got so much of it, that I was distress'd to think what I should do, in case of being call'd on to remit it. His Drinking continu'd about which we sometimes quarrel'd, for when a little intoxicated he was very fractious.

Franklin felt that using Vernon's money to support himself and Collins—who eventually departed for Barbados without reimbursing his friend—was "the first great errata of my life." His carelessness with this money convinced him that "my Father was not much out in his Judgment when he suppos'd me too young to manage Business of Importance." He gave his father's letter to Governor Keith, and abandoned his dreams of economic independence. But the Governor had different ideas.

*Autobiography*, 1771

Sir William, on reading his Letter, said he was too prudent. There was great Difference in Persons, and Discretion did not always accompany Years, nor was Youth always without it. And since he will not set you up, says he, I will do it my self. Give me an Inventory of the Things necessary to be had from England, and I will send for them. You shall repay me when you are able; I am resolv'd to have a good Printer here, and I am sure you must succeed. This was spoken with such an Appearance of Cordiality, that I had not the least doubt of his meaning what he said. I had hitherto kept the Proposition of my Setting up a Secret in Philadelphia, and I still kept it. Had it been known that I depended on the Governor, probably some Friend that knew him better would have advis'd me not to rely on him, as I afterwards heard it as his known Character to be liberal of Promises which he never meant to keep. . . .

I presented him an Inventory of a little Printing House, amounting by my Computation to about £100 Sterling. He lik'd it, but ask'd me if my being on the Spot in England to chuse the Types and see that every thing was good of the kind, might not be of some Advantage. Then, says he, when there, you may make Acquaintances and establish Correspondencies in the Bookselling and Stationary Way. I agreed that this might be advantageous. Then says he, get yourself ready to go with Annis; which was the annual Ship, and the only one at that Time usually passing between London and Philadelphia. But it would be some Months before Annis sail'd, so I continu'd working with Keimer, fretting about the Money Collins had got from me, and in daily Apprehensions of being call'd upon by Vernon, which however did not happen for some Years after.

While he was waiting for the ship that would take him to England, Franklin had a good time. Keimer provided a sideshow all by himself. He was one of those men who loved to argue about religion and display his wide but erratic reading. He soon found young Franklin was more than a match for him.

*Autobiography*, 1771

I us'd to work him so with my Socratic Method, and had trapann'd him so often by Questions apparently so distant from any Point we had in hand, and yet by degrees led to the Point, and brought him into Difficulties and Contradictions that at last he grew ridiculously cautious, and would hardly answer me the most common Question, without asking first, *What do you intend to infer from that*? However it gave him so high an Opinion of my Abilities in the Confuting Way, that he seriously propos'd my being his Colleague in a Project he had of setting up a new Sect. He was to preach the Doctrines, and I was to confound all Opponents. When he came to explain with me upon the Doctrines, I found several Conundrums which I objected to unless I might have my Way a little too, and introduce some of mine. Keimer wore his Beard at full Length, because somewhere in the Mosaic Law it is said, *thou shalt not mar the Corners of thy Beard*. He likewise kept the seventh day Sabbath; and these two Points were Essentials with him. I dislik'd both, but agreed to admit them upon Condition of his adopting the Doctrine of using no animal Food. I doubt, says he, my Constitution will not bear that. I assur'd him it would, and that he would be the better for it. He was usually a great Glutton, and I promis'd my self some Diversion in half-starving him. He agreed to try the Practice if I would keep him Company. I did so and we held it for three Months. We had our Victuals dress'd and brought to us regularly by a Woman in the Neighbourhood, who had from me a List of 40 Dishes to be prepar'd for us at different times, in all which there was neither Fish Flesh nor Fowl, and the whim suited me the better at this time from the Cheapness of it, not costing us above 18d. Sterling each, per Week. I have since kept several Lents most strictly, Leaving the common Diet for that, and that for the common, abruptly, without the least Inconvenience: So that I think there is little in the Advice of making those Changes by easy Gradations. I went on pleasantly, but poor Keimer suffer'd grievously, tir'd of the Project, long'd for the Flesh Pots of Egypt, and order'd a roast Pig. He invited me and two Women Friends to dine with him, but it being brought too soon upon table, he could not resist the Temptation, and ate it all up before we came.

Franklin also made friends with young men his own age, "All Lovers of Reading." Inadvertently, he encouraged one of them, James Ralph, to become America's first professional writer.

*Autobiography*, 1771

My chief Acquaintances at this time were, Charles Osborne, Joseph Watson, and James Ralph; All Lovers of Reading. . . . Many pleasant Walks we four had together on Sundays into the Woods near Skuylkill, where we read to one another and conferr'd on what we read.

Ralph was inclin'd to pursue the Study of Poetry, not doubting but he might become eminent in it and make his Fortune by it, alledging that the best Poets must when they first began to write, make as many Faults as he did. Osborne dissuaded him, assur'd him he had no Genius for Poetry, and advis'd him to think of nothing beyond the Business he was bred to; that in the mercantile way tho' he had no Stock, he might by his Diligence and Punctuality recommend himself to Employment as a Factor, and in time acquire wherewith to trade on his own Account. I

*Franklin departs for London aboard the* Annis *in 1724.*

approv'd the amusing one's self with Poetry now and then, so far as to improve one's Language, but no farther. On this it was propos'd that we should each of us at our next Meeting produce a Piece of our own Composing, in order to improve by our mutual Observations, Criticisms and Corrections. As Language and Expression was what we had in View, we excluded all Considerations of Invention, by agreeing that the Task should be a Version of the 18th Psalm, which describes the Descent of a Deity. When the Time of our Meeting drew nigh, Ralph call'd on me first, and let me know his Piece was ready. I told him I had been busy, and having little Inclination had done nothing. He then show'd me his Piece for my Opinion; and I much approv'd it, as it appear'd to me to have great Merit. Now, says he, Osborne never will allow the least Merit in any thing of mine, but makes 1000 Criticisms out of mere Envy. He is not so jealous of you. I wish therefore you would take this Piece, and produce it as yours. I will pretend not to have had time, and so produce nothing: We shall then see what he will say to it. It was agreed, and I immediately transcrib'd it that it might appear in my own hand. We met. Watson's Performance was read: there were some Beauties in it: but many Defects. Osborne's was read: It was much better. Ralph did it Justice, remark'd some Faults, but applauded the Beauties. He himself had nothing to produce. I was backward, seem'd desirous of being excus'd, had not had sufficient Time to correct; &c. but no Excuse could be admitted, produce I must. It was read and repeated; Watson and Osborne gave up the Contest; and join'd in applauding it immoderately. Ralph only made some Criticisms and propos'd some Amendments, but I defended my Text. Osborne was against Ralph, and told him he was no better a Critic than Poet; so he dropt the Argument. As they two went home together, Osborne express'd himself still more strongly in favour of what he thought my Production, having restrain'd himself before as he said, lest I should think it Flattery. But who would have imagin'd, says he, that Franklin had been capable of such a Performance; such Painting, such Force! such Fire! he has even improv'd the Original! In his common Conversation, he seems to have no Choice of Words; he hesitates and blunders; and yet, good God, how he writes! When we

41

next met, Ralph discover'd the Trick, we had plaid him, and Osborne was a little laught at. This Transaction fix'd Ralph in his Resolution of becoming a Poet.

Although he was married and had one child, Ralph decided to accompany Franklin to London in the fall of 1724. Franklin did not realize it at the time, but his friend, filled with dreams of literary glory, had no intention of returning. Franklin had a pressing personal matter of his own on his mind. For some time he had "made some Courtship" to Deborah Read, the young girl who had gazed in astonishment at his disheveled appearance on his first day in Philadelphia. He had proposed marriage, but her mother pointed out that they were both only eighteen, and Franklin was going on a long voyage. Perhaps it would be better to wait until he returned. So Deborah and Benjamin "interchang'd some Promises" and Franklin went aboard the *Annis*. When the man carrying Governor Keith's dispatches came aboard, Franklin asked for the Governor's letters of credit and introduction. He was told that they were all in the dispatch bag and when they landed in England the bag would be opened and he could pick out the ones that belonged to him. Satisfied, Franklin settled down to a long stormy voyage. He became very friendly with a Quaker merchant named Thomas Denham. But not even to him did Franklin reveal the purpose of his voyage. He soon found himself wishing that he had told his secret before he sailed.

*Autobiography*, 1771

When we came into the Channel, the Captain kept his Word with me, and gave me an Opportunity of examining the Bag for the Governor's Letters. I found none upon which my Name was put, as under my Care; I pick'd out 6 or 7 that by the Hand writing I thought might be the promis'd Letters, especially as one of them was directed to Basket the King's Printer, and another to some Stationer. We arriv'd in London the 24th of December, 1724. I waited upon the Stationer who came first in my Way, delivering the Letter as from Gov. Keith. I don't know such a Person, says he: but opening the Letter, O, this is from Riddlesden; I have lately found him to be a compleat Rascal, and I will have nothing to do with him, nor receive any Letters from him. So putting the Letter into my Hand, he turn'd on his Heel and left me to serve some Customer. I was surprized to find these were not the Governor's Letters. And after recollecting and comparing Circumstances, I began to doubt his Sincerity. I found my Friend Denham, and opened the whole Affair to him. He let me into Keith's Character, told me there was not the least Probability that he had written any Letters for me, that no one who knew him had the smallest Dependance on him, and he laught at the Notion of the Governor's giving me a Letter of Credit, having as he said no Credit to give.

In his later years, Franklin told friends in Paris that he was panicked by the thought of surviving on his own in London. He credited much of his survival to the friendship of a Boston physician, Zabdiel Boylston, who lent him twenty guineas and gave him advice and encouragement. Fortunately, Franklin also had his trade to support him and he soon found work at a large London printing house. For company, Franklin relied largely on Ralph, who was something of a problem.

*Autobiography*, 1771

Ralph and I were inseparable Companions. We took Lodgings together in Little Britain at 3*s*. 6*d*. per Week, as much as we could then afford. He found some Relations, but they were poor and unable to assist him. He now let me know his Intentions of remaining in London, and that he never meant to return to Philadelphia. He had brought no Money with him, the whole he could muster having been expended in paying his Passage. I had 15 Pistoles: So he borrowed occasionally of me, to subsist while he was looking out for Business. He first endeavoured to get into the Playhouse, believing himself qualify'd for an Actor; but Wilkes, to whom he apply'd, advis'd him candidly not to think of that, Employment, as it was impossible he should succeed in it. Then he propos'd to Roberts, a Publisher in Paternoster Row, to write for him a Weekly Paper like the Spectator, on certain Conditions, which Roberts did not approve. Then he endeavour'd to get Employment as a Hackney Writer to copy for the Stationers and Lawyers about the Temple: but could find no Vacancy.

I immediately got into Work at Palmer's then a famous Printing House in Bartholomew Close; and here I continu'd near a Year. I was pretty diligent; but spent with Ralph a good deal of my Earnings in going to Plays and other Places of Amusement. We had together consum'd all my Pistoles, and now just rubb'd on from hand to mouth. He seem'd quite to forget his Wife and Child, and I by degrees my Engagements with Miss Read, to whom I never wrote more than one Letter, and that was to let her know I was not likely soon to return. This was

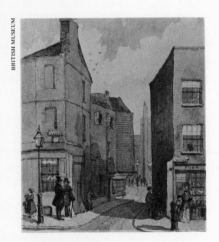

*Franklin's lodgings were here in London's "Little Britain."*

another of the great Errata of my Life, which I should wish to correct if I were to live it over again.

Having run short of money, young Franklin decided to sell a few odd items he had brought with him from America. He wrote the following letter to Sir Hans Sloane, physician to the King and a prominent member of the Royal Society, well known as a collector of natural history specimens. Later, in his *Autobiography*, Franklin turned this story inside out, saying Sloane "heard of" his curiosities and "persuaded" him to add them to his collection.

[London] June 2, 1725

Having lately been in the Nothern Parts of America, I have brought from thence a Purse made of the Stone Asbestus, a Piece of the Stone, and a Piece of Wood, the Pithy Part of which is of the same Nature, and call'd by the Inhabitants, Salamander Cotton. As you are noted to be a Lover of Curiosities, I have inform'd you of these; and if you have any Inclination to purchase them, or see 'em, let me know your Pleasure by a Line directed for me at the Golden Fan in Little Britain, and I will wait upon you with them.

Franklin also attracted some attention at this time by writing a religious pamphlet, entitled *A Dissertation on Liberty and Necessity, Pleasure and Pain.* Perhaps the best commentary on it was written by Franklin himself, fifty years later, in a letter to a British friend, Benjamin Vaughan.

Passy Nov. 9. 1779.

It was addres'd to Mr. J. R., that is James Ralph, then a Youth of about my age, and my intimate friend, afterwards a Political Writer and Historian. The Purport of it was to prove the Doctrine of fate, from the suppos'd attributes of God; in some such manner as this, that in creating and governing the World, as he was infinitely wise he knew what would be best; infinitely good, he must be disposed, and infinitely powerful, he must be able to execute it. Consequently *all is right*. There were only an hundred Copies printed, of which I gave a few to friends, and afterwards disliking the Piece, as conceiving it might have an ill Tendency, I burnt the rest except one Copy the Margin of which was filled with manuscript Notes by Lyons, author of the *Infallibility of Human Judgment*, who was at that time another of my Acquaintance in London. I was not 19 Years of age when

*An old cut of Palmer's printing house during Franklin's day*

*St. Bartholomew's Lady Chapel in London was once occupied by Palmer's printing house.*

it was written. In 1730 I wrote a Piece on the other side of the Question, which began with laying for its foundation this fact, *that almost all men in all ages and Country's, have at times made use of Prayer:* Thence I reasoned, that if all things are ordain'd, prayer must among the rest be ordain'd. But as prayer can produce no Change in Things that are ordain'd, Praying must then be useless and an absurdity. God would therefore not ordain Praying if everything else was ordain'd. But Praying exists, therefore all Things are not ordain'd &c. This Pamphlet was never printed, and the manuscript has been long lost. The great uncertainty I found in metaphysical reasonings disgusted me, and I quitted that kind of reading and study for others more satisfactory.

The master printer Samuel Palmer was impressed by the essay, although he told Franklin that the principles were "abominable." Through the attention it won, Franklin met several minor writers in local coffeehouses. Meanwhile, he and Ralph cane to a parting of the ways, and Franklin went to work for another printer, named Watts. At Watts's, Franklin drew on his Boston experience to save money and time. But his unorthodox ways clashed with the customs of the English printers.

*Autobiography,* 1771

At my first Admission into this Printing House, I took to working at Press, imagining I felt a Want of the Bodily Exercise I had been us'd to in America, where Presswork is mix'd with Composing. I drank only Water; the other Workmen, near 50 in Number, were great Guzzlers of Beer. On occasion I carried up and down Stairs a large Form of Types in each hand, when others carried but one in both Hands. They wonder'd to see from this and several Instances that the Water-American as they call'd me was *stronger* than themselves who drank *strong* Beer. We had an Alehouse Boy who attended always in the House to supply the Workmen. My Companion at the Press, drank every day a Pint before Breakfast, a Pint at Breakfast with his Bread and Cheese; a Pint between Breakfast and Dinner; a Pint at Dinner; a Pint in the Afternoon about Six o'Clock, and another when he had done his Day's-Work. I thought it a detestable Custom. But it was necessary, he suppos'd, to drink *strong* Beer that he might be *strong* to labour. I endeavour'd to convince him that the Bodily Strength afforded by Beer could only be in proportion to the Grain or Flour of the

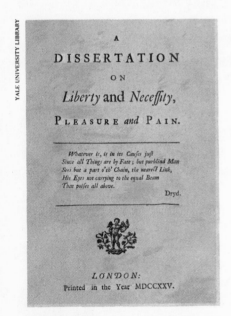

*Franklin both wrote and printed this pamphlet while he was working at Palmer's in 1725.*

45

*Franklin and printers supping on "hot Water-gruel" and bread*

*Pay table on Saturday nights; both from Holley's* Franklin

Barley dissolved in the Water of which it was made; that there was more Flour in a Penny-worth of Bread, and therefore if he would eat that with a Pint of Water, it would give him more Strength than a Quart of Beer. He drank on however, and had 4 or 5 Shillings to pay out of his Wages every Saturday Night for that muddling Liquor; an Expence I was free from. And thus these poor Devils keep themselves always under.

Watts after some Weeks desiring to have me in the Composing Room, I left the Pressmen. A new *Bienvenu* or Sum for Drink, being 5 *s.*, was demanded of me by the Compositors. I thought it an Imposition, as I had paid below. The Master thought so too, and forbad my Paying it. I stood out two or three Weeks, was accordingly considered as an Excommunicate, and had so many little Pieces of private Mischief done me, by mixing my Sorts, transposing my Pages, breaking my Matter, &c. &c. if I were ever so little out of the Room, and all ascrib'd to the Chapel Ghost, which they said ever haunted those not regularly admitted, that notwithstanding the Master's Protection, I found myself oblig'd to comply and pay the Money; convinc'd of the Folly of being on ill Terms with those one is to live with continually. I was now on a fair Footing with them, and soon acquir'd considerable Influence. I propos'd some reasonable Alterations in their Chapel Laws, and carried them against all Opposition. From my Example a great Part of them, left their muddling Breakfast of Beer and Bread and Cheese, finding they could with me be supply'd from a neighbouring House with a large Porringer of hot Water-gruel, sprinkled with Pepper, crumb'd with Bread, and a Bit of Butter in it, for the Price of a Pint of Beer, viz, three halfpence. This was a more comfortable as well as cheaper Breakfast, and kept their Heads clearer. Those who continu'd sotting with Beer all day, were often, by not paying, out of Credit at the Alehouse, and us'd to make Interest with me to get Beer, *their Light*, as they phras'd it, *being out*. I watch'd the Pay table on Saturday Night, and collected what I stood engag'd for them, having to pay some times near Thirty Shillings a Week on their Accounts. This, and my being esteem'd a pretty good Riggite, that is a jocular verbal Satyrist, supported my Consequence in the Society. My constant Attendance, (I never making a St. Monday), recommended me to the

Master; and my uncommon Quickness at Composing, occasion'd my being put upon all Work of Dispatch which was generally better paid. So I went on now very agreably.

At Watts's Printing House, Franklin made another friend, a youth named Wygate, who, like most of Franklin's friends, "lov'd Reading" and, unlike most printers, had a good education. He was, Franklin said, "a tolerable Latinist, spoke French." But Franklin's relationship with him took a strange turn when he taught him how to swim.

*Autobiography*, 1771

I taught him, and a Friend of his, to swim, at twice going into the River, and they soon became good Swimmers. They introduc'd me to some Gentlemen from the Country who went to Chelsea by Water to see the College and Don Saltero's Curiosities. In our Return, at the Request of the Company, whose Curiosity Wygate had excited, I stript and leapt into the River, and swam from near Chelsea to Blackfryars, performing on the Way many Feats of Activity both upon and under Water, that surpriz'd and pleas'd those to whom they were Novelties. I had from a Child been ever delighted with this Exercise, had studied and practis'd all Thevenot's Motions and Positions, added some of my own, aiming at the graceful and easy, as well as the Useful. All these I took this Occasion of exhibiting to the Company, and was much flatter'd by their Admiration. And Wygate, who was desirous of becoming a Master, grew more and more attach'd to me, on that account, as well as from the Similarity of our Studies. He at length propos'd to me travelling all over Europe together, supporting ourselves everywhere by working at our Business. I was once inclin'd to it. But mentioning it to my good Friend Mr. Denham, with whom I often spent an Hour, when I had Leisure. He dissuaded me from it, advising me to think only of returning to Pensilvania, which he was now about to do....

He now told me he ... should carry over a great Quantity of Goods in order to open a Store there: He propos'd to take me over as his Clerk, to keep his Books (in which he would instruct me) copy his Letters, and attend the Store. He added, that as soon as I should be acquainted with mercantile Business he would promote me by sending me with a Cargo of Flour and Bread &c. to the West Indies, and procure me Commissions from others; which would be profitable, and if I manag'd well, would establish me

*Illustrations from the* Art of Swimming, *including how to cut your toenails under water*

handsomely. The Thing pleas'd me, for I was grown tired of London, remember'd with Pleasure the happy Months I had spent in Pennsylvania, and wish'd again to see it. Therefore I immediately agreed, on the Terms of Fifty Pounds a Year, Pensylvania Money; less indeed than my present Gettings as a Compostor, but affording a better Prospect.

I now took Leave of Printing, as I thought for ever, and was daily employ'd in my new Business; going about with Mr. Denham among the Tradesmen, to purchase various Articles, and seeing them pack'd up, doing Errands, calling upon Workmen to dispatch, &c. and when all was on board, I had a few Days Leisure. On one of these Days I was to my Surprize sent for by a great Man I knew only by Name, a Sir William Wyndham and I waited upon him. He had heard by some means or other of my Swimming from Chelsey to Blackfryars, and of my teaching Wygate and another young Man to swim in a few Hours. He had two Sons about to set out on their Travels; he wish'd to have them first taught Swimming; and propos'd to gratify me handsomely if I would teach them. They were not yet come to Town and my Stay was uncertain, so I could not undertake it. But from this Incident I thought it likely, that if I were to remain in England and open a Swimming School, I might get a good deal of Money. And it struck me so strongly, that had the Overture been sooner made me, probably I should not so soon have returned to America.

*Old engraving of the interior of an eighteenth-century printing house*

On the voyage back to America in the summer of 1726, Franklin began the habit of keeping a journal. This fascinating document has come down to us, and it gives us a vivid picture of Franklin's interests at twenty. Already his inquiring mind was turning from religion to science. The following passages display both his acute observation and his inclination to experiment to prove a theory.

Friday, September 2 [1726]
This morning the wind changed, a little fair. We caught a couple of dolphins, and fried them for dinner. They tasted tolerably well. These fish make a glorious appearance in the water: their bodies are of a bright green, mixed with a silver colour, and their tails of a shining golden yellow; but all this vanishes presently after they are taken out of their element, and they change all over to a light grey. I observed that cutting off pieces of a just-caught living

dolphin for baits, those pieces did not lose their lustre and fine colours when the dolphin died, but retained them perfectly. Every one takes notice of that vulgar error of the painters, who always represent this fish monstrously crooked and deformed, when it is in reality as beautiful and well shaped a fish as any that swims. I cannot think what should be the original of this chimera of theirs, (since there is not a creature in nature that in the least resembles their dolphin) unless it proceeded at first from a false imitation of a fish in the posture of leaping, which they have since improved into a crooked monster with a head and eyes like a bull, a hog's snout, and a tail like a blown tulip. But the sailors give me another reason, though a whimsical one, viz. that as this most beautiful fish is only to be caught at sea, and that very far to the Southward, they say the painters wilfully deform it in their representations, lest pregnant women should long for what it is impossible to procure for them. . . .

Wednesday, September 28

We had very variable winds and weather last night, accompanied with abundance of rain; and now the wind is come about westerly again, but we must bear it with patience. This afternoon we took up several branches of gulf weed (with which the sea is spread all over from the Western Isles to the coast of America); but one of these branches had something peculiar in it. In common with the rest it had a leaf about three quarters of an inch long, indented like a saw, and small yellow berry filled with nothing but wind; besides which it bore a fruit of the animal kind, very surprising to see. It was a small shellfish like a heart, the stalk by which it proceeded from the branch being partly of a gristly kind. Upon this one branch of the weed there were near forty of these vegetable animals; the smallest of them near the end contained a substance somewhat like an oyster, but the larger were visibly animated, opening their shells every moment, and thrusting out a set of unformed claws, not unlike those of a crab; but the inner part was still a kind of soft jelly. Observing the weed more narrowly, I spied a very small crab crawling among it, about as big as the head of a ten-penny nail, and of a yellowish colour, like the weed itself. This gave me some reason to think that he was a native of the branch, that he had not long since been in the same condition with the rest of those little embrios that appeared in the shells, this being the method of their generation; and that consequently all the rest of this odd kind of fruit might be crabs in due time. To strengthen my conjecture, I have resolved to keep the weed in salt water, renewing it every day till we come on shore, by this experiment to see whether any more crabs will be produced or not in this manner....

Thursday, September 29

Upon shifting the water in which I had put the weed yesterday, I found another crab, much smaller than the former, who seemed to have newly left his habitation. But the weed begins to wither, and the rest of the embrios are dead. This new comer fully convinces me, that at least this sort of crabs are generated in this manner.

Friday, September 30

I took in some more gulf-weed to-day with the boat-hook, with shells upon it like that before mentioned, and three living perfect crabs, each less than the nail of my little finger. One of them had something particularly observable, to wit, a thin piece of the white shell which I before noticed as their covering while they remained in the condition of embrios, sticking close to his natural shell upon his back. This sufficiently confirms me in my opinion of the manner of their generation....

The long hours at sea also gave Franklin time to reflect on his life thus far. He drew up a plan to guide his future conduct. The manuscript has been lost. Only four points—but very important ones—survive.

[1726]

Those who write of the art of poetry teach us that if we would write what may be worth the reading, we ought always, before we begin, to form a regular plan and design of our piece: otherwise, we shall be in danger of incongruity. I am apt to think it is the same as to life. I have never fixed a regular design in life; by which means it has been a confused variety of different scenes. I am now entering upon a new one: let me, therefore, make some resolutions, and form some scheme of action, that, henceforth, I may live in all respects like a rational creature.

1.  It is necessary for me to be extremely frugal for some time, till I have paid what I owe.

2.  To endeavour to speak truth in every instance; to

give nobody expectations that are not likely to be answered, but aim at sincerity in every word and action— the most amiable excellence in a rational being.

3.  To apply myself industriously to whatever business I take in hand, and not divert my mind from my business by any foolish project of growing suddenly rich; for industry and patience are the surest means of plenty.

4.  I resolve to speak ill of no man whatever, not even in a matter of truth; but rather by some means excuse the faults I hear charged upon others, and upon proper occasions speak all the good I know of every body.

In the *Autobiography*, Franklin told how he also examined his religious beliefs, using a highly experimental approach—testing the effect of his skepticism on himself and his friends.

*Autobiography*, 1771

My Arguments perverted some others, particularly Collins and Ralph: but each of them having afterwards wrong'd me greatly without the least Compunction and recollecting Keith's Conduct towards me, (who was another Freethinker) and my own towards Vernon and Miss Read which at Times gave me great Trouble, I began to suspect that this Doctrine tho' it might be true, was not very useful. . . .

. . . I grew convinc'd that *Truth, Sincerity and Integrity* in Dealings between Man and Man, were of the utmost Importance to the Felicity of Life, and I form'd written Resolutions, (which still remain in my Journal Book) to practice them ever while I lived. Revelation had indeed no weight with me as such; but I entertain'd an Opinion, that tho' certain Actions might not be bad *because* they were forbidden by it, or good *because* it commanded them; yet probably those Actions might be forbidden *because* they were bad for us, or commanded *because* they were beneficial to us, in their own Natures, all the Circumstances of things considered. And this Persuasion, with the kind hand of Providence, or some guardian Angel, or accidental favourable Circumstances and Situations, or all together, preserved me (thro' this dangerous Time of Youth and the hazardous Situations I was sometimes in among Strangers, remote from the Eye and Advice of my Father) without any *wilful* gross Immorality or Injustice that might have been expected from my Want of Religion. I say *wilful*, because the Instances I have mentioned,

51

had something of *Necessity* in them, from my Youth, Inexperience, and the Knavery of others. I had therefore a tolerable Character to begin the World with, I valued it properly, and determin'd to preserve it.

Another explanation for Franklin's swing back to a religious attitude, if not orthodox convictions, was his brush with death and economic disaster soon after he landed in Philadelphia.

*Autobiography,* 1771

Mr. Denham took a Store in Water Street, where we open'd our Goods. I attended the Business diligently, studied Accounts, and grew in a little Time expert at selling. We lodg'd and boarded together, he counsell'd me as a Father, having a sincere Regard for me: I respected and lov'd him: and we might have gone on together very happily: But in the Beginning of Feby. 1726/7 when I had just pass'd my 21st Year, we both were taken ill. My Distemper was a Pleurisy, which very nearly carried me off: I suffered a good deal, gave up the Point in my own mind, and was rather disappointed when I found my Self recovering; regretting in some degree that I must now some time or other have all that disagreable Work to do over again. I forget what his Distemper was. It held him a long time, and at length carried him off. He left me a small Legacy in a nuncupative [oral] Will, as a Token of his Kindness for me, and he left me once more to the wide World. For the Store was taken into the Care of his Executors, and my Employment under him ended: My Brother-in-law Homes, being now at Philadelphia, advis'd my Return to my Business. And Keimer tempted me with an Offer of large Wages by the Year to come and take the Management of his Printing-House, that he might better attend his Stationer's Shop.... I try'd for farther Employment as a Merchant's Clerk; but not readily meeting with any, I clos'd again with Keimer.

Thus this second phase of Franklin's career came to a close with the young man seemingly back where he started when he first came to Philadelphia. He was working for Keimer again as a journeyman printer. But there were subtle, enormously important differences. The naïve runaway had become a man of the world. He had survived cynicism, atheism, the temptations of London, and the dangers of the Atlantic. Benjamin Franklin knew who he was now and a little, at least, of where he wanted to go.

# Chapter 3

# A Man of Business

Franklin was much too talented and too intelligent to remain an employee of a fool like Keimer for long. The master sensed this, and as soon as Franklin had put the print shop in order and trained the raw hands, Keimer invented a quarrel with Franklin and fired him. But one of the hands, Hugh Meredith, had in the meantime become a strong Franklin admirer. Meredith persuaded his father to put up the money so that he and Franklin could go into the printing business in a shop of their own, as partners. The business prospered. The elder Meredith sent customers to them, but most of their progress was due to Franklin's remarkable energy. In this passage from the *Autobiography* he recalls how hard he worked in those days when he was establishing himself in business.

*Autobiography*, 1771

Brientnal particulary procur'd us from the Quakers, the Printing 40 Sheets of their History, the rest being to be done by Keimer: and upon this we work'd exceeding hard, for the Price was low. It was a Folio, Pro Patria Size, in Pica with Long Primer Notes. I compos'd of it a Sheet a Day, and Meredith work'd it off at Press. It was often 11 at Night and sometimes later, before I had finish'd my Distribution for the next days Work: For the little Jobbs sent in by our other Friends now and then put us back. But so determin'd I was to continue doing a Sheet a Day of the Folio, that one Night when having impos'd my Forms, I thought my Days Work over, one of them by accident was broken and two Pages reduc'd to Pie, I immediately distributed and compos'd it over again before I went to bed. And this Industry visible to our Neighbours began to give us Character and Credit; particularly I was told, that mention being made of the new Printing Office at the Merchants every-night-Club, the general Opinion was that it must fail, there being already two Printers in the Place, Keimer and Bradford; but Doctor Baird . . . gave a contrary Opinion; for the Industry of that Franklin, says he, is superior to any thing I ever saw of the kind: I see him still at work when I go home from Club; and he is at Work again before his Neighbours are out of bed.

With James Franklin's experience as a guide, Franklin laid plans to found a newspaper. But the path to this turning point in his career proved by no means smooth. He told how he dealt with the obstacles that confronted him in this passage from the *Autobiography.*

*Autobiography,* 1771

George Webb, who had found a Female Friend that lent him wherewith to purchase his Time of Keimer, now came to offer himself as a Journeyman to us. We could not then imploy him, but I foolishly let him know, as a Secret, that I soon intended to begin a Newspaper, and might then have Work for him. My Hopes of Success as I told him were founded on this, that the then only Newspaper, printed by Bradford was a paltry thing, wretchedly manag'd, and no way entertaining; and yet was profitable to him. I therefore thought a good Paper could scarcely fail of good Encouragement. I requested Webb not to mention it, but he told it to Keimer, who immediately, to be beforehand with me, published Proposals for Printing one himself, on which Webb was to be employ'd. I resented this, and to counteract them, as I could not yet begin our Paper, I wrote several Pieces of Entertainment for Bradford's Paper, under the Title of the Busy Body which Brientnal continu'd some Months. By this means the Attention of the Publick was fix'd on that Paper, and Keimers Proposals which we burlesqu'd and ridicul'd, were disregarded. He began his Paper however, and after carrying it on three Quarters of a Year, with at most only 90 Subscribers, he offer'd it to me for a Trifle, and I having been ready some time to go on with it, took it in hand directly.

*Franklin trundled the papers himself.*

Keimer called his paper *The Universal Instructor in All Arts and Sciences: and Pennsylvania Gazette.* Franklin and Meredith shortened the title to *The Pennsylvania Gazette,* and thanks to Franklin's talent as a writer and printer, it swiftly became "extreamly profitable." The thorough professionalism of Franklin's approach is evident in this statement of policy, which appeared in the first issue under his editorship.

*First issue of* The Pennsylvania Gazette *under Franklin's aegis*

*The Pennsylvania Gazette,*
October 2, 1729

There are many who have long desired to see a good News-Paper in Pennsylvania; and we hope those Gentlemen who are able, will contribute towards the making This such. We ask Assistance, because we are fully sensible, that to publish a good News-Paper is not so easy an Undertaking as many People imagine it to be. The Author of a Gazette (in the Opinion of the Learned) ought to be qualified with an extensive Acquaintance with Languages, a great Easiness and Command of Writing and Relating Things cleanly and intelligibly, and in few Words; he should be able to speak of War both by Land and Sea; be well acquainted with Geography, with the History of the Time, with the several Interests of Princes and States, the Secrets of Courts, and the Manners and Customs of all Nations. Men thus accomplish'd are very rare in this remote Part of the World; and it would be well if the Writer of these Papers could make up among his Friends what is wanting in himself.

Upon the Whole, we may assure the Publick, that as far as the Encouragement we meet with will enable us, no Care and Pains shall be omitted, that may make the *Pennsylvania Gazette* as agreeable and useful an Entertainment as the Nature of the Thing will allow.

From the beginning, *The Pennsylvania Gazette* reflected Franklin's fundamental interests. He took up the clash between Governor William Burnet and the Massachusetts Assembly in a style that "struck the principal People, occasion'd the Paper and Manager of it to be much talk'd of, and in a few weeks brought them all to be our Subscribers." Here in Franklin's forthright prose is the story that started him on his way to success.

*The Pennsylvania Gazette,*
October 9, 1729

His Excellency Governor Burnet died unexpectedly. . . . And it was thought the Dispute would have ended with him, or at least have lain dormant till the Arrival of a new Governor from England, who possibly might, or might not be inclin'd to enter too rigorously into the Measures of his Predecessor. But our last Advices by the Post acquaint us, that his Honour the Lieutenant Governour (on whom the Government immediately devolves upon the Death or Absence of the Commander in Chief) has vigorously renew'd the Struggle on his own Account; of

For *BARBADOS* directly,
The SHIP
*INDUSTRY*,
*William Rankin*,
Commander ;
Will fail with all ex-
pedition.
For freight or paſſage, ap-
ply to ſaid commander on
board, or John Erwin, in
Strawberry Alley.

*Franklin greatly increased the
number of ads in the* Gazette; *this is
a notice of a ship sailing.*

which the Particulars will be seen in our Next.

Perhaps some of our Readers may not fully understand the Original or Ground of this warm Contest between the Governour and Assembly. It seems, that People have for these Hundred Years past, enjoyed the Privilege of Rewarding the Governour for the Time being, according to *their Sense* of his Merit and Services; and few or none of their Governors have hitherto complain'd, or had Reason to complain, of a too scanty Allowance. But the late Gov. Burnet brought with him Instructions to demand a *settled Salary* of £1000 *per Annum*, Sterling, on him and all his Successors, and the Assembly were required to fix it immediately. He insisted on it strenuously to the last, and they as constantly refused it. It appears by their Votes and Proceedings, that they thought it an Imposition, contrary to their own Charter, and to *Magna Charta*; and they judg'd that by the Dictates of Reason there should be a mutual Dependence between the *Governor* and the *Governed*, and that to make any Governour independent on his People, would be dangerous, and destructive of their Liberties, and the ready Way to establish Tyranny: They thought likewise, that the Province was not the less dependent on the Crown of Great-Britain, by the Governour's depending immediately on them and his own good Conduct for an ample Support, because all Acts and Laws which he might be induc'd to pass, must nevertheless be constantly sent Home for Approbation in Order to continue in Force. Many other Reasons were given and Arguments us'd in the Course of the Controversy, needless to particularize here, because all the material Papers relating to it, have been inserted already in our Publick news.

Much deserved Praise has the deceas'd Governour received, for his steady Integrity in adhering to his Instructions, notwithstanding the great Difficulty and Opposition he met with, and the strong Temptations offer'd from time to time to induce him to give up the Point. And yet perhaps something is due to the Assembly (as the Love and Zeal of that Country for the present Establishment is too well known to suffer any Suspicion of Want of Loyalty) who continue thus resolutely to Abide by what *they Think* their Right, and that of the People they represent, maugre all the Arts and Menaces of a Governour fam'd for his Cunning and Politicks, back'd with Instructions from

Home, and powerfully aided by the great Advantage such an Officer always has of engaging the principal Men of a Place in his Party, by conferring where he pleases so many Posts of Profit and Honour. Their happy Mother Country will perhaps observe with Pleasure, that tho' her gallant Cocks and matchless Dogs abate their native Fire and Intrepidity when transported to a Foreign Clime (as the common Notion is) yet her SONS in the remotest Part of the Earth, and even to the third and fourth Descent, still retain that ardent Spirit of Liberty, and that undaunted Courage in the Defence of it, which has in every Age so gloriously distinguished BRITONS and ENGLISH-MEN from all the Rest of Mankind.

At the same time, Franklin did not forget his family and friends in Massachusetts. The only surviving letter from this period is the one that follows, to his younger sister Jane. Captain Freeman, whom Franklin mentions in the first line, was a Boston friend of the family.

Philadelphia, January 6 [1727]

Dear Sister,

I am highly pleased with the account captain Freeman gives me of you. I always judged by your behaviour when a child that you would make a good, agreeable woman, and you know you were ever my peculiar favourite. I have been thinking what would be a suitable present for me to make, and for you to receive, as I hear you are grown a celebrated beauty. I had almost determined on a tea table, but when I considered that the character of a good housewife was far preferable to that of being only a pretty gentlewoman, I concluded to send you a *spinning wheel*, which I hope you will accept as a small token of my sincere love and affection.

Sister, farewell, and remember that modesty, as it makes the most homely virgin amiable and charming, so the want of it infallibly renders the most perfect beauty disagreeable and odious. But when that brightest of female virtues shines among other perfections of body and mind in the same person, it makes the woman more lovely than an angel. Excuse this freedom, and use the same with me. I am, dear Jenny, your loving brother,

B. Franklin

Sex was very much on Franklin's mind at this time. At first he tried to find a wife with a dowry large enough to pay off the debts he owed on his printing house. But he soon discovered that no dowries were forthcoming from parents of available girls. He then decided to correct one of the great errata of his life. While he was in England, Deborah Read, perhaps suffering from a broken heart, had married a ne'er-do-well named John Rogers, who soon revealed he had "a preceding Wife" in England and then, after running up a string of debts, absconded to the West Indies. This left Deborah a grass widow, an extremely unpleasant situation for a young woman in the eighteenth century. Franklin's solution was a common-law marriage.

*Autobiography*, 1771

... having turn'd my Thoughts to Marriage, I look'd round me, and made Overtures of Acquaintance in other Places; but soon found that the Business of a Printer being generally thought a poor one, I was not to expect Money with a Wife unless with such a one, as I should not otherwise think agreable. In the mean time, that hard-to-be-govern'd Passion of Youth, had hurried me frequently into Intrigues with low Women that fell in my Way, which were attended with some Expence and great Inconvenience, besides a continual Risque to my Health by a Distemper which of all Things I dreaded, tho' by great good Luck I escaped it.

A friendly Correspondence as Neighbours and old Acquaintances, had continued between me and Mrs. Read's Family, who all had a Regard for me from the time of my first Lodging in their House. I was often invited there and consulted in their Affairs, wherein I sometimes was of service. I pity'd poor Miss Read's unfortunate Situation, who was generally dejected, seldom chearful, and avoided Company. I consider'd my Giddiness and Inconstancy when in London as in a great degree the Cause of her Unhappiness; tho' the Mother was good enough to think the Fault more her own than mine, as she had prevented our Marrying before I went thither, and persuaded the other Match in my Absence. Our mutual Affection was revived, but there were now great Objections to our Union. That Match was indeed look'd upon as invalid, a preceding Wife being said to be living in England; but this could not easily be prov'd, because of the Distance. And tho' there was a Report of his Death, it was not certain. Then tho' it should be true, he had left many Debts which his Successor might be call'd on to pay. We ventured however, over all these Difficulties, and I [took] her to Wife Sept. 1. 1730. None of the

Inconveniences happened that we had apprehended, she prov'd a good and faithful Helpmate, assisted me much by attending the Shop, we throve together, and have ever mutually endeavour'd to make each other happy.

Not long after his marriage, Franklin brought home one of the results of his intrigues with low women that he did not mention in his *Autobiography* (except indirectly, where he alludes to "sinister events" in his life that he regretted). His illegitimate son, William, had been born about six months after his marriage. Franklin took the baby into his house and made him part of the family—a decision that caused no little inner turmoil in his wife. Otherwise, however, the marriage was happy. One reason was Franklin's policy of letting Deborah have her own way, recalled in this ironic passage from the second part of his *Autobiography*, composed in France in 1784.

*Autobiography*, 1784

*Deborah stitching pamphlets*

We have an English Proverb that says,

> He that would thrive
> Must ask his Wife;

it was lucky for me that I had one as much dispos'd to Industry and Frugality as my self. She assisted me chearfully in my Business, folding and stitching Pamphlets, tending Shop, purchasing old Linen Rags for the Papermakers, &c. &c. We kept no idle Servants, our Table was plain and simple, our Furniture of the cheapest. For instance my Breakfast was a long time Bread and Milk, (no Tea) and I ate it out of a twopenny earthen Porringer with a Pewter Spoon. But mark how Luxury will enter Families, and make a Progress, in Spite of Principle. Being call'd one Morning to Breakfast, I found it in a China Bowl with a Spoon of Silver. They had been bought for me without my Knowledge by my Wife, and had cost her the enormous Sum of three and twenty Shillings, for which she had no other Excuse or Apology to make, but that she thought *her* Husband deserv'd a Silver Spoon and China Bowl as well as any of his Neighbours.

In the fall of 1727, while he still was working as Keimer's chief assistant, Franklin organized the Junto. It was a club "formed of my ingenious acquaintances...for mutual improvement." Franklin found the idea in a book he had read in Boston, *Essays to Do Good*, by Cotton Mather. The Puritan minister's goal had been to promote religion and morality. Franklin's club was aimed at the betterment of its members, and of the city and Colony in which they lived. As its members rose to influence and wealth in Philadelphia, the Junto became a political powerhouse. With the help of the Junto, Franklin launched his "first Project of a public Nature," the creation of the first subscription library in North America. He told the story and the lessons he learned from it in his *Autobiography.*

*Autobiography,* 1784

At the time I establish'd my self in Pensylvania, there was not a good Bookseller's Shop in any of the Colonies to the Southward of Boston. In New-York and Philadelphia the Printers were indeed Stationers, they sold only Paper, &c., Almanacks, Ballads, and a few common School Books. Those who lov'd Reading were oblig'd to send for their Books from England. The Members of the Junto had each a few. We had left the Alehouse where we first met, and hired a Room to hold our Club in. I propos'd that we should all of us bring our Books to that Room, where they would not only be ready to consult in our Conferences, but become a common Benefit, each of us being at Liberty to borrow such as he wish'd to read at home. This was accordingly done, and for some time contented us. Finding the Advantage of this little Collection, I propos'd to render the Benefit from Books more common by commencing a Public Subscription Library. I drew a Sketch of the Plan and Rules that would be necessary, and got a skilful Conveyancer, Mr. Charles Brockden to put the whole in Form of Articles of Agreement to be subscribed; by which each Subscriber engag'd to pay a certain Sum down for the first Purchase of Books and an annual Contribution for encreasing them. So few were the Readers at that time in Philadelphia, and the Majority of us so poor, that I was not able with great Industry to find more than Fifty Persons, mostly young Tradesmen, willing to pay down for this purpose Forty shillings each, and Ten Shillings per Annum. On this little Fund we began. The Books were imported. The Library was open one Day in the Week for lending them to the Subscribers, on their Promisory Notes to pay Double the Value if not duly returned. The Institution soon manifested its Utility, was imitated by other Towns and in other Provinces, the Librarys were augmented by Donations, Reading became fashionable, and our People having no publick Amusements to divert their Attention from Study became better acquainted with Books, and in a few Years were observ'd by Strangers to be better instructed and more intelligent than People of the same Rank generally are in other Countries....

This Library afforded me the means of Improvement

*Book labels for the Library Company were printed on Franklin's presses, and he also composed the inscription for the building's cornerstone.*

by constant Study, for which I set apart an Hour or two each Day; and thus repair'd in some Degree the Loss of the Learned Education my Father once intended for me.

Meanwhile, *The Pennsylvania Gazette* thrived. Within a year friends advanced Franklin enough money to buy out his partner Meredith, who decided he would rather be a farmer than a printer. The *Gazette*'s success was due not only to Franklin's boldness in politics; he also exercised in its pages his talent for humor — under a number of pseudonyms. Among the *Gazette* correspondents were several descendants of Silence Dogood. Anthony Afterwit told how his wife spent him into bankruptcy. Celia Single was a born shrew who lectured the editor in scorching terms because of his partiality to men. Perhaps best of all was Alice Addertongue, who announced that she was organizing a kind of stock exchange for the sale and transfer of calumnies, slanders, and other reputation-wrecking pastimes of the gentler sex.

*The Pennsylvania Gazette,*
September 12, 1732

Mr. Gazetteer,

. . . I am a young Girl of about thirty-five, and live at present with my Mother. I have no Care upon my Head of getting a Living, and therefore find it my Duty as well as Inclination, to exercise my Talent at CENSURE, for the Good of my Country folks. There was, I am told, a certain generous Emperor, who if a Day had passed over his Head, in which he had conferred no Benefit on any Man, used to say to his Friends, in Latin, *Diem perdidi*, that is, it seems, *I have lost a Day*. I believe I should make use of the same Expression, if it were possible for a Day to pass in which I had not, or miss'd, an Opportunity to scandalize somebody: But, Thanks be praised, no such Misfortune has befel me these dozen Years.

Yet, whatever Good I may do, I cannot pretend that I first entred into the Practice of this Virtue from a Principle of Publick Spirit; for I remember that when a Child, I had a violent Inclination to be ever talking in my own Praise, and being continually told that it was ill Manners, and once severely whipt for it, the confin'd Stream form'd itself a new Channel, and I began to speak for the future in the Dispraise of others. This I find more agreable to Company, and almost as much so to my self: For what great Difference can there be, between putting your self up, or putting your Neighbour down? *Scandal*, like other Virtues, is in part its own Reward, as it gives us

*Home of the Library Company
of Philadelphia, completed in 1790*

the Satisfaction of making our selves appear better than others, or others no better than ourselves....

By Industry and Application, I have made my self the Center of all the *Scandal* in the Province, there is little stirring but I hear of it. I began the World with this Maxim, *That no Trade can subsist without Returns*; and accordingly, whenever I receiv'd a good story, I endeavour'd to give two or a better in the Room of it. My Punctuality in this Way of Dealing gave such Encouragement, that it has procur'd me an incredible deal of Business, which without Diligence and good Method it would be impossible for me to go through. For besides the Stock of Defamation thus naturally flowing in upon me, I practice an Art by which I can pump Scandal out of People that are the least enclin'd that way. Shall I discover my Secret? Yes; to let it die with me would be inhuman. If I have never heard ill of some Person, I always impute it to defective Intelligence; *for there are none without their Faults, no not one.* If she is a Woman, I take the first Opportunity to let all her Acquaintance know I have heard that one of the handsomest or best Men in Town has said something in Praise either of her Beauty, her Wit, her Virtue, or her good Management. If you know any thing of Humane Nature, you perceive that this naturally introduces a Conversation turning upon all her Failings, past, present, and to come. To the same purpose, and with the same Success, I cause every Man of Reputation to be praised before his Competitors in Love, Business, or Esteem on Account of any particular Qualification. Near the Times of *Election*, if I find it necessary, I commend every Candidate before some of the opposite Party, listning attentively to what is said of him in answer: (But Commendations in this latter Case are not always necessary, and should be used judiciously;) of late Years I needed only observe what they said of one another freely; and having for the Help of Memory taken Account of all Informations and Accusations received, whoever peruses my Writings after my Death, may happen to think, that during a certain Term, the People of Pennsylvania chose into all their Offices of Honour and Trust, the veriest Knaves, Fools and Rascals in the whole Province....

I mention'd above, that without good Method I could not go thro' my Business: In my Father's Life-time I had

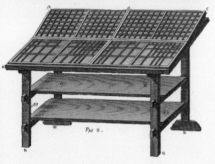

*Eighteenth-century type case used by printers, from the renowned* Diderot *Encyclopedia*

some Instruction in Accompts, which I now apply with Advantage to my own Affairs. I keep a regular Set of Books, and can tell at an Hour's Warning how it stands between me and the World. In my *Daybook* I enter every Article of Defamation as it is transacted; for Scandals *receiv'd in*, I give Credit; and when I pay them out again, I make the Persons to whom they respectively relate *Debtor*. In my *Journal*, I add to each Story by Way of Improvement, such probable Circumstances as I think it will bear, and in my *Ledger* the whole is regularly posted.

I suppose the Reader already condemns me in his Heart, for this particular of *adding Circumstances*; but I justify that part of my Practice thus. 'Tis a Principle with me, that none ought to have a greater Share of Reputation than they really deserve; if they have, 'tis an Imposition upon the Publick: I know it is every one's Interest, and therefore believe they endeavour, to conceal *all* their Vices and Follies; and I hold, that those People are *extraordinary* foolish or careless who suffer a *Fourth* of their Failings to come to publick Knowledge: Taking then the common Prudence and Imprudence of Mankind in a Lump, I suppose none suffer above *one Fifth* to be discovered: Therefore when I hear of any Person's Misdoing, I think I keep within Bounds if in relating it I only make it *three times* worse than it is; and I reserve to my self the Privilege of charging them with one Fault in four, which, for aught I know, they may be entirely innocent of. You see there are but few so careful of doing Justice as my self; what Reason then have Mankind to complain of *Scandal*? In a general way, the worst that is said of us is only half of what *might* be said, if all our Faults were seen.

But alas, two great Evils have lately befaln me at the same time; an extream Cold that I can scarce speak, and a most terrible Toothach that I dare hardly open my Mouth: For some Days past I have receiv'd ten Stories for one I have paid; and I am not able to ballance my Accounts without your Assistance. I have long thought that if you would make your Paper a Vehicle of Scandal, you would double the Number of your Subscribers. I send you herewith Account of *4 Knavish Tricks, 2 crackt M——n–ds, 5 Cu——ld–ms, 3 drub'd Wives,* and *4 Henpeck'd Husbands,* all within this Fortnight; which you may, as Articles of News, deliver to the Publick; and if my Toothach continues, shall send you more; being, in the mean time, Your constant Reader,

ALICE ADDERTONGUE

Franklin also utilized letters to the editor to shoot holes in his chief competition, Andrew Bradford's *The American Weekly Mercury.* Here is a sample of this tactic.

*The Pennsylvania Gazette,*
November 9, 1732

To the Printer of the *Gazette.*

As you sometimes take upon you to correct the Publick, you ought in your Turn patiently to receive publick Correction. My Quarrel against you is, your Practice of publishing under the Notion of News, old Transactions which I suppose you hope we have forgot. For Instance, in your Numb. 669, you tell us from London of July 20. That the Losses of our Merchants are laid before the Congress of Soissons, by Mr. Stanhope, &c. and that Admiral Hopson died the 8th of May last. Whereas 'tis certain, there has been no Congress at Soissons nor any where else these three Years at least; nor could Admiral Hopson possibly die in May last, unless he has made a Resurrection since his Death in 1728. And in your Numb. 670. among other Articles of equal Antiquity, you tell us a long Story of a Murder and Robbery perpetrated on the Person of Mr. Nath. Bostock, which I have read Word for Word not less than four Years since in your own Paper. Are these your *freshest Advices foreign and domestick?* I insist that you insert this in your next, and let us see how you justify yourself.

MEMORY

I need not say more in Vindication of my self against this Charge, than that the Letter is evidently wrong directed, and should have been *To the Publisher of the Mercury*: Inasmuch as the Numb. of my Paper is not yet amounted to 669, nor are those old Articles any where to be found in the *Gazette,* but in the *Mercury* of the two last Weeks.

But some of the correspondence was for the amusement of Franklin and his readers, and nothing else. The following exchange with the pretty creatures of Pennsylvania is definitely in this category.

*The Pennsylvania Gazette,*
November 20 and
November 27, 1735

Mr. Franklin,

Pray let the prettiest Creature in this Place know, (by publishing this) That if it was not for her Affectation, she would be absolutely irresistible.

*The little Epistle in our last, has produced no less than six, which follow in the order we receiv'd 'em.*

Mr. Franklin,

I cannot conceive who your Correspondent means by *the prettiest Creature* in this Place; but I can assure either him or her, that she who is truly so, has no Affectation at all.

Sir,

Since your last Week's Paper I have look'd in my Glass a thousand Times, I believe, in one Day; and if it was not for the Charge of Affectation I might, without Partiality, believe myself the Person meant.

Mr. Franklin,

I must own that several have told me, I am the prettiest Creature in this Place; but I believe I should not have been tax'd with Affectation if I could have thought as well of them as they do of themselves.

Sir,

Your Sex calls me pretty; my own affected. Is it from Judgment in the one, or Envy in the other?

Mr. Franklin,

They that call me affected are greatly mistaken; for I don't know that I ever refus'd a Kiss to any Body but a Fool.

Friend Benjamin,

I am not at all displeased at being charged with Affectation. Thou know'st the vain People call Decency of Behaviour by that Name.

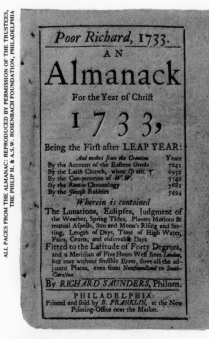

*The title page of Franklin's first* Poor Richard *almanac*

Almost every printer in Colonial America published an almanac—or wanted to publish one. They were widely read by farmers of the simpler sort, who sometimes took them seriously. Each almanac had a resident philomath who studied the stars, made his astronomical calculations and predictions, and split the profits with the printer. Franklin, with his usual shrewdness, noted that sensible people did not really believe in these predictions. Most people read almanacs for amusement, although they found in them such useful information as court dates and a calendar of other meeting dates. Franklin, therefore, decided to become his own philomath, inventing him as he did so many of his *Gazette* correspondents. His name was Richard Saunders and his candid introduction to the first edition explained why the work was titled *Poor Richard.*

*Poor Richard, 1733*

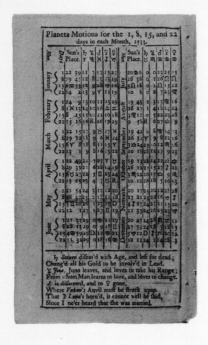

Courteous Reader,

I might in this place attempt to gain thy Favour, by declaring that I write Almanacks with no other View than that of the publick Good; but in this I should not be sincere; and Men are now a-days too wise to be deceiv'd by Pretences how specious soever. The plain Truth of the Matter is, I am excessive poor, and my Wife, good Woman, is, I tell her, excessive proud; she cannot bear, she says, to sit spinning in her Shift of Tow, while I do nothing but gaze at the Stars; and has threatned more than once to burn all my Books and Rattling-Traps (as she calls my Instruments) if I do not make some profitable Use of them for the good of my Family. The Printer has offer'd me some considerable share of the Profits, and I have thus begun to comply with my Dame's desire....

R. SAUNDERS

*Poor Richard* was soon the most successful almanac in America, selling more than ten thousand copies a year. The source of this success was not only the appeal of Poor Richard's ingenuous personality. His almanac's pages were crowded with amusing verses, proverbs, and aphorisms. Franklin took many of these from earlier almanacs and from collections of epigrams and sayings. But he constantly improved upon previous anthologists, by sharpening, simplifying, and balancing the epigrams that made "Poor Richard says" a household phrase throughout Colonial America. Here is a sampling of Franklin's best efforts, drawn from the twenty years during which he edited and wrote the *Almanack.*

Kings and Bears often worry their keepers.

He's a Fool that makes his Doctor his Heir.

Beware of meat twice boil'd, and an old foe reconcil'd.

The poor have little, beggars none, the rich too much, *enough* not one.

After 3 days men grow weary, of a wench, a guest, and weather rainy.

Men and Melons are hard to know.

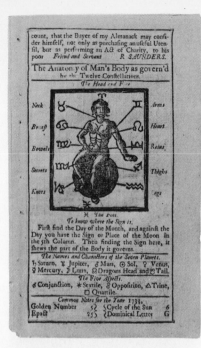

*Three additional pages from the 1733 almanac show calculations of the planets' motions, explanations of astrological signs common to most almanacs, and a prediction of eclipses.*

Where there's Marriage without Love, there will be Love without Marriage.

Neither a Fortress nor a Maidenhead will hold out long after they begin to parly.

An Egg today is better than a Hen tomorrow.

He that waits upon Fortune, is never sure of a Dinner.

Marry your Son when you will, but your Daughter when you can.

Approve not of him who commends all you say.

Three may keep a Secret, if two of them are dead.

Opportunity is the great Bawd.

Here comes the Orator! with his Flood of Words, and his Drop of Reason.

An old young man, will be a young old man.

Sal laughs at every thing you say. Why? Because she has fine Teeth.

Fish and Visitors stink in 3 days.

He that lives upon Hope, dies farting.

Let thy maidservant be faithful, strong, and homely.

Admiration is the Daughter of Ignorance.

She that paints her Face, thinks of her Tail.

A countryman between 2 Lawyers, is like a fish between two cats.

There are no ugly Loves, nor handsome Prisons.

Write with the learned, pronounce with the vulgar.

Keep your eyes wide open before marriage, half shut afterwards.

Thou can'st not joke an Enemy into a Friend; but thou may'st a Friend into an Enemy.

He that falls in love with himself, will have no Rivals.

To bear other People's afflictions, every one has Courage enough, and to spare.

Learn of the skilful: He that teaches himself, hath a fool for his master.

*Epitaph on a Scolding Wife by her Husband.* Here my poor Bridget's Corps doth lie, she is at rest—and so am I.

A Plowman on his Legs is higher than a Gentleman on his knees.

If your head is wax, don't walk in the Sun.

You can bear your own Faults, and why not a Fault in your Wife.

The Golden Age never was the present Age.

Old Boys have their Playthings as well as young Ones; the Difference is only in the Price.

The Proud hate Pride—in others.

He that is of Opinion Money will do every Thing, may well be suspected of doing every Thing for Money.

Love your Neighbor; yet don't pull down your Hedge.

Love your enemies, for they tell you your faults.

While the business flourished, a personal tragedy struck the Franklin family. Deborah had given birth to a son, whom they named Francis Folger Franklin. At the age of four, the boy died of smallpox. Franklin was to feel the bitter sorrow of the boy's death for the rest of his life, for he had hesitated to have him inoculated. The sorrowing parents placed on little Frankie's gravestone the words, "The DELIGHT of all that knew him." Good newspaperman that he was, Franklin tried to make his loss benefit the public, in the following story.

*The Pennsylvania Gazette,*
December 30, 1736

*Portrait engraving of Francis Folger Franklin, who died of smallpox*

Understanding 'tis a current Report, that my Son Francis, who died lately of the Small Pox, had it by Inoculation; and being desired to satisfy the Publick in that Particular; inasmuch as some People are, by that Report (join'd with others of the like kind, and perhaps equally groundless) deter'd from having that Operation perform'd on their Children, I do hereby sincerely declare, that he was not inoculated, but receiv'd the Distemper in the common Way of Infection: And I suppose the Report could only arise from its being my known Opinion, that Inoculation was a safe and beneficial Practice; and from my having said among my Acquaintance, that I intended to have my Child inoculated, as soon as he should have recovered sufficient Strength from a Flux with which he had been long afflicted.

B. FRANKLIN

Franklin's respect and affection for his father and mother continued to be a factor in his life, although he was now a mature man of thirty-two. This respect, however, did not prevent him from making it clear to them that he was no longer being guided by their religious beliefs. This letter was occasioned by an unfortunate incident, in which Franklin was involved. Some pranksters pretended to initiate a simple-minded apprentice named Daniel Rees into the Masons with a garish ceremony, which included a devil dressed in a cow's hide with horns. A bowl of brandy, lighted to add an eerie glow to the scene, was accidentally spilled on the boy, and he died of his burns two days later. Franklin was accused of being part of the hoax in Andrew Bradford's *Mercury*. The story spread to other papers, and was reprinted in Boston, where his parents heard about it and reacted with great alarm.

*Oldest American Masonic seal*

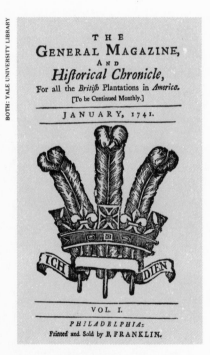

*Title page of Franklin's magazine, three days too late to be the first magazine published in America*

[Philadelphia] April 13. 1738

Honour'd Father and Mother

I have your Favour of the 21st of March in which you both seem concern'd lest I have imbib'd some erroneous Opinions. Doubtless I have my Share, and when the natural Weakness and Imperfection of Human Understanding is considered, with the unavoidable Influences of Education, Custom, Books and Company, upon our Ways of thinking, I imagine a Man must have a good deal of Vanity who believes, and a good deal of Boldness who affirms, that all the Doctrines he holds, are true; and all he rejects, are false. And perhaps the same may be justly said of every Sect, Church and Society of men when they assume to themselves that Infallibility which they deny to the Popes and Councils. I think Opinions should be judg'd of by their Influences and Effects; and if a Man holds none that tend to make him less Virtuous or more vicious, it may be concluded he holds none that are dangerous; which I hope is the Case with me. I am sorry you should have any Uneasiness on my Account, and if it were a thing possible for one to alter his Opinions in order to please others, I know none whom I ought more willingly to oblige in that respect than your selves: But since it is no more in a Man's Power *to think* than *to look* like another, methinks all that should be expected from me is to keep my Mind open to Conviction, to hear patiently and examine attentively whatever is offered me for that end; and if after all I continue in the same Errors, I believe your usual Charity will induce you rather to pity and excuse than blame me. In the mean time your Care and Concern for me is what I am very thankful for. . . .

. . . I am Your dutiful Son

BF

Nothing sums up Franklin's relationship with his wife better than the song to Deborah that he wrote some time in 1742. According to Franklin's friend Dr. John Bard, the inspiration came from a discussion, possibly at the Junto, about the number of poems written in praise of mistresses, and the far fewer written in praise of wives. The next morning Bard received the following verses from Franklin with a note asking him to sing them at their next meeting. "Joggy" was a term for a homely woman.

[*c.* 1742]

Song

Of their Chloes and Phillisses Poets may prate
   I sing my plain Country Joan
Now twelve Years my Wife, still the Joy of my Life
   Blest Day that I made her my own,
               My dear Friends
   Blest Day that I made her my own.

2

Not a Word of her Face, her Shape, or her Eyes,
   Of Flames or of Darts shall you hear;
Tho' I Beauty admire 'tis Virtue I prize,
   That fades not in seventy Years,
               My dear Friends

3

In Health a Companion delightfull and dear,
   Still easy, engaging, and Free,
In Sickness no less than the faithfullest Nurse
   As tender as tender can be,
               My dear Friends

4

In Peace and good Order, my Household she keeps
   Right Careful to save what I gain
Yet chearfully spends, and smiles on the Friends
   I've the Pleasures to entertain
               My dear Friends

5

She defends my good Name ever where I'm to blame,
   Friend firmer was ne'er to Man giv'n,
Her compassionate Breast, feels for all the Distrest,
   Which draws down the Blessing from Heav'n,
               My dear Friends

6

Am I laden with Care, she takes off a large Share,
   That the Burthen ne'er makes [me] to reel,
Does good Fortune arrive, the Joy of my Wife,
   Quite doubles the Pleasures I feel,
               My dear Friends

7

In Raptures the giddy Rake talks of his Fair,
   Enjoyment shall make him Despise,
I speak my cool sence, that long Experience,
   And Enjoyment have chang'd in no wise,
               My dear Friends

*Members of the Junto borrowing
each other's books to read*

[Some Faults we have all, and so may my Joan,
But then they're exceedingly small;
And now I'm us'd to 'em, they're just like my own,
I scarcely can see 'em at all,
My dear Friends,
I scarcely can see them at all.]
8
Were the fairest young Princess, with Million in Purse
To be had in Exchange for my Joan,
She could not be a better Wife, mought be a Worse,
So I'd stick to my Joggy alone
My dear Friends
I'd cling to my lovely ould Joan.

Perhaps it was his Boston birth, and his residence in Philadelphia, that gave Franklin a continental view of America. In this letter to William Strahan, a London printer who became a trusted correspondent, he revealed that, from a business point of view, he already thought of the Colonies as a whole. He had set up printers in Charleston, South Carolina, and New York, as well as operating his own shop in Philadelphia. The young man that Strahan sent over as a result of this letter was David Hall, a Scot who eventually became Franklin's partner. Mr. Read, mentioned in the first line, was a cousin of Deborah Read's.

Philada. July 10. 1743

Mr. Read has communicated to me part of a Letter from you, recommending a young Man whom you would be glad to see in better Business than that of a Journeyman Printer. I have already three Printing-Houses in three different Colonies, and purpose to set up a fourth if I can meet with a proper Person to manage it, having all Materials ready for that purpose. If the young Man will venture over hither, that I may see and be acquainted with him, we can treat about the Affair, and I make no doubt but he will think my Proposals reasonable; If we should not agree, I promise him however a Twelvemonths Good Work, and to defray his Passage back if he enclines to return to England.

Hall arrived carrying a friendly reply from Strahan, to which Franklin promptly responded. The letter is important not only because it marked the beginning of one of his most important friendships, but also because of the way Franklin wrote to the Londoner as a humble colonial.

Philada. July 4. 1744

I receiv'd your Favour per Mr. Hall, who arriv'd here

*Portrait of William Strahan
by Sir Joshua Reynolds*

about two Weeks since, and from the short Acquaintance I have had with him, I am persuaded he will answer perfectly the Character you had given of him. I make no doubt but his Voyage, tho' it has been expensive, will prove advantageous to him: I have already made him some Proposals, which he has under Consideration, and as we are like to agree on them, we shall not, I believe, differ on the Article of his Passage Money....

I have long wanted a Friend in London whose Judgment I could depend on, to send me from time to time such new Pamphlets as are worth Reading on any Subject (Religious Controversy excepted) for there is no depending on Titles and Advertisements. This Favour I take the Freedom to beg of you, and shall lodge Money in your Hands for that purpose.

We have seldom any News on our Side the Globe that can be entertaining to you on yours. All our Affairs are *petit*. They have a miniature Resemblance only, of the grand Things of Europe. Our Governments, Parliaments, Wars, Treaties, Expeditions, Factions, &c. tho' Matters of great and Serious Consequence to us, can seem but Trifles to you.

While he worked and prospered, Franklin never lost his interest in morality and religion, which he had inherited from Puritan Boston. He created his own set of religious exercises, some of which he recited daily. Even more interesting was his attempt to achieve moral perfection—and the conclusions he drew from the experiment. He told the story in his *Autobiography.*

*Autobiography,* 1771

It was about this time that I conceiv'd the bold and arduous Project of arriving at moral Perfection. I wish'd to live without committing any Fault at any time; I would conquer all that either Natural Inclination, Custom, or Company might lead me into. As I knew, or thought I knew, what was right and wrong, I did not see why I might not *always* do the one and avoid the other. But I soon found I had undertaken a Task of more Difficulty than I had imagined. While my *Attention was taken up* in guarding against one Fault, I was often surpriz'd by another. Habit took the Advantage of Inattention. Inclination was sometimes too strong for Reason. I concluded at length, that the mere speculative Conviction that it was our Interest to be compleatly virtuous, was not sufficient to prevent our Slipping, and that the contrary Habits must be broken and good ones acquired and established, before we can have any Dependence on a steady uniform Rectitude of Conduct. For this purpose I therefore contriv'd the following Method.

In the various Enumerations of the moral Virtues I had met with in my Reading, I found the Catalogue more or less numerous, as different Writers included more or fewer Ideas under the same Name. Temperance, for Example, was by some confin'd to Eating and Drinking, while by others it was extended to mean the moderating every other Pleasure, Appetite, Inclination or Passion, bodily or mental, even to our Avarice and Ambition. I propos'd to myself, for the sake of Clearness, to use rather more Names with fewer Ideas annex'd to each, than a few Names with more Ideas; and I included under Thirteen Names of Virtues all that at that time occurr'd to me as necessary or desirable, and annex'd to each a short Precept, which fully express'd the Extent I gave to its Meaning.

These names of Virtues with their Precepts were

### 1. TEMPERANCE.

Eat not to Dulness.

Drink not to Elevation.

### 2. SILENCE.

Speak not but what may benefit others or yourself. Avoid trifling Conversation.

### 3. ORDER.

Let all your Things have their Places. Let each Part of your Business have its Time.

### 4. RESOLUTION.

Resolve to perform what you ought. Perform without fail what you resolve.

### 5. FRUGALITY.

Make no Expence but to do good to others or yourself: i.e. Waste nothing.

### 6. INDUSTRY.

Lose no Time. Be always employ'd in something useful. Cut off all unnecessary Actions.

### 7. SINCERITY.

Use no hurtful Deceit.

Think innocently and justly; and, if you speak, speak accordingly.

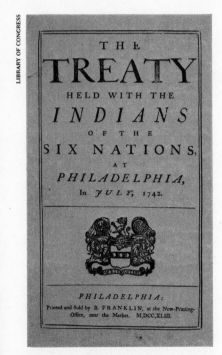

*Title page of one of Franklin's most elegant printing efforts*

73

### 8. JUSTICE.

Wrong none, by doing Injuries or omitting the Benefits that are your Duty.

### 9. MODERATION.

Avoid Extreams. Forbear resenting Injuries so much as you think they deserve.

### 10. CLEANLINESS.

Tolerate no Uncleanness in Body, Cloaths or Habitation.

### 11. TRANQUILITY.

Be not disturbed at Trifles, or at Accidents common or unavoidable.

### 12. CHASTITY.

Rarely use Venery but for Health or Offspring; Never to Dulness, Weakness, or the Injury of your own or another's Peace or Reputation.

### 13. HUMILITY.

Imitate Jesus and Socrates.

My Intention being to acquire the *Habitude* of all these Virtues, I judg'd it would be well not to distract my Attention by attempting the whole at once, but to fix it on one of them at a time, and when I should be Master of that, then to proceed to another, and so on till I should have gone thro' the thirteen. And as the previous Acquisition of some might facilitate the Acquisition of certain others, I arrang'd them with that View as they stand above. *Temperance* first, as it tends to procure that Coolness and Clearness of Head, which is so necessary where constant Vigilance was to be kept up, and Guard maintained, against the unremitting Attraction of ancient Habits, and the Force of perpetual Temptations. This being acquir'd and establish'd, *Silence* would be more easy, and my Desire being to gain Knowledge at the same time that I improv'd in Virtue, and considering that in Conversation it was obtain'd rather by the use of the Ears than of the Tongue, and therefore wishing to break a Habit I was getting into of Prattling, Punning and Joking, which only made me acceptable to trifling Company, I gave *Silence* the second Place. This, and the next, *Order,* I expected would allow me more Time for attending to my Project and my Studies; RESOLUTION, once become habitual, would keep me firm in my Endeavours to obtain all the subsequent Virtues; *Frugality* and *Industry*, by freeing me from my remaining Debt, and producing Affluence and Independance, would

M. T. CICERO's

*CATO MAJOR,*

OR HIS

DISCOURSE

OF

**OLD-AGE:**

With Explanatory NOTES.

*PHILADELPHIA:*
Printed and Sold by B. FRANKLIN,
MDCCXLIV.

*Title page of the* Cato Major,
*considered by Franklin to be his
most distinguished printed book*

make more easy the Practice of *Sincerity* and *Justice,* &c. &c. Conceiving then that agreable to the Advice of Pythagoras in his Golden Verses daily Examination would be necessary, I contriv'd the following Method for conducting that Examination.

I made a little Book in which I allotted a Page for each of the Virtues. I rul'd each Page with red Ink, so as to have seven Columns, one for each Day of the Week, marking each Column with a Letter for the Day. I cross'd these Columns with thirteen red Lines, marking the Beginning of each Line with the first Letter of one of the Virtues, on which Line and in its proper Column I might mark by a little black Spot every Fault I found upon Examination to have been committed respecting that Virtue upon that Day.

I determined to give a Week's strict Attention to each of the Virtues successively. Thus in the first Week my great Guard was to avoid every the least Offence against Temperance, leaving the other Virtues to their ordinary Chance, only marking every Evening the Faults of the Day. Thus if in the first Week I could keep my first Line marked T clear of Spots, I suppos'd the Habit of that virtue so much strengthen'd and its opposite weaken'd, that I might venture extending my Attention to include the next, and for the following Week keep both Lines clear of Spots. Proceeding thus to the last, I could go thro' a Course compleat in Thirteen Weeks, and four Courses in a Year. And like him who having a Garden to weed, does not attempt to eradicate all the bad Herbs at once, which would exceed his Reach and his Strength, but works on one of the Beds at a time, and having accomplish'd the first proceeds to a Second; so I should have, (I hoped) the encouraging Pleasure of seeing on my Pages the Progress I made in Virtue, by clearing successively my Lines of their Spots, till in the End by a Number of Courses, I should be happy in viewing a clean Book after a thirteen Weeks daily Examination. . . .

I enter'd upon the Execution of this Plan for Self Examination, and continu'd it with occasional Intermissions for some time. I was surpriz'd to find myself so much fuller of Faults than I had imagined, but I had the Satisfaction of seeing them diminish. To avoid the Trouble of renewing now and then my little Book, which by scraping out the Marks on the Paper of old Faults to make room for new Ones in a new Course, became full of Holes: I transferr'd my Tables and Precepts to the Ivory Leaves of a Memorandum Book, on which the Lines were drawn with red Ink that made a durable Stain, and on those Lines I mark'd my Faults with a black Lead Pencil, which Marks I could easily wipe out with a wet Sponge. After a while I went thro' one Course only in a Year, and afterwards only one in several Years, till at length I omitted them entirely, being employ'd in Voyages and Business abroad with a Multiplicity of Affairs, that interfered, but I always carried my little Book with me.

Franklin's search for moral perfection did not prevent him from writing this very cheerful drinking song around this time.

[ c. 1745]

The Antediluvians were all very sober
For they had no Wine, and they brew'd no October;
All wicked, bad Livers, on Mischief still thinking,
For there can't be good Living where there is not good
    Drinking.

                    Derry down

'Twas honest old Noah first planted the Vine,
And mended his Morals by drinking its Wine;
He justly the drinking of Water decry'd;
For he knew that all Mankind, by drinking it, dy'd.

                    Derry down

From this Piece of History plainly we find
That Water's good neither for Body or Mind;
That Virtue and Safety in Wine-bibbing's found
While all that drink Water deserve to be drown'd.

                    Derry down

So For Safety and Honesty put the Glass round.

As he grew older, Franklin did not lose his keen interest in sex. The following letter was for many years suppressed by various Franklin editors and librarians of his papers. Paul Leicester Ford, author of *The Many-Sided Franklin* (1899), for instance, thought it would "shock modern taste," and Albert Henry Smyth omitted it from his ten-volume edition, *The Writings of Benjamin Franklin* (1905-7), remarking that it would not be tolerated by "the public sentiment of the present age." Since 1926, when it was printed in a biography of Franklin by Phillips Russell, it has appeared in print frequently. No one knows to whom it was addressed. The editors of *The Papers of Benjamin Franklin* are inclined to believe that it is really an essay in the form of a letter; Franklin himself gave it the title "Old Mistresses Apologue."

June 25. 1745

My dear Friend,

I know of no Medicine fit to diminish the violent natural Inclinations you mention; and if I did, I think I should not communicate it to you. Marriage is the proper Remedy. It is the most natural State of Man, and therefore the State in which you are most likely to find solid Happiness. Your Reasons against entring into it at present, appear to me not well-founded. The circumstantial Advantages you have in View by postponing it, are not only uncertain, but they are small in comparison with that of the Thing itself, the being *married and settled.* It is the Man and Woman united that make the compleat human Being. Separate, she wants his Force of Body and Strength of Reason; he, her Softness, Sensibility and acute Discernment. Together they are more likely to succeed in the World. A single Man has not nearly the Value he would have in that State of Union. He is an incomplete Animal. He resembles the odd Half of a Pair of Scissars. If you get a prudent healthy Wife, your Industry in your Profession, with her good Oeconomy, will be a Fortune sufficient.

But if you will not take this Counsel, and persist in thinking a Commerce with the Sex inevitable, then I repeat my former Advice, that in all your Amours you should *prefer old Women to young ones.* You call this a Paradox, and demand my Reasons. They are these:

1.  Because as they have more Knowledge of the World and their Minds are better stor'd with Observations, their Conversation is more improving and more lastingly agreable.

2.  Because when Women cease to be handsome, they study to be good. To maintain their Influence over Men, they supply the Diminution of Beauty by an Augmentation of Utility. They learn to do a 1000 Services small and great, and are the most tender and useful of all Friends when you are sick. Thus they continue amiable. And hence there is hardly such a thing to be found as an old Woman who is not a good Woman.

3.  Because there is no hazard of Children, which

irregularly produc'd may be attended with much Inconvenience.

4. Because thro' more Experience, they are more prudent and discreet in conducting an Intrigue to prevent Suspicion. The Commerce with them is therefore safer with regard to your Reputation. And with regard to theirs, if the Affair should happen to be known, considerate People might be rather inclin'd to excuse an old Woman who would kindly take care of a young Man, form his Manners by her good Counsels, and prevent his ruining his Health and Fortune among mercenary Prostitutes.

5. Because in every Animal that walks upright, the Deficiency of the Fluids that fill the Muscles appears first in the highest Part: The Face first grows lank and wrinkled; then the Neck, then the Breast and Arms; the lower Parts continuing to the last as plump as ever: So that covering all above with a Basket, and regarding only what is below the Girdle, it is impossible of two Women to know an old from a young one. And as in the dark all Cats are grey, the Pleasure of corporal Enjoyment with an old Woman is at least equal, and frequently superior, every Knack being by Practice capable of Improvement.

6. Because the Sin is less. The debauching a Virgin may be her Ruin, and make her for Life unhappy.

7. Because the Compunction is less. The having made a young Girl *miserable* may give you frequent bitter Reflections; none of which can attend the making an old Woman *happy*.

8[thly and Lastly] They are *so grateful!!* Thus much for my Paradox. But still I advise you to marry directly; being sincerely Your affectionate Friend.

Around the same time, Franklin produced another famous bit of sexual foolery. "The Speech of Miss Polly Baker" was not printed in *The Pennsylvania Gazette*. Its first known public appearance was in the London newspaper *The General Advertiser* on April 15, 1747. Within a week, five London papers reprinted it, and they were soon imitated by five monthly magazines. Before the end of the year, many American newspapers followed suit. It was widely regarded in England, France, and many parts of America as fact. The Abbé Raynal cited it in his book, *Histoire Philosophique et Politique*, as an example of the supposed severity of laws in New England.

*The General Advertiser,*
April 15, 1747

The SPEECH of Miss POLLY BAKER, before a Court of
Judicature, at Connecticut near Boston in New-England;
where she was prosecuted the Fifth Time, for having a
Bastard Child: Which influenced the Court to dispense
with her Punishment, and induced one of her Judges to
marry her the next Day.

May it please the Honourable Bench to indulge me in
a few Words: I am a poor unhappy Woman, who have no
Money to fee Lawyers to plead for me, being hard put to
it to get a tolerable Living. I shall not trouble your
Honours with long Speeches; for I have not the Presumption to expect, that you may, by any Means, be
prevailed on to deviate in your Sentence from the Law,
in my Favour. All I humbly hope is, That your Honours
would charitably move the Governor's Goodness on my
Behalf, that my Fine may be remitted. This is the Fifth
Time, Gentlemen, that I have been dragg'd before your
Court on the same Account; twice I have paid heavy
Fines, and twice have been brought to Publick Punishment, for want of Money to pay those Fines. This may
have been agreeable to the Laws, and I don't dispute it;
but since Laws are sometimes unreasonable in themselves, and therefore repealed, and others bear too hard
on the Subject in particular Circumstances; and therefore there is left a Power somewhat to dispense with
the Execution of them; I take the Liberty to say, That
I think this Law, by which I am punished, is both unreasonable in itself, and particularly severe with regard
to me, who have always lived an inoffensive Life in the
Neighbourhood where I was born, and defy my Enemies
(if I have any) to say I ever wrong'd Man, Woman, or
Child. Abstracted from the Law, I cannot conceive (may
it please your Honours) what the Nature of my Offence
is. I have brought Five fine Children into the World, at
the Risque of my Life; I have maintain'd them well by
my own Industry, without burthening the Township,
and would have done it better, if it had not been for the
heavy Charges and Fines I have paid. Can it be a Crime
(in the Nature of Things I mean) to add to the Number
of the King's Subjects, in a new Country that really
wants People? I own it, I should think it a Praise-worthy,
rather than a punishable Action. I have debauched no

*An eighteenth-century printing house
as shown in Diderot's* Encyclopedia

other Woman's Husband, nor enticed any Youth; these Things I never was charg'd with, nor has any one the least Cause of Complaint against me, unless, perhaps, the Minister, or Justice, because I have had Children without being married, by which they have missed a Wedding Fee. But, can ever this be a Fault of mine? I appeal to your Honours. You are pleased to allow I don't want Sense; but I must be stupified to the last Degree, not to prefer the Honourable State of Wedlock, to the Condition I have lived in. I always was, and still am willing to enter into it; and doubt not my behaving well in it, having all the Industry, Frugality, Fertility, and Skill in Oeconomy, appertaining to a good Wife's Character. I defy any Person to say, I ever refused an Offer of that Sort: On the contrary, I readily consented to the only Proposal of Marriage that ever was made me, which was when I was a Virgin; but too easily confiding in the Person's Sincerity that made it, I unhappily lost my own Honour, by trusting to his; for he got me with Child, and then forsook me: That very Person you all know; he is now become a Magistrate of this Country; and I had Hopes he would have appeared this Day on the Bench, and have endeavoured to moderate the Court in my Favour; then I should have scorn'd to have mention'd it; but I must now complain of it, as unjust and unequal, That my Betrayer and Undoer, the first Cause of all my Faults and Miscarriages (if they must be deemed such) should be advanc'd to Honour and Power in the Government, that punishes my Misfortunes with Stripes and Infamy. I should be told, 'tis like, That were there no Act of Assembly in the Case, the Precepts of Religion are violated by my Transgressions. If mine, then, is a religious Offence, leave it to religious Punishments. You have already excluded me from the Comforts of your Church-Communion. Is not that sufficient? You believe I have offended Heaven, and must suffer eternal Fire: Will not that be sufficient? What Need is there, then, of your additional Fines and Whipping? I own, I do not think as you do; for, if I thought what you call a Sin, was really such, I could not presumptuously commit it. But, how can it be believed, that Heaven is angry at my having Children, when to the little done by me towards it, God has been pleased to add his Divine Skill and admirable Workmanship in the Formation of their

*The earliest known portrait of Franklin, attributed to Robert Feke, shows him as a prosperous business-man of around forty years of age.*

Bodies, and crown'd it, by furnishing them with rational and immortal Souls. Forgive me, Gentlemen, if I talk a little extravagantly on these Matters; I am no Divine, but if you, Gentlemen, must be making Laws, do not turn natural and useful Actions into Crimes, by your Prohibitions. But take into your wise Consideration, the great and growing Number of Batchelors in the Country, many of whom from the mean Fear of the Expences of a Family, have never sincerely and honourably courted a Woman in their Lives; and by their Manner of Living, leave unproduced (which is little better than Murder) Hundreds of their Posterity to the Thousandth Generation. Is not this a greater Offence against the Publick Good, than mine? Compel them, then, by Law, either to Marriage, or to pay double the Fine of Fornication every Year. What must poor young Women do, whom Custom have forbid to solicit the Men, and who cannot force themselves upon Husbands, when the Laws take no Care to provide them any; and yet severely punish them if they do their Duty without them; the Duty of the first and great Command of Nature, and of Nature's God, *Encrease and Multiply*. A Duty, from the steady Performance of which, nothing has been able to deter me; but for its Sake, I have hazarded the Loss of the Public Esteem, and have frequently endured Publick Disgrace and Punishment; and therefore ought, in my humble Opinion, instead of a Whipping, to have a Statue erected to my Memory.

By the age of forty-two, Franklin was a distinctly successful man. His printing business was earning him well over two thousand pounds a year. Looking back on his experience, he wrote an essay that was to be reprinted numerous times in subsequent years. The raw young man who had arrived in Philadelphia with only a dollar and a few pennies in his pocket now spoke with the seasoned voice of success.

[July 21, 1748]

ADVICE TO A YOUNG TRADESMAN, WRITTEN BY AN OLD ONE.

To my Friend A.B.

*As you have desired it of me, I write the following Hints, which have been of Service to me, and may, if observed, be so to you.*

Remember that TIME is Money. He that can earn Ten Shillings a Day by his Labour, and goes abroad, or sits idle one half of that Day, tho' he spends but Sixpence during his Diversion or Idleness, ought not to reckon That the only Expence; he has really spent or rather thrown away Five Shillings besides.

Remember that CREDIT is Money. If a Man lets his Money lie in my Hands after it is due, he gives me the Interest, or so much as I can make of it during that Time. This amounts to a considerable Sum where a Man has good and large Credit, and makes good Use of it.

Remember that Money is of a prolific generating Nature. Money can beget Money, and its Offspring can beget more, and so on. Five Shillings turn'd, is *Six*: Turn'd again, 'tis Seven and Three Pence; and so on 'til it becomes an Hundred Pound. The more there is of it, the more it produces every Turning, so that the Profits rise quicker and quicker. He that kills a breeding Sow, destroys all her Offspring to the thousandth Generation. He that murders a Crown, destroys all it might have produc'd, even Scores of Pounds.

Remember that Six Pounds a Year is but a Groat a Day. For this little Sum (which may be daily wasted either in Time or Expence unperceived) a Man of Credit may on his own Security have the constant Possession and Use of an Hundred Pounds. So much in Stock briskly turn'd by an industrious Man, produces great Advantage.

Remember this Saying, *That the good Paymaster is Lord of another Man's Purse.* He that is known to pay punctually and exactly to the Time he promises, may at any Time, and on any Occasion, raise all the Money his Friends can spare. This is sometimes of great Use: Therefore never keep borrow'd Money an Hour beyond the Time you promis'd, lest a Disappointment shuts up your Friends Purse forever.

The most trifling Actions that Affect a Man's Credit, are to be regarded. The Sound of your Hammer at Five in the Morning or Nine at Night, heard by a Creditor, makes him easy Six Months longer. But if he sees you at a Billiard Table, or hears your Voice in a Tavern, when you should be at Work, he sends for his Money the next Day. Finer Cloaths than he or his Wife wears, or greater Expence in any particular than he affords himself, shocks his Pride, and he duns you to humble you. Creditors are a kind of People, that have the sharpest Eyes and Ears, as well as the best Memories of any in the World.

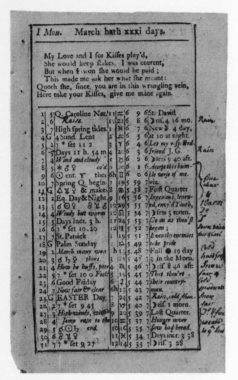

*Verse, weather predictions, and aphorisms were intermingled in* Poor Richard's *monthly pages, on which Franklin later made marginal notations of the actual weather.*

Good-natur'd Creditors (and such one would always chuse to deal with if one could) feel Pain when they are oblig'd to ask for Money. Spare 'em that Pain, and they will love you. When you receive a Sum of Money, divide it among 'em in Proportion to your Debts. Don't be asham'd of paying a small Sum because you owe a greater. Money, more or less, is always welcome; and your Creditor had rather be at the Trouble of receiving Ten Pounds voluntarily brought him, tho' at ten different Times or Payments, than be oblig'd to go ten Times to demand it before he can receive it in a Lump. It shews, besides, that you are mindful of what you owe; it makes you appear a careful as well as an honest Man; and that still encreases your Credit.

Beware of thinking all your own that you possess, and of living accordingly. 'Tis a Mistake that many People who have Credit fall into. To prevent this, keep an exact Account for some Time of both your Expences and your Incomes. If you take the Pains at first to mention Particulars, it will have this good Effect; you will discover how wonderfully small trifling Expences mount up to large Sums, and will discern what might have been, and may for the future be saved, without occasioning any great Inconvenience.

In short, the Way to Wealth, if you desire it, is as plain as the Way to Market. It depends chiefly on two Words, INDUSTRY and FRUGALITY; i.e. Waste neither Time nor Money, but make the best Use of both. He that gets all he can honestly, and saves all he gets (necessary Expences excepted) will certainly become RICH; If that Being who governs the World, to whom all should look for a Blessing on their honest Endeavours, doth not in his wise Providence otherwise determine.

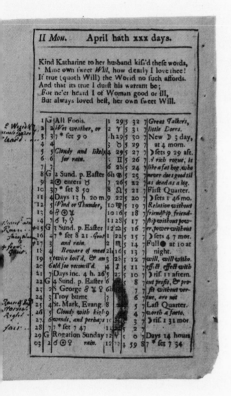

A new serenity was becoming an evident part of Franklin's life. Perhaps the best proof of this was his introduction to *Poor Richard* for 1746. Here the distinction between Franklin and Richard Saunders all but disappeared, and he painted a word picture of his way of life as he entered middle age.

*Poor Richard, 1746*

Who is Poor Richard? People oft enquire,
Where lives? What is he?—never yet the nigher.
Somewhat to ease your Curiositie,
Take these slight Sketches of my Dame and me.

Thanks to kind Readers and a careful Wife,
With Plenty bless'd, I lead an easy Life;
My Business Writing; hers to drain the Mead,
Or crown the barren Hill with useful Shade;
In the smooth Glebe to see the Plowshare worn,
And fill the Granary with needful Corn.
Press nectarous Cyder from my loaded Trees,
Print the sweet Butter, turn the drying Cheese.
Some Books we read, tho' few there are that hit
The happy Point where Wisdom joins with Wit;
That set fair Virtue naked to our View,
And teach us what is *decent*, what is *true*.
The Friend sincere, and honest Man, with Joy
Treating or treated oft our Time employ.
Our Table neat, Meals temperate; and our Door
Op'ning spontaneous to the bashful Poor.
Free from the bitter Rage of Party Zeal,
All those we love who seek the publick Weal.
Nor blindly follow Superstition's Lore,
Which cheats deluded Mankind o'er and o'er.
Not over righteous, quite beyond the Rule,
Conscience perplext by every canting Tool.
Nor yet when Folly hides the dubious Line,
Where Good and Bad their blended Colours join;
Rush indiscreetly down the dangerous Steep,
And plunge uncertain in the darksome Deep.
Cautious, if right; if wrong resolv'd to part
The Inmate Snake that folds about the Heart.
Observe the *Mean*, the *Motive* and the *End*;
Mending our selves, or striving still to mend.
Our Souls sincere, our Purpose fair and free,
Without Vain Glory or Hypocrisy:
Thankful if well; if ill, we kiss the Rod;
Resign with Hope, and put our Trust in GOD.

*Chapter* **4**

# America's Newton

In a letter to his mother in April, 1750, Franklin remarked that when he died he would rather have it said "he lived usefully, than he died rich." No sooner had he achieved financial security, than his spacious mind began seeking new frontiers to challenge. First, and most intriguing, was science. In the summer of 1747, Franklin offered David Hall, who was by then working as his foreman, an opportunity to become a partner in his printing business. Hall was to run the print shop, publish the newspaper and almanac, and pay Franklin 50 per cent of the profits. At the end of eighteen years, this arrangement would cease, and Hall would become the full owner of the business. Franklin, meanwhile, was free to devote all his time to the science that was to make him famous: electricity. The following letter was written to a man who was to play a very important role in Franklin's life—Peter Collinson, a London Quaker merchant with a strong interest in natural science.

> Philadelphia, March 28, 1747
>
> Your kind present of an electric tube, with directions for using it, has put several of us on making electrical experiments, in which we have observed some particular phaenomena that we look upon to be new. I shall, therefore communicate them to you in my next, though possibly they may not be new to you, as among the numbers daily employed in those experiments on your side of the water, 'tis probable some one or other has hit on the same observations. For my own part, I never was before engaged in any study that so totally engrossed my attention and my time as this has lately done; for what with making experiments when I can be alone, and repeating them to my Friends and Acquaintance, who, from the novelty of the thing, come continually in crouds to see them, I have, during some months past, had little leisure for any thing else.

Electricity was at this period more of a curiosity than a
science. It had attracted the attention of numerous learned men in Europe,
but no one knew what it was or how it worked. In another letter to Collinson,
Franklin moved toward one of his most significant discoveries, the importance
of pointed bodies in attracting and repelling electric current. From this discovery Franklin progressed to an even more significant insight, the creation
of the terms *negative* and *positive* to describe the two kinds of electricity that
caused bodies to repel and attract each other. "Watson's Sequel," which
Franklin mentions several times, was a book by the noted English electrical
scientist William Watson: *A Sequel to the Experiments and Observations
Tending to illustrate the Nature and Properties of Electricity.*

Philada. May 25. 1747

In my last I informed you that In pursuing our Electrical
Enquiries, we had observ'd some particular Phaenomena,
which we lookt upon to be new, and of which I promised
to give you some Account; tho' I apprehended they might
possibly not be new to you, as so many Hands are daily
employed in Electrical Experiments on your Side the
Water, some or other of which would probably hit on the
same Observations.

The first is the wonderful Effect of Points both in *drawing* off and *throwing* off the Electrical Fire. For Example,

Place an Iron shot of three or four Inches Diameter on
the Mouth of a clean dry Glass Bottle. By a fine silken
Thread from the Ceiling, right over the Mouth of the Bottle, suspend a small Cork Ball, about the Bigness of a
Marble: the Thread of such a Length, as that the Cork
Ball may rest against the Side of the Shot. Electrify the
Shot, and the Ball will be repelled to the Distance of 4 or
5 Inches, more or less according to the Quantity of Electricity. When in this State, if you present to the Shot the
Point of a long, slender, sharp Bodkin at 6 or 8 Inches Distance, the Repellency is instantly destroy'd, and the Cork
flies to it. A blunt Body must be brought within an Inch,
and draw a Spark to produce the same Effect. To prove
that the Electrical Fire is drawn off by the Point: if you
take the Blade of the Bodkin out of the wooden Handle,
and fix it in a Stick of Sealing Wax, and then present it at
the Distance aforesaid no such Effect follows; but slide
one Finger along the Wax till you touch the Blade, and the
Ball flies to the Shot immediately. If you present the Point
in the Dark, you will see, sometimes at a Foot Distance
and more, a Light gather upon it like that of a Fire-Fly or
Glow-Worm; the less sharp the Point, the nearer you must

bring it to observe this Light: and at whatever Distance you see the Light, you may draw off the Electrical Fire, and destroy the Repellency. If a Cork Ball, so suspended, be repelled by the Tube, and a Point be presented quick to it, tho' at a considerable Distance, tis surprizing to see how suddenly it flies back to the Tube. Points of Wood do as well as those of Metal, provided the Wood is not dry.

To shew that Points will *throw* off, as well as *draw* off the Electrical Fire: Lay a long sharp Needle upon the Shot, and you can not electrise the Shot, so as to make it repel the Cork Ball. Fix a Needle to the End of a suspended Gun Barrel, so as to point beyond it like a little Bayonet, and while it remains there, the Gun Barrel can not be electrised (by the Tube applied to the other End) so as to give a Spark; the Fire is continually running out silently at the Point. In the Dark you may see it make the same Appearance as it does in the Case before mentioned.

The Repellency between the Cork Ball and Shot is likewise destroy'd;  1. By sifting find Sand on it; this does it gradually: 2. By breathing on it: 3. By making a Smoke about it from burning Wood:  4. By Candle Light, even tho' the Candle is at a Foot Distance: These do it suddenly. The Light of a bright Coal from a Wood Fire, and the Light of a red-hot Iron do it likewise; but not at so great a Distance. Smoke from dry Rosin dropt into a little hot Letter Founders Ladle under the Shot does not destroy the Repellency; but is attracted by both the Shot and the Cork-Ball, forming proportionable Atmospheres round them, making them look beautifully; somewhat like some of the Figures in Burnets or Whiston's Theory of the Earth.

N.B. This Experiment should be made [in a closet] where the Air is very still.

The Light of the Sun thrown strongly on both Shot and Cork by a Looking Glass for a long Time together does not impair the Repellency in the least. This Difference between Fire Light and Sun Light is another Thing that seems new and extraordinary to us.

We had for some Time been of Opinion, that the Electrical Fire was not created by Friction, but collected, being an Element diffused among, and attracted by other Matter, particularly by Water and Metals. We had even discovered and demonstrated its Afflux to the Electrical Sphere, as well as its Efflux, by Means of little light Wind-Mill Wheels made of stiff Paper Vanes, fixt obliquely, and turning freely

*Peter Collinson of London*

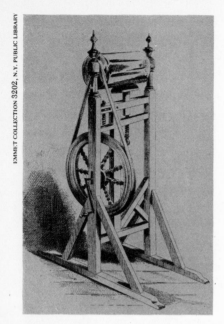

*Engraving of Franklin's crude
electrical generator, c. 1747*

on fine Wire Axes. Also by little Wheels of the same Matter, but formed like Water Wheels. Of the Disposition and Application of which Wheels, and the various Phaenomena resulting, I could, if I had Time, and it were necessary, fill you a Sheet.

The Impossibility of Electrising one's self (tho' standing on Wax) by Rubbing the Tube and drawing the Fire from it: and the Manner of doing it by passing the Tube near a Person, or Thing standing on the Floor &c. had also occurred to us some Months before Mr. Watsons ingenious *Sequel* came to hand; and these were some of the new Things I intended to have communicated to you: But now I need only mention some Particulars not hinted in that Piece, with our Reasonings thereon; tho' perhaps the latter might well enough be spared.

1. A Person standing on Wax and rubbing the Tube; and another Person on Wax drawing the Fire, they will both of them (provided they do not stand so as to touch one another) appear to be electrised to a Person standing on the Floor; that is, he will perceive a Spark on approaching each of them.

2. But if the Persons standing on Wax touch one another during the exciting of the Tube, neither of them will appear to be electrised.

3. If they touch one another after exciting the Tube, and drawing the Fire as aforesaid, there will be a stronger Spark between them than was between either of them and the Person on the Floor.

4. After such strong Spark, neither of them discovers any Electricity.

These Appearances we attempt to account for thus. We suppose as aforesaid, That Electrical Fire is a common Element, of which every one of the three Persons abovementioned has his equal Share before any Operation is begun with the Tube. *A* who stands on Wax, and rubs the Tube, collects the Electrical Fire from himself into the Glass; and his Communication with the common Stock being cut off by the Wax, his Body is not again immediately supply'd. *B*, who stands upon Wax likewise, passing his Knuckle along near the Tube, receives the Fire which was collected by the Glass from *A*; and his Communication with the common Stock being likewise cutt off, he retains the additional Quantity received. To *C*, standing on the Floor, both appear to be electrised; for he having only the middle Quantity of Electrical Fire receives a Spark on approaching *B*, who has an over-quantity, but gives one to *A*, who has an under-quantity. If *A* and *B* touch each other, the Spark between them is stronger, because the Difference between them is greater. After such Touch, there is no Spark between either of them and *C*; because the Electrical Fire in all is reduced to the original Equality. If they touch while Electrising, the Equality is never destroyed, the Fire only circulating. Hence have arisen some new Terms among us. We say *B* (and other Bodies alike circumstanced) are electrised *positively; A negatively*: Or rather *B* is electrised *plus* and *A minus*. And we daily in our Experiments electrise bodies *plus* or *minus* as we think proper. *These Terms* we may use till your Philosophers give us better.

Franklin's progress into the mystery of electricity was neither simple nor easy. He spent four years working on the new science. In this letter to Peter Collinson, he confessed to—and yet simultaneously exulted in—his difficulties.

Philada. Augt. 14. 1747

I have lately written two long Letters to you on the Subject of Electricity, one by the Governor's Vessel, the other per Mesnard. On some further Experiments since, I have observ'd a Phenomenon or two that I cannot at present account for on the Principles laid down in those Letters, and am therefore become a little diffident of my Hypothesis, and asham'd that I have express'd myself in so positive a manner. In going on with these Experiments, how many pretty Systems do we build, which we soon find ourselves oblig'd to destroy! If there is no other Use discover'd of Electricity, this, however, is something considerable, that it may *help to make a vain Man humble*. I must now request that you would not expose those Letters; or if you communicate them to any Friends, you would at least conceal my Name.

As he did with almost everything, Franklin injected an element of fun into his electrical investigations. This experiment, described in another letter to Peter Collinson, also has some interest for its symbolic, prophetic role in Franklin's life.

Philada. Apl. 29. 1749

The Magical Picture is made thus. Having a large Mezzotinto with a Frame and Glass (Suppose of the King, God

89

preserve him) Take out the Print, and cut a Pannel out of it, near two Inches all around distant from the Frame; if the Cut is thro' the Picture, tis not the Worse. With thin Paste or Gum Water, fix the Border, that is cut off, on the inside of the Glass, pressing it smoothe and close; then fill up the Vacancy by Gilding the Glass well with Leaf Gold or Brass; gild likewise the inner Edge of the Back of the Frame all round except the Top Part, and form a Communication between that Gilding and the Gilding behind the Glass: then put in the Board, and that side is finished. Turn up the Glass, and gild the foreside exactly over the Back Gilding; and when this is dry, cover it by pasting on the Pannel of the Picture that had been cut out, observing to bring the corresponding Parts of the Border and Picture together; by which the Picture will appear of a Piece as at first, only Part is behind the Glass and Part before. Hold the Picture horizontally by the Top, and place a little moveable gilt Crown on the Kings Head. If now the Picture be moderately electrified, and another Person take hold of the Frame with one Hand, so that his Fingers touch it's inside Gilding, and with the other Hand endeavour to take off the Crown, he will receive a terrible Blow and fail in the Attempt. If the Picture were highly charg'd, the Consequence might perhaps be as fatal as that of High Treason: For when the Spark is taken thro' a Quire of Paper laid on the Picture, by Means of a Wire Communication, it makes a fair Hole thro' every Sheet; that is thro' 48 Leaves (tho' a Quire of Paper is thought good Armour against the Push of a Sword, or even against a Pistol Bullet) and the Crack is exceeding loud. The Operator, who, to prevent its falling, holds the Picture by the upper End, where the inside of the Frame is not gilt, feels Nothing of the Shock, and may touch the Crown without Danger, which he pretends is a Test of his Loyalty. If a Ring of Persons take a Shock among them the Experiment is called the *Conspiracy....*

[Franklin ended the letter with a charming picture of Philadelphia's "Electricians" relaxing in the country.]

Chagrin'd a little that We have hitherto been able to discover Nothing in this Way of Use to Mankind, and the hot Weather coming on, when Electrical Experiments are not so agreable; 'tis proposed to put an End to them for this Season somewhat humorously in a Party of Pleasure on the Banks of Schuyl-Kill, (where Spirits are at the same

*An engraving of Franklin after the Mason Chamberlin portrait shows him looking at bells that rang when electricity passed through them; outside the window a storm swirls around his lightning rod.*

Time to be fired by a Spark sent from Side to Side thro'
the River). A Turky is to be killed for our Dinners by the
Electrical Shock; and roasted by the electrical Jack, before
a Fire kindled by the Electrified Bottle; when the Healths
of all the famous Electricians in England, France and
Germany, are to be drank in Electrified Bumpers, under
the Discharge of Guns from the Electrical Battery.

Even as he wrote these words, Franklin was moving to-
ward his most important practical discovery—the one that would make him
world-famous. He described his progress in a letter he wrote a few years
later to John Lining of Charleston, South Carolina.

Philadelphia, March 18, 1755
Your question, how I came first to think of proposing the
experiment of drawing down the lightning, in order to
ascertain its sameness with the electric fluid, I cannot
answer better than by giving you an extract from the
minutes I used to keep of the experiments I made, with
memorandums of such as I purposed to make, the reasons
for making them, and the observations that arose upon
them, from which minutes my letters were afterwards
drawn. By this extract you will see that the thought was
not so much "an out-of-the-way one," but that it might
have occurred to any electrician.

"Nov. 1, 1749. Electrical fluid agrees with lightning in
these particulars:   1. Giving light.   2. Colour of the light.
3. Crooked direction.   4. Swift motion.   5. Being conducted by metals.   6. Crack or noise in exploding.   7. Subsisting in water or ice.   8. Rending bodies it passes
through.   9. Destroying animals.   10. Melting metals.
11. Firing inflammable substances.   12. Sulphureous
smell. The electric fluid is attracted by points. We do not
know whether this property is in lightning. But since they
agree in all the particulars wherein we can already compare them, is it not probable they agree likewise in this?
Let the experiment be made."

By July 29, 1750, Franklin had worked out the details
for an experiment to prove that lightning and electricity were the same. Here
is a description of the event from a paper entitled "Opinions and Conjectures
concerning the Properties and Effects of the Electrical Matter, arising from
Experiments and Observations made in Philadelphia, 1749." A copy of the
paper was forwarded with a letter to his London correspondent Peter Collinson in mid-1750.

Philada. July 29 1750

21. To determine the Question, Whether the Clouds that contain Lightning are electrified or not, I would propose an Experiment to be try'd where it may be done conveniently.

On the Top of some high Tower or Steeple, place a Kind of Sentry Box big enough to contain a Man and an electrical Stand. From the Middle of the Stand let an Iron Rod rise, and pass bending out of the Door, and then upright 20 or 30 feet, pointed very sharp at the End. If the Electrical Stand be kept clean and dry, a Man standing on it when such Clouds are passing low, might be electrified, and afford Sparks, the Rod drawing Fire to him from the Cloud. If any Danger to the Man should be apprehended (tho' I think there would be none) let him stand on the Floor of his Box, and now and then bring near to the Rod, the Loop of a Wire, that has one End fastened to the Leads; he holding it by a Wax-Handle. So the Sparks, if the Rod is electrified, will Strike from the Rod to the Wire and not affect him.

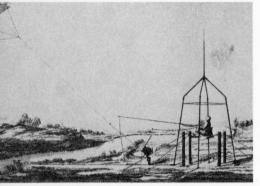

*An improvement of Franklin's electrical kite experiment is tested by a French scientist.*

In Europe this proposal was quickly dubbed the Philadelphia Experiment. Europeans learned about it from Franklin's collected letters, which Peter Collinson arranged to have published in 1751 as *Experiments and Observations on Electricity, Made in Philadelphia in America, by Mr. Benjamin Franklin.* Franklin himself did not attempt the experiment, because there was no structure high enough in Philadelphia to give it a chance to succeed. English scientists, who had no lack of church steeples to work from, were strangely uninterested in attempting it—an early example of the mother country's instinctive hauteur toward Americans. When *Experiments and Observations* was translated into French, in 1752, two French electricians, Delor and Dalibard, each successfully performed the sentry box experiment in the spring of that year. Word of their success crossed the Channel, and the English confirmed the triumph of Franklin's hypothesis several times during the summer of 1752. Meanwhile, in Philadelphia, Franklin was trying out an idea of his own. In June of 1752, before he heard about the success of the French and English experiments, he sent his conductor high enough to draw electricity from the clouds by flying it on a kite during a thunder shower. On October 19, 1752, Franklin reported the success of this experiment in a rather cryptic fashion, in *The Pennsylvania Gazette.*

Philadelphia, October 19 [1752]

As frequent Mention is made in the News Papers from Europe, of the Success of the Philadelphia Experiment for drawing the Electric Fire from Clouds by Means of

EXPERIMENTS

AND

OBSERVATIONS

ON

ELECTRICITY,

MADE AT

*Philadelphia* in *America*,

BY

Mr. BENJAMIN FRANKLIN,

AND

Communicated in several Letters to Mr. P. COLLINSON,
of *London*, F. R. S.

LONDON:

Printed and sold by E. CAVE, at *St. John's Gate*. 1751
(Price 2s. 6d.)

SUPPLEMENTAL

*Experiments and Observations*

ON

ELECTIRCITY,

PART II.

MADE AT

*Philadelphia* in *America*,

BY

BENJAMIN FRANKLIN, *Esq*;

AND

Communicated in several Letters to P. COLLINSON, *Esq;*
of *London*, F. R. S.

LONDON·

Printed and sold by E. CAVE, at *St. John's Gate*. 1753
(Price 6d)

*Title pages of the first and
supplemental editions of Franklin's
experiments reveal an embarrassing
spelling error in the key word.*

pointed Rods of Iron erected on high Buildings, &c. it may be agreeable to the Curious to be inform'd, that the same Experiment has succeeded in Philadelphia, tho' made in a different and more easy Manner, which any one may try, as follows.

Make a small Cross of two light Strips of Cedar, the Arms so long as to reach the four Corners of a large thin Silk Handkerchief when extended; tie the Corners of the Handkerchief to the Extremities of the Cross, so you have the Body of a Kite; which being properly accommodated with a Tail, Loop and String, will rise in the Air, like those made of Paper; but this being of Silk is fitter to bear the Wet and Wind of a Thunder Gust without tearing. To the Top of the upright Stick of the Cross is to be fixed a very sharp pointed Wire, rising a Foot or more above the Wood. To the End of the Twine, next the Hand, is to be tied a silk Ribbon, and where the Twine and the silk join, a Key may be fastened. This Kite is to be raised when a Thunder Gust appears to be coming on, and the Person who holds the String must stand within a Door, or Window, or under some Cover, so that the Silk Ribbon may not be wet; and Care must be taken that the Twine does not touch the Frame of the Door or Window. As soon as any of the Thunder Clouds come over the Kite, the pointed Wire will draw the Electric Fire from them, and the Kite, with all the Twine, will be electrified, and the loose Filaments of the Twine will stand out every Way, and be attracted by an approaching Finger. And when the Rain has wet the Kite and Twine, so that it can conduct the Electric Fire freely, you will find it stream out plentifully from the Key on the Approach of your Knuckle. At this Key the Phial may be charg'd; and from Electric Fire thus obtain'd, Spirits may be kindled, and all the other Electric Experiments be perform'd, which are usually done by the Help of a rubbed Glass Globe or Tube; and thereby the *Sameness* of the Electric Matter with that of Lightning compleatly demonstrated.

In *Poor Richard* for 1753, Franklin published the final phase of his discovery—the practical application known as the lightning rod.

*Poor Richard, 1753*

It has pleased God in his Goodness to Mankind, at length to discover to them the Means of securing their Habitations and other Buildings from Mischief by Thunder and Lightning. The Method is this: Provide a small Iron Rod (it may be made of the Rod-iron used by the Nailers) but of such a Length, that one End being three or four Feet in the moist Ground, the other may be six or eight Feet above the highest Part of the Building. To the upper End of the Rod fasten about a Foot of Brass Wire, the Size of a common Knitting-needle, sharpened to a fine Point; the Rod may be secured to the House by a few small Staples. If the House or Barn be long, there may be a Rod and Point at each End, and a middling Wire along the Ridge from one to the other. A House thus furnished will not be damaged by Lightning, it being attracted by the Points, and passing thro the Metal into the Ground without hurting any Thing. Vessels also, having a sharp pointed Rod fix'd on the Top of their Masts, with a Wire from the Foot of the Rod reaching down, round one of the Shrouds, to the Water, will not be hurt by Lightning.

As Franklin noted in his experiment on the magical picture, electricity was a powerful substance. He described how nearly fatal to him personally was one electrical experiment, in this letter that he wrote to his brother John Franklin.

Phila. Decr. 25. 1750
I have lately made an Experiment in Electricity that I desire never to repeat. Two nights ago being about to kill a Turkey by the Shock from two large Glass Jarrs containing as much electrical fire as forty common Phials, I inadvertently took the whole thro' my own Arms and Body, by receiving the fire from the united Top Wires with one hand, while the other held a Chain connected with the outsides of both Jars. The Company present (whose talking to me, and to one another I suppose occasioned my Inattention to what I was about) Say that the flash was very great and the crack as loud as a Pistol; yet my Senses being instantly gone, I neither Saw the one nor heard the other; nor did I feel the Stroke on my hand, tho' I afterwards found it raised a round swelling where the fire enter'd as big as half a Pistol Bullet by which you may judge of the Quickness of the Electrical Fire, which by this Instance Seems to be greater than that of Sound, Light and animal Sensation. What I can remember of the matter, is, that I was about to try whether the Bottles or Jars were fully charged, by the Strength and Length of the stream issuing to my hands as I commonly used to do, and which I might safely

*Exp. II.*

*One of the lightning rod illustrations from Franklin's book on electricity*

*Testing Franklin's experiment proved fatal to a Russian scientist.*

eno' have done if I had not held the chain in the other hand; I then felt what I know not how well to describe; an universal Blow thro'out my whole Body from head to foot which seem'd within as well as without; after which the first thing I took notice of was a violent quick Shaking of my body which gradually remitting, my sense as gradually return'd, and then I tho't the Bottles must be discharged but Could not conceive how, till att last I Perceived the Chain in my hand, and Recollected what I had been About to do: that part of my hand and fingers which held the Chain was left white as tho' the Blood had been Driven Out, and Remained so 8 or 10 Minutes After, feeling like Dead flesh, and I had a Numbness in my Arms and the back of my Neck, which Continued till the Next Morning but wore off. Nothing Remains now of this Shock but a Soreness in my breast Bone, which feels As if it had been Brused. I Did not fall, but Suppose I should have been Knocked Down if I had Received the Stroke in my head: the whole was Over in less than a minute.

You may Communicate this to Mr. Bowdoin As A Caution to him, but do not make it more Publick, for I am Ashamed to have been Guilty of so Notorious A Blunder; A Match for that of the Irishman, Sister Told me of, who to Divert his Wife pour'd the Bottle of Gun Powder on the live Coal; or of that Other, who being About to Steal Powder, made a Hole in the Cask with a Hott Iron.

Electricity was by no means the only science that absorbed Franklin's mind. He was also intensely interested in meteorology, and in this letter to his friend Jared Eliot, pastor of the Congregational Church in Killingworth, Connecticut, he explained an important discovery—the origin of northeast storms.

Philada. Feb. 13. 1749, 50 [1750]
You desire to know my Thoughts about the N.E. Storms beginning to Leeward. Some Years since there was an Eclipse of the Moon at 9 in the Evening, which I intended to observe, but before 8 a Storm blew up at NE., and continued violent all Night and all next Day, the Sky thick clouded, dark and rainy, so that neither Moon nor Stars could be seen. The Storm did a great deal of Damage all along the Coast, for we had Accounts of it in the News Papers from Boston, Newport, New York, Maryland and Virginia. But what surpriz'd me, was to find in the Boston Newspapers an Account of an Observation of that

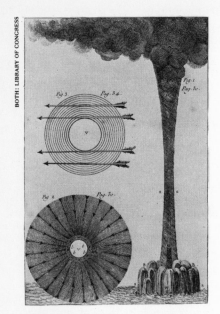

*Diagram of a waterspout used to illustrate Franklin's theory on the causes of this phenomenon of the sea*

Eclipse made there: For I thought, as the Storm came from the NE. it must have begun sooner at Boston than with us, and consequently have prevented such Observation. I wrote to my Brother about it, and he inform'd me, that the Eclipse was over there, an hour before the Storm began. Since which I have made Enquiries from time to time of Travellers, and of my Correspondents N Eastward and S. Westward, and observ'd the Accounts in the Newspapers from N England, N York, Maryland, Virginia and South Carolina, and I find it to be a constant Fact, that N East Storms begin to Leeward; and are often more violent there than farther to Windward. Thus the last October Storm, which with you was on the 8th. began on the 7th in Virginia and N Carolina, and was most violent there. As to the Reason of this, I can only give you my Conjectures. Suppose a great Tract of Country, Land and Sea, to wit Florida and the Bay of Mexico, to have clear Weather for several Days, and to be heated by the Sun and its Air thereby exceedingly rarefied; Suppose the Country North Eastward, as Pennsilvania, New England, Nova Scotia, Newfoundland, &c. to be at the same time cover'd with Clouds, and its Air chill'd and condens'd. The rarefied Air being lighter must rise, and the Dense Air next to it will press into its Place; that will be follow'd by the next denser Air, that by the next, and so on. Thus when I have a Fire in my Chimney, there is a Current of Air constantly flowing from the Door to the Chimney; but the beginning of the Motion was at the Chimney, where the air being rarefied by the Fire, rising, its Place was supply'd by the cooler Air that was next to it, and the Place of that by the next, and so on to the Door. So the Water in a long Sluice or Mill Race, being stop'd by a Gate, is at Rest like the Air in a Calm; but as soon as you open the Gate at one End to let it out, the Water next the Gate begins first to move, that which is next to it follows; and so tho' the Water proceeds forward to the Gate, the Motion which began there runs backwards, if one may so speak, to the upper End of the Race, where the Water is last in Motion. We have on this Continent a long Ridge of Mountains running from N east to S west; and the Coast runs the same Course. These may, perhaps, contribute towards the Direction [of the winds or at least influence] them in some Degree, [missing]. If these Conjectures do not [satisfy you, I wish] to have yours on the Subject.

Almost as important as electricity in winning Franklin fame as a scientist in his own time was his essay on population. Franklin wrote it in 1751—at a time when the British Iron Act of 1750, prohibiting the expansion of the iron industry in America, threatened the growth of the Colonies. Although he circulated the essay privately among his English and American friends, he did not consent to its publication until 1754. Thereafter, it was reprinted frequently and had a strong influence on other students of population, such as Thomas Malthus, and on economists, such as Adam Smith, who owned two copies of the essay. On English politicians, however, it seems to have had an opposite effect from the one Franklin intended. Instead of inspiring them to give the Colonies more freedom, the knowledge that America would soon match England in numbers and wealth made many politicians favor additional repressive measures. Franklin's prediction that the population of America would double every twenty years was amazingly accurate. It held true for a hundred years after he made it. It probably would have continued to hold true had not the massive influx of immigrants in the last half of the nineteenth century added a new, accelerating element to the nation's growth.

1751

OBSERVATIONS concerning the Increase of Mankind, Peopling of Countries, &c.

1.   Tables of the Proportion of Marriages to Births, of Deaths to Births, of Marriages to the Numbers of Inhabitants, &c. form'd on Observations made upon the Bills of Mortality, Christnings, &c. of populous Cities, will not suit Countries; nor will Tables form'd on Observations made on full settled old Countries, as Europe, suit new Countries, as America.

2.   For People increase in Proportion to the Number of Marriages, and that is greater in Proportion to the Ease and Convenience of supporting a Family. When Families can be easily supported, more Persons marry, and earlier in Life.

3.   In Cities, where all Trades, Occupations and Offices are full, many delay marrying, till they can see how to bear the Charges of a Family; which Charges are greater in Cities, as Luxury is more common: many live single during Life, and continue Servants to Families, Journeymen to Trades, &c. hence Cities do not by natural Generation supply themselves with Inhabitants; the Deaths are more than the Births.

4.   In Countries full settled, the Case must be nearly the same; all Lands being occupied and improved to the Heighth: those who cannot get Land, must Labour for

*When Franklin found that glasses "proper for Reading" were not best "for greater Distances," he was not long in making the first bifocals.*

# SCIENTIST, INVENTOR, AND GADGETEER

Franklin's scientific and inventive genius ran the gamut from his extraordinary discoveries in the field of electricity to a mathematical stunt of numbering squares so that the sums of every row, horizontal, perpendicular, or diagonal, should be equal (bottom). A British admirer said of him: "He could make an experiment with less apparatus . . . than any other philosopher we ever saw." The plate of diagrams at right is from Franklin's own copy of his *Experiments and Observations on Electricity* and the explanation of Fig. VI is in his own handwriting. Also by his own hand is the drawing of the "Boat for Pleasure on the Delaware River" (below, left), which illustrates how one would fix the sail in a horizontal position during a tempest. Other maritime inventions included a sea anchor to alleviate the problems illustrated by the two little ships below, which are in danger of having their anchor chains snapped in a storm; and on his various transatlantic crossings he determined the course of the Gulf Stream (bottom, far right). In 1753, he offered readers of *Poor Richard* a diagram charting the coming transit of Mercury across the face of the sun (bottom, left). But the invention that made his name a household word was the ingenious Franklin stove (bottom, near right), which vastly improved the heating of cold Colonial rooms.

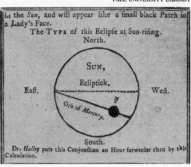

in the *Sun*, and will appear like a small black Patch in a Lady's Face.

The Type of this Eclipse at Sun-rising.

Dr. *Halley* puts this Conjunction an Hour forwarder than by this Calculation.

*A Magic Square of Squares.*

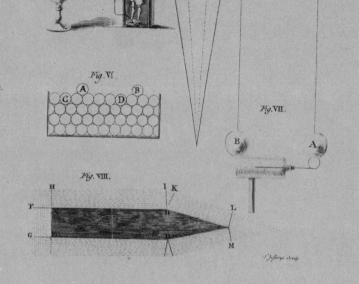

Fig. I. Fig. II. Fig. III. Fig. IV.

Fig. V. Fig. IX. Fig. X.

*Fig. VI. Profile of a Piece of Water. C & D are amongst the Particles of the Surface A & B above the Surface. Small Shot would represent it better than this Figure.*

Fig. VI.

Fig. VII.

Fig. VIII.

J. Jefferys Sculp.

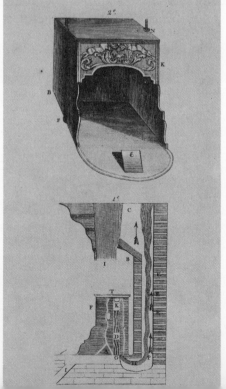

others that have it; when Labourers are plenty, their Wages will be low; by low Wages a Family is supported with Difficulty; this Difficulty deters many from Marriage, who therefore long continue Servants and single. Only as the Cities take Supplies of People from the Country, and thereby make a little more Room in the Country; Marriage is a little more incourag'd there, and the Births exceed the Deaths.

5.   Europe is generally full settled with Husbandsmen, Manufacturers, &c. and therefore cannot now much increase in People: America is chiefly occupied by Indians, who subsist mostly by Hunting. But as the Hunter, of all Men, requires the greatest Quantity of Land from whence to draw his Subsistence, (the Husbandman subsisting on much less, the Gardner on still less, and the Manufacturer requiring least of all), The Europeans found America as fully settled as it well could be by Hunters; yet these having large Tracks, were easily prevail'd on to part with Portions of Territory to the new Comers, who did not much interfere with the Natives in Hunting, and furnish'd them with many Things they wanted.

6. Land being thus plenty in America, and so cheap as that a labouring Man, that understands Husbandry, can in a short Time save Money enough to purchase a Piece of new Land sufficient for a Plantation, whereon he may subsist a Family; such are not afraid to marry; for if they even look far enough forward to consider how their Children when grown up are to be provided for, they see that more Land is to be had at Rates equally easy, all Circumstances considered.

7.   Hence Marriages in America are more general, and more generally early, than in Europe. And if it is reckoned there, that there is but one Marriage per Annum among 100 Persons, perhaps we may here reckon two; and if in Europe they have but 4 Births to a Marriage (many of their Marriages being late) we may here reckon 8, of which if one half grow up, and our Marriages are made, reckoning one with another at 20 Years of Age, our People must at least be doubled every 20 years.

8.   But notwithstanding this Increase, so vast is the Territory of North-America, that it will require many Ages to settle it fully; and till it is fully settled, Labour will never be cheap here, where no Man continues long a Labourer for others, but gets a Plantation of his own, no Man continues

*Thomas Malthus (above) and Adam Smith (below) were both influenced by Franklin's population study.*

long a Journeyman to a Trade, but goes among those new Settlers, and sets up for himself, &c. Hence Labour is no cheaper now, in Pennsylvania, than it was 30 Years ago, tho' so many Thousand labouring People have been imported.

9.   The Danger therefore of these Colonies interfering with their Mother Country in Trades that depend on Labour, Manufactures, &c. is too remote to require the Attention of Great-Britain.

10.   But in Proportion to the Increase of the Colonies, a vast Demand is growing for British Manufactures, a glorious Market wholly in the Power of Britain, in which Foreigners cannot interfere, which will increase in a short Time even beyond her Power of supplying, tho' her whole Trade should be to her Colonies: Therefore Britain should not much restrain Manufactures in her Colonies. A wise and good Mother will not do it. To distress, is to weaken, and weakening the Children, weakens the whole Family.

11.   Besides if the Manufactures of Britain (by Reason of the American Demands) should rise too high in Price, Foreigners who can sell cheaper will drive her Merchants out of Foreign Markets; Foreign Manufactures will thereby be encouraged and increased, and consequently foreign Nations, perhaps her Rivals in Power, grow more populous and more powerful; while her own Colonies, kept too low, are unable to assist her, or add to her Strength.

12.   'Tis an ill-grounded Opinion that by the Labour of Slaves, America may possibly vie in Cheapness of Manufactures with Britain. The Labour of Slaves can never be so cheap here as the Labour of working Men is in Britain. Any one may compute it. Interest of Money is in the Colonies from 6 to 10 per Cent. Slaves one with another cost £30 Sterling per Head. Reckon then the Interest of the first Purchase of a Slave, the Insurance or Risque on his Life, his Cloathing and Diet, Expences in his Sickness and Loss of Time, Loss by his Neglect of Business (Neglect is natural to the Man who is not to be benefited by his own Care or Diligence), Expence of a Driver to keep him at Work, and his Pilfering from Time to Time, almost every Slave being *by Nature* a Thief, and compare the whole Amount with the Wages of a Manufacturer of Iron or Wool in England, you will see that Labour is much cheaper there than it ever can

be by Negroes here. Why then will Americans purchase Slaves? Because Slaves may be kept as long as a Man pleases, or has Occasion for their Labour; while hired Men are continually leaving their Master (often in the midst of his Business,) and setting up for themselves.

13. As the Increase of People depends on the Encouragement of Marriages, the following Things must diminish a Nation, viz. 1. The being conquered; for the Conquerors will engross as many Offices, and exact as much Tribute or Profit on the Labour of the conquered, as will maintain them in their new Establishment, and this diminishing the Subsistence of the Natives discourages their Marriages, and so gradually diminishes them, while the Foreigners increase. 2. Loss of Territory. Thus the Britons being driven into Wales, and crowded together in a barren Country insufficient to support such great Numbers, diminished 'till the People bore a Proportion to the Produce, while the Saxons increas'd on their abandoned Lands; 'till the Island became full of English. And were the English now driven into Wales by some foreign Nation, there would in a few Years be no more Englishmen in Britain, than there are now People in Wales. 3. Loss of Trade. Manufactures exported, draw Subsistence from Foreign Countries for Numbers; who are thereby enabled to marry and raise Families. If the Nation be deprived of any Branch of Trade, and no new Employment is found for the People occupy'd in that Branch, it will also be soon deprived of so many People. 4. Loss of Food. Suppose a Nation has a Fishery, which not only employs great Numbers, but makes the Food and Subsistence of the People cheaper; If another Nation becomes Master of the Seas, and prevents the Fishery, the People will diminish in Proportion as the Loss of Employ, and Dearness of Provision, makes it more difficult to subsist a Family. 5. Bad Government and insecure Property. People not only leave such a Country, and settling Abroad incorporate with other Nations, lose their native Language, and become Foreigners; but the Industry of those that remain being discourag'd, the Quantity of Subsistence in the Country is lessen'd, and the Support of a Family becomes more difficult. So heavy Taxes tend to diminish a People. 6. The Introduction of Slaves. The Negroes brought into the English Sugar Islands, have greatly

*A page from a 1755 London reprint of Franklin's essay on population*

diminish'd the Whites there; the Poor are by this Means depriv'd of Employment, while a few Families acquire vast Estates; which they spend on Foreign Luxuries, and educating their Children in the Habit of those Luxuries; the same Income is needed for the Support of one that might have maintain'd 100. The Whites who have Slaves, not labouring, are enfeebled, and therefore not so generally prolific; the Slaves being work'd too hard, and ill fed, their Constitutions are broken, and the Deaths among them are more than the Births; so that a continual Supply is needed from Africa. The Northern Colonies having few Slaves increase in Whites. Slaves also pejorate the Families that use them; the white Children become proud, disgusted with Labour, and being educated in Idleness, are rendered unfit to get a Living by Industry.

14. Hence the Prince that acquires new Territory, if he finds it vacant, or removes the Natives to give his own People Room; the Legislator that makes effectual Laws for promoting of Trade, increasing Employment, improving Land by more or better Tillage; providing more Food by Fisheries; securing Property, &c. and the Man that invents new Trades, Arts or Manufactures, or new Improvements in Husbandry, may be properly called *Fathers* of their Nation, as they are the Cause of the Generation of Multitudes, by the Encouragement they afford to Marriage.

15. As to Privileges granted to the married, (such as the *Jus trium Liberorum* among the Romans), they may hasten the filling of a Country that has been thinned by War or Pestilence, or that has otherwise vacant Territory; but cannot increase a People beyond the Means provided for their Subsistence.

16. Foreign Luxuries and needless Manufactures imported and used in a Nation, do, by the same Reasoning, increase the People of the Nation that furnishes them, and diminish the People of the Nation that uses them. Laws therefore that prevent such Importations, and on the contrary promote the Exportation of Manufactures to be consumed in Foreign Countries, may be called (with Respect to the People that make them) *generative Laws*, as by increasing Subsistence they encourage Marriage. Such Laws likewise strengthen a Country, doubly, by increasing its own People and

diminishing its Neighbours....

18.    Home Luxury in the Great, increases the Nation's Manufacturers employ'd by it, who are many, and only tends to diminish the Families that indulge in it, who are few. The greater the common fashionable Expence of any Rank of People, the more cautious they are of Marriage. Therefore Luxury should never be suffer'd to become common.

19.    The great Increase of Offspring in particular Families, is not always owing to greater Fecundity of Nature, but sometimes to Examples of Industry in the Heads, and industrious Education; by which the Children are enabled to provide better for themselves, and their marrying early, is encouraged from the Prospect of good Subsistence.

20.    If there be a Sect therefore, in our Nation, that regard Frugality and Industry as religious Duties, and educate their Children therein, more than others commonly do; such Sect must consequently increase more by natural Generation, than any other Sect in Britain.

21.    The Importation of Foreigners into a Country that has as many Inhabitants as the present Employments and Provisions for Subsistence will bear; will be in the End no Increase of People; unless the New Comers have more Industry and Frugality than the Natives, and then they will provide more Subsistence, and increase in the Country; but they will gradually eat the Natives out. Nor is it necessary to bring in Foreigners to fill up any occasional Vacancy in a Country; for such Vacancy... will soon be filled by natural Generation....

22.    There is in short, no Bound to the prolific Nature of Plants or Animals, but what is made by their crowding and interfering with each others Means of Subsistence. Was the Face of the Earth vacant of other Plants, it might be gradually sowed and overspread with one Kind only; as, for Instance, with Fennel; and were it empty of other Inhabitants, it might in a few Ages be replenish'd from one Nation only; as, for Instance, with Englishmen. Thus there are suppos'd to be now upwards of One Million English Souls in North-America, (tho' 'tis thought scarce 80,000 have been brought over Sea) and yet perhaps there is not one the fewer in Britain, but rather many more, on Account of the Employment the Colonies afford to Manufacturers at Home. This Million doubling,

suppose but once in 25 Years, will in another Century be more than the People of England, and the greatest Number of Englishmen will be on this Side the Water. What an Accession of Power to the British Empire by Sea as well as Land! What Increase of Trade and Navigation! What Numbers of Ships and Seamen! We have been here but little more than 100 Years, and yet the Force of our Privateers in the late War, united, was greater, both in Men and Guns, than that of the whole British Navy in Queen Elizabeth's Time....

23.   In fine, A Nation well regulated is like a Polypus; take away a Limb, its Place is soon supply'd; cut it in two, and each deficient Part shall speedily grow out of the Part remaining. Thus if you have Room and Subsistence enough, as you may by dividing, make ten Polypes out of one, you may of one make ten Nations, equally populous and powerful; or rather, increase a Nation ten fold in Numbers and Strength.

And since Detachments of English from Britain sent to America, will have their Places at Home so soon supply'd and increase so largely here; why should the Palatine Boors be suffered to swarm into our Settlements, and by herding together establish their Language and Manners to the Exclusion of ours? Why should Pennsylvania, founded by the English, become a Colony of *Aliens,* who will shortly be so numerous as to Germanize us instead of our Anglifying them, and will never adopt our Language or Customs, any more than they can acquire our Complexion.

24.   Which leads me to add one Remark: That the Number of purely white People in the World is proportionably very small. All Africa is black or tawny. Asia chiefly tawny. America (exclusive of the new Comers) wholly so. And in Europe, the Spaniards, Italians, French, Russians and Swedes, are generally of what we call a swarthy Complexion; as are the Germans also, the Saxons only excepted, who with the English, make the principal Body of White People on the Face of the Earth. I could wish their Numbers were increased. And while we are, as I may call it, *Scouring* our Planet, by clearing America of Woods, and so making this Side of our Globe reflect a brighter Light to the Eyes of Inhabitants in Mars or Venus, why should we in the Sight of Superior Beings, darken its People? why increase the Sons of Africa, by Planting them

*Fanciful German version of the fresh air bath, an innovation Franklin suggested, and practiced, in 1768*

in America, where we have so fair an Opportunity, by excluding all Blacks and Tawneys, of increasing the lovely White and Red? But perhaps I am partial to the Complexion of my Country, for such Kind of Partiality is natural to Mankind.

Perhaps the most admirable thing about Franklin the scientist was his modesty. In a letter to his friend Jared Eliot he cheerfully dismissed, in typical Franklin style, the praise that had come his way as a result of his electrical discoveries.

Philada. April 12. 1753

The Tatler tells us of a Girl who was observ'd to grow suddenly proud, and none could guess the Reason, till it came to be known that she had got on a pair of new Silk Garters. Lest you should be puzzel'd to guess the Cause when you observe any thing of the kind in me, I think I will not hide my new Garters under my Petticoats, but take the Freedom to show them to you, in a Paragraph of our Friend Collinson's last Letter viz.—But I ought to mortify, and not indulge, this Vanity; I will not transcribe the Paragraph.—Yet I cannot forbear. "If any of thy Friends (says Peter) should take Notice that thy Head is held a little higher up than formerly, let them know; when the Grand Monarch of France strictly commands the Abbé Mazeas to write a Letter in the politest Terms to the Royal Society, to return the Kings Thanks and Compliments in an express Manner to Mr. Franklin of Pennsilvania, for the useful Discoveries in Electricity, and Application of the pointed Rods to prevent the terrible Effects of Thunderstorms. I say, after all this, is not some Allowance to be made if the Crest is a little elevated. There are four Letters containing very curious Experiments on thy Doctrine of Points and its Verification, which will be printed in the New Transactions. I think now I have stuck a Feather on thy Cap, I may be allowed to conclude in wishing thee long to wear it. Thine, P. Collinson." On reconsidering this Paragraph, I fear I have not so much Reason to be proud as the Girl had; for a Feather in the Cap is not so useful a Thing, or so serviceable to the Wearer, as a Pair of good Silk Garters.

Because of his reputation, soon grown to worldwide proportions, Franklin was sought out by other scientists for advice, information, and opinions. On a trip west in 1766, Franklin's friend George Croghan picked up some interesting fossils at a place in Kentucky appropriately called Big Bone Lick. Back in Philadelphia, Croghan split his collection in two and sent part to Lord Shelburne, the Secretary of State, and part to Franklin, also then in England. The shipment to Franklin included:

"Four great tusks, of different sizes.

One broken in halves, near six feet long.

One much decayed, the center looks like chalk, or lime.

A part was cut off from one of these teeth, that has all of the appearances of fine white ivory.

A joint of the vertebrae.

Three of the large pronged teeth; one has four rows of fangs."

Franklin acknowledged receipt of the interesting gift in a letter to Croghan and a few months later passed the fossils on to Abbé Jean Chappe d'Auteroche, a distinguished French astronomer, for another opinion. Following are the letters to Croghan and the Abbé Chappe.

London, Aug. 5, 1767.

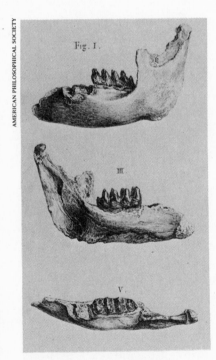

*Engravings of mastodon bones from Big Bone Lick, Kentucky*

I return you many thanks for the box of elephants' tusks and grinders. They are extremely curious on many accounts; no living elephants having been seen in any part of America by any of the Europeans settled there, or remembered in any tradition of the Indians. It is also puzzling to conceive what should have brought so many of them to die on the same spot; and that no such remains should be found in any other part of the continent, except in that very distant country Peru, from whence some grinders of the same kind formerly brought, are now in the museum of the Royal Society. The tusks agree with those of the African and Asiatic elephant, in being nearly of the same form and texture; and some of them, notwithstanding the length of time they must have lain, being still good ivory. But the grinders differ, being full of knobs, like the grinders of a carnivorous animal; when those of the elephant, who eats only vegetables, are almost smooth. But then we know of no other animal with tusks like an elephant to whom such grinders might belong. It is remarkable, that elephants now inhabit naturally only hot countries where there is no winter, and yet these remains are found in a winter country; and it is no uncommon thing to find elephants' tusks in Siberia, in great quantities, when their rivers overflow, and wash away the earth, though Siberia is still more a wintery country than that on the Ohio; which looks as if the earth had anciently been in another position, and the climates differently placed from what they are at present.

107

*Although Franklin was not deeply religious, his interest in linguistics may have drawn him to this revision of the Lord's Prayer.*

London, Jan. 31. 1768

I sent you sometime since, directed to the Care of M. Molini, a Bookseller near the Quây des Augustins a Tooth that I mention'd to you when I had the Pleasure of meeting with you at the Marquis de Courtanvaux's. It was found near the River Ohio in America, about 200 Leagues below Fort du Quesne, at what is called the Great Licking Place, where the Earth has a Saltish Taste that is agreable to the Bufaloes and Deer, who come there at certain Seasons in great Numbers to lick the same. At this [pla]ce have been found the Skeletons of near 30 [large?] Animals suppos'd to be Elephants, several Tusks like those of Elephants, being found with those Grinder Teeth. Four of these Grinders were sent me by the Gentleman who brought them from the Ohio to New York, together with 4 Tusks, one of which is 6 Feet long and in the thickest Part near 6 Inches Diameter, and also one of the Vertebrae. My Lord Shelbourn receiv'd at the same time 3 or four others with a Jaw Bone and one or two Grinders remaining in it. Some of Our Naturalists here, however, contend, that these are not the Grinders of Elephants but of some carnivorous Animal unknown, because such Knobs or Prominances on the Face of the Tooth are not to be found on those of Elephants, and only, as they say, on those of carnivorous Animals. But it appears to me that Animals capable of carrying such large and heavy Tusks, must themselves be large Creatures, too bulky to have the Activity necessary for pursuing and taking Prey; and therefore I am enclin'd to think those Knobs are only a small Variety, Animals of the same kind and Name often differing more materially, and that those Knobs might be as useful to grind the small Branches of Trees, as to chaw Flesh. However I should be glad to have your Opinion, and to know from you whether any of the kind have been found in Siberia.

Franklin the scientist is best remembered for his experiments with electricity, but his active mind continued to find other subjects for research and speculation. Indeed, his broad range of interests and his truly deep thinking on some subjects entitle him to be called "America's Newton." Although his American orientation usually inclined Franklin to look for practical applications of science, his mind continued to range widely over the whole field of knowledge, speculating on such things as the nature of matter and—in this letter to Barbeu-Dubourg—on raising the dead.

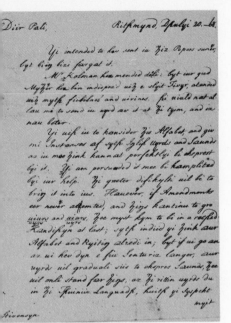

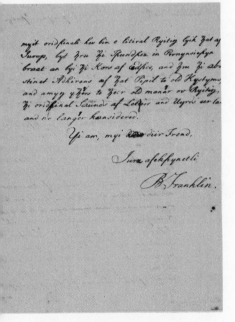

*Around 1768 Franklin became interested in phonetic spelling; this letter to Polly [Poli] Stevenson is the first known use of his new alphabet.*

[London, April–May, 1773]

Your observations on the causes of death, and the experiments which you propose for recalling to life those who appear to be killed by lightning, demonstrate equally your sagacity and your humanity. It appears that the doctrines of life and death in general are yet but little understood.

A toad buried in sand will live, it is said, till the sand becomes petrified; and then, being enclosed in the stone, it may still live for we know not how many ages. The facts which are cited in support of this opinion are too numerous, and too circumstantial, not to deserve a certain degree of credit. As we are accustomed to see all the animals with which we are acquainted eat and drink, it appears to us difficult to conceive how a toad can be supported in such a dungeon; but if we reflect that the necessity of nourishment which animals experience in their ordinary state proceeds from the continual waste of their substance by perspiration, it will appear less incredible that some animals in a torpid state, perspiring less because they use no exercise, should have less need of aliment; and that others, which are covered with scales or shells, which stop perspiration, such as land and sea turtles, serpents, and some species of fish, should be able to subsist a considerable time without any nourishment whatever. A plant, with its flowers, fades and dies immediately, if exposed to the air without having its root immersed in a humid soil, from which it may draw a sufficient quantity of moisture to supply that which exhales from its substance and is carried off continually by the air. Perhaps, however, if it were buried in quicksilver, it might preserve for a considerable space of time its vegetable life, its smell, and colour. If this be the case, it might prove a commodious method of transporting from distant countries those delicate plants, which are unable to sustain the inclemency of the weather at sea, and which require particular care and attention. I have seen an instance of common flies preserved in a manner somewhat similar. They had been drowned in Madeira wine, apparently about the time when it was bottled in Virginia, to be sent hither [to London]. At the opening of one of the bottles, at the house of a friend where I then was, three drowned flies fell into the first glass that was filled. Having heard it remarked that drowned flies were capable of being revived by the rays of the sun, I proposed making the experiment upon these; they were therefore exposed to the sun upon a sieve, which had been employed to strain them out of the wine. In less than three hours, two of them began by degrees to recover life. They commenced by some convulsive motions of the thighs, and at length they raised themselves upon their legs, wiped their eyes with their fore feet, beat and brushed their wings with their hind feet, and soon after began to fly, finding themselves in Old England, without knowing how they came thither. The third continued lifeless till sunset, when, losing all hopes of him, he was thrown away.

I wish it were possible, from this instance, to invent a method of embalming drowned persons, in such a manner that they may be recalled to life at any period, however distant; for having a very ardent desire to see and observe the state of America a hundred years hence, I should prefer to any ordinary death, the being immersed in a cask of Madeira wine, with a few friends, till that time, to be then recalled to life by the solar warmth of my dear country! But since in all probability we live in an age too early and too near the infancy of science, to hope to see such an art brought in our time to its perfection, I must for the present content myself with the treat, which you are so kind as to promise me, of the resurrection of a fowl or a turkey cock.

In a letter of October, 1750, to Cadwallader Colden, a fellow American scientist, who was also a prominent politician in New York, Franklin had cautioned against the scientist's natural inclination to abandon "Publick Business" completely. "But let not your Love of Philosophical Amusements have more than its due Weight with you. Had Newton been Pilot but of a single common Ship, the finest of his Discoveries would scarce have excus'd, or atton'd for his abandoning the Helm one Hour in Time of Danger; how much less if she had carried the Fate of the Commonwealth." This conviction soon forced Franklin to desert science for the far more uncertain world of politics.

*A Picture Portfolio*

# Ben Franklin's Philadelphia

## MAN OF THE CITY

Benjamin Franklin was decidedly an urban product. Raised in Boston, he matured and prospered in Philadelphia and later delighted in both London and Paris. The city for him was a stimulant and a challenge to which he responded with all his native ingenuity. In Philadelphia he never lived far from the heart of things, from the day in 1723 when he landed at the Market Street wharf, located to the left of the tallest spire—Christ Church—in the print opposite. The many places in which he lived and worked were all on this same busy street, then called High, close by the market houses (below). No picture of any of his homes is known to exist, but at his death in 1790, his grandson, using a standard newspaper cut of the day, advertised: "To be Let—the Mansion House of the late Dr. Franklin."

## A REASONABLE MARRIAGE

Franklin took Deborah Read to wife in Philadelphia in 1730, perhaps as much to help him avoid "Intrigues with low Women" as for any other reason. She was no match for her brilliant husband, but he fondly wrote in his *Autobiography:* "...she prov'd a good and faithful Helpmate, assisted me much

by attending the Shop, we throve together, and have ever mutually endeavour'd to make each other happy." For the long years he would be separated from her on his missions abroad, he had Benjamin Wilson paint their portraits to be hung together in their Philadelphia home.

## SUBSCRIPTION LIBRARY

Franklin's contributions to Philadelphia were legion. In 1727, he started a congenial club called the Junto, which met once a week in a tavern to discuss the topics of the day. Its need for books led Franklin to set up a subscription library, and thus the Library Company of Philadelphia came into being. Among Franklin's contributions to the infant company was a copy of *Logic* bearing his signature (right), possibly the earliest example of his handwriting. When the library later moved into the handsome new building below, in 1790, the year Franklin died, he was honored by a statue in the niche above the door.

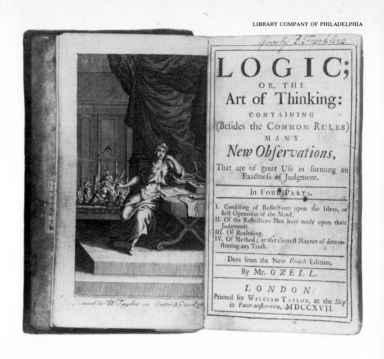

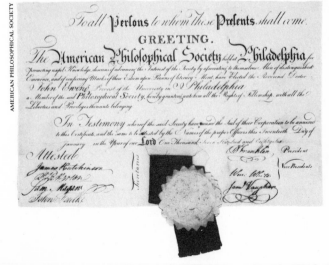

## PHILOSOPHERS' HAVEN

Another remarkable institution that owed its existence to Franklin was the American Philosophical Society, whose building adjoining the State House is seen behind the trees above. Modeled on the Royal Society of London, it attracted a select group of scientifically minded men, with Franklin as their energetic organizing secretary. As its president from 1769 until his death, Franklin signed membership certificates like the one at left, admitting John Ewing, provost of the University of Pennsylvania to the society.

117

118

## URBAN IMPROVEMENTS

Colonial cities were prone to devastating fires and to violence
in their dimly lit streets. Franklin responded to such problems
in characteristic fashion by proposing a regular paid corps of
watchmen, instead of volunteers, and by suggesting that both
their watchboxes (far left) and all street lamps be equipped
with four panes of glass instead of the old globes to facilitate
replacing and keeping them clean. To reduce the wild confusion at the scene of fires, Franklin recommended forming vol-
unteer fire companies trained both in putting out fires and in
rescue work, as in the eighteenth-century engraving below. He
is shown at left, below, in the white chief's hat of his own Union
Fire Company, the first in Philadelphia. Although this painting
was done a century after the fact, the fire mark of the four
clasped hands at left dates from 1752, the year Franklin
founded the first successful fire insurance company in the Colonies. These emblems were nailed to the face of insured buildings and warned firefighters to be careful in their work.

## PLAIN TRUTH:

### OR,

### SERIOUS CONSIDERATIONS

On the PRESENT STATE of the

### CITY of PHILADELPHIA,

AND

### PROVINCE of PENNSYLVANIA.

By a TRADESMAN of *Philadelphia.*

*Capta urbe, nihil fit reliqui victis. Sed, per Deos immortales, vos ego appello, qui semper domos, villas, signa, tabulas vestras, tanti æstimationis fecistis ; si ista, cujuscunque modi sint, quæ amplexamini, retinere, si voluptatibus vestris etiam præbere vultis ; expergiscimini aliquando, & capessite rempublicam. Non agitur nunc de sociorum injuriis ; LIBERTAS & ANIMA nostra in dubio est. Dux hostium cum exercitu sæpe caput est. Vos cunctamini etiam nunc, & dubitatis quid faciatis ? Scilicet, res ipsa aspera est, sed vos non timetis eam. Imo vero maxime ; sed inertia & mollitia animi, alius alium expectante, cunctamini ; videlicet, Diis immortalibus confisi, qui hanc rempublicam in maximis periculis servavere. NON VOTIS, NEQUE SUPPLICIIS MULIEBRIBUS, AUXILIA DEORUM PARANTUR : vigilando, agendo, bene consulendo, prospere omnia cedunt. Ubi socordiæ tte atque ignaviæ tradideris, nequicquam Deos implores ; irati, infestique sunt.*
M. POR. CAT. in SALUST.

Printed in the YEAR MDCCXLVII.

# AN OUNCE OF PREVENTION

In 1747, with England at war against France and Spain, Franklin tried to prod the Pennsylvania Assembly into providing for its defense by writing the pamphlet *Plain Truth* (below, left) urging a "voluntary Association of the People." Its frontispiece was a woodcut (far left), thought to be the first attempt printed in America to symbolize a political situation; it shows a farmer praying for help to Hercules, who is telling him to help himself. When the Assembly failed to act, Franklin held a lottery and with its proceeds saw that a fort was erected on the Delaware River to protect Philadelphia and where "among the rest I regularly took my turn of duty . . . as a common soldier." Nine years later, he was appointed special commissioner in charge of the Pennsylvania frontier. Traveling to the Moravian outposts of Bethlehem (left) and Gnadenhütten, where the Indians had been dangerously hostile, he built several forts and organized the local militias. On his return, although he was now a man of fifty and going to fat, Franklin had achieved sufficient military stature to be elected colonel of the city's militia regiment, supported by regular British troops, seen below in their Philadelphia barracks.

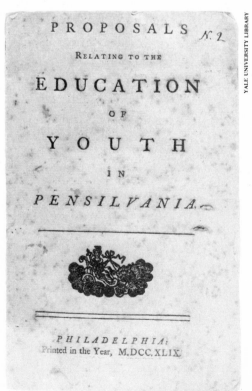

## KNOWLEDGE FOR THE YOUNG

Spurred on by an anonymous pamphlet (below, left), actually written and printed by Franklin, the "principal inhabitants" of Philadelphia dug into their pocketbooks for the funds necessary to establish an academy, later to become the University of Pennsylvania. Opened in 1751, in the old Whitefield tabernacle on Fourth Street (seen at left in a contemporary sketch by Pierre Eugène Du Simitière), its first provost was an Anglican clergyman, William Smith (below), with Franklin as president of the board of trustees. The two men did not remain friends, and Franklin was to write in 1763: "I made that Man my Enemy by doing him too much Kindness. Tis the honestest Way of acquiring an Enemy. And since 'tis convenient to have at least one Enemy, who by his Readiness to revile one on all Occasions may make one careful of one's Conduct, I shall keep him an Enemy for that purpose . . . ."

*A South-East Prospect of the Pensylvania Hospi...*
*This Building, by the Bounty of the Government, And of many private Persons, Was*
*Montgomery and Winter Del. Printed and Sold by Rob. Kennedy Philad.* *Built A Dom. 1755. from N.1 to 2*
*TAKE CARE OF HIM NI WILL REPAY THEE*

## "RELIEF OF THE SICK AND MISERABLE"

"There is no such thing as carrying through a public-spirited project without you are concerned in it," wrote Franklin's intimate friend Dr. Thomas Bond in regard to the foundation of a privately managed hospital for Philadelphians. Thanks to Franklin's energy and propaganda skills—he used the builder's intended plan (above) and an account of the creation (right) to get the necessary aid from the Colonial assembly—the building "for the Relief of the Sick and Miserable" was opened in 1756. The original manuscript of Franklin's inscription for the hospital's cornerstone is at upper right—dated in a year during which George II was "happily reigning" and Philadelphia was "flourishing."

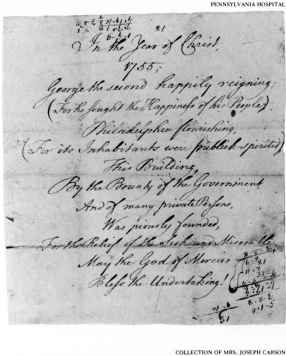

SOME

# ACCOUNT

OF THE

## Pennsylvania Hospital;

From its first RISE, to the Beginning
of the *Fifth Month*, called *May*, 1754.

*PHILADELPHIA:*
Printed by B. FRANKLIN, and D. HALL. MDCCLIV.

the *Elevation* of the intended *Plan*.
*ounded*, for the *Relief* of the *Sick and Miserable*

# MONEY AND THE MAIL

Franklin's first attempt to sway public opinion with a book explained the need for a paper currency (below, far right). It was so successful that he ended up with the job of printing the money, for which he cleverly designed a leaf pattern to discourage counterfeiting (below, right). He was appointed Postmaster of Philadelphia in 1737 and immediately set about streamlining the system and keeping records (below, left), running the Post Office from his own shop in Market Street. From 1753 until his dismissal in 1774 he was Deputy Postmaster General of America. In 1775, when the Post Office was located in the London Coffee House (right), the Continental Congress—recognizing that it was now necessary to supersede the royal authority—nominated Franklin, just home from London, first Postmaster General of the budding nation. He promptly issued a circular using the rude woodcut of a post rider (below), and used as his official frank "B. *Free*, Franklin" (bottom) in place of "*Free*, B. Franklin," in a humorous display of patriotism.

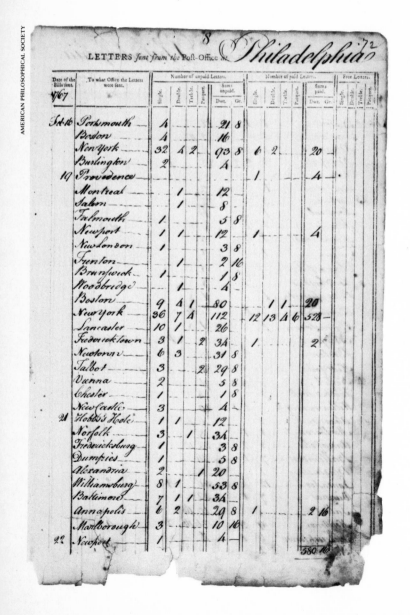

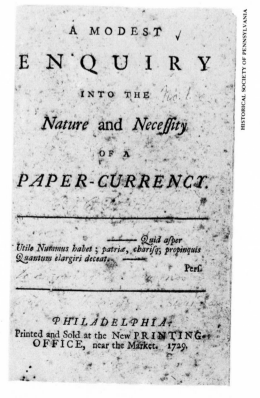

127

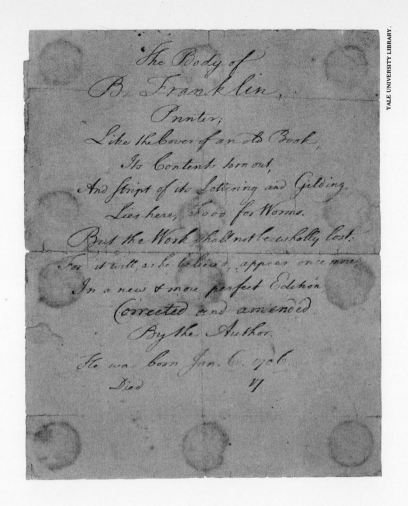

## PHILADELPHIA'S PATRIARCH

Unquestionably Philadelphia's most prominent citizen, Franklin was sent to London in 1757 to represent the people of Pennsylvania as their Colonial agent. When he returned nearly twenty years later, after war had broken out between England and her Colonies, he was promptly elected to the Second Continental Congress. Serving ably on numerous committees, he was often observed by his colleague John Adams as being "fast asleep in his chair," and indeed he appears to be dozing in the painting at left depicting Congress voting for independence on July 2, 1776. Dispatched abroad again that same year to negotiate a treaty of alliance with France, he did not return to his beloved Philadelphia until 1785. Given a hero's welcome, he was elected President of the Supreme Executive Council of Pennsylvania and, at the age of eighty-one, he became a delegate to the Constitutional Convention. Three years later death claimed him, but he had farsightedly provided his own famous epitaph (above), written sixty-two years earlier. The whole world mourned him, and it has been perfectly said that "no other town burying its great man ever buried more of itself than Philadelphia with Franklin."

# Chapter 5

# Pennsylvania Politician

Even when Franklin's researches into electricity were at their most intense, he did not abandon his strong interest and rising influence in Pennsylvania politics. In 1747, he was chiefly responsible for creating the Colony's first militia, to defend Pennsylvania against possible French and Spanish attacks during the War of the Austrian Succession, known in America as King George's War. Previously he had played a leading role in the creation of Philadelphia's first fire department and had persuaded his fellow citizens to hire watchmen to guard the streets at night—the first tentative step toward a police department. Next he helped found the Academy of Philadelphia, from which the University of Pennsylvania eventually grew. In 1751, the Pennsylvania Hospital was chartered, again under Franklin's leadership. On August 13, 1751, his fellow citizens acknowledged his talent for political and social leadership by electing him to the Pennsylvania Assembly. Although some of the letters and essays he wrote in connection with these local activities are lively and vivid, they no longer hold as much interest for modern readers as does Franklin's response to the larger political problems of the American Colonies as a whole. One of the liveliest expressions of his interest in politics was the letter he wrote on May 9, 1751, to *The Pennsylvania Gazette* under the pseudonym Americanus. Recent editions of the *Gazette* had carried numerous stories about the murders, robberies, and other criminal acts committed by convict servants in Virginia, Maryland, and Pennsylvania.

May 9, 1751

To the Printers of the Gazette.

By a Passage in one of your late Papers, I understand that the Government at home will not suffer our mistaken Assemblies to make any Law for preventing or discouraging the Importation of Convicts from Great Britain, for this kind Reason, *"That such Laws are against* the *Publick Utility, as they tend to prevent the* IMPROVEMENT *and* WELL PEOPLING of the Colonies."

Such a tender *parental* Concern in our *Mother Country* for the *Welfare* of her Children, calls aloud for the highest *Returns* of Gratitude and Duty. This every one must be sensible of: But 'tis said, that in our present Circumstances it is absolutely impossible for us to make *such* as are adequate to the Favour. I own it; but nevertheless let us do our Endeavour. 'Tis something to show a grateful Disposition.

In some of the uninhabited Parts of these Provinces, there are Numbers of these venomous Reptiles we call RATTLE–SNAKES; Felons-convict from the Beginning of the World: These, whenever we meet with them, we put to Death, by Virtue of an old Law, *Thou shalt bruise his Head.* But as this is a sanguinary Law, and may seem too cruel; and as however mischievous those Creatures are with us, they may possibly change their Natures, if they were to change the Climate; I would humbly propose, that this general Sentence of *Death* be changed for *Transportation.*

In the Spring of the Year, when they first creep out of their Holes, they are feeble, heavy, slow, and easily taken; and if a small Bounty were allow'd *per* Head, some Thousands might be collected annually, and *transported* to Britain. There I would propose to have them carefully distributed in St. James's Park, in the Spring-Gardens and other Places of Pleasure about London; in the Gardens of all the Nobility and Gentry throughout the Nation; but particularly in the Gardens of the *Prime Ministers*, the *Lords of Trade* and *Members of Parliament*; for to them we are *most particularly* obliged.

There is no human Scheme so perfect, but some Inconveniencies may be objected to it: Yet when the Conveniencies far exceed, the Scheme is judg'd rational, and fit to be executed. Thus Inconveniencies have been objected to that *good* and *wise* Act of Parliament, by virtue of which all the Newgates and Dungeons in Britain are emptied into the Colonies. It has been said, that these Thieves and Villains introduc'd among us, spoil the Morals of Youth in the Neighbourhoods that entertain them, and perpetrate many horrid Crimes: But let not *private Interests* obstruct *publick Utility.* Our *Mother* knows what is best for us. What is a little *Housebreaking,*

By the Honourable the PRESIDENT and COUNCIL of the Province of *Pennsylvania,*

A PROCLAMATION
For a GENERAL FAST.

FORASMUCH as it is the Duty of Mankind, on all suitable Occasions, to acknowledge their Dependance on the DIVINE BEING, to give Thanks for the Mercies received, and no less to deprecate his Judgments, and humbly pray for his Protection...

*This rare broadside proclaimed a general fast that Franklin proposed to the Council in 1747 and which "they Embraced"; it was one of Franklin's efforts to unite the people of Philadelphia in self-defense.*

131

*One of the Colonial flags of
the Pennsylvania "Associators" was
designed by Franklin in 1747.*

*Shoplifting*, or *Highway Robbing*; what is a *Son* now and then *corrupted* and *hang'd*, a Daughter *debauch'd* and *pox'd*, a Wife *stabb'd*, a Husband's *Throat cut*, or a Child's *Brains beat out* with an Axe, compar'd with this "IMPROVEMENT and WELL PEOPLING of the Colonies!"

Thus it may perhaps be objected to my Scheme, that the *Rattle-Snake* is a mischievous Creature, and that his changing his Nature with the Clime is a mere Supposition, not yet confirm'd by sufficient Facts. What then? Is not Example more prevalent than Precept? And may not the honest rough British Gentry, by a Familiarity with these Reptiles, learn to *creep*, and to *insinuate*, and to *slaver*, and to *wriggle* into Place (and perhaps to *poison* such as stand in their Way) Qualities of no small Advantage to Courtiers! In comparison of which "*Improvement* and *Publick Utility*," what is a *Child* now and then kill'd by their venomous Bite,—or even a favourite *Lap-Dog*? . . .

AMERICANUS

Although Franklin said in his *Autobiography* that he never sought an office, or resigned one, the fact is that he could not resist the opportunity to become Deputy Postmaster General of America. He got into the postal business almost in self-defense. Newspaper publishers in all the Colonies sought the appointment because it enabled them to send their papers free while barring their local competition. Franklin had become Postmaster of Philadelphia in 1737. The ensuing years gave him the chance to study the American postal system, which was very poorly run. In the following letter to Peter Collinson, Franklin, after a few lines about the flourishing state of the library and the academy, got down to the business of asking Collinson's help. The appointment came two years later, in 1753, and he held office for two decades, until his dismissal in 1774 for pro-Colonial activities considered disloyal to the Crown.

Philada. May 21. 1751

The Occasion of my writing this, viâ Ireland, is, That I have just receiv'd Advice that the Deputy-Postmaster General of America (Mr. Elliot Benger residing in Virginia) who has for some time been in a declining Way, is tho't to be near his End. My Friends advise me to apply for that Post, and Mr. Allen (our Chief Justice) has wrote the enclos'd to his Correspondent Mr. Simpson in my favour, requesting his Interest and Application in the Affair, and impowering him to advance a considerable Sum if it should be necessary. I have not heretofore made much Scruple of giving you Trouble when the Publick Good was to be promoted by it; but 'tis with great Reluctance that I think of asking you to interest yourself in my private Concerns, as I know you have little Time to spare. The Place is in the Disposal of the Postmasters General of Britain, with some of whom or their Friends you may possibly have Acquaintance. Mr. Allen has desir'd Mr. Simpson to confer with you on the Affair, and if you can, without much Inconvenience to your self, advise and assist in endeavouring to secure the Success of this Application, you will, whatever may be the Event, add greatly to the Obligations you have already confer'd on me; and if it succeeds, I hope that as my *Power* of doing Good increases, my *Inclination* will always at least keep pace with it.

I am quite a Stranger to the Manner of Managing these Applications, so can offer no particular Instructions. I enclose a Copy of the Commission of a former Dep. Postmaster General, which may be of some Use: The Articles of Agreement refer'd to in the Commission I have never seen, but suppose they have always been nearly the same whoever is appointed, and have been usually sent over to America to be executed by the new Officer; for I know neither of the three last Officers went to England for the Commission. The Place has been commonly reputed worth about £150 a Year, but would be otherways very suitable to me, particularly as it would enable me to execute a Scheme long since form'd, of which I send you enclos'd a Copy, and which I hope would soon produce something agreable to you and to all Lovers of Useful Knowledge, for I have now a large Acquaintance among ingenious Men in America. I need not tell you, that Philadelphia being the Center of the Continent Colonies, and having constant Communication with the West India Islands, is by much a fitter Place for the Situation of a General Post Office than Virginia, and that it would be some Reputation to our Province, to have it establish'd here. ...I have heard £200 was given for this Office by Mr. Benger, and the same by his Predecessor; I know not whose Perquisite it was: But lest that should not be Sufficient, and there may be some contingent Fees and Charges, Mr. Allen has ordered £300. However, the less it costs the better, as 'tis an Office for Life only, which is a very uncertain Tenure.

*Post rider of Franklin's day*

Meanwhile, the pulse of world politics began to quicken, and its beat was felt in Pennsylvania. France and England were girding for the climactic conflict that would decide which would rule North America. In the winter of 1754 an obscure Virginia militia officer named George Washington had carried a message from the Governor of Virginia, warning the French to cease their penetration of the Ohio country. The French returned the warning with insults, and then, in an aggressive move that clearly endangered both Pennsylvania and Virginia, swept down the Ohio and routed the Virginians who were building a fort at the forks of the Ohio River, on the site of present-day Pittsburgh. Franklin instantly recognized the essence of the French threat to the thirteen English Colonies. The French were united and had a plan. In this news story from *The Pennsylvania Gazette* (which he sent to Richard Partridge, Pennsylvania's agent in London, suggesting that he have it inserted in "some of your most publick Papers"), Franklin summed up the threat and presented his solution — backed up with America's first political cartoon.

*The Pennsylvania Gazette,*
*May 9, 1754*

Friday last an Express arrived here from Major Washington, with Advice, that Mr. Ward, Ensign of Capt. Trent's Company, was compelled to surrender his small Fort in the Forks of Monongahela to the French, on the 17th past.... We hear farther, that some few of the English Traders on the Ohio escaped, but 'tis supposed the greatest Part are taken, with all their Goods, and Skins, to the Amount of near £20,000. The Indian Chiefs, however, have dispatch'd Messages to Pennsylvania, and Virginia, desiring that the English would not be discouraged, but send out their Warriors to join them, and drive the French out of the Country before they fortify; otherwise the Trade will be lost, and, to their great Grief, an eternal Separation made between the Indians and their Brethren the English, 'Tis farther said, that besides the French that came down from Venango, another Body of near 400, is coming up the Ohio; and that 600 French Indians, of the Chippaways and Ottaways, are coming down Siota River, from the Lake, to join them; and many more French are expected from Canada; the Design being to establish themselves, settle their Indians, and build Forts just on the Back of our Settlements in all our Colonies; from which Forts, as they did from Crown-Point, they may send out their Parties to kill and scalp the Inhabitants, and ruin the Frontier Counties. Accordingly we hear, that the Back Settlers in Virginia,

*America's first political cartoon,*
*probably designed by Franklin*

are so terrify'd by the Murdering and Scalping of the Family last Winter, and the Taking of this Fort, that they begin already to abandon their Plantations, and remove to Places of more Safety.—The Confidence of the French in this Undertaking seems well-grounded on the present disunited State of the British Colonies, and the extreme Difficulty of bringing so many different Governments and Assemblies to agree in any speedy and effectual Measures for our common Defence and Security; while our Enemies have the very great Advantage of being under one Direction, with one Council, and one Purse. Hence, and from the great Distance of Britain, they presume that they may with Impunity violate the most solemn Treaties subsisting between the two Crowns, kill, seize and imprison our Traders, and confiscate their Effects at Pleasure (as they have done for several Years past) murder and scalp our Farmers, with their Wives and Children, and take an easy Possession of such Parts of the British Territory as they find most convenient for them; which if they are permitted to do, must end in the Destruction of the British Interest, Trade and Plantations in America.

A few weeks later, in a letter to Peter Collinson, Franklin added new depth to his vision of Colonial unity. Collinson had written from London, the preceding March, to express his concern over the "Comotion" in the Virginia and New York legislatures—and to state that it was difficult for anyone to determine who was right unless he could hear both sides.

Philada: 28th May. 1754

I am heartily concern'd with you, at the Dissensions so unseasonably kindling in the Colony Assemblies, when unanimity is became more than ever necessary to Frustrate the Designs of the French. May I presume to whisper my Sentiments in a private Letter? Britain and her Colonies should be considered as one Whole, and not as different States with separate Interests.

Instructions from the Crown to the Colonies, should have in View the Common Weal of that Whole, to which partial Interests ought to give way: And they should never Aim at extending the Prerogative beyond its due Bounds, nor abridging the just Liberties of the people: In short, they should be plainly just and reasonable, and rather savour of Fatherly Tenderness and Affection, than of Masterly harshness and Severity. Such Instructions might safely be made publick; but if they are of a different kind, they must be kept secret. Then the Representatives of the People, knowing nothing of the Instructions, frame Laws which cannot pass. Governors not daring to produce the Instructions invent other Reasons for refusing the Bill. False Reasons seldom appear good, their Weakness is discover'd and expos'd. The Governor persists and is despised. The people lose their Respect for him, grow Angry and rude. And if at length the Instruction appears, perhaps to justify the Governor's conduct, they say, why was it not produc'd before? for then all this Time spent in Framing the Bill, and disputing the point, might have been saved, the heavy charge of long Sessions prevented and Harmony preserved. —But enough of this.

The British, aware that some degree of Colonial unity was a military necessity, ordered the royal governors to convene an intercolonial congress at Albany to discuss a coordinated policy toward the Indians, who were showing signs of going over en masse to the French. Franklin was chosen by his fellow Pennsylvanians as one of the delegates, or commissioners, as they were called, to this conference. In New York, Franklin met an old friend, James Alexander, a prominent merchant and New Jersey landowner. The conversation turned to the problems of uniting the Colonies, and Franklin remarked that he thought he had a plan that might be workable. Alexander eagerly asked for something in writing, and Franklin sent him the following rough outline of what eventually became known to historians as the Albany Plan of Union.

N York June 8. 1754

Short hints towards a scheme for uniting the Northern Colonies

A Governour General

To be appointed by the King.

To be a Military man

To have a Salary from the Crown

To have a negation on all acts of the Grand Council, and carry into execution what ever is agreed on by him and that Council.

Grand Council

One member to be chosen by the Assembly of each of the smaller Colonies and two or more by each of the larger, in proportion to the Sums they pay Yearly into the General Treasury.

Members Pay

—Shillings sterling per Diem deuring their sitting and mileage for Travelling Expences.

Place and Time of meeting

To meet — times in every Year, at the Capital of each Colony in Course, unless particular circumstances and emergencies require more frequent meetings and Alteration in the Course, of places. The Governour General to Judge of those circumstances &c. and call by his Writts.

General Treasury

Its Fund, an Excise on Strong Liquors pretty equally drank in the Colonies or Duty on Liquor imported, or — shillings on each Licence of Publick House or Excise on Superfluities as Tea &c. &c. all which would pay in some proportion to the present wealth of· each Colony, and encrease as that wealth encreases, and prevent disputes about the Inequality of Quotas.

To be Collected in each Colony, and Lodged in their Treasury to be ready for the payment of Orders issuing from the Governour General and Grand Council jointly.

DUTY AND POWER

of the Governour General and Grand Council

To order all Indian Treaties.

make all Indian purchases not within proprietary Grants

make and support new settlements by building Forts, raising and paying Soldiers to Garison the Forts, defend the frontiers and annoy the Ennemy.

equip Grand Vessels to scour the Coasts from Privateers in time of war, and protect the Trade

and every thing that shall be found necessary for the defence and support of the Colonies in General, and encreasing and extending their settlements &c.

For the Expence they may draw on the fund in the Treasury of any Colony.

Manner of forming this Union

The scheme being first well considered corrected and improved by the Commissioners at Albany, to be sent home, and an Act of Parliament obtain'd for establishing it.

Franklin's Plan of Union was accepted with only minor changes by the Albany Congress, but it was either rejected or ignored by every Colony, including Franklin's Pennsylvania, which caused him, he admitted in his *Autobiography* "no small mortification." In a letter of

December 29, 1754, to Peter Collinson, he was candid about his disillusionment with his fellow Americans. "Every Body cries, a Union is absolutely necessary; but when they come to the Manner and Form of the Union, their weak Noddles are presently distracted. So if ever there be an Union, it must be form'd at home by the Ministry and Parliament." Meanwhile, Governor William Shirley of Massachusetts, one of the most far-seeing and competent Crown officials in America, discussed the plan with Franklin when he visited Boston. Shirley offered an alternative plan. Franklin's plan had called for a kind of American parliament or grand council, composed of representatives from the assemblies of each Colony. Shirley's alternative was a much smaller council composed of the governors of all the Colonies, plus one or two members of their respective councils. Such an arrangement would have effectively excluded the people from choosing any representatives to the council, since all the governors except those of Rhode Island and Connecticut were appointed by the Crown, as were their councilors. Franklin and Shirley discussed the two plans in an exchange of letters. Franklin all but predicted the American Revolution as he explained to the Royal Governor why Americans would resent being taxed by a governing body in which they had no representatives.

Boston. December 4. 1754

Sir,

I mention'd it Yesterday to your Excellency as my Opinion, that Excluding the People of the Colonies from all Share in the Choice of the Grand Council would probably give extreme Dissatisfaction, as well as the Taxing them by Act of Parliament where they have no Representative. In Matters of General Concern to the People, and especially where Burthens are to be laid upon them, it is of Use to consider as well what they will *be apt* to think and say, as what they *ought* to think: I shall, therefore, as your Excellency requires it of me, briefly mention what of either Kind occurs at present, on this Occasion.

First, they will say, and perhaps with Justice, that the Body of the People in the Colonies are as loyal, and as firmly attach'd to the present Constitution and reigning Family, as any Subjects in the King's Dominions; that there is no Reason to doubt the Readiness and Willingness of their Representatives to grant, from Time to Time, such Supplies, for the Defence of the Country, as shall be judg'd necessary, so far as their Abilities will allow: That the People in the Colonies, who are to feel the immediate Mischiefs of Invasion and Conquest by an Enemy, in the Loss of their Estates, Lives and Liberties,

*Governor William Shirley*

are likely to be better Judges of the Quantity of Forces necessary to be raised and maintain'd, Forts to be built and supported, and of their own Abilities to bear the Expence, than the Parliament of England at so great a Distance. That Governors often come to the Colonies meerly to make Fortunes, with which they intend to return to Britain, are not always Men of the Best Abilities and Integrity, have no Estates here, nor any natural Connections with us, that should make them heartily concern'd for our Welfare; and might possibly be sometimes fond of raising and keeping up more Forces than necessary, from the Profits accruing to themselves, and to make Provision for their Friends and Dependents. That the Councellors in most of the Colonies, being appointed by the Crown, on the Recommendation of Governors, are often of small Estates, frequently dependant on the Governors for Offices, and therefore too much under Influence. That there is therefore great Reason to be jealous of a Power in such Governors and Councils, to raise such Sums as they shall judge necessary, by Draft on the Lords of the Treasury, to be afterwards laid on the Colonies by Act of Parliament, and paid by the People here; since they might abuse it, by projecting useless Expeditions, harrassing the People, and taking them from their Labour to execute such Projects, and meerly to create Offices and Employments, gratify their Dependants and divide Profits. That the Parliament of England is at a great Distance, subject to be misinform'd by such Governors and Councils, whose united Interests might probably secure them against the Effect of any Complaints from hence. That it is suppos'd an undoubted Right of Englishmen not to be taxed but by their own Consent given thro' their Representatives. That the Colonies have no Representatives in Parliament. That to propose taxing them by Parliament, and refusing them the Liberty of chusing a Representative Council, to meet in the Colonies, and consider and judge of the Necessity of any General Tax and the Quantum, shews a Suspicion of their Loyalty to the Crown, or Regard for their Country, or of their Common Sense and Understanding, which they have not deserv'd. That compelling the Colonies to pay Money without their Consent would be rather like raising Contributions in an Enemy's Country, than taxing of Englishmen for their own publick Benefit. That it would be treating them as a conquer'd People, and not as true British Subjects. That a Tax laid by the Representatives of the Colonies might easily be lessened as the Occasions should lessen, but being once laid by Parliament, under the Influence of the Representations made by Governors, would probably be kept up and continued, for the Benefit of Governors, to the grievous Burthen and Discouragement of the Colonies, and preventing their Growth and Increase. That a Power in Governors to march the Inhabitants from one End of the British and French Colonies to the other, being a Country of at least 1500 Miles square, without the Approbation or Consent of their Representatives first obtain'd to such Expeditions, might be grievous and ruinous to the People, and would put them on a Footing with the Subjects of France in Canada, that now groan under such Oppression from their Governor, who for two Years past has harrass'd them with long and destructive Marches to the Ohio. That if the Colonies in a Body may be well governed by Governors and Councils appointed by the Crown, without Representatives, particular Colonies may as well or better by so governed; a Tax may be laid on them all by Act of Parliament, for Support of Government, and their Assemblies be dismiss'd as a useless Part of their Constitution. That the Powers propos'd, by the Albany Plan of Union to be vested in a Grand Council representative of the People, even with Regard to Military Matters, are not so great as those the Colonies of Rhode-Island and Connecticut are intrusted with, and have never abused; for by this Plan the President-General is appointed by the Crown, and controlls all by his Negative; but in those Governments the People chuse the Governor, and yet allow him no Negative. That the British Colonies, bordering on the French, are properly Frontiers of the British Empire; and that the Frontiers of an Empire are properly defended at the joint Expence of the Body of People in such Empire.... if the Frontiers in America must bear the Expence of their own Defence, it seems hard to allow them no Share in Voting the Money, judging of the Necessity and Sum, or advising the Measures. That besides the Taxes necessary for the Defence of the Frontiers, the Colonies pay yearly great Sums to the Mother Country unnotic'd: For Taxes, paid in Britain by the Land holder or Artificer, must enter into and increase the Price of the Produce of Land, and of Manufactures made of it; and great Part of this is paid by Consumers in the Colonies, who thereby pay a considerable Part of the British Taxes. We are restrain'd in our Trade with Foreign Nations, and where we could be supplied with any Manufactures cheaper from them, but must buy the same dearer from Britain, the Difference of Price is a clear Tax to Britain. We are oblig'd to carry great Part of our Produce directly to Britain, and where the Duties there laid upon it lessens its Price to the Planter, or it sells for less than it would in Foreign Markets, the Difference is a Tax paid to Britain. Some Manufactures we could make, but are forbid, and must take them of British Merchants; the whole Price of these is a Tax paid to Britain. By our greatly increasing the *Consumption* and *Demand* of British Manufactures, their Price is considerably rais'd of late Years; the Advance is clear Profit to Britain, and enables its People better to pay great Taxes; and much of it being paid by us is clear Tax to Britain. In short, as we are not suffer'd to regulate our Trade, and restrain the Importation and Consumption of British Superfluities, (as Britain can the Consumption of Foreign Superfluities) our whole Wealth centers finally among the Merchants and Inhabitants of Britain, and if we make them richer, and enable them better to pay their Taxes, it is nearly the same as being taxed ourselves, and equally beneficial to the Crown. These Kind of Secondary Taxes, however, we do not complain of, tho' we have no Share in the Laying or Disposing of them; but to pay immediate heavy Taxes, in the Laying Appropriation or Disposition of which, we have no Part, and which perhaps we may know to be as unnecessary as grievous, must seem hard Measure to Englishmen, who cannot conceive, that by hazarding their Lives and Fortunes in subduing and settling new Countries, extending the Dominion and encreasing the Commerce of their Mother Nation, they have forfeited the native Rights of Britons, which they think ought rather to have been given them, as due to such Merit, if they had been before in a State of Slavery.

These, and such Kind of Things as these, I apprehend will be thought and said by the People, if the propos'd Alteration of the Albany Plan should take Place. Then, the Administration of the Board of Governors and Council so appointed, not having any Representative Body of the People to approve and unite in its Measures, and conciliate the Minds of the People to them, will probably become suspected and odious. Animosities and dangerous Feuds will arise between the Governors and Governed, and every Thing go into confusion.

During this visit to Boston, Franklin, aged forty-nine, had a kind of May-December romance with twenty-four-year-old Catherine Ray. She had come to Boston to visit her sister, who had married into the Boston branch of the Franklin family. She traveled with Franklin to Westerly, Rhode Island, where they visited her sister Anna, wife of Samuel Ward. Then "Katy" was hastily summoned back to Block Island to the bedside of her critically ill father. Franklin continued his journey to Philadelphia, where he wrote her the first of many letters they were to exchange.

Philada. March 4. 1755

It gives me great Pleasure to hear that you got home safe and well that Day. I thought too much was hazarded, when I saw you put off to Sea in that very little Skiff, toss'd by every Wave. But the Call was strong and just, a sick Parent. I stood on the Shore, and look'd after you, till I could no longer distinguish you, even with my Glass; then returned to your Sister's, praying for your safe Passage. Towards Evening all agreed that you must certainly be arriv'd before that time, the Weather having been so favourable; which made me more easy and chearful, for I had been truly concern'd for you.

I left New England slowly, and with great Reluctance: Short Days Journeys, and loitering Visits on the Road, for three or four Weeks, manifested my Unwillingness to quit a Country in which I drew my first Breath, spent my earliest and most pleasant Days, and had now received so many fresh Marks of the People's Goodness and Benevolence, in the kind and affectionate Treatment I had every where met with. I almost forgot I had a Home; till I was more than half-way towards it; till I had, one by one, parted with all my New England Friends, and was got into the western Borders of Connecticut, among meer Strangers: then, like an old Man, who, having buried all he lov'd in this World, begins to think of Heaven, I begun to think of and wish for Home; and as I drew nearer, I found the Attraction stronger and stronger, my Diligence and Speed increas'd with my Impatience, I drove on violently, and made such long Stretches that a very few Days brought me to my

*Sketch by Charles Willson Peale of Franklin and one of his lady friends*

own House, and to the Arms of my good old Wife and Children, where I remain, Thanks to God, at present well and happy.

Persons subject to the Hyp, complain of the North East Wind as increasing their Malady. But since you promis'd to send me Kisses in that Wind, and I find you as good as your Word, 'tis to me the gayest Wind that blows, and gives me the best Spirits. I write this during a N. East Storm of Snow, the greatest we have had this Winter: Your Favours come mixd with the Snowy Fleeces which are pure as your Virgin Innocence, white as your lovely Bosom, — and as cold: — But let it warm towards some worthy young Man, and may Heaven bless you both with every kind of Happiness.

The war that Franklin had foreseen in his *Gazette* story on Major Washington's dispatch now began in earnest. The British sent Major General Edward Braddock with two regiments of regular troops to drive the French from the fort they had seized from the Virginians. In this passage from the section of his *Autobiography* composed late in his life, Franklin told how he became involved in the expedition.

*Autobiography,* 1788

The British Government not chusing to permit the Union of the Colonies, as propos'd at Albany, and to trust that Union with their Defence, lest they should thereby grow too military, and feel their own Strength, Suspicions and Jealousies at this time being entertain'd of them; sent over General Braddock with two Regiments of Regular English Troops for that purpose. He landed at Alexandria in Virginia, and thence march'd to Frederic Town in Maryland, where he halted for Carriages. Our Assembly apprehending, from some Information, that he had conceived violent Prejudices against them, as averse to the Service, wish'd me to wait upon him, not as from them, but as Postmaster General, under the guise of proposing to settle with him the Mode of conducting with most Celerity and Certainty the Dispatches between him and the Governors of the several Provinces, with whom he must necessarily have continual Correspondence, and of which they propos'd to pay the Expence. My Son accompanied me on this Journey. We found the General at Frederic Town, waiting impatiently for the Return of those he had sent thro' the back Parts of Maryland and Virginia to collect Waggons. I staid with him several

Days, Din'd with him daily, and had full Opportunity of removing all his Prejudices, by the Information of what the Assembly had before his Arrival actually done and were still willing to do to facilitate his Operations.

When I was about to depart, the Returns of Waggons to be obtain'd were brought in, by which it appear'd that they amounted only to twenty-five, and not all of those were in serviceable Condition. The General and all the Officers were surpriz'd, declar'd the Expedition was then at an End, being impossible, and exclaim'd against the Ministers for ignorantly landing them in a Country destitute of the Means of conveying their Stores, Baggage, &c. not less than 150 Waggons being necessary. I happen'd to say, I thought it was pity they had not been landed rather in Pennsylvania, as in that Country almost every Farmer had his Waggon. The General eagerly laid hold of my Words, and said, "Then you, Sir, who are a Man of Interest there, can probably procure them for us; and I beg you will undertake it." I ask'd what Terms were to be offer'd the Owners of the Waggons; and I was desir'd to put on Paper the Terms that appear'd to me necessary. This I did, and they were agreed to, and a Commission and Instructions accordingly prepar'd immediately.

*Battery proposed by Franklin for the defense of Philadelphia*

In two weeks, Braddock had 150 wagons and 259 pack horses in his camp. But this help from Franklin only facilitated his advance to the forest ambush that destroyed him and his army. Franklin wrote that he sensed trouble well before the disaster occurred.

*Autobiography*, 1788

This General was I think a brave Man, and might probably have made a Figure as a good Officer in some European War. But he had too much self-confidence, too high an Opinion of the Validity of Regular Troops, and too mean a One of both Americans and Indians. George Croghan, our Indian Interpreter, join'd him on his March with 100 of those People, who might have been of great Use to his Army as Guides, Scouts, &c. if he had treated them kindly; but he slighted and neglected them, and they gradually left him.

In Conversation with him one day, he was giving me some Account of his intended Progress. "After taking Fort Du Quesne, says he, I am to proceed to Niagara; and having taken that, to Frontenac, if the Season will allow time; and I suppose it will; for Duquesne can hardly

*Engraving of the "Defeat and Death of General Braddock" from Russel's* History of England

detain me above three or four Days; and then I see nothing that can obstruct my March to Niagara." Having before revolv'd in my Mind the long Line his Army must make in their March, by a very narrow Road to be cut for them thro' the Woods and Bushes; and also what I had read of a former Defeat of 1500 French who invaded the Iroquois Country, I had conceived some Doubts and some Fears for the Event of the Campaign. But I ventur'd only to say, To be sure, Sir, if you arrive well before Duquesne, with these fine Troops so well provided with Artillery, that Place, not yet compleatly fortified, and as we hear with no very strong Garrison, can probably make but a short Resistance. The only Danger I apprehend of Obstruction to your March, is from the Ambuscades of Indians, who by constant Practice are dextrous in laying and executing them. And the slender Line near four Miles long, which your Army must make, may expose it to be attack'd by Surprize in its Flanks, and to be cut like a Thread into several Pieces, which from their Distance cannot come up in time to support each other. He smil'd at my Ignorance, and reply'd, "These Savages may indeed be a formidable Enemy to your raw American Militia; but upon the King's regular and disciplin'd Troops, Sir, it is impossible they should make any Impression." I was conscious of an Impropriety in my Disputing with a military Man in Matters of his Profession, and said no more.

In Pennsylvania, meanwhile, Franklin found himself caught in the middle of a continuing quarrel between the Proprietors (the sons of Pennsylvania's founder, William Penn) and the people. The core of the argument was the Proprietors' insistence that their lands be exempted from any tax levied to raise funds for the defense of the province. The Proprietors and their supporters in Pennsylvania attempted to defend their position by attacking the Quakers, who composed the bulk of the majority party, arguing that the refusal of the Quakers to bear arms in defense of the country was a far more serious dereliction. In this letter to Peter Collinson, Franklin summed up the situation. The "Brief State" that he mentioned was a pamphlet, A *Brief State of the Province of Pennsylvania*, attacking Franklin and the Quaker Party. It had in fact been written by William Smith, the Anglican clergyman whom Franklin had hired to head the Academy of Philadelphia. Franklin had not yet perceived Smith's devious character.

Philada. Augt. 27. 1755.

We are all in Flames, as you will see by the Papers. I

145

have wrote to our Agent, Mr. Partridge, a short, but I believe a clear Account of our late Bill for giving £50,000 refus'd by the Governor because the Proprietary Estate was thereby to be taxed with others. He will show it to you if you desire it, as I have not now time to repeat it. These Obstructions of the General Interest from particular Disputes in the Colonies, show more and more the Necessity of the projected UNION, which I hope will be compleated soon; for depend on it, no American War will ever be well carried on without it.

I wrote to you, via New York, a full Account of our shameful Defeat on the Ohio. The General presum'd too much, and was too secure. This the Event proves; but it was my Opinion from the time I saw him and convers'd with him. . . .

I do not find that our Assembly have any Inclination to answer the Brief State. They think it below them. Perhaps they slight it too much. The design was to get Quakers out of the Assembly, on this Principle, or at least on this Pretence, *That they could not or would not do the Duty of Assembly-men in defending the Country.* Great Pains was taken to this Purpose at our last Election, when I was absent in New England, but in vain. If the End was, simply, to get the Country defended by Grants of Money, the Quakers have now shown that they can give and dispose of Money for that purpose as freely as any People. If this does not give Satisfaction, the Pique against them must seem to be personal and private, and not founded on Views for the publick Good. I know the Quakers now think it their Duty, when chosen, to consider themselves as Representatives of the *Whole People,* and not of their own Sect only; they consider the public Money as raised from and belonging to the *whole Publick,* and not to their Sect only; and therefore, tho' they can neither bear Arms themselves, nor compel others to do it, yet very lately, when our Frontier Inhabitants, who are chiefly Presbyterians or Churchmen, thought themselves in Danger, and the Poor among them were unable to provide Arms, and petitioned the House, a Sum was voted for that purpose, and put into the Hands of a Committee to procure and supply them. I have accordingly purchas'd and sent up a considerable Quantity; with the Governor's Approbation, as to the Disposition; for as he is Captain General we think it our Duty not to

*Scene in a Quaker meeting house*

arm the People without his Consent, tho' we are otherwise at Variance with him.... A Number of Falshoods are now privately propagated to blast my Character, of which I shall take no Notice 'till they grow bold enough to show their Faces in publick. Those who caress'd me a few Months since, are now endeavouring to defame me every where by every base Art.... if I did not love the Country and the People, [I] would remove immediately into a more quiet Government, Connecticut, where I am also happy enough to have many Friends.

Franklin's correspondence with young Catherine Ray gave him an opportunity to escape from Pennsylvania politics.

Philada. Sept. 11. 1755

Begone, Business, for an Hour, at least, and let me chat a little with my Katy....

You ask in your last, How I do, and what I am doing, and whether every body loves me yet, and why I make 'em do so? In [the first place, I am so well?] Thanks to God, that I do not remember I was ever better. I still relish all the Pleasures of Life that a temperate Man can in reason desire, and thro' Favour I have them all in my Power. This happy Situation shall continue as long as God pleases, who knows what is best for his Creatures, and I hope will enable me to bear with Patience and dutiful Submission any Change he may think fit to make that is less agreable. As to the second Question, I must confess, (but don't you be jealous) that many more People love me now than ever did before: For since I saw you, I have been enabled to do some general Services to the Country, and to the Army, for which both have thank'd and prais'd me; and say they love me; they *say so*, as you us'd to do; and if I were to ask any Favours of them, would, perhaps, as readily refuse me: So that I find little real Advantage in being belov'd, but it pleases my Humour.

Now it is near four Months since I have been favour'd with a single Line from you; but I will not be angry with you, because 'tis my fault. I ran in debt to you three or four Letters, and as I did not pay, you would not trust me any more, and you had some Reason: But believe me, I am honest, and tho' I should never make equal Returns, you shall see I'll keep fair Accounts. Equal Returns I can never make, tho' I should write to you by every Post: For

*Quakers going to meeting*

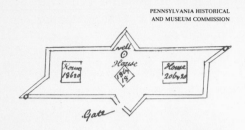

*Top, Franklin's own sketch of Fort Allen; center, building the stockade of the fort; below, back from the frontier, he parades in triumph with the men of his regiment.*

the Pleasure I receive from one of yours, is more than you can have from two of mine. . . .

I long to hear whether you have continu'd ever since in that Monastery; or have broke into the World again, doing pretty Mischief; how the Lady Wards do, and how many of them are married, or about it; what is become of Mr. B. and Mr. L. and what the State of your Heart is at this Instant? but that, perhaps I ought not to know; and therefore I will not conjure, as you sometimes say I do. . . .

I commend your prudent Resolutions in the Article of granting Favours to Lovers: But if I were courting you, I could not heartily approve such Conduct. I should even be malicious enough to say you were too *knowing.* . . .

You have spun a long Thread, 5022 Yards! It will reach almost from Block Island hither. I wish I had hold of one End of it, to pull you to me: But you would break it rather than come. The Cords of Love and Friendship are longer and stronger, and in Times past have drawn me farther; even back from England to Philadelphia. I guess that some of the same kind will one day draw you out of that Island.

I was extreamly pleas'd with the Turff you sent me. The Irish People who have seen it, say, 'tis the right Sort; but I cannot learn that we have anything like it here. The Cheeses, particularly one of them, were excellent: All our Friends have tasted it, and all agree that it exceeds any English Cheese they ever tasted. Mrs. Franklin was very proud, that a young Lady should have so much Regard for her old Husband, as to send him such a Present. We talk of you every Time it comes to Table; She is sure you are a sensible Girl, and a notable Housewife; and talks of bequeathing me to you as a Legacy; But I ought to wish you a better, and hope she will live these 100 Years; for we are grown old together, and if she has any faults, I am so us'd to 'em that I don't perceive 'em. . . . Indeed I begin to think she has none, as I think of you. And since she is willing I should love you as much as you are willing to be lov'd by me; let us join in wishing the old Lady a long Life and a happy.

Pennsylvania soon summoned Franklin back to duty — duty that included his assumption of the role of general. With Braddock's army defeated, and its survivors having retreated all the way to New Jersey, the Pennsylvania frontier was left almost totally exposed to marauding

French and Indians. The town of Gnadenhütten in the Lehigh Gap was burned and its inhabitants massacred. Early in January, 1756, Franklin led some three hundred volunteers out of Philadelphia to restore order in the western counties. His son William accompanied him and handled the military details of the expedition. The mission was successful. The two Franklins organized local militia in frontier towns and then marched to Gnadenhütten, where they built a fort. In that desolate place, Franklin wrote the following cheerful letter to his wife Deborah. He addressed her in the sentimental phrase they both used when they wrote to each other: "My dear child."

Gnadenhathen, January 25, 1756.

My Dear Child,

This day week we arrived here, I wrote to you the same day, and once since. We all continue well, thanks be to God. We have been hindered with bad weather, yet our fort is in a good defensible condition, and we have every day, more convenient living. Two more are to be built, one on each side of this, at about fifteen miles distance. I hope both will be done in a week or ten days, and then I purpose to bend my course homewards.

We have enjoyed your roast beef, and this day began on the roast veal; all agree that they are both the best that ever were of the kind. Your citizens, that have their dinners hot and hot, know nothing of good eating; we find it in much greater perfection when the kitchen is four score miles from the dining room. . . .

As to our lodging, 'tis on deal feather beds, in warm blankets, and much more comfortable than when we lodged at our inn, the first night after we left home, for the woman being about to put very damp sheets on the bed we desired her to air them first; half an hour afterwards, she told us the bed was ready, and the sheets *well aired.* I got into bed, but jumped out immediately, finding them as cold as death, and partly frozen. She had *aired* them indeed, but it was out upon the *hedge.* I was forced to wrap myself up in my great coat and woollen trowsers, every thing else about the bed was shockingly dirty. . . .

B FRANKLIN

*Order to pay Captain Edward Croston for troop provisions, written in Franklin's hand and signed by all seven of the provincial commissioners*

Returning to Philadelphia, Franklin found sad news. His favorite brother, John, had died of the bladder ailment that had distressed him for many years. Writing to John's stepdaughter, Elizabeth Hubbart, Franklin composed a letter about life and death that quickly achieved fame. At first it was copied by hand to solace others similarly bereaved, and later it was frequently printed.

Philadelphia, February 22, 1756

I condole with you, we have lost a most dear and valuable relation, but it is the will of God and Nature that these mortal bodies be laid aside, when the soul is to enter into real life; 'tis rather an embrio state, a preparation for living; a man is not completely born until he be dead: Why then should we grieve that a new child is born among the immortals? A new member added to their happy society? We are spirits. That bodies should be lent us, while they can afford us pleasure, assist us in acquiring knowledge, or doing good to our fellow creatures, is a kind and benevolent act of God—when they become unfit for these purposes and afford us pain instead of pleasure—instead of an aid, become an incumbrance and answer none of the intentions for which they were given, it is equally kind and benevolent that a way is provided by which we may get rid of them. Death is that way. We ourselves prudently choose a partial death. In some cases a mangled painful limb, which cannot be restored, we willingly cut off. He who plucks out a tooth, parts with it freely since the pain goes with it, and he that quits the whole body, parts at once with all pains and possibilities of pains and diseases it was liable to, or capable of making him suffer.

Our friend and we are invited abroad on a party of pleasure—that is to last for ever. His chair was first ready and he is gone before us. We could not all conveniently start together, and why should you and I be grieved at this, since we are soon to follow, and we know where to find him.

*John Franklin's bookplate*

Later that year, Franklin wrote another letter, which did not achieve fame but foreshadowed one of the most important preoccupations of his later years—founding a colony on the Ohio River. It was written to George Whitefield, famous as a preacher both in America and England.

New York, July 2. 1756

You mention your frequent Wish that you were a Chaplain to an American Army. I sometimes wish, that you and I were jointly employ'd by the Crown to settle a Colony on the Ohio. I imagine we could do it effectually, and without putting the Nation to much Expence. But I fear we shall never be call'd upon for such a Service. What a glorious Thing it would be, to settle in that fine Country a large Strong Body of Religious and Industrious

*Reverend George Whitefield*

People! What a Security to the other Colonies; and Advantage to Britain, by Increasing her People, Territory, Strength and Commerce. Might it not greatly facilitate the Introduction of pure Religion among the Heathen, if we could, by such a Colony, show them a better Sample of Christians than they commonly see in our Indian Traders, the most vicious and abandoned Wretches of our Nation? Life, like a dramatic Piece, should not only be conducted with Regularity, but methinks it should finish handsomely. Being now in the last Act, I begin to cast about for something fit to end with. Or if mine be more properly compar'd to an Epigram, as some of its few Lines are but barely tolerable, I am very desirous of concluding with a bright Point. In such an Enterprize I could spend the Remainder of Life with Pleasure; and I firmly believe God would bless us with Success, if we undertook it with a sincere Regard to his Honour, the Service of our gracious King, and (which is the same thing) the Publick Good.

Relations between the Pennsylvania Assembly and the proprietary government worsened steadily. The Proprietors stubbornly insisted that their lands should be exempted from taxation, and the Quaker Assembly in return refused to vote any money for the defense of the Colony or contribute any of its much-needed resources to the war with France. Finally, Franklin and the other members of the Assembly decided that the only answer to the impasse was direct negotiations with the Proprietors in England. In this letter to his London friend and fellow printer William Strahan, Franklin predicted his early arrival in the British capital and the beginning of another phase in his career. The son Billy he mentioned was Strahan's boy, who the two friends hoped would marry Franklin's daughter Sarah, then thirteen. "Smouting" is printer's slang for part-time work.

[Philadelphia,] Jan. 31. 1757

It gives me great Pleasure to hear so good an Account of our Son Billy. In Return, let me tell you, that our Daughter Sally is indeed a very good Girl, affectionate, dutiful and industrious, has one of the best Hearts, and tho' not a Wit, is for one of her Years, by no means deficient in Understanding. She already takes off part of her Mother's Family Cares. This must give you and Mrs. Strahan Pleasure: So that Account is partly ballanced.

Our Assembly talk of sending me to England speedily. Then look out sharp, and if a fat old Fellow should come to your Printing House and request a little Smouting, depend upon it, 'tis Your affectionate Friend and humble Servant

B Franklin

On the point of leaving for England, Franklin did not forget his Boston relatives. His older half sister, Elizabeth Douse, was living in a house he owned in Boston. Another sister, Jane Mecom, and some additional members of the family thought that it would be more economical to sell the house and furniture, and move the old woman in with them. In this wise letter to his sister Jane, Franklin demurred.

New York, April 19. 1757

I wrote a few Lines to you yesterday, but omitted to answer yours relating to Sister Douse: As *having their own Way,* is one of the greatest Comforts of Life, to old People, I think their Friends should endeavour to accommodate them in that, as well as in any thing else. When they have long liv'd in a House, it becomes natural to them, they are almost as closely connected with it as the Tortoise with his Shell, they die if you tear them out of it. Old Folks and old Trees, if you remove them, tis ten to one that you kill them. So let our good old Sister be no more importun'd on that head. We are growing old fast ourselves, and shall expect the same kind of Indulgencies. If we give them, we shall have a Right to receive them in our Turn.

And as to her few fine Things, I think she is in the right not to sell them, and for the Reason she gives, that they will fetch but little. When that little is spent, they would be of no farther use to her; but perhaps the Expectation of Possessing them at her Death, may make that Person tender and careful of her, and helpful to her, to the amount of ten times their Value. If so, they are put to the best Use they possibly can be.

I hope you visit Sister as often as your Affairs will permit, and afford her what Assistance and Comfort you can, in her present Situation. *Old Age, Infirmities,* and *Poverty,* join'd, are Afflictions enough; the *Neglect and Slight* of Friends and near Relations, should never be added. People in her Circumstances are apt to suspect this sometimes without Cause; *Appearances* should therefore be attended to, in our Conduct towards them, as well as *Realities.* . . .

We expect to sail in about a Week, so that I can hardly hear from you again on this Side the Water.

On the voyage to England, Franklin prepared the text for *Poor Richard* of 1758. With plenty of time on his hands, he went through all his previous volumes, and wrote an introductory essay, *The Way to Wealth,* which was to become one of his most famous compositions—with a very unfortunate effect on his reputation. Poor Richard's advice on how to get rich achieved wide fame in Franklin's lifetime and was reprinted repeatedly in the hundred years after his death. It made Franklin's name synonymous with saving, and even with penny-pinching—an ironic fate for a man who abandoned what he called "the pursuit of wealth to no purpose" at the age of forty–two. Franklin did pinch his pennies as a young man, starting out in business with heavy debts. But, as his letters have already demonstrated, once he achieved financial security, he was generous and open-handed. The essay, in which Franklin created another of his memorable characters, wise old Father Abraham, was really more of an intellectual exercise. The tone is highly ironic and at times is even close to parody. Franklin was actually laughing just a little at himself and Poor Richard and the whole notion of persuading men to save money—while simultaneously working into the text a maximum number of quotations from his previous almanacs. Appropriately, it was the last Franklin himself wrote.

*Poor Richard, 1758*

...a great Number of People were collected at a Vendue [auction] of Merchant Goods. The Hour of Sale not being come, they were conversing on the Badness of the Times, and one of the Company call'd to a plain clean old Man, with white Locks, *Pray, Father Abraham, what think you of the Times? Won't these heavy Taxes quite ruin the Country? How shall we be ever able to pay them? What would you advise us to?*—Father Abraham stood up, and reply'd, If you'd have my Advice, I'll give it you in short, for a *Word to the Wise is enough,* and *many Words won't fill a Bushel,* as *Poor Richard says.* They join'd in desiring him to speak his Mind, and gathering round him, he proceeded as follows;

"Friends, says he, and Neighbours, the Taxes are indeed very heavy, and if those laid on by the Government were the only Ones we had to pay, we might more easily discharge them; but we have many others, and much more grievous to some of us. We are taxed twice as much by our *Idleness,* three times as much by our *Pride,* and four times as much by our *Folly,* and from these Taxes the Commissioners cannot ease or deliver us by allowing an Abatement. However let us hearken to good Advice, and something may be done for us; *God helps them that help themselves,* as Poor Richard says, in his Almanack

FATHER
## Abraham's
# SPEECH
To a great Number of People, at a *Vendue* of Merchant-Goods ;

Introduced to the PUBLICK by

*Poor Richard,*

A famous PENNSYLVANIA Conjurer, and Almanack-Maker,

In Anfwer to the following QUESTIONS.

*Pray,* Father Abraham, *what think you of the Times? Won't thefe heavy Taxes quite ruin the Country? How fhall we be ever able to pay them? What would you advife us to?*

*To which are added,*
SEVEN *curious* PIECES *of* WRITING.

BOSTON, NEW-ENGLAND,
*Printed and Sold by* Benjamin Mecom, *at* The NEW PRINTING-OFFICE, *Oppofite to the* Old-Brick Meeting, *near the* Court-Houfe.

NOTE, Very good Allowance to thofe who take them by the Hundred or Dozen, to fell again.

*The title page of* Father Abraham's Speech, *first published in 1758*

Father Abraham's Speech *became best known by its later title,* The Way to Wealth, *published in many editions, such as this 1807 British version.*

of 1733.

It would be thought a hard Government that should tax its People one tenth Part of their *Time,* to be employed in its Service. But *Idleness* taxes many of us much more, if we reckon all that is spent in absolute *Sloth,* or doing of nothing, with that which is spent in idle Employments or Amusements, that amount to nothing. *Sloth,* by bringing on Diseases, absolutely shortens Life. *Sloth, like Rust, consumes faster than Labour wears, while the used Key is always bright,* as Poor Richard says. But *dost thou love Life, then do not squander Time, for that's the Stuff Life is made of,* as Poor Richard says. How much more than is necessary do we spend in Sleep! forgetting that *The sleeping Fox catches no Poultry,* and that *there will be sleeping enough in the Grave,* as Poor Richard says. If Time be of all Things the most precious, *wasting Time* must be, as Poor Richard says, *the greatest Prodigality,* since, as he elsewhere tells us, *Lost Time is never found again;* and what we call *Time-enough, always proves little enough:* Let us then be up and be doing, and doing to the Purpose; so by Diligence shall we do more with less Perplexity. *Sloth makes all Things difficult, but Industry all easy,* as Poor Richard says; and *He that riseth late, must trot all Day, and shall scarce overtake his Business at Night.* While *Laziness travels so slowly, that Poverty soon overtakes him,* as we read in Poor Richard, who adds, *Drive thy Business, let not that drive thee;* and *Early to Bed, and early to rise, makes a Man healthy, wealthy and wise.*

So what signifies *wishing* and *hoping* for better Times. We may make these Times better if we bestir ourselves. *Industry need not wish,* as Poor Richard says, and *He that lives upon Hope will die fasting. There are no Gains, without Pains;* then *Help Hands, for I have no Lands,* or if I have, they are smartly taxed. And, as Poor Richard likewise observes, *He that Hath a Trade hath an Estate,* and *He that hath a Calling hath an Office of Profit and Honour;* but then the *Trade* must be worked at, and the *Calling* well followed, or neither the *Estate,* nor the *Office,* will enable us to pay our Taxes. If we are industrious we shall never starve; for, as Poor Richard says, *At the working Man's House Hunger looks in, but dares not enter.* Nor will the Bailiff nor the Constable enter, for *Industry pays Debts, while Despair encreaseth them,* says Poor Richard. What though you have found no Treasure, nor has any rich Relation left you a Legacy, *Diligence is the Mother of Good luck,* as Poor Richard says, and *God gives all Things to Industry.* Then *plough deep, while Sluggards sleep, and you shall have Corn to sell and to keep,* says Poor Dick. Work while it is called To-day, for you know not how much you may be hindered To-morrow, which makes Poor Richard say, *One To-day is worth two To-morrows;* and farther, *Have you somewhat to do To-morrow, do it To-day.* If you were a Servant, would you not be ashamed that a good Master should catch you idle? Are you then your own Master, *be ashamed to catch yourself idle,* as Poor Dick says. When there is so much to be done for yourself, your Family, your Country, and your gracious King, be up by Peep of Day; *Let not the Sun look down and say, Inglorious here he lies.* Handle your Tools without Mittens; remember that *the Cat in Gloves catches no Mice,* as Poor Richard says. 'Tis true there is much to be done, and perhaps you are weak handed, but stick to it steadily, and you will see great Effects, for *constant Dropping wears away Stones,* and by *Diligence and Patience the Mouse ate in two the Cable;* and *Little Strokes fell great Oaks,* as Poor Richard says in his Almanack, the Year I cannot just now remember.

Methinks I hear some of you say, *Must a Man afford himself no Leisure?* I will tell thee, my Friend, what Poor Richard says, *Employ thy Time well if thou meanest to gain Leisure;* and, *since thou art not sure of a Minute, throw not away an Hour.* Leisure, is Time for doing something useful; this Leisure the diligent Man will obtain, but the lazy Man never; so that, as Poor Richard says, a *Life of Leisure and a Life of Laziness are two Things.* Do you imagine that Sloth will afford you more Comfort than Labour? No, for as Poor Richard says, *Trouble springs from Idleness, and grievous Toil from needless Ease. Many without Labour, would live by their* Wits *only, but they break for want of Stock.* Whereas Industry gives Comfort, and Plenty, and Respect: *Fly Pleasures, and they'll follow you. . . .*

But with our Industry, we must likewise be *steady, settled* and *careful,* and oversee our own Affairs *with our own Eyes,* and not trust too much to others; for, as Poor Richard says. . .

*Illustrations from the 1807 British edition with* Poor Richard *sayings: "The cat in gloves catches no mice"; "There will be sleeping enough in the grave"; and "Never leave that till tomorrow, which you can do today."*

*He that by the Plough would thrive,*
*Himself must either hold or drive.*

And again, *The Eye of a Master will do more Work than both his Hands*; and again, *Want of Care does us more Damage than Want of Knowledge*; and again, *Not to oversee Workmen, is to leave them your Purse open.* . . . And farther, *If you would have a faithful Servant, and one that you like, serve yourself.* . . .

So much for Industry, my Friends, and Attention to one's own Business; but to these we must add *Frugality*, if we would make our *Industry* more certainly successful. A Man may, if he knows not how to save as he gets, *keep his Nose all his Life to the Grindstone*, and die not worth a *Groat* at last. *A fat Kitchen makes a lean Will.* . . . and, *If you would be wealthy*, says he, in another Almanack, *think of Saving as well as of Getting: The Indies have not made Spain rich, because her* Outgoes *are greater than her* Incomes. Away then with your expensive Follies, and you will not have so much Cause to complain of hard Times, heavy Taxes, and chargeable Families; for, as Poor Dick says,

*Women and Wine, Game and Deceit,*
*Make the Wealth small, and the Wants great.*

And farther, *What maintains one Vice, would bring up two Children.* You may think perhaps, That a *little* Tea, or a *little* Punch now and then, Diet a *little* more costly, Clothes a *little* finer, and a *little* Entertainment now and then, can be no *great* Matter; but remember what Poor Richard says . . . *Beware of* little *Expences; a small Leak will sink a great Ship*; and again, *Who Dainties love, shall Beggars prove.* . . .

Here you are all got together at this Vendue of *Fineries* and *Knicknacks.* You call them *Goods,* but if you do not take Care, they will prove *Evils* to some of you. You expect they will be sold *cheap,* and perhaps they may for less than they cost; but if you have no Occasion for them, they must be *dear* to you. Remember what Poor Richard says, *Buy what thou hast no Need of, and ere long thou shalt sell thy Necessaries.* And again, *At a great Pennyworth pause a while:* He means, that perhaps the Cheapness is *apparent* only, and not *real*; or the Bargain, by straitning thee in thy Business, may do thee more Harm than Good. . . . Many a one, for the Sake of Finery on the Back, have gone with a hungry Belly, and

*Eight panels from an 1859 engraving, "Poor Richard Illustrated," with "Lessons for the Young and Old on Industry, Temperance, Frugality &c by Benjamin Franklin"*

half starved their Families; *Silks and Satins, Scarlet and Velvets,* as Poor Richard says, *put out the Kitchen Fire.* These are not the *Necessaries* of Life; they can scarcely be called the *Conveniencies,* and yet only because they look pretty, how many *want* to *have* them. The *artificial* Wants of Mankind thus become more numerous than the *natural;* and, as Poor Dick says, *For one* poor *Person, there are an hundred* indigent. By these, and other Extravagancies, the Genteel are reduced to Poverty, and forced to borrow of those whom they formerly despised, but who through *Industry* and *Frugality* have maintained their Standing; in which Case it appears plainly, that a *Ploughman on his Legs is higher than a Gentleman on his Knees,* as Poor Richard says. Perhaps they have had a small Estate left them, which they knew not the Getting of; they think *'tis Day, and will never be Night;* that a little to be spent out of *so much,* is not worth minding; *(a Child and a Fool,* as Poor Richard says, *imagine Twenty Shillings and Twenty Years can never be spent)* but, *always taking out of the Meal-tub, and never putting in, soon comes to the Bottom;* then, as Poor Dick says, *When the Well's dry, they know the Worth of Water.* But this they might have known before, if they had taken his Advice; *If you would know the Value of Money, go and try to borrow some;* for, *he that goes a borrowing goes a sorrowing....*

> *Fond* Pride of Dress, *is sure a very Curse;*
> *E'er* Fancy *you consult, consult your Purse.*

...When you have bought one fine Thing you must buy ten more, that your Appearance may be all of a Piece; but Poor Dick says, *'Tis easier to* suppress *the first Desire, than to* satisfy *all that follow it....*

But what Madness must it be to *run in Debt* for these Superfluities! We are offered, by the Terms of this Vendue, *Six Months Credit;* and that perhaps has induced some of us to attend it, because we cannot spare the ready Money, and hope now to be fine without it. But, ah, think what you do when you run in Debt; *You give to another Power over your Liberty.* If you cannot pay at the Time, you will be ashamed to see your Creditor; you will be in Fear when you speak to him; you will make poor pitiful sneaking Excuses, and by Degrees come to lose your Veracity, and sink into base downright lying; for, as Poor Richard says, *The second Vice is*

*Lying, the first is running in Debt.* And again, to the same Purpose, *Lying rides upon Debt's Back. . . .*

And now to conclude, *Experience keeps a dear School, but Fools will learn in no other, and scarce in that;* for it is true, *we may give Advice, but we cannot give Conduct,* as Poor Richard says: However, remember this, *They that won't be counselled, can't be helped,* as Poor Richard says. . . .

Thus the old Gentleman ended his Harangue. The People heard it, and approved the Doctrine, and immediately practised the contrary, just as if it had been a common Sermon; for the Vendue opened, and they began to buy extravagantly, notwithstanding all his Cautions, and their own Fear of Taxes.

War was still raging between France and England when Franklin sailed from America. In this vivid passage from his *Autobiography*, Franklin told how close his ship came to disaster, because of the captain's fear of capture by the French.

*Autobiography,* 1788

We were several times chas'd on our Passage, but out-sail'd every thing, and in thirty Days had Soundings. We had a good Observation, and the Captain judg'd himself so near our Port, (Falmouth) that if we made a good Run in the Night we might be off the Mouth of that Harbour in the Morning, and by running in the Night might escape the Notice of the Enemy's Privateers, who often cruis'd near the Entrance of the Channel. Accordingly all the Sail was set that we could possibly make, and the Wind being very fresh and fair, we went right before it, and made great Way. The Captain after his Observation, shap'd his Course as he thought so as to pass wide of the Scilly Isles; but it seems there is sometimes a strong Indraught setting up St. George's Channel which deceives Seamen. . . . This Indraught was probably the Cause of what happen'd to us. We had a Watchman plac'd in the Bow to whom they often call'd, *Look well out before, there;* and he as often answer'd, *Aye, aye!* But perhaps had his Eyes shut, and was half asleep at the time: they sometimes answering as is said mechanically: For he did not see a Light just before us which had been hid by the Studding Sails from the Man at Helm and from the rest of the Watch; but by an accidental Yaw of the Ship was discover'd, and occasion'd a great Alarm, we being very near it, the light appearing to me as big as a Cart Wheel. It was Midnight, and Our Captain fast asleep. But Capt. Kennedy jumping upon Deck, and seeing the Danger, ordered the Ship to wear round, all Sails standing, An Operation dangerous to the Masts, but it carried us clear, and we escap'd Shipwreck, for we were running right upon the Rocks on which the Lighthouse was erected. This Deliverance impress'd me strongly with the Utility of Lighthouses and made me resolve to encourage the building more of them in America, if I should live to return there.

In the Morning it was found by the Soundings, &c. that we were near our Port, but a thick Fog hid the Land from our Sight. About 9 a Clock the Fog began to rise, and seem'd to be lifted up from the Water like the Curtain at the Play-house, discovering underneath the Town of Falmouth, the Vessels in its Harbour, and the Fields that surrounded it. A most pleasing Spectacle to those who had been so long without any other Prospects, than the uniform View of a vacant Ocean!

William Franklin, now twenty-six years old, accompanied his father as his secretary. He also planned to study law in England and be admitted to the bar. For some years he had been reading in the law office of Joseph Galloway, Franklin's loyal lieutenant in the Pennsylvania Assembly. Father and son paused to sightsee a little on the three-hundred-mile trip from Falmouth, viewing Stonehenge, the prehistoric ruin on Salisbury Plain, and the Roman antiquities collected by Lord Pembroke in his house and gardens at Wilton. They arrived in London on July 26, 1757, and took rooms at the Bear Inn on the Southwark end of old London Bridge. The next day they visited Peter Collinson, and from his offices Franklin dashed off this note to Deborah reporting their safe arrival.

London, July 27. 1757

My dear Child

We arrived here well last Night, only a little fatigued with the last Day's Journey, being 70 Miles. I write only this Line, not knowing of any Opportunity to send it; but Mr. Collinson will enquire for one, as he is going out. If he finds one, I shall write more largely. I have just seen Mr. Strahan, who is well with his Family. Billy is with me here at Mr. Collinson's, and presents his Duty to you, and Love to his Sister. My Love to all. I am, my dear Child, Your loving Husband

B FRANKLIN

# Chapter 6

# To England with Love

Afew days after Franklin arrived in London, and met the friends whom he had known only by correspondence, William Strahan and Peter Collinson, he declared himself ready to tackle the Penns. Collinson and another Quaker friend of Pennsylvania, Dr. John Fothergill, a prominent London physician, advised Franklin against complaining to Crown officials. They recommended negotiating directly with the Proprietors to work out a compromise, and Dr. Fothergill arranged an interview between Franklin and the Penns. Thomas Penn, as principal Proprietor, was the spokesman. Here, from the *Autobiography*, is Franklin's version of the meeting.

*Autobiography,* 1789–90

After some Days, Dr. Fothergill having spoken to the Proprietaries, they agreed to a Meeting with me at Mr. T. Penn's House in Spring Garden. The Conversation at first consisted of mutual Declarations of Disposition to reasonable Accommodation; but I suppose each Party had its own ideas of what should be meant by *reasonable.* We then went into Consideration of our several Points of Complaint which I enumerated. The Proprietaries justify'd their Conduct as well as they could, and I the Assembly's. We now appeared very wide, and so far from each other in our Opinions, as to discourage all Hope of Agreement. However, it was concluded that I should give them the Heads of our Complaints in Writing, and they promis'd then to consider them. I did so soon after; but they put the Paper into the Hands of the Solicitor Ferdinando John Paris, who manag'd for them all their Law Business in their great Suit with the neighbouring Proprietary of Maryland, Lord Baltimore, which had subsisted 70 Years, and wrote for them all their Papers and Messages in their

Dispute with the Assembly. He was a proud angry Man; and as I had occasionally in the Answers of the Assembly treated his Papers with some Severity, they being really weak in point of Argument, and haughty in Expression, he had conceiv'd a mortal Enmity to me, which discovering itself whenever we met, I declin'd the Proprietary's Proposal that he and I should discuss the Heads of Complaint between our two selves, and refus'd treating with any one but them.

In the midst of this discouraging business, Franklin contracted one of the few serious illnesses of his life. He took to his bed, and not until November 22, 1757, did he have the strength to write Deborah and tell her of his ordeal. "Cupping" refers to bloodletting, a standard medical treatment of the day. The "bark" is quinine, frequently prescribed to fight fever. That Franklin survived this heroic approach to medicine is a tribute to his tough constitution.

London, Nov. 22. 1757

The 2d of September I wrote to you that I had had a violent cold and something of a fever, but that it was almost gone. However, it was not long before I had another severe cold, which continued longer than the first, attended by great pain in my head, the top of which was very hot, and when the pain went off, very sore and tender. These fits of pain continued sometimes longer than at others; seldom less than 12 hours, and once 36 hours. I was now and then a little delirious: they cupped me on the back of the head which seemed to ease me for the present; I took a great deal of bark, both in substance and infusion, and too soon thinking myself well, I ventured out twice, to do a little business and forward the service I am engaged in, and both times got fresh cold and fell down again; my good Doctor grew very angry with me, for acting so contrary to his Cautions and Directions, and oblig'd me to promise more Observance for the future. He attended me very carefully and affectionately; and the good Lady of the House nursed me kindly; Billy was also of great Service to me, in going from place to place, where I could not go myself, and Peter was very diligent and attentive. I took so much bark in various ways that I began to abhor it; I durst not take a vomit, for fear of my head; but at last I was seized one morning with a vomiting and purging, the latter of which continued the greater part of the day, and I believe was a

*Trade card of an English "cupper"*

161

kind of crisis to the distemper, carrying it clear off; for ever since I feel quite lightsome, and am every day gathering strength; so I hope my seasoning is over, and that I shall enjoy better health during the rest of my stay in England. . . .

I make no doubt but Reports will be spread by my Enemies to my Disadvantage, but let none of them trouble you. If I find I can do my Country no Good, I will take care, at least, not to do it any Harm. I will neither seek nor accept of any thing for my self; and though I may perhaps not be able to obtain for the People what they wish and expect, no Interest shall induce me to betray the Trust they have repos'd in me. . . .

Had I been well, I intended to have gone round among the Shops, and bought some pretty things for you and my dear good Sally, (whose little hands you say eased your headache) to send by this ship, but I must now defer it to the next, having only got a crimson satin cloak for you, the newest fashion, and the black-silk for Sally; but Billy sends her a scarlet feather, muff, and tippet, and a box of fashionable linen for her dress; . . .

The agreable Conversation I meet with among Men of Learning, and the Notice taken of me by Persons of Distinction, are the principal Things that sooth me for the present under this painful Absence from my Family and Friends; yet those would not detain me here another Week, if I had not other Inducements, Duty to my Country and Hopes of being able to do it Service.

*Trade card of the kind of London fabric shop frequented by Franklin*

On January 14, 1758, Franklin told Deborah that he was growing "daily stronger and better," but was not yet his old self: "much writing still disorders me." He added that he "would be glad if I could tell you when I expected to be at home, but that is still in the dark." His report of a recent conference with the Penns, sent the same day to Isaac Norris, Speaker of the Pennsylvania Assembly, made it sound very much as though the argument was going to continue for a long time. The letter survives only in an extract that Norris made from it. But the third person opening quickly shifts to the first person, and undoubtedly contains most of Franklin's real language—language that outraged the Penns, when they heard about the letter through their informants in Pennsylvania.

[London] Dated Janry: 14. 1758.
Extract from Mr. Franklin's Letter.

Benjamin Franklin insisted in a Conference with the Proprietaries, that if, when Commissioners were named

*Thomas Penn, "the principal Proprietor" of Pennsylvania, and his brother Richard (below)*

in a Bill, the Governor might not strike out or change them at his Pleasure, as none but his own Creatures might be admitted, and the Assembly might as well trust him with the whole, and this it was an undoubted Right of the House of Commons to name Commissioners in Bills in all Cases where they thought it necessary and proper, and to have such Commissioners so named stand without Alteration and Amendment and therefore our Assembly claimed the said Privileges; To which He answered that in such Cases, that before the House of Commons inserted the Names of Commissioners in Bills, the List was privately settled with the Ministry by the Committees; but tho' it might be a Privilege of the House of Commons, it did not follow that it was the Privilege of a Pennsylvania Assembly. That We were only a kind of Corporation acting by a Charter from the Crown and could have no Privileges or Rights but what was granted by that Charter, in which no such Privilege as We now claim was any where mentioned. *But says I* Your Father's Charter expressly says that the Assembly of Pennsylvania shall have all the Power and Privileges of an Assembly according to the Rights of the Freeborn Subjects of England, and as is usual in any of the British Plantations in America. *Yes says he* but, if my Father granted Privileges he was not by the Royal Charter impowered to grant, Nothing can be claim'd by such Grant. *I said,* If then your Father had no Right to grant the Privileges He pretended to grant, and published all over Europe as granted those who came to settle in the Province upon the Faith of that Grant and in Expectation of enjoying the Privileges contained in it, were deceived, cheated and betrayed. *He answered* they should have themselves looked to that. That the Royal Charter was no Secret; they who came into the Province on my Father's Offer of Privileges, if, they were deceiv'd, it was their own Fault; and that He said with a Kind of triumphing laughing Insolence, such as a low Jockey might do when a Purchaser complained that He had cheated him in a Horse. I was astonished to see him thus meanly give up his Father's Character and conceived that Moment a more cordial and thorough Contempt for him than I ever before felt for any Man living — A Contempt that I cannot express in Words, but I believe my Countenance expressed it strongly. And that his Brother was looking at me, must have observed it; however finding myself grow warm I

163

made no other Answer to this than that the poor People were no Lawyers themselves and confiding in his Father did not think it necessary to consult any.

Franklin's interest in his English ancestors inspired him to take a journey into Northamptonshire to find out more about the history of his family. In this long letter to Deborah, he told much of what he summarized in his *Autobiography* about the English Franklins. But this has the charm of added detail and fresh news. He began his journey after being feted at Cambridge's commencement in July.

*Cambridge University looked like this when Franklin and his son attended commencement ceremonies there early in July of 1758.*

London, September 6, 1758. After the commencement, we went from Cambridge, through Huntingdonshire into Northamptonshire, and at Wellingborough; on inquiry we found still living Mary Fisher, whose maiden name was Franklin, daughter and only child of Thomas Franklin, my father's eldest brother: she is five years older than sister Douse, and remembers her going away with my father and his then wife, and two other children to New England, about the year, 1685. We have had no correspondence with her since my uncle Benjamin's death, now near 30 years. I knew she had lived at Wellingborough, and had married there to one Mr. Richard Fisher, a grazier and tanner, about fifty years ago, but did not expect to see either of them alive, so inquired for their posterity; I was directed to their house and we found them both alive, but weak with age, very glad however to see us; she seems to have been a very smart, sensible woman. They are wealthy, have left off business, and live comfortably. They have had only one child, a daughter, who died, when about thirty years of age, unmarried; she gave me several of my uncle Benjamin's letters to her, and acquainted me where the other remains of the family lived, of which I have, since my return to London, found out a daughter of my father's only sister, very old, and was never married. She is a good clever woman, but poor, though vastly contented with her situation and very cheerful. The others are in different parts of the country: I intend to visit them, but they were too much out of our tour in that journey. From Wellingborough we went to Ecton, about three or four miles, being the village where my father was born, and where his father, grandfather, and great-grandfather had lived, and how many of the family before we know not. We went first to see the old house and grounds; they came to Mr.

*In Ecton Franklin visited the small house where his father was born and the church where his ancestors had worshiped and were buried.*

Fisher with his wife, and after letting them for some years finding his rent something ill paid, he sold them. The land is now added to another farm, and a school kept in the house: it is a decayed old stone building, but still known by the name of Franklin House. Thence we went to visit the rector of the parish, who lives close by the church, a very antient building. He entertained us very kindly, and showed us the old church register, in which were the births, marriages, and burials of our ancestors for 200 years, as early as his book began. His wife a good-natured chatty old lady, (grandaughter of the famous archdeacon Palmer, who formerly had that parish, and lived there,) remembered a great deal about the family; carried us out into the church-yard, and showed us several of their grave stones, which were so covered with moss that we could not read the letters till she ordered a hard brush and basin of water, with which Peter scoured them clean, and then Billy copied them. She entertained and diverted us highly with stories of Thomas Franklin, Mrs. Fisher's father, who was a conveyancer, something of a lawyer, clerk of the county courts, and clerk to the archdeacon, in his visitations; a very leading man in all county affairs, and much employed in public business. He set on foot a subscription for erecting chimes in their steeple, and completed it, and we heard them play. He found out an easy method of saving their village meadows from being drowned, as they used to be sometimes by the river, which method is still in being; but when first proposed, nobody could conceive how it could be; but however they said if Franklin says he knows how to do it, it will be done. His advice and opinion was sought for on all occasions, by all sorts of people, and he was looked upon, she said, by some, as something of a conjurer.

In the autumn of 1759, Franklin, with his son, journeyed to Scotland, where he received a degree of Doctor of Laws from the University of St. Andrews. He made many friends in the course of this journey, including the philosopher David Hume and the jurist and man of letters Henry Home, Lord Kames. His lordship was famous as a practical joker, but he met his match in Franklin. Visiting the Kames estate in Berwick, Franklin startled the jurist by declaring, one evening, that the Old Testament recommended toleration. Presbyterian educated, Kames knew his Bible well, and he emphatically disagreed. Franklin called for a Bible, and proceeded to recite the following passage, which he introduced as a chapter from Genesis.

*Lord Kames*

*Milne Square in Edinburgh, where Franklin lodged in 1759*

### CHAP. XXVII

1. And it came to pass after these Things, that Abraham sat in the Door of his Tent, about the going down of the Sun.

2. And behold a Man, bowed with Age, came from the Way of the Wilderness, leaning on a Staff.

3. And Abraham arose and met him, and said unto him, Turn in, I pray thee, and wash thy Feet, and tarry all Night, and thou shalt arise early on the Morrow, and go on thy Way.

4. And the Man said, Nay, for I will abide under this Tree.

5. But Abraham pressed him greatly; so he turned, and they went into the Tent; and Abraham baked unleavened Bread, and they did eat.

6. And when Abraham saw that the Man blessed not God, he said unto him, Wherefore dost thou not worship the most high God, Creator of Heaven and Earth?

7. And the Man answered and said, I do not worship the God thou speakest of; neither do I call upon his Name; for I have made to myself a God, which abideth alway in mine House, and provideth me with all Things.

8. And Abraham's Zeal was kindled against the Man; and he arose, and fell upon him, and drove him forth with Blows into the Wilderness.

9. And at Midnight God called unto Abraham, saying, Abraham, where is the Stranger?

10. And Abraham answered and said, Lord, he would not worship thee, neither would he call upon thy Name; therefore have I driven him out from before my Face into the Wilderness.

11. And God said, Have I born with him these hundred ninety and eight Years, and nourished him, and cloathed him, notwithstanding his Rebellion against me, and couldst not thou, that art thyself a Sinner, bear with him one Night?

12. And Abraham said, Let not the Anger of my Lord wax hot against his Servant. Lo, I have sinned; forgive me, I pray Thee:

13. And Abraham arose and went forth into the Wilderness, and sought diligently for the Man, and found him, and returned with him to his Tent; and when he had entreated him kindly, he sent him away on the Morrow with Gifts.

14.   And God spake again unto Abraham, saying, For this thy Sin shall thy Seed be afflicted four Hundred Years in a strange Land:

15.   But for thy Repentance will I deliver them; and they shall come forth with Power, and with Gladness of Heart, and with much Substance.

This "Parable against Persecution," as it has come to be known, was, of course, another Franklin hoax—a skillful imitation of the King James version of the Bible. Franklin wrote several similar imitations in the course of his life, recommending various virtues, such as brotherly love. With learned conversations, new friendships, jokes, and an honorary degree to treasure, Franklin looked back on his weeks in Scotland as "the densest happiness" he had ever experienced in his life. He returned to London to find the British celebrating another kind of triumph. General James Wolfe had won a magnificent victory on the Plains of Abraham, before Quebec, on September 13, 1759. It meant the end of French rule in North America and the imminent close of the Seven Years' War. Almost immediately, politically minded Britons began discussing peace terms. What, they asked, should be done with the rich sugar island of Guadeloupe in the West Indies, captured from the French earlier in the war. At this point in history, the West Indies produced far more wealth for England than did the North American Colonies, and thus generated substantial support in Parliament. Some politicians recommended that Britain return Canada to France in the peace negotiations and retain Guadeloupe. To Franklin this was not only idiocy, it was a callous disregard of America's safety and security. Without the French in Canada to supply the Indians with weapons and ammunition, there was at least a hope that the bloody border wars that had distressed Pennsylvania and neighboring Colonies for generations might finally come to an end. Franklin leaped into the debate over Canada with a series of letters in British newspapers, and finally with a closely reasoned essay, *The Interest of Great Britain Considered*, published in April, 1760. A brief, humorous version of this argument, which probably expressed more of Franklin's real feelings toward the notion of returning Canada, appeared anonymously in William Strahan's paper, *The London Chronicle*.

[London, December 27, 1759]

Mr. Chronicle,

We Britons are a nation of statesmen and politicians; we are privy councellors by birthright; and therefore take it much amiss when we are told by some of your correspondents, "that it is not proper to expose to public view the many good reasons there are for restoring Canada," (*if we reduce it.*)

I have, with great industry, been able to procure a full

account of those reasons, and shall make no secret of them among ourselves. Here they are. Give them to all your readers; that is, to all that can read, in the King's dominions.

1. We should restore Canada; because an uninterrupted trade with the Indians throughout a vast country, where the communication by water is so easy, would encrease our commerce, *already too great*, and occasion a large additional demand for our manufactures, *already too dear.*

2. We should restore it, lest, thro' a greater plenty of beaver, broad-brimmed hats become cheaper to that unmannerly sect, the Quakers.

3. We should restore Canada, that we may *soon* have a new war, and another opportunity of spending two or three millions a year in America; there being great danger of our growing too rich, our European expences not being sufficient to drain our immense treasures.

4. We should restore it, that we may have occasion constantly to employ, in time of war, a fleet and army in those parts; for otherwise we might be too strong at home.

5. We should restore it, that the French may, by means of their Indians, carry on, (as they have done for these 100 years past even in times of peace between the two crowns) a constant scalping war against our colonies, and thereby stint their growth; for, otherwise, the children might in time be as tall as their mother.

6. What tho' the blood of thousands of unarmed English farmers, surprized and assassinated in their fields; of harmless women and children murdered in their beds; doth at length call for vengeance;—what tho' the Canadian measure of iniquity be full, and if ever any country did, that country now certainly does, deserve the judgment of *extirpation:*—yet let not us be the executioners of Divine justice;—it will look as if Englishmen were revengeful.

7. Our colonies, 'tis true, have exerted themselves beyond their strength, on the expectations we gave them of driving the French from Canada; but tho' we ought to keep faith with our Allies, it is not necessary with our children. That might teach them (against Scripture) to *put their trust in Princes:* Let 'em learn to trust in God.

8. Should we not restore Canada, it would look as if our statesmen had *courage* as well as our soldiers; but what have statesmen to do with *courage?* Their proper

character is *wisdom*.

9. What can be *braver,* than to show all Europe we can afford to lavish our best blood as well as our treasure, in conquests we do not intend to keep? . . .

10. The French have long since openly declar'd, *"que les Anglois et les François sont incompatible dans cette partie de l'Amerique;" "*that our people and theirs were incompatible in that part of the continent of America:" *"que rien n'etoit plus important à l'etat, que de delivrer leur colonie du facheux voisinage des Anglois;"* "that nothing was of more importance to France, than delivering its colony from the troublesome neighbourhood of the English;" . . . Now, if we do not fairly leave the French in Canada, till they have a favourable opportunity of putting their *burning* and *ruining* schemes in execution, will it not look as if we were afraid of them? . . .

I will not dissemble, Mr. Chronicle; that in answer to all these reasons and motives for restoring Canada, I have heard one that appears to have some weight on the other side of the question. It is said, that nations, as well as private persons, should, for their honour's sake, take care to preserve a *consistence of character*: that it has always been the character of the English to fight strongly, and negotiate weakly; generally agreeing to restore, at a peace, what they ought to have kept, and to keep what they had better have restored: then, if it would really, according to the preceding reasons, be prudent and right to restore Canada, we ought, say these objectors, to keep it; otherwise *we shall be inconsistent with ourselves.* I shall not take upon myself to weigh these different reasons, but offer the whole to the consideration of the public. Only permit me to suggest, that there is one method of avoiding fairly all future dispute about the propriety of *keeping* or *restoring* Canada; and that is, *let us never take it.* The French still hold out at Montreal and Trois Rivieres, in hopes of succour from France. Let us be but *a little too late* with our ships in the river St. Laurence, so that the enemy may get their supplies up next spring, as they did the last, with reinforcements sufficient to enable them to recover Quebec. . . .

The following letter to Deborah gives us a glimpse of a Franklin family drama. William Strahan had become more and more insistent that Franklin settle in England. He had urged Deborah to come over

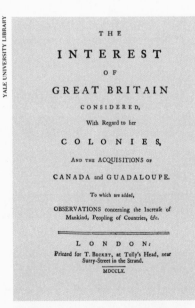

THE

INTEREST

OF

GREAT BRITAIN

CONSIDERED,

With Regard to her

COLONIES,

AND THE ACQUISITIONS OF

CANADA and GUADALOUPE.

To which are added,

OBSERVATIONS concerning the Increase of Mankind, Peopling of Countries, &c.

LONDON:

Printed for T. BECKET, at Tully's Head, near Surry-Street in the Strand.

MDCCLX.

*Franklin's essay on the Canada question was published in London.*

before some Englishwoman captured her husband. He then made a serious proposal of marriage between his son and Sally.

London, March 5. 1760

I receiv'd the Enclos'd some time since from Mr. Strahan. I afterwards spent an Evening in Conversation with him on the Subject. He was very urgent with me to stay in England and prevail with you to remove hither with Sally. He propos'd several advantageous Schemes to me which appear'd reasonably founded. His Family is a very agreable one; Mrs. Strahan a sensible [and] good Woman, the Children of amiable [char]acters and particularly the young Man, [who is] sober, ingenious and industrious, and a [desirable] Person. In Point of Circumstances [there can] be no Objection, Mr. Strahan being [in so thriving] a Way, as to lay up a Thousand [Pounds] every Year from the Profits of his Business, after maintaining his Family and paying all Charges. I gave him, however, two Reasons why I could not think of removing hither. One, my Affection to Pensilvania, and long established Friendships and other Connections there: The other, your invincible Aversion to crossing the Seas. And without removing hither, I could not think of parting with my Daughter to such a Distance. I thank'd him for the Regard shown us in the Proposal; but gave him no Expectation that I should forward the Letters.

*John Baskerville*

The opportunity to play a joke on a supposed expert was something that Franklin frequently found irresistible. In this letter to the English printer John Baskerville, whom he had met in Birmingham, Franklin deliciously described one of his most successful gambits. Baskerville's typeface was thicker in the heavy strokes, finer in the light ones, and sharper at the angles than the more familiar Caslon type. Many conservatives declared it difficult to read, and it took many years for Baskerville to win popularity. When he published his Cambridge Bible in August, 1763, Baskerville, conscious of the widespread criticism, included an extract of this letter from Franklin.

Craven-Street, London [1760?]

Dear Sir,

Let me give you a pleasant Instance of the Prejudice some have entertained against your Work. Soon after I returned, discoursing with a Gentleman concerning the Artists of Birmingham, he said you would be a Means of blinding all the Readers in the Nation, for the Strokes of your Letters being too thin and narrow, hurt the Eye,

*Baskerville's Cambridge Bible*

and he could never read a Line of them without Pain. I thought, said I, you were going to complain of the Gloss on the Paper, some object to: No, no, says he, I have heard that mentioned, but it is not that; 'tis in the Form and Cut of the Letters themselves; they have not that natural and easy Proportion between the Height and Thickness of the Stroke, which makes the common Printing so much more comfortable to the Eye. You see this Gentleman was a Connoisseur. In vain I endeavoured to support your *Character* against the Charge; he knew what he felt, he could see the Reason of it, and several other Gentlemen among his Friends had made the same Observation, &c. Yesterday he called to visit me, when, mischievously bent to try his Judgment, I stept into my Closet, tore off the Top of Mr. Caslon's Specimen, and produced it to him as yours brought with me from Birmingham, saying, I had been examining it since he spoke to me, and could not for my Life perceive the Disproportion he mentioned, desiring him to point it out to me. He readily undertook it, and went over the several Founts, shewing me every-where what he thought Instances of that Disproportion; and declared, that he could not then read the Specimen without feeling very strongly the Pain he had mentioned to me. I spared him that Time the Confusion of being told, that these were the Types he had been reading all his Life with so much Ease to his Eyes; the Types his adored Newton is printed with, on which he has pored not a little; nay, the very Types his own Book is printed with, for he is himself an Author; and yet never discovered this painful Disproportion in them, till he thought they were yours.

Franklin was a deeply paternal man. He converted almost every circle in which he moved into a kind of family, with himself as the father. His life in London was no exception to this pattern. Soon after his arrival, he and William had rented four rooms at Number 7, Craven Street, within easy walking distance of the government offices in Whitehall and the Houses of Parliament. Mrs. Stevenson, his landlady, was a widow, and her eighteen-year-old daughter Mary, known to the family as Polly, was an intelligent and sensitive young girl, who soon came to regard Franklin as her second father. He was delighted when she showed an interest in science, and this letter was the beginning of a series in which Franklin attempted to answer her scientific questions.

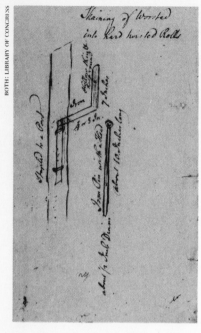

*Benjamin Franklin's letters to Polly Stevenson were often scientific and occasionally contained sketches, like this device for "Skeining of Worsted."*

Cravenstreet, June 11. 1760

Dear Polly,

'Tis a very sensible Question you ask, how the Air can affect the Barometer, when its Opening appears covered with Wood? If indeed it was so closely covered as to admit of no Communication of the outward Air to the Surface of the Mercury, the Change of Weight in the Air could not possibly affect it. But the least Crevice is sufficient for the Purpose; a Pinhole will do the Business. And if you could look behind the Frame to which your Barometer is fixed, you would certainly find some small Opening. . . .

Your Observation on what you have lately read concerning Insects, is very just and solid. Superficial Minds are apt to despise those who make that Part of Creation their Study, as mere Triflers; but certainly the World has been much oblig'd to them. Under the Care and Management of Man, the Labours of the little Silkworm afford Employment and Subsistence to Thousands of Families, and become an immense Article of Commerce. The Bee, too, yields us its delicious Honey, and its Wax useful to a multitude of Purposes. Another Insect, it is said, produces the Cochineal, from whence we have our rich Scarlet Dye. The Usefulness of the Cantharides, or Spanish Flies, in Medicine, is known to all, and Thousands owe their Lives to that Knowledge. By human Industry and Observation, other Properties of other Insects may possibly be hereafter discovered, and of equal Utility. A thorough Acquaintance with the Nature of these little Creatures, may also enable Mankind to prevent the Increase of such as are noxious or secure us against the Mischiefs they occasion. . . .

There is, however, a prudent Moderation to be used in Studies of this kind. The Knowledge of Nature may be ornamental, and it may be useful, but if to attain an Eminence in that, we neglect the Knowledge and Practice of essential Duties, we deserve Reprehension. For there is no Rank in Natural Knowledge of equal Dignity and Importance with that of being a good Parent, a good Child, a good Husband, or Wife, a good Neighbour or Friend, a good Subject or Citizen, that is, in short, a good Christian. Nicholas Gimcrack, therefore, who neglected the Care of his Family, to pursue Butterflies, was a just Object of Ridicule. . . .

In England Franklin busied himself with another invention—the armonica. The idea of a musical instrument made of glasses was not new. By 1761, the instrument had become so popular in London that one of the more skillful professional performers published a set of instructions on how to play it. A friend in the Royal Society introduced the pastime to Franklin, who had inherited from his father a strong interest in music and a modest talent. It did not take him long to find the armonicas then in use very unsatisfactory. The glasses had to be filled with just the right amount of water before each performance, and providing enough glasses to give the instrument a decent range created armonicas so large that it was impossible to play them seated from a single position. In this letter to the Italian scientist and writer Giovanni Battista Beccaria, Franklin told of his improved version of the instrument. It became extremely popular on the Continent, and two of Franklin's protégées, Marianne and Cecilia Davies, gave public concerts across Europe, culminating in Vienna, where they played and sang at the marriage of the Archduchess Amalia to Duke Ferdinand of Parma. Mozart, Beethoven, and several other famous musicians composed music for the armonica. Eventually, however, the instrument got a very bad reputation, because its remarkably sweet and ethereal music was thought to have a depressing effect on the players, even to producing numerous nervous breakdowns.

London, July 13, 1762

Rev. Sir,

I once promised myself the pleasure of seeing you at Turin, but as that is not now likely to happen, being just about returning to my native country, America, I sit down to take leave of you (among others of my European friends that I cannot see) by writing.

I thank you for the honourable mention you have so frequently made of me in your letters to Mr. Collinson and others, for the generous defence you undertook and executed with so much success, of my electrical opinions; and for the valuable present you have made me of your new work, from which I have received great information and pleasure. I wish I could in return entertain you with any thing new of mine on that subject; but I have not lately pursued it. Nor do I know of any one here that is at present much engaged in it.

Perhaps, however, it may be agreeable to you, as you live in a musical country, to have an account of the new instrument lately added here to the great number that charming science was before possessed of: As it is an instrument that seems peculiarly adapted to Italian music, especially that of the soft and plaintive kind, I

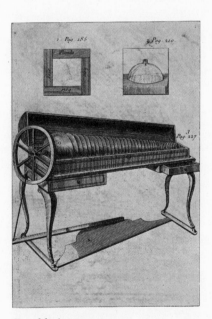
*Franklin's armonica*

will endeavour to give you such a description of it, and of the manner of constructing it, that you, or any of your friends may be enabled to imitate it, if you incline so to do, without being at the expence and trouble of the many experiments I have made in endeavouring to bring it to its present perfection.

You have doubtless heard the sweet tone that is drawn from a drinking glass, by passing a wet finger round its brim. One Mr. Puckeridge, a gentleman from Ireland, was the first who thought of playing tunes, formed of these tones. He collected a number of glasses of different sizes, fixed them near each other on a table, and tuned them by putting into them water, more or less, as each note required. The tones were brought out by passing his fingers round their brims. He was unfortunately burnt here, with his instrument, in a fire which consumed the house he lived in. Mr. E. Delaval, a most ingenious member of our Royal Society, made one in imitation of it, with a better choice and form of glasses, which was the first I saw or heard. Being charmed with the sweetness of its tones, and the music he produced from it, I wished only to see the glasses disposed in a more convenient form, and brought together in a narrower compass, so as to admit of a greater number of tones, and all within reach of hand to a person sitting before the instrument, which I accomplished, after various intermediate trials....

My largest glass is a G a little below the reach of a common voice, and my highest G, including three compleat octaves. To distinguish the glasses the more readily to the eye, I have painted the apparent parts of the glasses within side, every semitone white and the other notes of the octave with the seven prismatic colours, *viz.* C, red; D, orange; E, yellow; F, green; G, blue; A, Indigo; B, purple; and C, red again; so that glasses of the same colour (the white excepted) are always octaves to each other.

This instrument is played upon, by sitting before the middle of the set of glasses as before the keys of a harpsichord, turning them with the foot, and wetting them now and then with a spunge and clean water. The fingers should first be a little soaked in water and quite free from all greasiness; a little fine chalk upon them is sometimes useful, to make them catch the glass and bring out the tone more readily. Both hands are used, by which means different parts are played together. Observe, that the tones

*Ticket to the coronation of George III on September 22, 1761, which Franklin attended*

are best drawn out when the glasses turn *from* the ends of the fingers, not when they turn *to* them.

The advantages of this instrument are, that its tones are incomparably sweet beyond those of any other; that they may be swelled and softened at pleasure by stronger or weaker pressures of the finger, and continued to any length; and that the instrument, being once well tuned, never again wants tuning.

In honour of your musical language, I have borrowed from it the name of this instrument, calling it the Armonica.

By this time, Franklin had received another honorary degree, Doctor of Civil Law from Oxford University. He also completed his negotiations with the Penns. In a compromise, Franklin won the Privy Council's approval for taxing the Proprietors' lands on an equitable basis in return for having agreed to abandon a few other minor points in dispute. By now a new king was on the throne. George III had succeeded his grandfather, George II, on October 25, 1760. William Pitt resigned as Secretary of State, and the Peace Party soon had control of the government. His business almost completed, Franklin made plans to go home. But he stayed long enough to win another victory. William Franklin had by this time obtained his law degree, and his father, through friends that were influential with the new king, obtained for him the Royal Governorship of New Jersey. Although Franklin had tried to arrange a marriage between him and Polly Stevenson, William now married a "West Indian charmer"—Elizabeth Downes, whom he had been courting for a number of years. In the following letters, Franklin said good-bye to Polly Stevenson and to William Strahan, who had become his closest friend in England.

Portsmouth, Augt. 11. 1762

My dear Polly

This is the best Paper I can get at this wretched Inn, but it will convey what is intrusted to it as faithfully as the finest. It will tell my Polly, how much her Friend is afflicted, that he must, perhaps never again, see one for whom he has so sincere an Affection, join'd to so perfect an Esteem; whom he once flatter'd himself might become his own in the tender Relation of a Child; but can now entertain such pleasing hopes no more; Will it tell *how much* he is afflicted? No, it cannot.

Adieu, my dearest Child: I will call you so; Why should I not call you so, since I love you with all the Tenderness, all the Fondness of a Father? Adieu. May the God of all Goodness shower down his choicest Blessings upon you, and make you infinitely Happier than that Event could

175

have made you. Adieu. And wherever I am, believe me to be, with unalterable Affection, my dear Polly, Your sincere Friend

B FRANKLIN

Portsmouth, Monday, Augt. 23. 1762

Dear Sir,

I have been two Nights on board expecting to sail, but the Wind continuing contrary, am just now come on shore again, and have met with your kind Letter of the 20th. I thank you even for the Reproofs it contains, tho' I have not altogether deserved them. I cannot, I assure you, quit even this disagreable Place without Regret, as it carries me still farther from those I love, and from the Opportunities of hearing of their Welfare. The Attraction of *Reason* is at present for the other Side of the Water, but that of *Inclination* will be for this side. You know which usually prevails. I shall probably make but this one Vibration and settle here for ever. Nothing will prevent it, if I can, as I hope I can, prevail with Mrs. F. to accompany me; especially if we have a Peace. I will not tell you, that to be near and with you and yours, is any part of my Inducement: It would look like a Complement extorted from me by your Pretences to Insignificancy. Nor will I own that your Persuasions and Arguments have wrought this Change in my former Resolutions: tho' it is true that they have frequently intruded themselves into my Consideration whether I would or not. I trust, however, that we shall once more see each other and be happy again together, which God, etc.

My Love to Mrs. Strahan, and your amiable and valuable Children. Heaven bless you all, whatever becomes of Your much obliged and affectionate Friend

B FRANKLIN

Chapter 7

# Birth of an Ambassador

Franklin returned to Philadelphia with an annoying worry nagging his mind. His enemy, William Smith, now provost of the College of Philadelphia, had spread numerous lies in England about Franklin's loss of popularity in Pennsylvania. This explains the note of triumph in the following letter to William Strahan describing the warm welcome Franklin had met in Philadelphia. Dr. Hawkesworth, mentioned in the opening line, was a writer and editor, who helped his wife run a school at Bromley, Kent; "my little Wife" refers to Strahan's daughter Margaret Penelope, a girl of eleven.

Philada. Dec. 2. 1762

Dear Straney,

As good Dr. Hawkesworth calls you, to whom my best Respects. I got home well the 1st. of November, and had the Happiness to find my little Family perfectly well; and that Dr. Smith's Reports of the Diminution of my Friends were all false. My House has been full of a Succession of them from Morning to Night ever since my Arrival, congratulating me on my Return with the utmost Cordiality and Affection. My Fellow Citizens while I was on the Sea, had, at the annual Election, chosen me unanimously, as they had done every Year while I was in England, to be their Representative in Assembly; and would, they say, if I had not disappointed them by coming privately to Town before they heard of my Landing, have met me with 500 Horse. Excuse my Vanity in writing this to you, who know what has provok'd me to it. My Love to good Mrs. Strahan, and your Children, particularly my little Wife. I shall write more fully per next Opportunity, having now only time to add, that I am, with unchangeable Affection, my dear Friend, Yours sincerely

B FRANKLIN

Back in Philadelphia, Franklin exchanged greetings with two of his favorite female correspondents, Catherine Ray, who had married her second cousin, William Greene, Jr., on April 30, 1758; and Jane Franklin Mecom. Although Franklin did not stay in England for William's wedding to Elizabeth Downes—"the Promotion and Marriage" of his son mentioned by Jane Mecom—he obviously liked his new daughter-in-law. So did William Strahan, who called her "as good a soul as breathes."

Philada: Nov 25th. 1762.

I received your kind congratulations on my return, and thank you cordially. It gives me great pleasure to hear you are married and live happily. You are a good Girl for complying with so essential a duty, and God will bless you. Make my compliments acceptable to your spouse; and fulfil your promise of writing to me; and let me know everything that has happened to you and your friends since my Departure, for I interest myself as much as ever in whatever relates to your Happiness. My best Respects to your Brother and Sister Ward, and Compliments on his advancement to the Government of your Colony; and believe me ever, My dear Caty Your affectionate Friend and humble servant

B FRANKLIN.

Philada. Nov. 25. 1762

Dear Sister,

I thank you for your obliging Letter of the 12th. Instant. My Wife says she will write to you largely by next Post, being at present short of Time. As to the Promotion and Marriage you mention, I shall now only say that the Lady is of so amiable a Character, that the latter gives me more Pleasure than the former, tho' I have no doubt but that he will make as good a Governor as Husband: for he has good Principles and good Dispositions, and I think is not deficient in good Understanding. I am as ever Your affectionate Brother

B FRANKLIN

But Franklin could not forget the happiness he had experienced during his years in England. In this letter to Polly Stevenson, he commented on it in the strongest possible terms.

Philada. March 25. 1763

Your pleasing Favour of Nov. 11 is now before me. It found me as you suppos'd it would, happy with my American Friends and Family about me; and it made me more happy in showing me that I am not yet forgotten by the dear Friends I left in England. And indeed why should I fear they will ever forget me, when I feel so strongly that I shall ever remember them! . . .

Of all the enviable Things England has, I envy it most its People. Why should that petty Island, which compar'd to America is but like a stepping Stone in a Brook, scarce enough of it above Water to keep one's Shoes dry; why, I say, should that little Island, enjoy in almost every Neighbourhood, more sensible, virtuous and elegant Minds, than we can collect in ranging 100 Leagues of our vast Forests.

Early in 1763, William Franklin arrived in Philadelphia with his wife. A few days later father and son journeyed to New Jersey, where William was installed as the province's new governor. In this letter to Strahan, Franklin told of that journey, commented on peace with France, and alluded to the possibility of his returning to England.

Philada. March 28. 1763

I have received your Favours of Oct. 20 and Nov. 1 by my Son who is safely arrived with my new Daughter. I thank you for your Friendly Congratulations on his Promotion. I am just return'd from a Journey I made with him thro' his Government, and had the Pleasure of seeing him every where receiv'd with the utmost Respect and even Affection by all Ranks of People. So that I have great Hopes of his being now comfortably settled.

As to myself, I mention'd to you in a former Letter, that I found my Friends here more numerous and as hearty as ever. It had been industriously reported, that I had lived very extravagantly in England, and wasted a considerable Sum of the Publick Money which I had received out of your Treasury for the Province; but the Assembly, when they came to examine my Accounts and allow me for my Services, found themselves Two Thousand two hundred and fourteen Pounds 10s. 7d. Sterling in my Debt; to the utter Confusion of the Propagators of that Falshood, and the Surprize of all they had made to believe it. The House accordingly order'd that Sum to be paid me, and that the Speaker

*Detail from a 1764 cartoon showing Franklin (left) holding a paper on which is written: "Resolves, ye Proprietaries are knave and tyrant."*

should moreover present me with their Thanks for my Fidelity, &c. in transacting their Affairs.

I congratulate you on the glorious Peace your Ministry have made, the most advantageous to Britain, in my Opinion, of any your Annals have recorded. As to the Places left or restor'd to France, I conceive our Strength will now soon increase to so great a degree in North America, that in any future War we may with ease reduce them all; and therefore I look on them as so many Hostages or Pledges of good Behaviour from that perfidious Nation. Your Pamphlets and Papers therefore that are wrote against the Peace with some Plausibility, give one Pleasure, as I hope the French will read them, and be persuaded they have made an excellent Bargain....

I do not forget any of your Reasons for my Return to England. The Hint you add in your last, is good and wise; it could not have been wiser or better if you had drank ever so much Madeira. It is however, impossible for me to execute that Resolution this ensuing Summer, having many Affairs first to arrange; but I trust I shall see you before you look much older.

In the summer of 1763 Franklin turned his attention to the condition of the Post Office. He instituted various improvements in the service, as he made clear in this letter to Anthony Todd, Secretary of the British Post Office.

[Philadelphia, January 16, 1764]
In my last I wrote you that Mr. Foxcroft, my Colleague, was gone to Virginia where and in Maryland some offices are yet unsettled. We are to meet again in April at Annapolis, and then shall send you a full Account of our Doings. I will now only just mention, that we hope in the Spring to expedite the Communication between Boston and New York, as we have already that between New York and Philadelphia, by making the Mails travel by Night as well as by Day, which has never heretofore been done in America. It passes now between Philadelphia and New York, so quick that a Letter can be sent from one place to another, and an Answer received the Day following, which before took a week, and when our Plan is executed between Boston and New York, Letters may be sent and answers received in four Days, which before took a fortnight; and between Philadelphia and Boston in Six days, which before required Three

Weeks. We think this expeditious Communication will greatly encrease the Number of Letters from Philadelphia and Boston by the Packets to Britain.

In spite of peace in Europe, the American frontier remained restless. In this letter to Richard Jackson, the member of Parliament who was now serving as Pennsylvania's agent, Franklin suggested how England might raise money in America in order to support the fourteen battalions the British high command felt it needed to keep the Indians quiet. He then added a succinct narration of an episode that shook Pennsylvania to its foundations. Presbyterian Irish from the township of Paxton murdered a group of peaceful Christian Indians in retaliation for the depredations committed by marauding tribes during the uprising known as Pontiac's War. Franklin condemned the murders in a scorching pamphlet. The frontiersmen reacted by marching on Philadelphia. Franklin hastily organized the Philadelphia militia and then rode out to negotiate a truce with the leaders of the rebels. The opening paragraphs are an interesting indication of Franklin's conservative attitude at this point in his life. "Mr. W." is John Wilkes, the English agitator whose defiance of Parliament and of the laws of libel was roiling London.

*"The March of the Paxton Men," a cartoon from 1764, showing Franklin (right) cheering his supporters*

Philada. Feb. 11. 1764

I have just received your Favour by the extra Packet of Nov. 26. and am pleas'd to find a just Resentment so general in your House against Mr. W.'s seditious Conduct, and to hear that the present Administration is like to continue.

If Money *must* be raised from us to support 14 Batallions, as you mention, I think your Plan the most advantageous to both the Mother Country and Colonies of any I have seen. A moderate Duty on Foreign Mellasses maybe collected; when a high one could not. The same on foreign Wines; and a Duty not only on Tea, but on all East India Goods might perhaps not be amiss, as they are generally rather Luxuries than Necessaries; and many of your Manchester Manufactures might well supply their Places. The Duty on Negroes I could wish large enough to obstruct their Importation, as they every where prevent the Increase of Whites. But if you lay such Duties as may destroy our Trade with the Foreign Colonies, I think you will greatly hurt your own Interest as well as ours. I need not explain this to you, who will readily see it. The American Fishery, too, should be as little burthened as possible. It is to no purpose to enlarge on these Heads, as probably your Acts are pass'd

*In another cartoon of 1764, Franklin (foreground) eyes a group of his Quaker friends, who are expressing their fears of the "Paxton spirit."*

before this can reach you.

In my last I mention'd to you the Rioting on our Frontiers, in which 20 peaceable Indians were kill'd, who had long liv'd quietly among us. The Spirit of killing all Indians, Friends and Foes, spread amazingly thro' the whole Country: The Action was almost universally approved of by the common People; and the Rioters thence receiv'd such Encouragement, that they projected coming down to this City, 1000 in Number, arm'd, to destroy 140 Moravian and Quaker Indians, under Protection of the Government. To check this Spirit, and strengthen the Hands of the Government by Changing the Sentiments of the Populace, I wrote the enclos'd Pamphlet, which we had only time to circulate in this City and Neighbourhood, before we heard that the Insurgents were on their March from all Parts. It would perhaps be Vanity in me to imagine so slight a thing could have any extraordinary Effect. But however that may be, there was a sudden and very remarkable Change; and above 1000 of our Citizens took Arms to support the Government in the Protection of those poor Wretches. Near 500 of the Rioters had rendezvous'd at Germantown, and many more were expected; but the Fighting Face we put on made them more willing to hear Reason, and the Gentlemen sent out by the Governor and Council to discourse with them, found it no very difficult Matter to persuade them to disperse and go home quietly. They came from all Parts of our Frontier, and were armed with Rifle Guns and Tomhawks. You may judge what Hurry and Confusion we have been in for this Week past. I was up two Nights running, all Night, with our Governor; and my Rest so broken by Alarms on the other Nights, that the whole Week seems one confus'd Space of Time, without any such Distinction of Days, as that I can readily and certainly say, on such a Day such a thing happened. At present we are pretty quiet, and I hope that Quiet will continue. A Militia Bill is ordered by the House to be brought in, our Want of such a Law appearing on this Occasion to every-body; but whether we shall be able to frame one that will pass, is a Question. The Jealousy of an Addition of Power to the Proprietary Government, which is universally dislik'd here, will prevail with the House not to leave the sole Appointment of the Militia Officers in the Hands of the Governor; and he, I suppose, will insist upon it, and so the Bill will probably fall through; which perhaps is no great Matter, as your 14 Battallions will make all Militias in America needless, as well as put them out of Countenance.

The experience disgusted Franklin and made a collision between him and the proprietary government almost inevitable. The break came when the new proprietary governor refused to keep the agreement that Franklin had made with the Penns in England. The governor insisted that the Proprietors' lands could only be taxed at a rate no higher than the poorest quality land owned by other people. He also insisted that the Penns' town lots be exempted. Franklin and his followers now rammed through the Assembly a petition calling on the king to place Pennsylvania under a royal government. In this letter to Richard Jackson, Franklin declared war.

Philada. March 29. 1764

In my last I inform'd you that the Agreement between the Governor and Assembly was not likely long to continue. The enclos'd Paper will show you that the Breach is wider now than ever. And 'tis thought there will be a general Petition from the Inhabitants to the Crown, to take us under its immediate Government. I send you this early Notice of what is intended that you may prepare Minds for it, as they fall in your Way. If I can have time I will send you a Copy of the Bill we last sent up, and which was refused. But if it goes not by this Vessel, we shall send it via Lisbon in one that sails in a few Days.

Be assured, that we all think it impossible to go on any longer under a Proprietary Government. By the Resolves you will see, that never was greater Unanimity in any Assembly. Enclos'd I send you a Draft of what I think will be pretty nearly the Petition, that you may see the Tenor of it. Note, There was an Agreement between the First Proprietor W. Penn, and the Crown, for the Sale of the Government at £11,000 of which £2,000 was paid him. Note also, that the Crown has a great Sum in the Proprietaries Hands, half the Quitrents of the Lower Counties belonging to the Crown, of which the Proprietaries are Receivers, and I believe have never render'd any Account.

You will endear yourself to us forever, if you can get this Change of Government compleated.

I write in great haste. . . .

THYRSIS, with a Pr*fb*t*rian Nofe.    CORIN, with a Q**k*ronian Nofe.

*A 1764 book,* The Squabble, A Pastoral Ecologue, *contains this rare caricature of Franklin (right) and criticizes his role in the Paxton case.*

The decision to oust the Proprietors provoked a tremendous political battle in Pennsylvania. They and their followers in turn mustered all their strength to oust Franklin's party from control of the Assembly. Pamphlets flew back and forth, and not a little verbal mud flew with them. Franklin was in the thick of the battle. Five days after the Assembly adjourned, he published explanatory remarks on the Assembly's Resolves and followed this up with a long essay, *Cool Thoughts on the Present Situation of Our Publick Affairs*. The proprietary party fought back with the publication of a speech by one of their leading spokesmen, John Dickinson. The preface to the speech was a panegyric on William Penn in the form of an epitaph. It was cleverly composed of phrases from Assembly documents between the years 1719 and 1756. William Penn's character was, of course, not really in dispute, and Franklin could not resist the opportunity to parody his opponents' efforts to make political capital out of the saintly Quaker founder. In a preface written for the publication of a speech by his political lieutenant Joseph Galloway, Franklin composed this counterepitaph on Penn's sons.

COOL THOUGHTS

ON THE

PRESENT SITUATION

OF OUR

PUBLIC AFFAIRS.

IN A LETTER TO A FRIEND IN THE COUNTRY.

PHILADELPHIA:
PRINTED BY W. DUNLAP. M,DCC,LXIV.

*Franklin's opponents complained that this pamphlet was "distributed gratis by thousands" in Pennsylvania.*

[Philadelphia, August 11, 1764]
Be this a Memorial
Of T         and R         P         ,
P         of P
Who with Estates immense,
Almost beyond Computation,
When their own Province,
And the whole British Empire
Were engag'd in a bloody and most expensive War,
Begun for the Defence of those Estates,
Could yet meanly desire
To have those very Estates
Totally or Partially
Exempted from Taxation,
While their Fellow-Subjects all around them,
Groan'd
Under the universal Burthen.
To gain this Point,
They refus'd the necessary Laws
For the Defence of their People
And suffer'd their Colony to welter in its Blood,
Rather than abate in the least
Of these their dishonest Pretentions.
The Privileges granted by their Father
Wisely and benevolently
To encourage the first Settlers of the Province.
They,

184

Foolishly and cruelly,
Taking Advantage of public Distress,
Have extorted from the Posterity of those Settlers;
And are daily endeavouring to reduce them
To the most abject Slavery:
Tho' to the Virtue and Industry of those People
In improving their Country,
They owe all that they possess and enjoy.
A striking Instance
Of human Depravity and Ingratitude;
And an irrefragable Proof,
That Wisdom and Goodness
Do not descend with an Inheritance;
But that ineffable Meanness
May be connected with unbounded Fortune.

The fiercely fought election of 1764 had a curious outcome. Franklin and Galloway were both narrowly defeated for reelection, but their party retained firm control of the Assembly. Undaunted, the anti-proprietary party promptly appointed Franklin a special agent to return to London and present their petition to remove the Proprietors and place Pennsylvania under the direct rule of the Crown. Franklin told the story in this brief letter to Richard Jackson.

Philada. Oct. 11. 1764

I have now only time to cover the enclos'd, and acquaint you that I am no longer in the Assembly. The Proprietary Party by great Industry against great Security carried the Election of this County and City by about 26 Votes against me and Mr. Galloway; the Voters near 4000. They carried (would you think it!) above 1000 Dutch from me, by printing part of my Paper sent to you 12 Years since on Peopling new Countries where I speak of the Palatine *Boors herding* together, which they explain'd that I call'd them a *Herd of Hogs.* This is quite a laughing Matter. But the Majority of the last Assembly remain, and will I believe still be for the Measure of Changing the Proprietary for a Royal Governor. I am, with great Respect Dear Sir, Your most humble Servant

B FRANKLIN

*Detail from a contemporary cartoon depicting Franklin's defeat in the 1764 election; Franklin is portrayed listening to the Devil.*

HISTORICAL SOCIETY OF PENNSYLVANIA

While the Proprietors' followers fumed, three hundred of Franklin's friends escorted him to Chester, where he went aboard the *King of Prussia* on November 7, 1764. As cannons boomed, everyone cheered lustily and sang a parody of "God Save the King:"

O LORD our GOD arise,
Scatter our Enemies,
   And make them fall.
Confound their Politicks,
Frustrate such Hypocrites,
Franklin, on Thee we fix,
   GOD Save us all.

The following night, aboard the ship as it anchored farther down the Delaware, Franklin's thoughts turned to his family. His chief concern was his daughter, who he feared would meet with numerous snubs and insults from his political enemies in Philadelphia. In the campaign they had attacked him scurrilously, dredging up the scandal of William's illegitimate birth and accusing Franklin of being a secret enemy of both the Germans and the Quakers. Out of this deep concern he wrote the following wise and tender letter to Sarah Franklin.

*It was in this scurrilous pamphlet that Franklin's enemies dredged up the scandal of William's illegitimacy.*

Reedy Island Nov. 8. 1764
7 at Night.

My dear Child, the natural Prudence and goodness of heart that God has blessed you with, make it less necessary for me to be particular in giving you Advice; I shall therefore only say, that the more attentively dutiful and tender you are towards your good Mama, the more you will recommend your self to me; But why shou'd I mention *me*, when you have so much higher a Promise in the Commandment, that such a conduct will recommend you to the favour of God. You know I have many Enemies (all indeed on the Public Account, for I cannot recollect that I have in a private Capacity given just cause of offence to any one whatever) yet they are Enemies and very bitter ones, and you must expect their Enmity will extend in some degree to you, so that your slightest Indiscretions will be magnified into crimes, in order the more sensibly to wound and afflict me. It is therefore the more necessary for you to be extreamly circumspect in all your Behaviour that no Advantage may be given to their Malevolence. Go constantly to Church whoever preaches. The Acts of Devotion in the common Prayer Book, are your principal Business there; and if properly attended to, will do more towards mending the Heart than Sermons generally can do. For they were composed by Men of much greater Piety and Wisdom, than our common Composers of Sermons can pretend to be. And therefore I wish you wou'd never miss the Prayer Days. Yet I do not mean that you shou'd despise Sermons even of the

Preachers you dislike, for the Discourse is often much better than the Man, as sweet and clear Waters come to us thro' very dirty Earth. I am the more particular on this Head, as you seem'd to express a little before I came away some Inclination to leave our Church, which I wou'd not have you do.

For the rest I would only recommend to you in my Absence to acquire those useful Accomplishments Arithmetick, and Bookkeeping. This you might do with Ease, if you wou'd resolve not to see Company on the Hours you set apart for those Studies. . . .

We expect to be at Sea to morrow if this Wind holds, after which I shall have no opportunity of Writing to you till I arrive (if it pleases God that I do arrive) in England. I pray that *his* Blessing may attend you which is of more worth than a Thousand of mine, though they are never wanting. Give my Love to your Brother and Sister, as I cannot now write to them; and remember me affectionately to the young Ladies your Friends, and to our good Neighbours. I am, my dear Sally, Your ever Affectionate Father

B. FRANKLIN

His friends had wished Franklin thirty days' fair wind, and he gratefully reported to Deborah one month later that their wish had come true. He debarked from the *King of Prussia* on December 9, 1764, at Portsmouth and hurried on to London. A few days after he arrived, he dashed off the following note to Polly Stevenson.

[December 12–16, 1764]

I have once more the Pleasure of writing a Line to my dear Polly from Cravenstreet, where I arrived on Monday Evening in about 30 days from Philadelphia. Your good Mama was not at home, and the Maid could not tell where to find her, so I sat me down and waited her Return, when she was a good deal surpriz'd to find me in her Parlour.

Franklin wrote frequently to his wife Deborah, assuring her that he had no intention of staying in London very long. On February 14, 1765, he told her that "a few months I hope will finish affairs here to my wish, and bring me to that retirement and repose with my little family, so suitable to my years, and which I have so long set my heart upon." But London was almost a second home to him by now, and he was soon busily involved in writing and politicking, while he laid the groundwork for his petition to the king. One bit of politics that Franklin did not even bother to mention—at least it does not appear in any of his surviving letters from the early months of 1765—was his involvement with agents of other American Colonies in seeking to dissuade the British government, and the First Minister, George Grenville, in particular, to abandon the plan of raising money in America through a stamp tax on newspapers, legal documents, and numerous other items. In a conference with Franklin and three other agents on February 2, Grenville asked if they knew of a better way of raising the revenue that the British government needed to maintain troops in the border forts and pay the other expenses of the royal government in America. In letters from Pennsylvania the year before, Franklin had commented unfavorably on the idea of a stamp tax, and he now proposed to Grenville a plan for a system of Colonial paper currency under the regulation of Parliament. The users would pay a 6 per cent interest on the money, which would go to the Crown. To bolster his standing with Grenville, and make a better impression, Franklin persuaded Thomas Pownall, former Governor of Massachusetts and a recognized British authority on America, to join him in recommending the plan. With this letter, written on February 12, they submitted a long, detailed draft of how the scheme would work. If Grenville had taken Franklin's advice at this point, the American Revolution might never have taken place. But as Franklin told Joseph Galloway over a year later, Grenville was "besotted with his Stamp Scheme, which he rather chose to carry through."

London Feb. 12. 1765

Sir

We have taken the liberty to enclose and beg leave to submitt to your consideration a measure calculated for supplying the Colonies with a Paper Currency, become absolutely necessary to their Circumstances, by which Measure a certain and very considerable Revenue will arise to the crown.

We are from our Experience and the having been employed in the Public Service in America, intirely confident and certain of the Effect of this measure; And if we shall be so happy as to see it adopted, We are ready to explain the manner of carrying it into Execution—and beg Leave to offerr our services in the Administration and Execution of it on such Terms as Government upon consideration shall find most conducive to the Public Benefit. With the most perfect esteem we have the honour to be Sir Your most Obedient and most humble Servants.

T POWNALL
B FRANKLIN

*George Grenville*

188

Throughout the first half of 1765, Franklin was optimistic about the chances of unseating the Penns. But the unsettled state of British politics made progress difficult, as he explained in this letter to his old Junto friend, Hugh Roberts. The ministry he mentioned was that headed by George Grenville.

London July 7th. 1765

Your kind Favour of May 20th. by the Hand of our good Friend Mr. Neave, gave me great Pleasure. I find on these Occasions, that Expressions of Steady continued Friendship such as are contain'd in your Letter, tho' but from one or a few honest and sensible Men who have long known us, afford a Satisfaction that far outweighs the clamorous Abuse of 1000 Knaves and Fools.

While I enjoy the Share I have so Long had in the Esteem of my old Friends, the Bird-and Beast-People you mention may peck and snarl and bark at me, as much as they think proper.

There is only some Danger that I should grow too Vain on their Disapprobation. . . .

Our Affairs are at a total Stop here by the Present unsettled State of the Ministry. But will go forward again as soon as that is fix'd. Nothing yet appears that is Discourageing. . . .

I wish you would continue to meet the Junto, notwithstanding that some Effects of our publick Political Misunderstandings may some times Appear there. 'Tis now perhaps one of the *oldest* Clubs, as I think it was formerly one of the *best*, in the Kings Dominions: it wants but about two Years of Forty since it was establish'd; We loved and still Love one another, we are Grown Grey together and yet it is to Early to Part. Let us Sit till the Evening of Life is spent, the Last Hours were allways the most joyous; when we can Stay no Longer 'tis time enough then to bid each other good Night, separate, and go quietly to bed.

*Thomas Pownall*

News from America soon shook Franklin's optimism. Philadelphia friends sent Franklin at least four different copies of a series of Resolves adopted by the Virginia House of Burgesses at the instance of one of their youngest and most eloquent members, Patrick Henry. The Virginia Resolves rejected Parliament's right to impose such taxes as those of the Stamp Act. In Pennsylvania, the proprietary party used the Stamp Act as a weapon against the Franklin-Galloway plan to remove the Penns. Galloway gloomily told Franklin that "the Prop—y Party and men in power here...

189

prevail on the People to give every Kind of opposition to the Execution of this Law. To incense their Minds against the King Lords and Commons, and to alienate their Affections from the Mother Country." The opposition to the Stamp Act in other Colonies was no less determined, and in Massachusetts it was tinged with violence. Franklin soon realized that he was in an extremely embarrassing situation. Grenville, in order to make the act more palatable to Americans, had asked Colonial agents to recommend reliable men for the job of stamp commissioners in the various Colonies. For Pennsylvania, Franklin recommended his friend John Hughes. This made it seem to many in Pennsylvania that Franklin not only approved of the act but had actually played a part in helping to pass it. As soon as news of his appointment arrived, Hughes became a target of violent political attacks and threats. He wrote an unhappy letter to Franklin, describing his plight, and Franklin replied in the following cautious terms. The "bill of fees" refers to money Franklin laid out to purchase Hughes's commission. The "petition" is, of course, the plea to remove the Penns. In spite of what he had already heard, Franklin still could not quite believe that the furor over the Stamp Act would or could obscure this issue, so important to him personally.

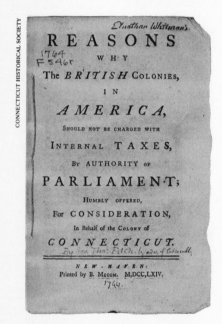

*A pamphlet printed in New Haven, Connecticut, in 1764 by Benjamin Mecom, son of Franklin's sister Jane*

London, Aug. 9. 1765

Since my last I have received your Favour of June 20. The Account you give me of the Indiscretion of some People with you, concerning the Government here, I do not wonder at. 'Tis of a Piece with the rest of their Conduct. But the Rashness of the Assembly in Virginia is amazing! I hope however that ours will keep within the Bounds of Prudence and Moderation; for that is the only way to lighten or get clear of our Burthens.

As to the Stamp-Act, tho' we purpose doing our Endeavour to get it repeal'd, in which I am sure you would concur with us, yet the Success is uncertain. If it continues, your undertaking to execute it may make you unpopular for a Time, but your Acting with Coolness and Steadiness, and with every Circumstance in your Power of Favour to the People, will by degrees reconcile them. In the meantime, a firm Loyalty to the Crown and faithful Adherence to the Government of this Nation, which it is the Safety as well as Honour of the Colonies to be connected with, will always be the wisest Course for you and I to take, whatever may be the Madness of the Populace or their blind Leaders, who can only bring themselves and Country into Trouble, and draw on greater Burthens by Acts of rebellious Tendency.

In mine of June 29. I sent you the Bill of Fees I had paid, amounting to £5 10s. 0d. Since which I have paid another Demand of £2 4s. 6d. Treasury Fees for a second Warrant, &c. the first not having included the Lower Counties. I now send with this, your Commission, with a Letter from the Secretary of the Stamp Office, with whom you are to correspond.

As to our Petition, the new Secretary of State, General Conway, has appointed next Wednesday to give us an Audience upon it, when I suppose it will be presented. And I have very little doubt of a favourable Progress and advantageous Issue.

Hughes and others were soon writing Franklin letters that brought home to him the seriousness and significance of the American resistance to the Stamp Act. Hughes frankly discussed the possibility of being murdered, and told Franklin how he was "well-arm'd" and "determin'd to stand a Siege" in his Philadelphia home. William Franklin lamented the total lack of directions from the ministry relative to the Stamp Act, and told him that in New York Franklin's old friend Cadwallader Colden, now the acting governor, had moved his son, who was appointed Stamp Commissioner for New York, into New York's fort and had marshaled soldiers and men-of-war to protect the stamps when they arrived. "The Boston Writers have basely spirited up the People there to rise and destroy Mr. Oliver's House, on Account of his being the Stamp Officer, &c.," William added. In this letter to his printing partner, David Hall, Franklin revealed some of the agitation that the crisis was stirring in him. The "quartering clause" refers to an alteration that Franklin had obtained in a bill Parliament had passed earlier in the year, outlining procedures for quartering troops in the Colonies. The original version of the act would have permitted the army to quarter the troops in private homes.

London, Sept. 14. 1765

You tell me "you should have been glad if I could have done anything to prevent the Stamp Act, as nothing could have contributed so much to have *removed the Prejudices* of many of the People against me, who stick not now to say that instead of doing anything to prevent it, I helped to plan it when last in England." To you who know me, I need not defend myself against such base Calumnies, and Time will open the Eyes of others. In the Heat of Party, Abuse is receiv'd greedily, and Vindications coldly. And it is my Opinion, that if I had actually prevented the Stamp Act, (which God knows I did all in my Power to prevent) neither the Malice of the bigotted Abettors of Indian Murder, nor the Malice of the interested Abettors of Proprietary Injustice, would have been in the least abated towards me. Those I have made my Enemies, by exposing their Wickedness and Folly to the World. They are my only Enemies, and they will continue my Enemies, let me do what I will that deserves their Friendship: Otherwise they would have given me some Credit for the Services I did last Winter, in opposing and preventing the Quartering Clause, and obtaining sundry favourable Changes in the Acts of Trade, of which, tho' I do not pretend to the whole Merit, I certainly had a considerable Share: but the Abatement of Postage near 30 per Cent. is, I may say, wholly owing to me, and will save more in the Pockets of Trading People, than all the Stamps they are to pay can amount to: And yet what Effect has that had towards *removing Prejudices?* By your Letter it seems none at all. It shall be my Endeavour, with God's Help, to act uprightly; and if I have the Approbation of the Good and Wise, which I shall certainly have sooner or later, the Enmity of Knaves and Fools will give me very little Concern.

The climax to this stream of bad news from America was a report from Deborah that mobs had threatened her and Sally in the house that Franklin had completed building shortly before he left for England. In a letter she wrote on September 22, 1765, Deborah told her husband how she had stood her ground with the aid of her relations and Franklin's friends. "I sente to aske my Brother to Cume and bring his gun all so so we maid one room into a Magazin. I ordored sum sorte of defens up Stairs such as I Cold manaig my self." On November 9, 1765, Franklin replied in a letter that has unfortunately been torn and worn by the passage of time and is reproduced here with modern interpolations in brackets. "The pious Presbyterian Countryman" was Samuel Smith, a Philadelphia merchant born in New England. The "Test" was the Test Act, which required office-holders in England to swear allegiance to the Church of England.

London, Nov. 9. 1765

Dear Debby,

I received yours and Sally's kind Letters of Sept. 22. and Brother Read's. Also one from our good Neighbour Thomson, and one from Brother Peter; one from Mr. Hall and one from Mr. Parker: All which I pray you to acknowledge for me, with Thanks, as I find I can not have time to write to them by this Packet. I honour much the Spirit and Courage you show'd, and the prudent Preparations you made in that [Time] of Danger. The [Woman?]

deserves a good [House] that [is?] determined [*torn*] to defend it. I hope that Mr. Hughes [recovers?] from that Illness. [*Torn and illegible*] and affectionately [to everyone on?] that List [that] you give me, who were so kind as to visit you [that] Evening. I shall long remember their Kindn[ess. As] to that pious Presbyterian Countryman of mine [whom you] say sets the People a madding, by telling them [that I] plann'd the Stamp Act, and am endeavo[uring to] bring the Test over to America, I thank him he does not charge me (as they do their God) with having plann'd Adam's Fall, and the Damnation of Mankind. It might be affirm'd with equal Truth and Modesty. He certainly was intended for a Wise Man; for he has the wisest Look of any Man I know; and if he would only nod and wink, and could but hold his Tongue, he might deceive an Angel. Let us pity and forget him. I am, my dear Girl, Your ever loving Husband

B FRANKLIN

*Protesting the stamp tax, a New Jersey revolutionary paper made use of Franklin's segmented snake.*

Franklin now went to work on a full-time campaign to get the Stamp Act repealed. In this letter to William Franklin he gave a vivid picture of his activities and arguments. Lord Rockingham had recently replaced George Grenville as First Minister. Lord Dartmouth was another nobleman sympathetic to America.

London, Novr. 9, 1765

Mr. Cooper, Secretary of the Treasury, is our old Acquaintance, and expresses a hearty Friendship for us both. Enclosed I send you his Billet proposing to make me acquainted with Lord Rockingham. I dine with his Lordship To-morrow.

I had a long Audience on Wednesday with Lord Dartmouth. He was highly recommended to me by Lords Grantham and Bessborough, as a young Man of excellent Understanding and the most amiable Dispositions. They seem'd extremely intent on bringing us together. I had been to pay my Respects to his Lordship on his Appointment to preside at the Board of Trade; but during the Summer he has been much out of Town, so that I had not till now the Opportunity of conversing with him. I found him all they said of him. He even exceeded the Expectations they had raised in me. If he continues in that Department, I foresee much Happiness from it to American Affairs. He enquired kindly after you, and spoke of you handsomely.

*With its issue of October 31, 1765,* The Pennsylvania Journal *stopped publication to protest the purchase of stamps—*"EXPIRING: *In Hopes of a Resurrection to Life again.*"

I gave it him as my Option, that the general Execution of the Stamp Act would be impracticable without occasioning more Mischief than it was worth, by totally alienating the Affections of the Americans from this Country, and thereby lessening its Commerce. I therefore wish'd that Advantage might be taken of the Address expected over (if express'd, as I hop'd it would be, in humble and dutiful Terms) to suspend the Execution of the Act for a Term of Years, till the Colonies should be more clear of Debt, and better able to bear it, and then drop it on some other decent Pretence, without ever bringing the Question of Right to a Decision. And I strongly recommended either a thorough Union with America, or that Government here would proceed in the old Method of Requisition, by which I was confident more would be obtained in the Way of voluntary Grant, than could probably be got by compulsory Taxes laid by Parliament. That particular Colonies might at Times be backward, but at other Times, when in better Temper, they would make up for that Backwardness, so that on the whole it would be nearly equal. That to send Armies and Fleets to enforce the Act, would not, in my Opinion, answer any good End; That the Inhabitants would probable take every Method to encourage the Soldiers to desert, to which the high Price of Labour would contribute, and the Chance of being never apprehended in so extensive a Country, where the Want of Hands, as well as the Desire of wasting the Strength of an Army come to oppress, would encline every one to conceal Deserters, so that the Officers would probably soon be left alone. That Fleets might indeed easily obstruct their Trade, but withal must ruin great Part of the Trade of Britain; as the Properties of American and British or London Merchants were mix'd in the same Vessels, and no Remittances could be receiv'd here; besides the Danger, by mutual Violences, Excesses and Severities, of creating a deep-rooted Aversion between the two Countries, and laying the Foundation of a future total Separation. I added, that notwithstanding the present Discontents, there still remain'd so much Respect in America for this Country, that Wisdom would do more towards reducing Things to order, than all our Force; And that, if the Address expected from the Congress of the Colonies should be unhappily such as could not be made the Foundation of a Suspension of the Act, in that Case three or four wise and good Men, Personages of some Rank and Dignity, should be sent over to America, with a Royal Commission to enquire into Grievances, hear Complaints, learn the true State of Affairs, giving Expectations of Redress where they found the People really aggriev'd, and endeavouring to convince and reclaim them by Reason, where they found them in the Wrong. That such an Instance of the Considerateness, Moderation and Justice of this Country towards its remote Subjects would contribute more towards securing and perpetuating the Dominion, than all its Force, and be much cheaper. A great deal more I said on our American Affairs; too much to write. His Lordship heard all with great Attention and Patience. As to the Address expected from the Congress, he doubted some Difficulty would arise about receiving it, as it was an irregular Meeting, unauthoriz'd by any American Constitution. I said, I hoped Government here would not be too nice on that Head; That the Mode was indeed new, but to the People there it seem'd necessary, their separate Petitions last Year being rejected. And to refuse hearing Complaints and Redressing Grievances, from Punctilios about Form, had always an ill Effect, and gave great Handle to those turbulent factious Spirits who are ever ready to blow the Coals of Dissension. He thank'd me politely for the Visit, and desired to see me often.

It is true that Inconveniences may arise to Government here by a Repeal of the Act, as it will be deem'd a tacit giving up the Sovereignty of Parliament: And yet I think the Inconveniences of persisting much greater, as I have said above. The present Ministry are truely perplex'd how to act on the Occasion: as, if they relax, their Predecessors will reproach them with giving up the Honour, Dignity, and Power of this Nation. And yet even they, I am told, think they have carry'd Things too far; So that if it were indeed true that I had plann'd the Act (as you say it is reported with you) I believe we should soon hear some of them exculpating themselves by saying I had misled them. I need not tell you that I had not the least Concern in it. It was all cut and dry'd, and every Resolve fram'd at the Treasury ready for the House, before I arriv'd in England, or knew any thing of the Matter; so that if they had given me a Pension on that Account (as is said by some, I am told) it would have been very dishonest in me to accept of it.

Meanwhile, in the English newspapers, Franklin began a task that was to occupy him for the next ten years—defending America's reputation against the volleys of abuse fired at the Colonies by outraged Britons, who could see no reason why Americans should not pay the same taxes they paid at home. The following letter attacked a correspondent who, signing himself Tom Hint, condemned the anti-Stamp Act rioting in New York and called upon the British army to punish Americans. Franklin did not try very hard to disguise his identity, signing "F.B." at the close of the letter.

December 20, 1765

To the PRINTER.

I beg room in your impartial paper for a word or two with your correspondent of Friday Last, who subscribes himself TOM HINT.

He tells us, that he lived many years in that part of the world, and is pleased to assert roundly, that "the most opulent inhabitants of America are of selfish, mean dispositions, void of public spirit; and that they took every occasion (during the late war, it seems) of obstructing the King's measures, when they in the least interfered with their particular interests."

It is a heavy charge this: and as I too have lived many years in that country, I have reason to know that it is a charge without foundation; and that the very reverse is true.

I would therefore ask this writer, if he has never learnt that calumniating even a single person behind his back, to increase differences between friends, is unworthy a gentleman; and that stabbing in the dark is unbecoming a soldier and an officer? Whether he does not think that calumniating the principal people of twelve or thirteen colonies, to incite the mother country to sheath the sword in the bowels of her children, is not infinitely more wicked? and the doing this under a feigned name, at three thousand miles distance from the parties injured, proportionably more mean, base, and cowardly?

I call upon him, therefore, to name those opulent persons, and point out the instances, putting his own name openly and fairly to his accusation; or take to himself in private the conscious shame that belongs to such baseness, aggravated by a recollection of the generous hospitality he personally met with in the country he has so unworthily abused.

In Strahan's London *Chronicle,* from February 6 to 8, 1766, Franklin published for the first time his letters to William Shirley, which were graphic proof that America's hostility to taxation without representation had deep roots. Meanwhile, in Parliament, Edmund Burke, the Irish-born private secretary of Lord Rockingham, decided that what the House of Commons needed was information, not more windy rhetoric. He proceeded to arrange for a series of experts on America to testify. One of these was Benjamin Franklin. Knowing the importance of his testimony, because of his worldwide reputation, the supporters of the ministry did their utmost to make it as effective as possible. In the days preceding Franklin's appearance, they conferred with him and worked out a series of questions that they would ask him from the floor. He prepared careful answers to these queries. There would inevitably be questions from the opposition, as well. For these, Franklin would have to depend upon his native wit.

[February 13, 1766]

The EXAMINATION of Doctor BENJAMIN FRANKLIN, before an AUGUST ASSEMBLY, relating to the Repeal of the STAMP ACT, &c.

Q.  What is your name, and place of abode?

A.  Franklin, of Philadelphia.

Q.  Do the Americans pay any considerable taxes among themselves?

A.  Certainly many, and very heavy taxes.

Q.  What are the present taxes in Pennsylvania, laid by the laws of the colony?

A.  There are taxes on all estates real and personal, a poll tax, a tax on all offices, professions, trades and businesses, according to their profits; and excise on all wine, rum, and other spirits; and a duty of Ten Pounds per head on all Negroes imported, with some other duties.

Q.  For what purpose are those taxes laid?

A.  For the support of the civil and military establishments of the country, and to discharge the heavy debt contracted in the last war.

Q.  How long are those taxes to continue?

A.  Those for discharging the debt are to continue till 1772, and longer, if the debt should not be then all discharged. The others must always continue.

Q.  Was it not expected that the debt would have been sooner discharged?

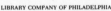

*The only known original example of Franklin's Stamp Act cartoon showing "Britannia" dismembered*

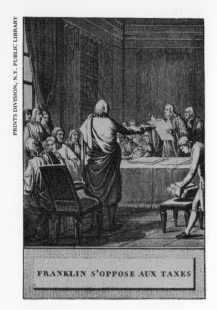

FRANKLIN S'OPPOSE AUX TAXES

*Contemporary French engraving illustrating Franklin's examination before the House of Commons*

A. It was, when the peace was made with France and Spain—But a fresh war breaking out with the Indians, a fresh load of debt was incurred, and the taxes, of course, continued longer by a new law.

Q. Are not all the people very able to pay those taxes?

A. No. The frontier counties, all along the continent, having been frequently ravaged by the enemy, and greatly impoverished, are able to pay very little tax. And therefore, in consideration of their distresses, our late tax laws do expressly favour those counties, excusing the sufferers; and I suppose the same is done in other governments.

Q. Are not you concerned in the management of the Post-Office in America?

A. Yes. I am Deputy Post-Master General of North-America.

Q. Don't you think the distribution of stamps, by post, to all the inhabitants, very practicable, if there was no opposition?

A. The posts only go along the sea coasts; they do not, except in a few instances, go back into the country; and if they did, sending for stamps by post would occasion an expence of postage, amounting, in many cases, to much more than that of the stamps themselves. . . .

Q. From the thinness of the back settlements, would not the stamp-act be extreamly inconvenient to the inhabitants, if executed?

A. To be sure it would; as many of the inhabitants could not get stamps when they had occasion for them, without taking long journeys, and spending perhaps Three or Four Pounds, that the Crown might get Sixpence.

Q. Are not the Colonies, from their circumstances, very able to pay the stamp duty?

A. In my opinion, there is not gold and silver enough in the Colonies to pay the stamp duty for one year.

Q. Don't you know that the money arising from the stamps was all to be laid out in America?

A. I know it is appropriated by the act to the American service; but it will be spent in the conquered Colonies, where the soldiers are, not in the Colonies that pay it. . . .

Q. How many white men do you suppose there are in

North-America?

A.   About 300,000, from sixteen to sixty years of age.

Q.   What may be the amount of one year's imports into Pennsylvania from Britain?

A.   I have been informed that our merchants compute the imports from Britain to be above 500,000 Pounds.

Q.   What may be the amount of the produce of your province exported to Britain?

A.   It must be small, as we produce little that is wanted in Britain. I suppose it cannot exceed 40,000 Pounds.

Q.   How then do you pay the ballance?

A.   The Ballance is paid by our produce carried to the West-Indies, and sold in our own islands, or to the French, Spaniards, Danes and Dutch; by the same carried to other colonies in North-America, as to New-England, Nova-Scotia, Newfoundland, Carolina and Georgia; by the same carried to different parts of Europe, as Spain, Portugal and Italy. In all which places we receive either money, bills of exchange, or commodities that suit for remittance to Britain; which, together with all the profits on the industry of our merchants and mariners, arising in those circuitous voyages, and the freights made by their ships, center finally in Britain, to discharge the ballance, and pay for British manufactures continually used in the province, or sold to foreigners by our traders....

Q.   Do you think it right that America should be protected by this country, and pay no part of the expence?

A.   That is not the case. The Colonies raised, cloathed and paid, during the last war, near 25000 men, and spent many millions.

Q.   Were you not reimbursed by parliament?

A.   We were only reimbursed what, in your opinion, we had advanced beyond our proportion, or beyond what might reasonably be expected from us; and it was a very small part of what we spent. Pennsylvania, in particular, disbursed about 500,000 Pounds, and the reimbursements, in the whole, did not exceed 60,000 Pounds....

Q.   Do not you think the people of America would submit to pay the stamp duty, if it was moderated?

A. No, never, unless compelled by force of arms....

Q. What was the temper of America towards Great-Britain before the year 1763?

A. The best in the world. They submitted willingly to the government of the Crown, and paid, in all their courts, obedience to acts of parliament. Numerous as the people are in the several old provinces, they cost you nothing in forts, citadels, garrisons or armies, to keep them in subjection. They were governed by this country at the expence only of a little pen, ink and paper. They were led by a thread. They had not only a respect, but an affection, for Great-Britain, for its laws, its customs and manners, and even a fondness for its fashions, that greatly increased the commerce. Natives of Britain were always treated with particular regard; to be an Old Englandman was, of itself, a character of some respect, and gave a kind of rank among us.

Q. And what is their temper now?

A. O, very much altered.

Q. Did you ever hear the authority of parliament to make laws for America questioned till lately?

A. The authority of parliament was allowed to be valid in all laws, except such as should lay internal taxes. It was never disputed in laying duties to regulate commerce.

Q. In what proportion hath population increased in America?

A. I think the inhabitants of all the provinces together, taken at a medium, double in about 25 years. But their demand for British manufactures increases much faster, as the consumption is not merely in proportion to their numbers, but grows with the growing abilities of the same numbers to pay for them. In 1723, the whole importation from Britain to Pennsylvania, was but about 15,000 Pounds Sterling; it is now near Half a Million....

Q. What is your opinion of a future tax, imposed on the same principle with that of the stamp-act; how would the Americans receive it?

A. Just as they do this. They would not pay it.

Q. Have you not heard of the resolutions of this house, and of the house of lords, asserting the right of parliament relating to America, including a power to tax

*Crude anti-Stamp Act woodcut from* The Pennsylvania Journal, *1765*

the people there?

A. Yes, I have heard of such resolutions.

Q. What will be the opinion of the Americans on those resolutions?

A. They will think them unconstitutional, and unjust....

Q. You say the Colonies have always submitted to external taxes, and object to the right of parliament only in laying internal taxes; now can you shew that there is any kind of difference between the two taxes to the Colony on which they may be laid?

A. I think the difference is very great. An external tax is a duty laid on commodities imported; that duty is added to the first cost, and other charges on the commodity, and when it is offered to sale, makes a part of the price. If the people do not like it at that price, they refuse it; they are not obliged to pay it. But an internal tax is forced from the people without their consent, if not laid by their own representatives. The stamp-act says, we shall have no commerce, make no exchange of property with each other, neither purchase nor grant, nor recover debts; we shall neither marry, nor make our wills, unless we pay such and such sums, and thus it is intended to extort our money from us, or ruin us by the consequences of refusing to pay it.

Q. But supposing the external tax or duty to be laid on the necessaries of life imported into your Colony, will not that be the same thing in its effects as an internal tax?

A. I do not know a single article imported into the Northern Colonies, but what they can either do without, or make themselves....

Q. Considering the resolutions of parliament, as to the right, do you think, if the stamp-act is repealed, that the North Americans will be satisfied?

A. I believe they will.

Q. Why do you think so?

A. I think the resolutions of right will give them very little concern, if they are never attempted to be carried into practice. The Colonies will probably consider themselves in the same situation, in that respect, with Ireland; they know you claim the same right with regard to Ireland, but you never exercise it. And they may believe you never will exercise it

*Example of British stamp used in the Colonies under the Stamp Act*

*Earthenware teapot, circa 1765, with
a decorative protest to the Stamp Act*

COLONIAL WILLIAMSBURG COLLECTION

in the Colonies, any more than in Ireland, unless on some very extraordinary occasion.

Q. But who are to be the judges of that extraordinary occasion? Is it not the parliament?

A. Though the parliament may judge of the occasion, the people will think it can never exercise such right, till representatives from the Colonies are admitted into parliament, and that whenever the occasion arises, representatives will be ordered....

Q. Can any thing less than a military force carry the stamp-act into execution?

A. I do not see how a military force can be applied to that purpose.

Q. Why may it not?

A. Suppose a military force sent into America, they will find nobody in arms; what are they then to do? They cannot force a man to take stamps who chooses to do without them. They will not find a rebellion; they may indeed make one.

Q. If the act is not repealed, what do you think will be the consequences?

A. A total loss of the respect and affection the people of America bear to this country, and of all the commerce that depends on that respect and affection.

Q. How can the commerce be affected?

A. You will find, that if the act is not repealed, they will take very little of your manufactures in a short time....

Q. Supposing the stamp-act continued, and enforced, do you imagine that ill humour will induce the Americans to give as much for worse manufactures of their own, and use them, preferably to better of ours?

A. Yes, I think so. People will pay as freely to gratify one passion as another, their resentment as their pride....

Q. If the stamp act should be repealed, would not the Americans think they could oblige the parliament to repeal every external tax law now in force?

A. It is hard to answer questions of what people at such a distance will think.

Q. But what do you imagine they will think were the motives of repealing the act?

A. I suppose they will think that it was repealed from

a conviction of its inexpediency; and they will rely upon it, that while the same inexpediency subsists, you will never attempt to make such another.

Q. What do you mean by its inexpediency?

A. I mean its inexpediency on several accounts; the poverty and inability of those who were to pay the tax; the general discontent it has occasioned; and the impracticability of enforcing it.

Q. If the act should be repealed, and the legislature should shew its resentment to the opposers of the stamp-act, would the Colonies acquiesce in the authority of the legislature? What is your opinion they would do?

A. I don't doubt at all, that if the legislature repeal the stamp-act, the Colonies will acquiesce in the authority....

Q. Do you think...that the taking possession of the King's territorial rights, and strengthening the frontiers, is not an American interest?

A. Not particularly, but conjointly a British and an American interest.

Q. You will not deny that the preceding war, the war with Spain, was entered into for the sake of America; was it not occasioned by captures made in the American seas?

A. Yes; captures of ships carrying on the British trade there, with British manufactures.

Q. Was not the late war with the Indians, since the peace with France, a war for America only?

A. Yes; it was more particularly for America than the former, but it was rather a consequence or remains of the former war, the Indians not having been thoroughly pacified, and the Americans bore by much the greatest share of the expence. It was put an end to by the army under General Bouquet; there were not above 300 regulars in that army, and above 1000 Pennsylvanians....

Q. If the stamp-act should be repealed, and an act should pass, ordering the assemblies of the Colonies to indemnify the sufferers by the riots, would they obey it?

A. That is a question I cannot answer.

Q. Suppose the King should require the Colonies to grant a revenue, and the parliament should be against their doing it, do they think they can grant a revenue to the King, without the consent of the parliament of G. Britain?

A.  That is a deep question. As to my own opinion, I should think myself at liberty to do it, and should do it, if I liked the occasion....

Q.  If the stamp-act should be repealed, and the Crown should make a requisition to the Colonies for a sum of money, would they grant it?

A.  I believe they would....

Q.  If the stamp-act should be repealed, would it induce the assemblies of America to acknowledge the rights of parliament to tax them, and would they erase their resolutions?

A.  No, never.

Q.  Is there no means of obliging them to erase those resolutions?

A.  None that I know of; they will never do it unless compelled by force of arms.

Q.  Is there a power on earth that can force them to erase them?

A.  No power, how great soever, can force men to change their opinions....

Q.  What used to be the pride of the Americans?

A.  To indulge in the fashions and manufactures of Great-Britain.

Q.  What is now their pride?

A.  To wear their old cloaths over again, till they can make new ones.

It is always fascinating to catch a glimpse of history and its impact on a man almost at the moment it was being made. At two o'clock on the morning of February 22, the committee of the whole House of Commons voted 275 to 167 to repeal the Stamp Act. Only a few hours later, an exultant Franklin dashed off the following letter to his wife Deborah.

London, Feb. 22. 1766

My dear Child,

I am excessively hurried, being every Hour that I am awake either abroad to speak with Members of Parliament or taken up with People coming to me at home, concerning our American Affairs, so that I am much behind-hand in answering my Friends Letters. But tho' I cannot by this Opportunity write to others, I must not omit a Line to you who kindly write me so many. I am well; 'tis all I can say at present, except that I am just now made very happy by a Vote of the Commons for the Repeal of the Stamp Act. Your ever loving Husband

B FRANKLIN

By March 8, the repeal of the Stamp Act had received the royal assent. William Strahan rushed a stenographic copy of Franklin's examination to David Hall in Philadelphia with these expansive words: "To this very examination, more than to anything else, you are indebted to the *speedy* and *total* repeal of this odious law." Strahan may have been laying on the praise a bit thick, to bolster his friend Franklin's reputation. But there is no doubt that Franklin's appearance did play a major role in repealing the Stamp Act, and restoring a state of temporary calm between England and America. As a result, Franklin's political reputation soared to hitherto unknown heights. He was hailed as the savior of America, and the examination was reprinted in Massachusetts, Virginia, and New York, and became required reading throughout the Colonies. Franklin did not allow this abrupt and welcome reversal to go to his head. In this letter to Charles Thomson, he summed up his mature opinion of the tangled skein.

London, Sept. 27. 1766

Dear Friend and Neighbour

I received your very kind Letter of May 20. which came here while I was absent in Germany. The favourable Sentiments you express of my Conduct with regard to the Repeal to the Stamp Act, give me real Pleasure; and I hope in every other matter of publick Concern, so to behave myself as to stand fair in the Opinions of the Wise and Good: What the rest think and say of me will then give me less Concern.

That Part of your Letter which related to the Situation of People's Minds in America before and after the Repeal, was so well exprest, and in my Opinion so proper to be generally read and understood here, that I had it printed in the London Chronicle. I had the Pleasure to find that it did Good in several Instances within my Knowledge.

There are Claimers enow of Merit in obtaining the Repeal. But if I live to see you, I will let you know what an Escape we had in the Beginning of the Affair, and how much we were obliged to what the Profane would call *Luck*, and the Pious *Providence*.

You will give an old Man Leave to say My Love to Mrs. Thomson. With sincere Regard, I am, Your affectionate Friend. . . .

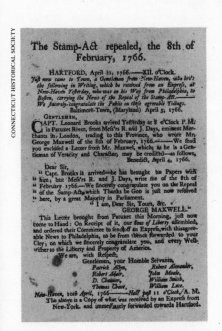

*Broadside announcing the repeal of the Stamp Act on February 8, 1766, which did not reach Hartford, Connecticut, until April 11*

Franklin knew there was still formidable opposition to America in Parliament. He used his favorite weapon, ridicule, to attack the die-hards in the following newspaper essay. Where it first appeared— sometime in February or March, 1766— is not known; it was reprinted in the *Pennsylvania Chronicle* for March 16–23, 1767.

[February–March 1766]

To the PRINTER.

It is reported, I know not with what Foundation, that there is an Intention of obliging the Americans to pay for all the Stamps they ought to have used, between the Commencement of the Act, and the Day on which the Repeal takes Place, viz. from the first of November 1765, to the first of May 1766; that this is to make Part of an Act, which is to give Validity to the Writings and Law Proceedings, that contrary to Law have been executed without Stamps, and is to be the Condition on which they are to receive that Validity. Shall we then keep up for a Trifle the Heats and Animosities that have been occasioned by the Stamp-Act? and lose all the Benefit of Harmony and good Understanding between the different Parts of the Empire, which were expected from a generous total Repeal? Is this Pittance likely to be a Whit more easily collected than the whole Duty? Where are Officers to be found who will undertake to collect it? Who is to protect them while they are about it? In my Opinion, it will meet with the same Opposition, and be attended with the same Mischiefs that would have attended an Enforcement of the Act entire.

But I hear, that this is thought necessary, to raise a Fund for defraying the Expence that has been incurred by stamping so much Paper and Parchment for the Use of America, which they have refused to take and turn'd upon our Hands; and that since they are highly favour'd by the Repeal, they cannot with any Face of Decency refuse to make good the Charges we have been at on their Account. The whole Proceeding would put one in Mind of the Frenchman that used to accost English and other Strangers on the Pont-Neuf, with many Compliments, and a red hot Iron in his Hand; *Pray Monsieur Anglois,* says he, *Do me the Favour to let me have the Honour of thrusting this hot Iron into your Backside?* Zoons, what does the Fellow mean! Begone with your Iron, or I'll break your Head! *Nay, Monsieur,* replies he, *if you do not chuse it, I do not insist upon it. But at least,*

*To celebrate the repeal of the Stamp Act an obelisk was erected in Boston. This view of one of its sides is a detail from a large etching by Paul Revere and includes representations of Queen Charlotte, King George, and other distinguished patriots.*

*you will in Justice have the Goodness to pay me some-thing for the heating of my Iron.*

F.B.

Only a few weeks after the Stamp Act was repealed, Parliament reaffirmed that it had no intention of abandoning its traditional attitude toward the Colonies, by considering a bill renewing England's right to transport felons to America and extending the right to Scotland. Franklin drew up this satiric petition, which he permitted Pennsylvania's agent, Richard Jackson, to pass around to his fellow M.P.'s, unofficially. It "occasion'd some laughing," but the bill passed without debate.

[April 12–15, 1766]

To the honourable the Knights Citizens and Burgesses of Great Britain in Parliament assembled,

The Petition of BF. Agent for the Province of Pensilvania, Most humbly Sheweth,

That the Transporting of Felons from England to the Plantations in America, is and hath long been a great Grievance to the said Plantations in general.

That the said Felons being landed in America, not only continue their evil Practices, to the Annoyance of his Majesty's good Subjects there, but contribute greatly to corrupt the Morals of the Servants and poorer People among whom they are mixed.

That many of the said Felons escape from the Servitude to which they were destined, into other Colonies, where their Condition is not known and wandering at large from one populous Town to another commit many Burglaries Robberies and Murders, to the great Terror of the People, and occasioning heavy Charges for the apprehending and securing such Felons, and bringing them to Justice.

That your Petitioner humbly conceives the Easing one Part of the British Dominions of their Felons by burthening another Part with the same Felons, cannot increase the common Happiness of his Majesty's Subjects; and that therefore the Trouble and Expence of transporting them is upon the whole altogether useless.

That your Petitioner nevertheless observes with extream Concern, in the Votes of Friday last, that Leave is given to bring in a Bill, for extending to Scotland the Act made in the 4th. Year of the Reign of King George the First, whereby the aforesaid Grievances are (as he understands) to be greatly increas'd by allowing Scotland

*A detail from an English cartoon following the Stamp Act's repeal shows George Grenville, holding coffin of "Miss Americ-Stamp," and other Tory ministers filing behind him into the family vault.*

also to transport its Felons to America.

Your Petitioner therefore humbly prays, in behalf of Pensilvania and the other Plantations in America that the House wou'd take the Premisses into Consideration, and in their great Wisdom and Goodness repeal all Acts and Clauses of Acts for Transporting of Felons; or if this may not at present be done, that they would at least reject the propos'd Bill for extending of the said Acts to Scotland; or, if it be thought fit to allow of such Extension, that then the said Extension may be carried farther, and the Plantations be also by an equitable Clause in the same Bill permitted to transport their Felons to Scotland.

Already, the Boston runaway, the journeyman printer, the Philadelphia businessman, was quietly assuming the role he had created for himself in the Stamp Act crisis — unofficial ambassador for a yet-unborn American nation. It had been a long journey for Franklin. Looking back across forty crowded years to his youth, he undoubtedly thought that the repeal of the Stamp Act was that "bright point" with which he wished to end his life. He had no way of knowing that the best and most dramatic years were yet to come — with a "point" far brighter than even he dared to imagine.

# Chapter 8

# Spokesman for America

With the Stamp Act repealed, Franklin felt himself on a firmer and broader political foundation than he had ever known before. He was now an unofficial spokesman, not merely for Pennsylvania but for all the Colonies. In the higher levels of the British Government, he had acquired a name that inspired considerable respect, if not always admiration. With peace between the mother country and Colonies seemingly assured, Franklin decided to put this new-found prestige at the service of one of his oldest and most ambitious dreams—the founding of a western colony. The impetus came from his son William Franklin, the Governor of New Jersey. A group of William's friends, notably Samuel Wharton of the important Philadelphia firm of Baynton, Wharton and Morgan, had come up with the idea of petitioning the Crown for a grant of lands in the West to repay them and other traders such as George Croghan for the heavy losses they had suffered during the Indian war known as Pontiac's Uprising, 1763–64. William suggested the idea of petitioning for a colony, rather than a simple grant of land, which the British Government would be more likely to resist. Governor Franklin brought Joseph Galloway into the project, and explained to his father that they hoped to obtain the land from the Indians through the diplomacy of Sir William Johnson, the Indian Superintendent, who was also a secret partner in the company formed to run the colony. Franklin promptly replied on May 10, 1766, that he liked the project "and will forward it to my utmost here." The same day he wrote Galloway that it was "a most desirable measure" and that "the Proposal is much listened to here." In the following letter to William, Franklin discussed the numerous wheels that had begun to turn in pursuit of this scheme. Lord Hillsborough was the new head of the Board of Trade, which had a strong influence in American affairs. General Lyman was Phineas Lyman, a Connecticut soldier who had distinguished himself in the French and Indian War. George Croghan was negotiating with Illinois country Indians on behalf of the British. Lord Adam Gordon was a British soldier and member of Parliament, who had traveled widely in America. "Our friend Sargent" was John Sargent, a London banker.

September 12th, 1766

I have just received Sir William's open letter to Secretary Conway, recommending your plan for a colony in the Ilinois, which I am glad of. I have closed and sent it to him. He is not now in that department; but it will of course go to Lord Shelburne, whose good opinion of it I have reason to hope for; and I think Mr. Conway was rather against distant posts and settlements in America. We have, however, suffered a loss in Lord Dartmouth, who I know was inclined to a grant there in favor of the soldiery, and Lord Hillsborough is said to be terribly afraid of dispeopling Ireland. General Lyman has been long here soliciting such a grant, and will readily join the interest he has made with ours, and I should wish for a body of Connecticut settlers, rather than all from our frontiers. I purpose waiting on Lord Shelburne on Tuesday, and hope to be able to send you his sentiments by Falconer, who is to sail about the twentieth.

A good deal, I imagine, will depend on the account, when it arrives, of Mr. Croghan's negotiation in that country. This is an affair I shall seriously set about, but there are such continual changes here, that it is very discouraging to all applications to be made to the ministry. I thought the last set well established, but they are broken and gone. The present set are hardly thought to stand very firm, and God only knows whom we are to have next.

The plan is I think well drawn, and I imagine Sir William's approbation will go a great way in recommending it, as he is much relied on in all affairs, that may have relation to the Indians. Lord Adam Gordon is not in town, but I shall take the first opportunity of conferring with him. I thank the Company for their willingness to take me in, and one or two others that I may nominate. I have not yet concluded whom to propose it to; but I suppose our friend Sargent should be one. I wish you had allowed me to name more, as there will be in the proposed country, by my reckoning, near sixty-three millions of acres, and therefore enough to content a great number of reasonable people, and by numbers we might increase the weight of interest here.

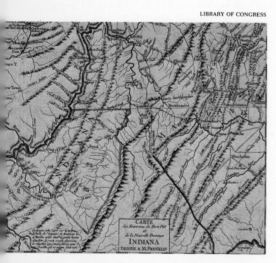

"Indiana" was one of several names suggested for the large western colony assiduously promoted by Franklin.

As always, Franklin found time to maintain a personal correspondence with those he loved. Jane Mecom was one of these, although she was at times a difficult correspondent. She quarreled frequently with her famous brother by mail, taking offense—sometimes theological, sometimes personal—at his opinions and remarks. On his side, Franklin obviously enjoyed discussing religion with her, since she was such a perfect foil for his unorthodox beliefs. In this letter, he tried to relieve the pessimism she felt after having read some harsh criticism of Franklin in American newspapers. His enemies' treatment of him, she said, "makes the world Apear a misereable world to me not withstanding your good opinyon of it."

London, March 2. 1767

Dear Sister

I received your kind Letter of Nov. 8. for which I thank you. It rejoices me to hear that you and your Children continue well. I thank God that I too enjoy a greater Share of Health, Strength and Activity than is common with People of my Years, being now Three-score and one. You mention my Opinion of this being a good sort of World, in which you differ from me. Every one should speak as they find. Hitherto I have found it so, and I should be ungrateful to Providence if I did not own it. As to the Abuses I meet with, which you bring as an Argument against my Opinion, you must know I number them among my Honours. One cannot behave so as to obtain the Esteem of the Wise and Good, without drawing on one's self at the same time the Envy and Malice of the Foolish and Wicked, and the latter is a Testimony of the former. The best Men have always had their Share of this Treatment, and the more of it in proportion to their different and greater degrees of Merit. A Man has therefore some Reason to be asham'd of himself when he meets with none of it. And the World is not to be condemn'd in the Lump because some bad People live in it. Their Number is not great, the Hurt they do is but small, as real good Characters always finally surmount and are established, notwithstanding these Attempts to keep them down. And in the mean time such Enemies do a Man some good; while they think they are doing him harm, by fortifying the Character they would destroy; for when he sees how readily imaginary Faults and Crimes are laid to his Charge, he must be more apprehensive of the Danger of committing real Ones, as he can expect no Quarter, and therefore is more on his Guard to avoid or least to conceal them.

A more serious personal matter that absorbed Franklin at this time was the marriage of his daughter Sally to Richard Bache. Franklin did not look with favor on the match. English-born, the thirty-year-old Bache had worked with his brother as a merchant in New York in 1765 and in 1766 had moved to Philadelphia, where he opened a dry goods store. He was soon in financial difficulty. Franklin's business friends in Philadelphia told William Franklin that Bache was "a mere Fortune Hunter, who wants to better his Circumstances [by] marrying into a Family that will support him." William confessed that he did not "know what to make of all the different Accounts I hear of him." But he was certain that Bache was involved "in a Load of Debt greatly more than he is worth, and that if Sally marries him they must both be entirely dependent on you for Subsistence." A prudent man, William concluded his letter, "Do burn this." Though his father also made some frosty comments on Bache, he had enough confidence in Deborah's judgment to leave the final decision to her.

London, June 22. 1767

It seems now as if I should stay here another Winter, and therefore I must leave it to your Judgment to act in the Affair of your Daughter's Match as shall seem best. If you think it a suitable one, I suppose the sooner it is compleated, the better. In that case, I would only advise that you do not make an expensive feasting Wedding, but conduct every thing with Frugality and Oeconomy, which our Circumstances really now require to be observed in all our Expences; For since my Partnership with Mr. Hall is expired, a great Source of our Income is cut off; and if I should lose the Post Office, which among the many Changes here is far from being unlikely, we should be reduc'd to our Rent and Interest of Money for a Subsistence, which will by no means afford the chargeable Housekeeping and Entertainments we have been used to; for my own Part I live here as frugally as possible not to be destitute of the Comforts of Life, making no Dinners for any body, and contenting myself with a single Dish when I dine at home; and yet such is the Dearness of Living here in every Article, that my Expences amaze me. I see too by the Sums you have received in my Absence, that yours are very great, and I am very sensible that your Situation naturally brings you a great many Visitors which occasion an Expence not easily to be avoided, especially when one has been long in the Practice and Habit of it: But when People's Incomes are lessened, if they cannot proportionably lessen their Outgoings, they must come to Poverty. If we were young enough to

*Franklin's daughter, Sarah Franklin Bache, in a portrait by John Hoppner*

begin Business again, it might be another Matter; but I doubt we are past it; and Business not well managed ruins one faster than no Business. In short, with Frugality and prudent Care we may subsist decently on what we have, and leave it entire to our Children: but without such Care, we shall not be able to keep it together; it will melt away like Butter in the Sunshine; and we may live long enough to feel the miserable Consequences of our Indiscretion.

I know very little of the Gentleman or his Character, nor can I at this Distance. I hope his Expectations are not great of any Fortune to be had with our Daughter before our Death. I can only say, that if he proves a good Husband to her, and a good Son to me, he shall find me as good a Father as I can be: but at present I suppose you would agree with me that we cannot do more than fit her out handsomely in Cloaths and Furniture, not exceeding in the whole Five Hundred Pounds, of Value. For the rest, they must depend as you and I did, on their own Industry and Care: as what remains in our Hands will be barely sufficient for our Support, and not enough for them when it comes to be divided at our Decease.

A few weeks later Franklin wrote again about the impending marriage, suggesting that it might be best to delay it for a time, while Sally visited England. But this advice was ignored, and Sally and Richard Bache were married in the fall of 1767. Meanwhile, the confused state of English politics gave Franklin little peace of mind. In a letter to Joseph Galloway he acutely analyzed Parliament's drift toward another clash with America.

London, Aug 8. 1767

The Confusion among our Great Men still continues as great as ever, and a melancholy thing it is to consider, that instead of employing the present Leisure of Peace in such Measures as might extend our Commerce, pay off our Debts, secure Allies, and encrease the Strength and Ability of the Nation to support a future War, the whole Time seems wasted in Party Contentions about Power and Profit, in Court Intrigues and Cabals, and in abusing one another.

There has lately been an Attempt to make a kind of Coalition of Parties in a new Ministry; but it is fallen through, and the present Set is like to continue for some time longer, which I am rather pleas'd with, as some of

*Joseph Galloway*

those who were propos'd to be introduc'd, are profess'd Adversaries to America, which is now made one of the Distinctions of Party here; those who in the two last Sessions have shown a Disposition to favor us, being called by Way of Reproach *Americans;* while the others, Adherents to Grenville and Bedford, value themselves on being true to the Interest of Britain, and zealous for maintaining its Dignity and Sovereignty over the Colonies. This Distinction will, it is apprehended, be carried much higher in the next Session, for the political Purpose of influencing the ensuing Election. It is already given out, that the Compliance of New York in providing for the Quarters, without taking Notice of its being done in Obedience to the Act of Parliament, is evasive and unsatisfactory: that it is high time to put the Right and Power of this Country to tax the Colonies, out of dispute, by an Act of Taxation effectually carried into Execution, and that all the Colonies should be oblig'd explicitly to acknowledge that Right. Every Step is taking to render the Taxing of America a popular Measure, by continually insisting on the Topics of our Wealth and flourishing Circumstances, while this Country is loaded with Debt, great Part of it incurr'd on our Account the Distress of the Poor here by the Multitude and Weight of Taxes, &c. &c. And tho' the Traders and Manufacturers may possibly be kept in our Interest, the Idea of an American Tax is very pleasing to the landed Men, who therefore readily receive and propagate these Sentiments wherever they have Influence. If such a Bill should be brought in, it is hard to say what would be Event of it, or what would be the Effects. Those who oppose it, tho' they should be strong enough to throw it out, would be stigmatiz'd at the next Election as Americans, Betrayers of Old England, &c.—and perhaps our Friends by this means being excluded, a Majority of our Adversaries may get in, and then the Act infallibly passes the following Session. To avoid the Danger of such Exclusion, perhaps little or no Opposition will be given, and then it passes immediately. I know not what to advise on this Occasion, but that we should all do our Endeavours on both sides the Water, to lessen the present Unpopularity of the American Cause; conciliate the Affections of the People here towards us; increase by all possible Means the Number of our Friends, and be careful not to weaken their Hands and strengthen those of our Enemies, by rash Proceedings on our side, the Mischiefs of which are inconceivable.

Meanwhile, Franklin's interest in the western colony remained strong. In a letter to William Franklin he told of further efforts with Lord Shelburne, the Secretary of State for American Affairs.

London, August 8, 1767.

Last week I dined at Lord Shelburne's, and had a long conversation with him and Mr. Conway (there being no other company), on the subject of reducing American expence. They have it in contemplation to return the management of Indian affairs into the hands of the several provinces on which the nations border, that the colonies may bear the charge of treaties, &c. which they think will then be managed more frugally, the treasury being tired with the immense drafts of the superintendants, &c. I took the opportunity of urging it as one means of saving expence in supporting the outposts, that a settlement should be made in the Illinois country; expatiated on the various advantages, viz. furnishing provisions cheaper to the garrisons, securing the country, retaining the trade, raising a strength there which on occasion of a future war, might easily be poured down the Missisippi upon the lower country, and into the Bay of Mexico, to be used against Cuba, or Mexico itself, &c. I mentioned your plan, its being approved by Sir William Johnson, the readiness and ability of the gentlemen concerned to carry the settlement into execution with very little expence to the crown, &c. &c. The Secretaries appeared finally to be fully convinced, and there remained no obstacle but the Board of Trade, which was to be brought over privately before the matter should be referred to them officially....

Du Guerchy the French Ambassador is gone home, and Monsieur Durand is left Minister Plenipotentiary. He is extremely curious to inform himself in the affairs of America; pretends to have a great esteem for me, on account of the abilities shown in my examination; has desired to have all my political writings, invited me to dine with him, was very inquisitive, treated me with great civility, makes me visits, &c. I fancy that intriguing nation would like very well to meddle on occasion, and blow up the coals between Britain and her colonies;

*Sir William Johnson*

but I hope we shall give them no opportunity.

I write this in a great hurry, being setting out in an hour on another journey with my steady good friend Sir John Pringle. We propose to visit Paris. Durand has given me letters of recommendation to the Lord knows who. I am told I shall meet with great respect there; but winds change and perhaps it will be full as well if I do not. We shall be gone about six weeks.

Franklin returned from France to find another tempest brewing between England and the Colonies. Charles Townshend, Chancellor of the Exchequer in the rather disorganized Ministry nominally headed by William Pitt, now Lord Chatham, decided to take the Americans at their word when they claimed to have no objection to external taxes. He proceeded to impose duties on glass, lead, painters' colors, tea, and paper—all imported in large amounts by the Colonies. The Americans responded by reviving the boycott on imports that had proved successful against the Stamp Act. The turmoil resulted in a Cabinet reshuffle that eliminated Lord Shelburne, who had been in favor of the Franklins' new colony. Wills Hill, Lord Hillsborough, became Secretary of State for Colonies, and he was inclined to take a negative view of all things American. He was particularly opposed to a new colony, because he feared it might depopulate Ireland, where he had vast estates. Hillsborough's attitude and the continued American agitation over the Townshend Acts produced a distinct change in Franklin's thinking. He discussed the change in this letter. The "Farmer's letters" are a reference to John Dickinson's tract, *Letters from a Farmer in Pennsylvania,* which argued that the Townshend Acts were unconstitutional because they were designed not to regulate trade but to raise revenue, and hence were in the same category as the Stamp Act. Later in the year Franklin wrote a preface for the English edition. The letter also reveals the strong concern Franklin felt for his son's career. But the final paragraphs, with their harsh criticism of England, are perhaps most important. The love affair between Franklin and the mother country was already beginning to sour.

London, March 13, 1768.

My Lord H. mentioned the Farmer's letters to me, said he had read them, that they were well written, and he believed he could guess who was the author, looking in my face at the same time as if he thought it was me. He censured the doctrines as extremely wild, &c. I have read them as far as No. 8. I know not if any more have been published. I should have thought they had been written by Mr. Delancey, not having heard any mention of the others you point out as joint authors. I am not yet master of the idea these and the New England writers

*A view of Hayes Place in Kent, the seat of William Pitt, Lord Chatham*

have of the relation between Britain and her colonies. I know not what the Boston people mean by the "subordination" they acknowledge in their Assembly to Parliament, while they deny its power to make laws for them, nor what bounds the Farmer sets to the power he acknowledges in Parliament to "regulate the trade of the colonies," it being difficult to draw lines between duties for regulation and those for revenue, and if the Parliament is to be the judge, it seems to me that establishing such principles of distinction will amount to little. The more I have thought and read on the subject the more I find myself confirmed in opinion, that no middle doctrine can be well maintained, I mean not clearly with intelligible arguments. Something might be made of either of the extremes; that Parliament has a power to make *all laws* for us, or that it has a power to make *no laws* for us; and I think the arguments for the latter more numerous and weighty than those for the former. Supposing that doctrine established, the colonies would then be so many separate states, only subject to the same King, as England and Scotland were before the Union. And then the question would be, whether a union like that with Scotland would or would not be advantageous to *the whole*. I should have no doubt of the affirmative, being fully persuaded that it would be best for *the whole,* and that though particular parts might find particular disadvantages in it, they would find greater advantages in the security arising to every part from the increased strength of the whole. But such union is not likely to take place, while the nature of our present relation is so little understood on both sides the water, and sentiments concerning it remain so widely different. As to the Farmers' combating, as you say they intend to do, my opinion, that the Parliament might lay duties though not impose internal taxes, I shall not give myself the trouble to defend it. Only to you, I may say, that not only the Parliament of Britain, but every state in Europe claims and exercises a right of laying duties on the exportation of its own commodities to foreign countries. A duty is paid here on coals exported to Holland, and yet England has no right to lay an internal tax on Holland. All goods brought out of France to England, or any other country, are charged with a small duty in France, which the consumers pay, and yet France has no

217

right to tax other countries. And in my opinion the grievance is not that Britain puts duties upon her own manufactures exported to us, but that she forbids us to buy the like manufactures from any other country. This she does however in virtue of her allowed right to regulate the commerce of the whole empire, allowed I mean by the Farmer, though I think whoever would dispute that right might stand upon firmer ground and make much more of the argument: but my reasons are too many and too long for a letter.

Mr. Grenville complained in the House that the Governor of New Jersey, New Hampshire, East and West Florida, had none of them obeyed the orders sent them, to give an account of the manufactures carried on in their respective provinces. Upon hearing this I went, after the House was up and got a sight of the reports made by the other governors. They are all much in the same strain, that there are no manufactures of any consequence; in Massachusetts, a little coarse woollen only made in families for their own wear: glass and linen have been tried and failed. Rhode Island, Connecticut, and New York much the same. Pennsylvania has tried a linen manufactory but it is dropped, it being imported cheaper; there is a glass-house in Lancaster county, but it makes only a little coarse wear for the country neighbours. Maryland is clothed all with English manufactures. Virginia the same, except that in their families, they spin a little cotton of their own growing. South Carolina and Georgia none. All speak of the dearness of labour that makes manufactures impracticable. Only the Governor of North Carolina parades with a large manufacture in his country that may be useful to Britain of *pine boards*; they having fifty saw mills on one river. These accounts are very satisfactory here, and induce the parliament to despise and take no notice of the Boston resolutions. I wish you would send your account before the meeting of next parliament. You have only to report a glass-house for coarse window glass and bottles, and some domestic manufactures of linen and woollen for family use that do not half clothe the inhabitants, all the finer goods coming from England and the like. I believe you will be puzzled to find any other, though I see great puffs in the papers.

The parliament is up and the nation in a ferment with

the new elections. Great complaints are made that the natural interests of country gentlemen in their neighbouring boroughs, is overborne by the monied interest of the new people who have got sudden fortunes in the Indies, or as contractors, &c. £4000 is now the market price for a borough. In short this whole venal nation is now at market, will be sold for about Two Millions; and might be bought out of the hands of the present bidders (if he would offer half a million more) by the very devil himself....

I am your affectionate father,

B. FRANKLIN

As a wise man and a loving father, Franklin was sensible enough to reconcile himself to the marriage his daughter had entered against his better judgment. In a letter to Richard Bache he began to thaw.

London, Aug. 13. 1768

Loving Son,

I received yours of May 20, as also the preceding Letters mentioned in it. You must have been sensible that I thought the Step you had taken, to engage yourself in the Charge of a Family, while your Affairs bore so unpromising an Aspect with Regard to the probable Means of maintaining it, a very rash and precipitate one. I could not therefore but be dissatisfy'd with it, and displeas'd with you whom I look'd upon as an Instrument of bringing future Unhappiness on my Child, by involving her in the Difficulty and Distress that seem'd connected with your Circumstances, you having not merely Nothing beforehand, but being besides greatly in Debt. In this Situation of my Mind, you should not wonder that I did not answer your Letters. I could say nothing agreable: I did not chuse to write, what I thought, being unwilling to give Pain where I could not give Pleasure. Time has made me easier. I hope too, that the Accounts you give me of your better Prospects are well-founded, and that by an industrious Application to Business you may retrieve your Losses. I can only add at present, that my best Wishes attend you, and that if you prove a good Husband & Son, you will find in me an Affectionate Father,

B FRANKLIN

My Love to Sally. I have sent her by Mr. Coleman, who left us this Day, a new Watch & Buckles.

*Richard Bache by John Hoppner*

219

Politics continued to be Franklin's main absorption. In a letter to Joseph Galloway he all but abandoned hope for the mission that brought him to England—ousting the Penns from Pennsylvania. The shift from Pennsylvania agent to American spokesman was becoming more and more pronounced. Jeffery Amherst, mentioned in the closing lines, was the British commander in chief in America during the French and Indian War. He was much admired by the Americans, who considered him one of their staunchest supporters in England. He had been made Governor of Virginia and Colonel of the 60th (Royal American) Regiment, both sinecures that enabled him to remain in England while the Colony was ruled by a lieutenant governor and the regiment was run by a lieutenant colonel.

London, August 20. 1768

I wrote a pretty long Letter to you by Falconer, in which I acquainted you with what had heretofore pass'd between Lord Hillsborough and myself relating to the Change of our Government; and that I proposed waiting on him again in a few Days, in consequence of an Intimation I had received that he was now disposed to favour the Petition. I have accordingly been with him, and had a long Audience of him upon the Subject, the Particulars of which I cannot at present give you, but the Conclusion was, that we parted without agreeing on any thing, the Advice he gave us in order to obtain the Change, being such as I assur'd him we could not take. I shall therefore move the Matter no farther during the Administration of a Minister that appears to have a stronger Partiality for Mr Penn than any of his Predecessors. I stay however a little longer here, till I see what Turn American Affairs are like to take. The next News from America, which is anxiously expected, will probably enable us to judge. A Party is now growing in our Favour, which I shall endeavour to increase and strengthen by every Effort of Tongue and Pen. Possibly by our united Endeavours (I wish I could say *probably*) the Repeal of the late offensive Duties may be obtained. If it should be resolv'd by the Ministry to make us easy, I know not but I may still return this Fall. But otherwise, I shall stay the Session, to see if the new Parliament can be brought to disapprove of the violent Measures talked of, and to repeal the Act. Sir Jeffery Amherst's being stript of his Offices, gives great Offence to all the Military People here, and tho' the Measure of requiring a chief Governor to reside in his Government was not in itself a wrong thing, yet Advantage is taken of it by the Opposition, to arraign the

Conduct of Lord Hillsborough, and render him odious. Please to present my best Respects and Duty to the Assembly, and assure them of my most faithful Services.

The struggle over the Townshend Acts did not reach a climax, in the pattern of the Stamp Act crisis. But the British Government finally reacted to the nonimportation agreements, which Americans were maintaining with considerable determination. Franklin rushed news to America of a major shift in the British position. The letter went to Noble Wimberly Jones, Speaker of the Georgia House of Representatives. The Colony had appointed Franklin its agent in 1768.

London, June 7, 1769

I did myself the Honour of Writing to you on the 3d. of the last Month, since when the Parliament has risen without repealing the Duties that have been so generally complain'd of. But we are now assured by the Ministry, that the Affairs of America have been lately considered in Council; that it was the unanimous Opinion no new Acts for the purpose of Raising a Revenue in America should be made here; and that it was the full Intention of his Majesty's Servants to propose early in the ensuing Session the Repeal of the Duties on Glass, Paper, and Painters Colours. Believing this News would be agreable to our Friends, I take the first Opportunity of communicating it to you; and hope that nothing will happen in the mean time, to change the favourable Sentiments towards us, which apparently begin to take place in the Minds of his Majesty and his Ministers. Possibly we may not at first obtain all we desire, or all that ought to be granted to us; but the giving Ground to us in some degree has a good Aspect, and affords room to hope that gradually every Obstruction to that cordial Amity so necessary for the Welfare of the whole Empire, will be removed. Indeed I wish, as I think it would be best, that this could be done at once: But 'tis perhaps too much to expect, considering the Pride natural to so great a Nation, the Prejudices that have so universally prevailed here with regard to the Point of Right, and the Resentment at our disputing it.

The opposition of Lord Hillsborough completely stalled plans for the western colony, as conceived by William Franklin and his American friends. Finally, in 1769, taking Benjamin Franklin's advice, they reorganized the company with a British base, retaining most of the

American partners but opening up shares to many more British partners. Franklin joined forces with banker Thomas Walpole, nephew of a former prime minister, and together they shrewdly selected a cross section of the British establishment, representing all parties and shades of political opinion. In this letter Franklin invited Grey Cooper, one of the Secretaries of the Treasury, to join the group.

> Craven Street, Tuesday July 11. 1769
> An Application being about to be made for a Grant of Lands in the Territory on the Ohio lately purchased of the Indians, I cannot omit acquainting you with it, and giving you my Opinion, that they will very soon be settled by People from the neighbouring Provinces, and be of great Advantage in a few Years to the Undertakers. As you have those fine Children, and are likely to have many more, I wish for their Sakes, you may incline to take this Opportunity of making a considerable Addition to their future Fortunes, as the Expence will be a Trifle. If therefore you will give me leave, I shall put your Name down among us for a Share (40,000 Acres). Your Neighbour Mr Dagge will call upon you some Day and explain the Particulars more fully.

Franklin's letters during these years reflect a steady growth toward a conviction that America must become independent of England. This letter informed Samuel Cooper, pastor of Boston's Brattle Square Church, that the Townshend duties—as a reaction to Colonial non-importation agreements—had been limited to tea. The quartering of British troops in America remained a disputed issue.

> London, June 8, 1770.
> I received duly your favour of March 28. With this I send you two Speeches in Parliament on our Affairs by a Member that you know. The Repeal of the whole late Act would undoubtedly have been a prudent Measure, and I have reason to believe that Lord North was for it, but some of the other Ministers could not be brought to agree to it. So the Duty on Tea, with that obnoxious Preamble, remains to continue the dispute. But I think the next Session will hardly pass over without repealing them; for the Parliament must finally comply with the Sense of the Nation. As to the Standing Army kept up among us in time of Peace, without the Consent of our Assemblies, I am clearly of Opinion that it is not agreable to the Constitution. Should the King by the Aid of his Parliaments in Ireland and the Colonies, raise an Army

*Thomas Walpole*

and bring it into England, quartering it here in time of Peace without the Consent of the Parliament of Great Britain, I am persuaded he would soon be told that he had no Right so to do, and the Nation would ring with Clamours against it. I own that I see no Difference in the Cases. And while we continue so many distinct and separate States, our having the same Head or Sovereign, the King, will not justify such an Invasion of the separate Right of each State to be consulted on the Establishment of whatever Force is proposed to be kept up within its Limits, and to give or refuse its Consent as shall appear most for the Public Good of that State. That the Colonies originally were constituted distinct States, and intended to be continued such, is clear to me from a thorough Consideration of their original Charters, and the whole Conduct of the Crown and Nation towards them until the Restoration. Since that Period, the Parliament here has usurp'd an Authority of making Laws for them, which before it had not. We have for some time submitted to that Usurpation, partly thro' Ignorance and Inattention, and partly from our Weakness and Inability to contend. I hope when our Rights are better understood here, we shall, by prudent and proper Conduct be able to obtain from the Equity of this Nation a Restoration of them. And in the mean time I could wish that such Expressions as, *The Supreme Authority of Parliament; The Subordinacy of our Assemblies to the Parliament* and the like, (which in Reality mean nothing if our Assemblies with the King have a true Legislative Authority) I say, I could wish that such Expressions were no more seen in our publick Pieces. They are too strong for Compliment, and tend to confirm a Claim [of] Subjects in one Part of the King's Dominions to be Sovereigns over their Fellow-Subjects in another Part of his Dominions; when [in] truth they have no such Right, and their Claim is founded only on Usurpation, the several States having equal Rights and Liberties, and being only connected, as England and Scotland were before the Union, by having one common Sovereign, the King. This kind of Doctrine the Lords and Commons here would deem little less than Treason against what they think their Share of the Sovereignty over the Colonies. To me those Bodies seem to have been long encroaching on the Rights of their and our Sovereign, assuming too much of his

*Drawing of Number 7 Craven Street,
where Franklin lived in London*

Authority, and betraying his Interests. By our Constitution he is, with [his] Plantation Parliaments, the sole Legislator of his American Subjects, and in that Capacity is and ought to be free to exer[cise] his own Judgment unrestrain'd and unlimited by his Parliament here. And our Parliaments have right to grant him Aids without the Consent of this Parliament, a Circumstance which, by the [way] begins to give it some Jealousy. Let us therefore hold fast [our] Loyalty to our King (who has the best Disposition towards us, and has a Family-Interest in our Prosperity); as that steady Loyalty is the most probable Means of securing us from the arbitrary Power of a corrupt Parliament, that does not like us, and conceives itself to have an Interest in keeping us down and fleecing us. If they should urge the *Inconvenience* of an Empire's being divided into so many separate States, and from thence conclude that we are not so divided; I would answer, that an Inconvenience proves nothing but itself. England and Scotland were once separate States, under the same King. The Inconvenience found in their being separate States, did not prove that the Parliament of England had a right to govern Scotland. A formal Union was thought necessary, and England was an hundred Years soliciting it, before she could bring it about. If Great Britain now think such a Union necessary with us, let her propose her Terms, and we may consider of them. Were the general Sentiments of this Nation to be consulted in the Case, I should hope the Terms, whether practicable or not, would at least be equitable: for I think that except among those with whom the Spirit of Toryism prevails, the popular Inclination here is, to wish us well, and that we may preserve our Liberties.

Polly Stevenson married Dr. William Hewson early in July, 1770. In September, Mrs. Stevenson took a trip to the country, and Polly and her husband came to Craven Street to run the house. To amuse himself and his friends, Franklin composed *The Craven Street Gazette,* a delightful burlesque of contemporary British newspapers. Miss Franklin was a young English cousin who spent much of her time at Craven Street. The *"great* person" was, of course, Benjamin Franklin himself.

Saturday, Sept. 22. 1770
This Morning Queen Margaret, accompanied by her first Maid of Honour, Miss Franklin, set out for Rochester. Immediately on their Departure, the whole street was

in tears—from a heavy Shower of Rain.

It is whispered, that the new Family Administration which took place on her Majesty's Departure, promises, like all other new Administrations, to govern much better than the old one.

We hear that the *great* person (so called from his enormous Size), of a certain Family in a certain Street, is grievously affected at the late Changes, and could hardly be comforted this Morning, tho' the new Ministry promised him a roasted Shoulder of Mutton, and Potatoes, for his dinner.

It is said, that the same *great* Person intended to pay his Respects to another great Personage this Day, at St. James's, it being Coronation-Day; hoping thereby a little to amuse his grief; but was prevented by an accident, Queen Margaret, or her Maid of Honour having carried off the Key of the Drawers, so that the Lady of the Bedchamber could not come at a laced Shirt for his Highness. Great Clamours were made on this Occasion against her Majesty.

Other Accounts say, that the Shirts were afterwards found, tho' too late, in another Place. And some suspect, that the Wanting a Shirt from those Drawers was only a ministerial Pretence to excuse Picking the Locks, that the new Administration might have every thing at Command.

We hear that the Lady Chamberlain of the Household went to Market this Morning by her own self, gave the Butcher whatever he ask'd for the Mutton, and had no Dispute with the Potatoe Woman—to their great Amazement—at the Change of Times!

It is confidently asserted, that this Afternoon, the Weather being wet, the great *Person* a little chilly, and no body at home to find fault with the Expence of Fuel, he was indulg'd with a Fire in his Chamber. It seems the Design is, to make him contented, by Degrees, with the Absence of the Queen.

A Project has been under Consideration of Government, to take the Opportunity of her Majesty's Absence, for doing a Thing she was always averse to, viz. Fixing a new Lock on the Street Door, or getting a Key made to the old one; it being found extreamly inconvenient, that one or other of the Great Officers of State, should, whenever the Maid goes out for a Ha'p worth of Sand or

*"Cries of London," a series of
water colors painted in 1759 by Paul
Sandby, included an inkseller (top),
cane chair weaver, and shrimp girl.*

a Pint of Porter, be obliged to attend the Door to let her in again. But Opinions, being divided, which of the two Expedients to adopt, the Project is for the present laid aside.

We have good Authority to assure our Readers, that a Cabinet Council was held this Afternoon at Tea; the Subject of which was a Proposal for the Reformation of Manners, and a more strict Observation of the Lord's Day. The Result was a unanimous Resolution, that no Meat should be dress'd tomorrow; whereby the Cook and the first Minister will both be at Liberty to go to Church, the one having nothing to do, and the other no Roast to rule. It seems the cold Shoulder of Mutton, and the Apple pye, were thought sufficient for Sunday's Dinner. All pious People applaud this Measure, and 'tis thought the new Ministry will soon become popular....

Sunday, Sept. 23.

It is now found by sad Experience, that good Resolutions are easier made than executed. Notwithstanding yesterday's solemn Order of Council, no body went to Church to day. It seems the *great* Person's broad-built-bulk lay so long abed, that Breakfast was not over 'till it was too late to dress. At least this is the Excuse. In fine, it seems a vain thing to hope Reformation from the Example of our great Folks. The Cook and the Minister, however, both took Advantage of the Order so far, as to save themselves all Trouble, and the Clause of *cold Dinner* was enforc'd, tho' the *going to Church* was dispens'd with; just as the common working People observe the Commandments; *the seventh day thou shalt rest,* they think a sacred Injunction; but the other *Six Days shalt thou labour* is deem'd a mere Piece of Advice, which they may practise when they want Bread and are out of Credit at the Alehouse, and may neglect whenever they have Money in their Pockets. It must nevertheless be said in justice to our Court, that whatever Inclination they had to Gaming, no Cards were brought out to Day....

Monday, Sept. 24.

We are credibly informed, that the *great* Person dined this Day with the Club at the Cat-and-Bagpipes in the City, on cold Round of boil'd Beef. This, it seems, he was under some Necessity of Doing (tho' he rather dislikes Beef) because truly the Ministers were to be all abroad somewhere to dine on hot roast Venison. It is thought

*The hot pudding- (top), green vegetable-, and mop-venders, as drawn by Sandby, were all familiar London street sights to Franklin.*

that if the Queen had been at home, he would not have been so slighted. And tho' he shows outwardly no Marks of Dissatisfaction, it is suspected that he begins to wish for her Majesty's Return. . . .

This evening there was high Play at the Groom Porter's in Cravenstreet House. The Great Person lost Money. It is supposed the Ministers, as is usually supposed of all Ministers, shared the Emoluments among them.

Tuesday, Sept. 25.

This morning the good Lord Hutton call'd at Cravenstreet House, and enquired very respectfully & affectionately concerning the Welfare of the absent Queen. He then imparted to the big Man a Piece of Intelligence important to them both, which he had just received from Lady Hawkesworth, viz. That [the] amiable and excellent Companion Miss Dorothea Blount had made a Vow to marry absolutely him of the two, whose Wife should first depart this Life. It is impossible to express with Words the various Agitations of Mind appearing in both their Faces on this Occasion. *Vanity* at the Preference given them to the rest of Mankind; *Affection* to their present Wives; *Fear* of losing them; *Hope,* (if they must lose them) to obtain the propos'd Comfort; *Jealousy* of each other, in case both Wives should die together; &c. &c. &c. all working at the same time, jumbled their Features into inexplicable Confusion. They parted at length with Professions & outward Appearances indeed of ever-during Friendship; but it was shrewdly suspected that each of them sincerely wished Health & long Life to the other's Wife; & that however long either of these Friends might like to live himself, the other would be very well pleas'd to survive him. . . .

The Publick may be assured, that this Morning a certain *great Person* was ask'd very complaisantly by the Mistress of the Household, if he would chuse to have the Blade Bone of Saturday's Mutton that had been kept for his Dinner to Day, *broil'd* or *cold.* He answer'd gravely, *If there is any Flesh on it, it may be broil'd; if not, it may as well be cold.* Orders were accordingly given for broiling it. But when it came to Table, there was indeed so very little Flesh, or rather none, (Puss having din'd on it yesterday after Nanny) that if our new Administration had been as good Oeconomists as they would be thought, the Expence of Broiling might well have been saved to the Publick, and carried to the Sinking Fund. It is assured the great Person bears all with infinite Patience. But the Nation is astonish'd at the insolent Presumption, that dares treat so much Mildness in so cruel a manner.

A terrible Accident had *like to have happened* this Afternoon at Tea. The Boiler was set too near the End of the little square Table. The first Ministress was sitting at one End of the Table to administer the Tea; the great Person was about to sit down at the other End where the Boiler stood. By a sudden Motion, the Lady gave the Table a Tilt. Had it gone over, the great *person* must have been scalded; perhaps to Death. Various are the Surmises and Observations on this Occasion. The Godly say, it would have been a just Judgment on him, for preventing, by his Laziness, the Family's going to Church last Sunday. The Opposition do not stick to insinuate that there was a Design to scald him, prevented only by his quick Catching the Table. The Friends of the Ministry give out, that he carelessly jogg'd the Table himself, & would have been inevitably scalded had not the Ministress sav'd him. It is hard for the Publick to come at the Truth in these Cases.

At six o'Clock this Afternoon News came by the Post, that her Majesty arrived safely at Rochester on Saturday Night. The Bells immediately rang—for Candles, to illuminate the Parlour; the Court went into Cribbidge, and the Evening concluded with every other Demonstration of Joy. . . .

We hear that from the Time of her Majesty's leaving Craven Street House to this Day, no Care is taken to file the Newspapers; but they lie about in every Room, in every Window, and on every Chair, just where the Doctor lays them when he reads them. It is impossible Government can long go on in such Hands.

From America came news that Franklin had become a grandfather. Sally had given birth to a boy, who was named Benjamin Franklin Bache. In this letter Franklin responded with some good-humored advice to Deborah on the art of grandmothership.

London, October 3, 1770

My dear Child,

I received your kind Letter of Aug. 16, which gave me a great deal of Satisfaction. I am glad your little Grandson recovered so soon of his Illness, as I see you are quite in

Love with him, and your Happiness wrapt up in his; since your whole long Letter is made up of the History of his pretty Actions. It was very prudently done of you not to interfere when his Mother thought fit to correct him; which pleases me the more, as I feared, from your Fondness of him, that he would be too much humoured, and perhaps spoiled. There is a Story of two little Boys in the Street; one was crying bitterly; the other came to him to ask what was the Matter? I have been, says he, "for a pennyworth of Vinegar, and I have broke the Glass, and spilt the Vinegar, and my Mother will whip me." *No, she won't whip you* says the other. Indeed, she will, says he. *What,* says the other, *have you then got ne'er a Grandmother?*

From Boston came even more unexpected news. Thanks largely to the letter he had written to Samuel Cooper on June 8, 1770, Franklin had been appointed the agent of Massachusetts. In reply to Cooper's letter telling him of this action, Franklin called the appointment "one of the greatest honours." But it was in many respects also a profound embarrassment to him. Since Boston was regarded as the most radical and troublesome of the Colonies, whoever represented it was almost *de facto* out of favor with the British Ministry. Moreover, Franklin was only the agent of the Assembly. The Governor, Thomas Hutchinson, and his Council, retained other agents in London to represent their views, which sharply differed from those of the Assembly. A month after Franklin wrote to Cooper accepting the appointment, the new agent wrote another letter, describing the reception he received from Lord Hillsborough when he attempted to inform that stiff-necked noble of his appointment.

London, Feb. 5. 1771

I have just received your kind Favour of January 1 by Mr. Bowdoin, to whom I should be glad to render any Service here. I wrote to you some Weeks since in Answer to yours of July and November, expressing my Sentiments without the least Reserve on Points that require free Discussion, as I know I can confide in your Prudence not to hurt my Usefulness here, by making me more obnoxious than I must necessarily be from that known Attachment to the American Interest, which my Duty as well as Inclination demands of me.

In the same Confidence I send you the inclosed Extract from my Journal, containing a late Conference between the Secretary and your Friend, in which you will see a little of his Temper: It is one of the many Instances of his Behaviour and Conduct, that have given me the very mean Opinion I entertain of his Abilities and Fitness for his Station. His Character is Conceit, Wrongheadedness, Obstinacy, and Passion. Those, who would speak most favourably of him, allow all this; they only add, that he is an honest Man, and means well. If that be true, as perhaps it may, I wish him a better Place, where only Honesty and Well-meaning are required, and where his other Qualities can do no harm. Had the War taken place, I have reason to believe he would have been removed. He had, I think, some Apprehensions of it himself at the Time I was with him. I hope, however, that our Affairs will not much longer be perplex'd and embarass'd by his perverse and senseless Management. I have since heard, that his Lordship took great Offence at some of my last Words, which he calls extreamly rude and abusive. He assured a Friend of mine, that they were equivalent to telling him to his Face, that the Colonies could expect neither Favour nor Justice during his Administration. I find he did not mistake me.

It is true, as you have heard, that some of my Letters to America have been echo'd back hither; but that has not been the Case with any that were written to you. Great Umbrage was taken, but chiefly by Lord Hillsborough, who was disposed before to be angry with me, and therefore the Inconvenience was the less; and, whatever the Consequences are of his Displeasure, putting all my Offences together, I must bear them as well as I can. Not but that, if there is to be War between us, I shall do my best to defend myself and annoy my Adversary, little regarding the story of the Earthen Pot and Brazen Pitcher. One encouragement I have, the knowledge, that he is not a whit better lik'd by his Colleagues in the Ministry, than he is by me, that he cannot probably continue where he is much longer, and that he can scarce be succeeded by anybody, who will not like me the better for his having been at Variance with me. . . .

*Minutes of the Conference mentioned in the preceeding Letter.*

Wednesday, January 16, 1771.

I went this morning to wait on Lord Hillsborough. The porter at first denied his Lordship, on which I left my name and drove off. But, before the coach got out of the square, the coachman heard a call, turned, and went back to the door, when the porter came and said, "His Lordship will see you, Sir." I was shown into the levee I have lately made a Tour thro' Ireland and Scotland. room, where I found Governor Bernard, who, I understand, attends there constantly. Several other gentlemen were there attending, with whom I sat down a few minutes, when Secretary Pownall came out to us, and said his Lordship desired I would come in.

I was pleased with this ready admission and preference, having sometimes waited three or four hours for my turn; and, being pleased, I could more easily put on the open, cheerful countenance, that my friends advised me to wear. His Lordship came towards me and said, "I was dressing in order to go to court; but, hearing that you were at the door, who are a man of business, I determined to see you immediately." I thanked his Lordship, and said that my business at present was not much; it was only to pay my respects to his Lordship, and to acquaint him with my appointment by the House of Representatives of Massachusetts Bay to be their agent here, in which station if I could be of any service —(I was going on to say—"to the public, I should be very happy;" but his Lordship, whose countenance changed at my naming that province, cut me short by saying, with something between a smile and a sneer,)

L. H.  I must set you right there, Mr. Franklin, you are not agent.

B. F.  Why, my Lord?

L. H.  You are not appointed.

B. F.  I do not understand your Lordship; I have the appointment in my pocket.

L. H.  You are mistaken; I have later and better advices. I have a letter from Governor Hutchinson; he would not give his assent to the bill.

B. F.  There was no bill, my Lord; it was a vote of the House.

L. H.  There was a bill presented to the governor for the purpose of appointing you and another, one Dr. Lee, I think he is called, to which the governor refused his assent.

B. F.  I cannot understand this, my Lord; I think there must be some mistake in it. Is your Lordship quite sure that you have such a letter?

*Wills Hill, Lord Hillsborough*

*Portrait of Governor Thomas
Hutchinson by Edward Truman*

L. H.   I will convince you of it directly. (*Rings the
bell.*) Mr. Pownall will come in and satisfy you.

B. F.   It is not necessary, that I should now detain
your Lordship from dressing. You are going to court. I
will wait on your Lordship another time.

L. H.   No, stay; he will come immediately. (*To the
servant.*) Tell Mr. Pownall I want him.

(*Mr. Pownall comes in.*)

L. H.   Have not you at hand Governor Hutchinson's
letter, mentioning his refusing his assent to the bill for
appointing Dr. Franklin agent?

Sec. P.   My Lord?

L. H.   Is there not such a letter?

Sec. P.   No, my Lord; there is a letter relating to
some bill for the payment of a salary to Mr. De Berdt,
and I think to some other agent, to which the governor
had refused his assent.

L. H.   And is there nothing in the letter to the purpose
I mention?

Sec. P.   No, my Lord.

B. F.   I thought it could not well be, my Lord; as my
letters are by the last ships, and they mention no such
thing. Here is the authentic copy of the vote of the
House appointing me, in which there is no mention of
any act intended. Will your Lordship please to look at
it? (*With seeming unwillingness he takes it, but does not
look into it.*)

L. H.   An information of this kind is not properly
brought to me as Secretary of State. The Board of Trade
is the proper place.

B. F.   I will leave the paper then with Mr. Pownall
to be—

L. H.   (*Hastily.*) To what end would you leave it
with him?

B. F.   To be entered on the minutes of that Board,
as usual.

L. H.   (*Angrily.*) It shall not be entered there. No such
paper shall be entered there, while I have any thing to
do with the business of that Board. The House of Representatives has no right to appoint an agent. We shall take
no notice of any agents, but such as are appointed by
acts of Assembly, to which the governor gives his assent.
We have had confusion enough already. Here is one
agent appointed by the Council, another by the House
of Representatives. Which of these is agent for the

province? Who are we to hear in provincial affairs? An agent appointed by act of Assembly we can understand. No other will be attended to for the future, I can assure you.

B. F.    I cannot conceive, my Lord, why the consent of the governor should be thought necessary to the appointment of an agent for the people. It seems to me that—

L. H.    (*With a mixed look of anger and contempt.*) I shall not enter into a dispute with YOU, Sir, upon this subject.

B. F.    I beg your Lordship's pardon; I do not presume to dispute with your Lordship; I would only say, that it seems to me, that every body of men, who cannot appear in person, where business relating to them may be transacted, should have a right to appear by an agent. The concurrence of the governor does not seem to me necessary. It is the business of the people, that is to be done; he is not one of them; he is himself an agent.

L. H.    (*Hastily.*) Whose agent is he?

B. F.    The King's, my Lord.

L. H.    No such matter. He is one of the corporation by the province charter. No agent can be appointed but by an act, nor any act pass without his assent. Besides, this proceeding is directly contrary to express instructions.

B. F.    I did not know there had been such instructions. I am not concerned in any offence against them, and—

L. H.    Yes, your offering such a paper to be entered is an offence against them. (*Folding it up again without having read a word of it.*) No such appointment shall be entered....

B. F.    (*Reaching out his hand for the paper, which his Lordship returned to him.*) I beg your Lordship's pardon for taking up so much of your time. It is, I believe, of no great importance whether the appointment is acknowledged or not, for I have not the least conception that an agent can *at present* be of any use to any of the colonies. I shall therefore give your Lordship no further trouble. (*Withdrew.*)

Around this time Franklin wrote a song, "The Mother Country," which summed up in an amusing and ironic way his complex feelings toward England.

We have an old Mother that peevish is grown,
She snubs us like Children that scarce walk alone;
She forgets we're grown up and have Sense of our own;
> *Which nobody can deny, deny,*
> *Which nobody can deny.*

If we don't obey Orders, whatever the Case;
She frowns, and she chides, and she loses all Patience,
and sometimes she hits us a Slap in the Face,
> *Which nobody can deny, &c.*

Her Orders so odd are, we often suspect
That Age has impaired her sound Intellect:
But still an old Mother should have due Respect,
> *Which nobody can deny, &c.*

Let's bear with her Humours as well as we can:
But why should we bear the Abuse of her Man?
When Servants make Mischief, they earn the Rattan,
> *Which nobody can deny, &c.*

Know too, ye bad Neighbours, who aim to divide
The Sons from the Mother, that still she's our Pride;
And if ye attack her we're all of her side,
> *Which nobody can deny, &c.*

We'll join in her Lawsuits, to baffle all those,
Who, to get what she has, will be often her Foes:
For we know it must all be our own, when she goes,
> *Which nobody can deny, deny,*
> *Which nobody can deny.*

Meanwhile, at Craven Street, Polly Stevenson Hewson had given birth to a son; Franklin was his godfather. The "Place" he mentioned in the first line of this letter to her was the Yorkshire home of his son-in-law, Richard Bache, who had come to England to meet Franklin.

Preston, Nov. 25, 1771.

Dear Friend,

I came to this Place on Saturday night, right well, and untir'd with a 70 miles' Journey that day. I met with your and my Dolly's joint Letter, which would have refreshed me with its kindness, if I had been ever so weary....

I thank you for your Intelligence about my Godson. I believe you are sincere, when you say you think him as fine a Child as you wish to see. He had cut two Teeth, and three, in another Letter, make five; for I know you never write Tautologies. If I have over-reckon'd, the Number will be right by this Time. His being like me in so many Particulars pleases me prodigiously; and I

*Eighteenth-century "Irish Cabbin"*

am persuaded there is another, which you have omitted, tho' it must have occurr'd to you while you were putting them down. Pray let him have every thing he likes; I think it of great Consequence while the Features of the Countenance are forming; it gives them a pleasant Air, and, that being once become natural and fix'd by Habit, the Face is ever after the handsomer for it, and on that much of a Person's good Fortune and Success in Life may depend. Had I been cross'd as much in my Infant Likings and Inclinations as you know I have been of late Years, I should have been, I was going to say, not near so handsome; but as the Vanity of that Expression would offend other Folk's Vanity, I change it, out of regard to them, and say, a great deal more homely.

Franklin's visit to Ireland made a deep impression on him. He saw in grisly detail what happened to a country that totally surrendered its independence to another nation. In a letter to Dr. Joshua Babcock, postmaster of Westerly, Rhode Island, he gave a vivid description of Ireland's degradation.

*An Irish day laborer*

London, Jan. 13. 1772

I have lately made a Tour thro' Ireland and Scotland. In those Countries a small Part of the Society are Landlords, great Noblemen, and Gentlemen, extreamly opulent, living in the highest Affluence and Magnificence: The Bulk of the People Tenants, extreamly poor, living in the most sordid Wretchedness, in dirty Hovels of Mud and Straw, and cloathed only in Rags.

I thought often of the Happiness of New England, where every Man is a Freeholder, has a Vote in publick Affairs, lives in a tidy, warm House, has plenty of good Food and Fewel, with whole cloaths from Head to Foot, the Manufacture perhaps of his own Family. Long may they continue in this Situation! But if they should ever envy the Trade of these Countries, I can put them in a Way to obtain a Share of it. Let them with three fourths of the People of Ireland live the Year round on Potatoes and Buttermilk, without Shirts, then may their Merchants export Beef, Butter, and Linnen. Let them, with the Generality of the Common People of Scotland, go Barefoot, then may they make large Exports in Shoes and Stockings: And if they will be content to wear Rags, like the Spinners and Weavers of England, they may make Cloths and Stuffs for all Parts of the World.

Farther, if my Countrymen should ever wish for the honour of having among them a gentry enormously wealthy, let them sell their Farms & pay rack'd Rents; the Scale of the Landlords will rise as that of the Tenants is depress'd, who will soon become poor, tattered, dirty, and abject in Spirit. Had I never been in the American Colonies, but was to form my Judgment of Civil Society by what I have lately seen, I should never advise a Nation of Savages to admit of Civilization: For I assure you, that, in the Possession & Enjoyment of the various Comforts of Life, compar'd to these People every Indian is a Gentleman: And the Effect of this kind of Civil Society seems only to be, the depressing Multitudes below the Savage State that a few may be rais'd above it.

Franklin fought a war on two fronts with Lord Hillsborough, the Secretary of State for Colonies. He opposed Hillsborough's policy of repression and severity toward America in general, and behind the scenes he lobbied intensively for the western colony, which Hillsborough was blocking. Negotiations for the colony reached a climax when Hillsborough, as president of the Board of Trade, issued a report against it. Franklin and his friends demanded a hearing before the Privy Council; and Samuel Wharton, who had come over to England to assist Franklin in pushing the plan, made a long speech that reads as though it was composed by Franklin, or written under his direction and advice. The Privy Council rejected the Board of Trade's decision and declared in favor of the colony. Hillsborough, mortified, had no alternative but to resign. The Council's decision was undoubtedly affected by the presence among its members of several sharers in the Grand Ohio Company, as the founding organization was now called. In these letters to his son William, Franklin carefully restrained his exultation over this triumph. One reason may well have been his knowledge that his letters were being opened by the Ministry.

London, August 17, 1772.

At length we have got rid of Lord Hillsborough, and Lord Dartmouth takes his place, to the great satisfaction of all the friends of America. You will hear it said among you, I suppose, that the interest of the Ohio planters has ousted him; but the truth is, what I wrote you long since, that all his brother ministers disliked him extremely, and wished for a fair occasion of tripping up his heels; so, seeing that he made a point of defeating our scheme, they made another of supporting it, on purpose to mortify him, which they knew his pride could not bear. I do not mean they would have done this, if they had thought our proposal bad in itself, or his opposition well founded; but I believe, if he had been on good terms with them, they would not have differed with him for so small a matter. The King, too, was tired of him and of his administration, which had weakened the affection and respect of the colonies for a royal government, of which (I may say it to you) I used proper means from time to time that his Majesty should have due information and convincing proofs. More of this when I see you.

The King's dislike made the others more firmly united in the resolution of disgracing Hillsborough, by setting at nought his famous report. But, now that business is done, perhaps our affair may be less regarded in the cabinet and suffered to linger, and possibly may yet miscarry. Therefore let us beware of every word and action, that may betray a confidence in its success, lest we render ourselves ridiculous in case of disappointment....

I am writing by Falconer, and therefore in this only add, that I am ever your affectionate father,

B FRANKLIN

P.S.  The regard Lord Dartmouth has always done me the honour to express for me, gives me room to hope being able to obtain more in favour of our colonies upon occasion, than I could for some time past.

London, August 19, 1772.

As to my situation here, nothing can be more agreeable, especially as I hope for less embarrassment from the new minister; a general respect paid me by the learned, a number of friends and acquaintance among them, with whom I have a pleasing intercourse; a character of so much weight, that it has protected me when some in power would have done me injury, and continued me in an office they would have deprived me of; my company so much desired, that I seldom dine at home in winter, and could spend the whole summer in the country-houses of inviting friends, if I chose it. Learned and ingenious foreigners, that come to England, almost all make a point of visiting me; for my reputation is still higher abroad than here. Several of the foreign ambassadors have assiduously cultivated my acquaintance, treating me as one of their *Corps,* partly I believe from the desire they have, from time to time, of hearing something of American

*Engraving of Lord Dartmouth after a portrait by Sir Joshua Reynolds*

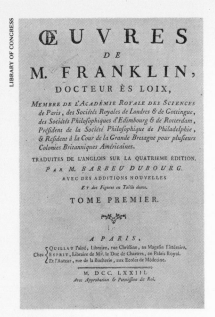

*A French edition of Franklin's works, published in 1773, lists him as a member of the Royal Academy.*

affairs, an object become of importance in foreign courts, who begin to hope Britain's alarming power will be diminished by the defection of her colonies; and partly that they may have an opportunity of introducing me to the gentlemen of their country who desire it. The King, too, has lately been heard to speak of me with great regard.

These are flattering circumstances, but a violent longing for home sometimes seizes me, which I can no otherwise subdue but by promising myself a return next spring or next fall, and so forth. As to returning hither, if I once go back, I have no thoughts of it. I am too far advanced in life to propose three voyages more....

*August 22d.*—I find I omitted congratulating you on the honour of your election into the Society for propagating the Gospel. There you match indeed my Dutch honour. But you are again behind, for last night I received a letter from Paris, of which the enclosed is an extract, acquainting me that I am chosen *Associé Etranger* [foreign member] of the Royal Academy there. There are but eight of these *Associés Etrangers* in all Europe, and those of the most distinguished names of science. The vacancy I have the honour of filling was made by the death of the late celebrated Van Swieten of Vienna. This mark of respect from the first academy in the world, which Abbé Nollet, one of its members, took so much pains to prejudice against my doctrines, I consider as a kind of victory without ink-shed, since I never answered him. I am told he has but one of his sect now remaining in the Academy. All the rest, who have in any degree acquainted themselves with electricity, are as he calls them *Franklinists.*

Although Franklin himself, earlier in his life, had owned one or two slaves, who worked for him as house servants, he very soon imbibed a deep detestation for slavery from his close association with Philadelphia's Quakers. In this letter to Anthony Benezet, a Quaker who devoted his life to the abolition of the slave trade, Franklin linked the origins of slavery to British imperial policy.

London, August 22: 1772.

I made a little extract from yours of April 27, of the number of slaves imported and perishing, with some close remarks on the hypocrisy of this country, which encourages such a detestable commerce by laws for promoting the Guinea trade; while it piqued itself on its virtue, love of liberty, and the equity of its courts, in setting free a single negro. This was inserted in the *London Chronicle*, of the 20th of June last.

I thank you for the Virginia address, which I shall also publish with some remarks. I am glad to hear that the disposition against keeping negroes grows more general in North America. Several pieces have been lately printed here against the practice, and I hope in time it will be taken into consideration and suppressed by the legislature. Your labours have already been attended with great effects. I hope, therefore, you and your friends will be encouraged to proceed.

On the whole, Franklin was in a buoyant mood in 1772. The western colony seemed within his grasp, and something close to a détente seemed to prevail between England and America. In this sunny atmosphere, he tossed off one of his most delightful letters to Georgiana Shipley, daughter of Jonathan Shipley, the Bishop of St. Asaph. It was at the Shipleys' country home, in the village of Twyford, that Franklin wrote the first part of his autobiography. Mungo was an American squirrel whom Franklin had given to the Shipleys. He escaped from their garden and was killed by a neighbor's dog.

London, September 26, 1772.

I LAMENT with you most sincerely the unfortunate end of poor MUNGO. Few squirrels were better accomplished; for he had had a good education, had travelled far, and seen much of the world. As he had the honour of being, for his virtues, your favourite, he should not go, like common skuggs, without an elegy or an epitaph. Let us give him one in the monumental style and measure, which, being neither prose nor verse, is perhaps the properest for grief; since to use common language would look as if we were not affected, and to make rhymes would seem trifling in sorrow.

EPITAPH.

Alas! poor Mungo!
Happy wert thou, hadst thou known
Thy own felicity.
Remote from the fierce bald eagle,
Tyrant of thy native woods,
Thou hadst nought to fear from his piercing talons,
Nor from the murdering gun
Of the thoughtless sportsman.
Safe in thy wired castle,

*Century* MAGAZINE, 1898

*Georgiana Shipley*

GRIMALKIN never could annoy thee.

Daily wert thou fed with the choicest viands,
By the fair hand of an indulgent mistress;
But, discontented,
Thou wouldst have more freedom.
Too soon, alas! didst thou obtain it;
And wandering,
Thou art fallen by the fangs of wanton, cruel RANGER!

Learn hence,
Ye who blindly seek more liberty,
Whether subjects, sons, squirrels or daughters,
That apparent restraint may be real protection;
Yielding peace and plenty
With security.

You see, my dear Miss, how much more decent and proper this broken style is, than if we were to say, by way of epitaph,

Here SKUGG
Lies snug,
As a bug
In a rug.

and yet, perhaps, there are people in the world of so little feeling as to think that this would be a good-enough epitaph for poor Mungo.

Suddenly the pace of politics quickened. The British Government became deeply entangled in the problems of the East India Company. In a letter written to William Franklin around this time, Franklin almost mordantly discussed "how the continued refusal of North America to take tea" had come close to wrecking the company. Numerous bankruptcies, caused by the abrupt plunge of the company's stock, had given "such a shock to credit" as England had not experienced since the collapse of the great speculation known as the South Sea Bubble about fifty years earlier. Manufacturers in turn were forced to lay off thousands of hands, and there was serious unrest in the manufacturing towns. "Blessed effects of pride, pique and passion in government, which should have no passions," Franklin said. This turmoil did not augur much progress for the western colony. In this letter to Joseph Galloway, Franklin discussed these and other matters.

London, April 6, 1773.

The Parliament is busy about India Affairs, and as yet see no End of the Business. It is thought they will sit till the End of June. An Alliance with France and

Spain is talk'd of; and a War with Prussia. But this may blow over. A War with France and Spain would be of more Advantage to American Liberty; Every Step would then be taken to conciliate our Friendship, our Grievances would be redress'd, and our Claims allow'd. And this will be the Case sooner or later. For as the House of Bourbon is most vulnerable in its American Possessions, our hearty Assistance in a War there must be of the greatest Importance.

The Affair of the Grant goes on but slowly. I do not yet clearly see Land. I begin to be a little of the Sailor's Mind when they were handing a Cable out of a Store into a Ship, and one of 'em said: "Tis a long, heavy Cable. I wish we could see the End of it." "D—n me," says another, "if I believe it has any End; somebody has cut it off."

In Boston, the political pot also began to boil again. A town meeting, organized by Samuel Adams, produced a report summarizing all the irritations and grievances that existed between England and America. Governor Thomas Hutchinson called it "a declaration of independency" and convened the General Court (or Massachusetts Assembly) to answer it. Franklin's low opinion of Hutchinson was part of the reason why he took a step that was to have enormous consequences both for him and for America. Early in 1773, a friend showed him some letters that Hutchinson and Lieutenant Governor Andrew Oliver had written to Thomas Whately, an undersecretary in the British Cabinet and a political follower of George Grenville. The letters had been stolen from Whately's files after his death. In these letters, Hutchinson and Oliver recommended a severe policy of repression to handle the unrest in Boston. Franklin forwarded copies of these explosive missives to Boston, with the proviso that they should be shown only to a small circle of leading men. The more radical Boston leaders decided to ignore this prohibition, and the letters were soon published, edited to make Governor Hutchinson and Lieutenant Governor Oliver appear in the most odious light possible. In this letter to Samuel Cooper, Franklin discussed the motives he had for sending the letters to Boston.

London, July 25, 1773.

I am glad to know your Opinion, that those Letters came seasonably, and may be of public Utility. I accompanied them with no Restriction relating to myself. My duty to the Province, as their Agent, I thought required the Communication of them, as far as I could. I was sensible I should make Enemies there, and perhaps might offend government here; but those Apprehensions I disregarded. I did not expect and hardly still expect that my sending them could be kept a Secret; but since it is so hitherto, I now wish it may continue so, because the Publication of the Letters, contrary to my Engagement, has changed the Circumstances. If they serve to diminish the Influence and demolish the Power of the Parties, whose Correspondence has been, and would probably have continued to be so mischievous to the Interest and Rights of the Province, I shall on that Account be more easy under any inconveniences I may suffer, either here or there; and shall bear, as well as I can, the Imputation of not having taken sufficient Care to insure the Performance of my Promise.

The situation in Boston made Franklin very touchy about his relationship with Crown officials. In this letter to William Franklin, he also revealed a significant turn in his thinking about the causes of the trouble between England and America. Lord North was First Minister in the reorganized British Cabinet.

London, July 14, 1773.

I am glad to find by yours of May 4 that you have been able to assist Josiah Davenport a little, but vex'd that he and you should think of putting me upon a Solicitation, which it is impossible for me to engage in. I am not upon Terms with Lord North, to ask any such Favour from him. Displeased with something he said relating to America, I have never been at his Levees, since the first. Perhaps he has taken that amiss. For the last Week we met occasionally at Lord Le Despencer's, in our Return from Oxford, where I had been to attend the Solemnity of his Installation, and he seemed studiously to avoid speaking to me. I ought to be asham'd to say that on such occasions I feel myself to be as proud as anybody. His Lady indeed was more gracious. She came, and sat down by me on the same Sopha, and condescended to enter into a Conversation with me agreably enough, as if to make some Amends. Their Son and Daughter were with them. They staied all Night, so that we din'd, supp'd, and breakfasted together, without exchanging three Sentences. But had he ever so great a Regard for me, I could not ask that Office, trifling as it is, for any Relation of mine. And detesting as I do the whole System of American Customs, believing they will one Day bring on a Breach, through the Indiscretion and Insolence of those

*Andrew Oliver*

*Lord North, after a Ramsay portrait*

concern'd in the Collection, I should never wish to see one so near to me in that Business....I am glad you stand so well with Lord Dartmouth. I am likewise well with him, but he never spoke to me of augmenting your Salary. He is truly a good Man, and wishes sincerely a good Understanding with the Colonies, but does not seem to have Strength equal to his Wishes. Between you and I, the late Measures have been, I suspect, very much the King's own, and he has in some Cases a great Share of what his Friends call *Firmness.* Yet, by some Painstaking and proper Management, the wrong Impressions he has received may be removed, which is perhaps the only Chance America has for obtaining *soon* the Redress she aims at. This entirely to yourself.

A few weeks later Franklin wrote to William about a more personal matter. In England before his marriage, William—himself illegitimate—had fathered an illegitimate son, whom he had named William Temple Franklin. Benjamin Franklin had paid for the boy's education in a school outside of London, and Temple had grown up thinking he was a distant relation of the Franklin family. By now the boy was almost thirteen and he no doubt knew who his father was. Lord le Despencer, whose gardens Franklin was enjoying, was head of the British Post Office. The buttons his son had sent him were actually pebbles from a beach near Philadelphia that Franklin had dubbed "Button-mold Bay."

West Wycombe, Lord le Despencer's,
Aug. 3. 1773.

Temple is just return'd to School from his Summer Vacation. He always behaves himself so well, as to encrease my Affection for him every time he is with me.

As you are like to have a considerable Landed Property, it would be well to make your Will, if you have not already done it, and secure that Property to him. Our Friend Galloway will advise you in the Manner. Whatever he may come to possess, I am persuaded he will make a good Use of it, if his Temper and Understanding do not strangely alter.

I am in this House as much at my Ease as if it was my own; and the Gardens are a Paradise. But a pleasanter Thing is the kind Countenance, the facetious and very intelligent Conversation of mine Host, who having been for many Years engaged in publick Affairs, seen all Parts of Europe, and kept the best Company in the World, is himself the best existing.

I wear the Buttons (for which I thank you) on a suit of light gray which matches them. All the *connoisseurs* in natural Productions are puzzeled with them, not knowing any thing similar.

Throughout these years Franklin continued to campaign in the newspapers on behalf of America. Scarcely a month passed without one of his essays appearing. Most of them debated with the numerous critics of America, who were also busy writing to the papers. But in 1773, as a new storm brewed between England and America, Franklin abruptly shifted his tone from vigorous debate to savage satire. On September 11, 1773, the *Public Advertiser* published an essay, "Rules by which a Great Empire May be Reduced to a Small One." Addressed to "All ministers who have the management of extensive dominions," it laid down twenty rules that were guaranteed to destroy a great empire, all of which, it soon became obvious to the reader, the British Ministry was already faithfully following. Eleven days later, the *Public Advertiser* published another essay, "An Edict by the King of Prussia." Both essays caused something of a sensation in England. The "Edict" was far more popular, and in fact sold out the paper.

Dantzic, Sept. 5, [1773]

"FREDERICK, by the grace of God, King of Prussia, &c. &c. &c., to all present and to come, (*à tous présens et à venir,*) Health. The peace now enjoyed throughout our dominions, having afforded us leisure to apply ourselves to the regulation of commerce, the improvement of our finances, and at the same time the easing our domestic subjects in their taxes: For these causes, and other good considerations us thereunto moving, we hereby make known, that, after having deliberated these affairs in our council, present our dear brothers, and other great officers of the state, members of the same, we, of our certain knowledge, full power, and authority royal, have made and issued this present Edict, viz.

"Whereas it is well known to all the world, that the first German settlements made in the Island of Britain, were by colonies of people, subject to our renowned ducal ancestors, and drawn from their dominions, under the conduct of Hengist, Horsa, Hella, Uff, Cerdicus, Ida, and others; and that the said colonies have flourished under the protection of our august house for ages past; have never been emancipated therefrom; and yet have hitherto yielded little profit to the same: And whereas we ourself have in the last war fought for and defended the said colonies, against the power of France, and thereby enabled them to make conquests from the said power of America, for which we have not yet received adequate compensation: And whereas it is just and expedient that a revenue should be raised from the said colonies in Britain, towards our indemnification; and that those who are descendants of our ancient subjects, and thence still owe us due obedience, should contribute to the replenishing of our royal coffers as they must have done, had their ancestors remained in the territories now to us appertaining: We do therefore hereby ordain and command, that, from and after the date of these presents, there shall be levied and paid to our officers of the *customs,* on all goods, wares, and merchandizes, and on all grain and other produce of the earth, exported from the said Island of Britain, and on all goods of whatever kind imported into the same, a duty of four and a half per cent *ad valorem,* for the use of us and our successors. And that the said duty may more effectually be collected, we do hereby ordain, that all ships or vessels bound from Great Britain to any other part of the world, or from any other part of the world to Great Britain, shall in their respective voyages touch at our port of Koningsberg, there to be unladen, searched, and charged with the said duties.

"And whereas there hath been from time to time discovered in the said island of Great Britain, by our colonists there, many mines or beds of iron-stone; and sundry subjects, of our ancient dominion, skilful in converting the said stone into metal, have in time past transported themselves thither, carrying with them and communicating that art; and the inhabitants of the said island, presuming that they had a natural right to make the best use they could of the natural productions of their country for their own benefit, have not only built furnaces for smelting the said stone into iron, but have erected plating-forges, slitting-mills, and steel-furnaces, for the more convenient manufacturing of the same; thereby endangering a diminution of the said manufacture in our ancient dominion;—we do therefore hereby farther ordain, that, from and after the date hereof, no mill or other engine for slitting or rolling of iron, or any plating-forge to work with a tilt-hammer, or any furnace for making steel, shall be erected or continued in the said island of Great Britain: And the Lord Lieutenant of

*A serene view of West Wycombe, home of Lord and Lady le Despencer, where Franklin was "as much at my Ease as if it were my own."*

every county in the said island is hereby commanded, on information of any such erection within his county, to order and by force to cause the same to be abated and destroyed; as he shall answer the neglect thereof to us at his peril. But we are nevertheless graciously pleased to permit the inhabitants of the said island to transport their iron into Prussia, there to be manufactured, and to them returned; they paying our Prussian subjects for the workmanship, with all the costs of commission, freight, and risk, coming and returning; any thing herein contained to the contrary notwithstanding.

"We do not, however, think fit to extend this our indulgence to the article of wool; but, meaning to encourage, not only the manufacturing of woollen cloth, but also the raising of wool, in our ancient dominions, and to prevent both, as much as may be, in our said island, we do hereby absolutely forbid the transportation of wool from thence, even to the mother country, Prussia; and that those islanders may be farther and more effectually restrained in making any advantage of their own wool in the way of manufacture, we command that none shall be carried out of one country into another; nor shall any worsted, bay, or woollen yarn, cloth, says, bays, kerseys, serges, frizes, druggets, cloth-serges, shalloons, or any other drapery stuffs, or woollen manufactures whatsoever, made up or mixed with wool in any of the said counties, be carried into any other county, or be waterborne even across the smallest river or creek, on penalty of forfeiture of the same, together with the boats, carriages, horses, &c., that shall be employed in removing them. Nevertheless, our loving subjects there are hereby permitted (if they think proper) to use all their wool as manure for the improvement of their lands. . . .

"And, lastly, being willing farther to favor our said colonies in Britain, we do hereby also ordain and command, that all the *thieves,* highway and street robbers, house-breakers, forgerers, murderers, s—d—tes, and villains of every denomination, who have forfeited their lives to the law in Prussia; but whom we, in our great clemency, do not think fit here to hang, shall be emptied out of our gaols into the said island of Great Britain, for the better peopling of that country.

"We flatter ourselves, that these our royal regulations and commands will be thought just and reasonable by our much-favoured colonists in England; the said regulations being copied from their statutes of 10 and 11 William III. c. 10, 5 Geo. II. c. 22, 23, Geo. II. c. 29, 4 Geo. I. c. 11, and from other equitable laws made by their parliaments; or from instructions given by their Princes; or from resolutions of both Houses, entered into for the good government of their *own colonies in Ireland and America. . . .*"

In a letter to his son, Franklin discussed the impact of his satires and included a vivid account of how totally the "Edict" fooled his English friends. But the letter is more important for an early paragraph in which Franklin stated his conclusion on the essential quarrel with England —and noted the ominous fact that his son did not agree with him.

London, October 6, 1773.

From a long and thorough consideration of the subject, I am indeed of opinion, that the parliament has no right to make any law whatever, binding on the colonies; that the king, and not the king, lords, and commons collectively, is their sovereign; and that the king, with their respective parliaments, is their only legislator. I know your sentiments differ from mine on these subjects. You are a thorough government man, which I do not wonder at, nor do I aim at converting you. I only wish you to act uprightly and steadily, avoiding that duplicity, which in Hutchinson, adds contempt to indignation. If you can promote the prosperity of your people, and leave them happier than you found them, whatever your political principles are, your memory will be honoured.

I have written two pieces here lately for the *Public Advertiser,* on American affairs, designed to expose the conduct of this country towards the colonies in a short, comprehensive, and striking view, and stated, therefore, in out-of-the-way forms, as most likely to take the general attention. The first was called *"Rules by which a Great Empire may be reduced to a small one;"* the second, *"An Edict of the King of Prussia."* I sent you one of the first, but could not get enough of the second to spare you one, though my clerk went the next morning to the printer's, and wherever they were sold. . . .

I am not suspected as the author, except by one or two friends; and have heard the latter spoken of in the highest terms, as the keenest and severest piece that has appeared here for a long time. Lord Mansfield, I hear, said of it, that it *was very* ABLE *and very* ARTFUL *indeed;* and would do mischief by giving here a bad impression of the measures of government; and in the colonies, by encouraging them in their contumacy....

What made it the more noticed here was, that people in reading it were, as the phrase is, *taken in,* till they had got half through it, and imagined it a real edict, to which mistake I suppose the King of Prussia's *character* must have contributed. I was down at Lord Le Despencer's, when the post brought that day's papers. Mr. Whitehead was there, too, (Paul Whitehead, the author of "Manners,") who runs early through all the papers, and tells the company what he finds remarkable. He had them in another room, and we were chatting in the breakfast parlour, when he came running in to us, out of breath, with the paper in his hand. Here! says he, here's news for ye! *Here's the King of Prussia, claiming a right to this kingdom!* All stared, and I as much as anybody; and he went on to read it. When he had read two or three paragraphs, a gentleman present said, *Damn his impudence, I dare say, we shall hear by next post that he is upon his march with one hundred thousand men to back this.* Whitehead, who is very shrewd, soon after began to smoke it, and looking in my face said, *I'll be hanged if this is not some of your American jokes upon us.* The reading went on, and ended with abundance of laughing, and a general verdict that it was a fair hit: and the piece was cut out of the paper and preserved in my Lord's collection.

Violent events now led one to another in England and America. The uproar over the Hutchinson letters caused a tremendous reaction inside the British Government. When the Massachusetts General Court directed Franklin to submit a petition to the King, asking for the removal of Hutchinson and Oliver, the issue swiftly spread to the newspapers and aroused vigorous debate. William Whately, brother of the man who had received the letters, accused John Temple, an American friend of Franklin's, of stealing them. Temple, who had been a customs commissioner in Boston, returned to England to defend himself against accusations of favoring American smugglers and challenged Whately to a duel, which took place in Hyde Park and left Whately slightly wounded. Franklin, hearing that Whately intended to renew the combat as soon as he recovered, published the following letter on Christmas Day, 1773, admitting that he was the man who had sent the letters to Boston. Franklin later noted, as a kind of footnote to this letter, that Hutchinson had "the same idea of *duty* when he procured copies of Dr. Franklin's letters to the Assembly, and sent them to the Ministry of England."

[London, December 25, 1773]

Finding that two gentlemen have been unfortunately engaged in a duel about a transaction and its circumstance, of which both of them are totally ignorant and innocent; I think it incumbent upon me to declare (for the prevention of farther mischief, as far as such a declaration may contribute to prevent it), that I alone am the person who obtained and transmitted to Boston the letters in question. Mr. W. could not communicate them, because they were never in his possession; and for the same reason, they could not be taken from him by Mr. T. They were not of the nature of *private* letters between friends. They were written by public officers to persons in public stations, on public affairs, and intended to procure public measures; they were therefore handed to other public persons who might be influenced by them to produce those measures. Their tendency was to incense the mother country against her colonies and, by the steps recommended, to widen the breach; which they effected. The chief caution expressed with regard to privacy was, to keep their contents from the colony agents, who, the writers apprehended, might return them, or copies of them to America. That apprehension was, it seems, well founded; for the first agent who laid his hands on them, thought it his duty to transmit them to his constituents.

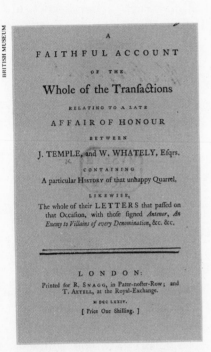

A
FAITHFUL ACCOUNT
OF THE
Whole of the Transactions
RELATING TO A LATE
AFFAIR OF HONOUR
BETWEEN
J. TEMPLE, and W. WHATELY, Esqrs.
CONTAINING
A particular History of that unhappy Quarrel,
LIKEWISE,
The whole of their LETTERS that passed on
that Occasion, with those signed *Antenor*, *An
Enemy to Villains of every Denomination*, &c. &c.

LONDON:
Printed for R. SNAGG, in Pater-noster-Row; and
T. AXTELL, at the Royal-Exchange.
M DCC LXXIV.
[ Price One Shilling. ]

*A 1774 account of the duel between
John Temple and William Whately*

Fourteen days later, Franklin was mildly astonished to discover that the petition of the Massachusetts Assembly was to receive a formal hearing before the Privy Council's Committee for Plantation Affairs on the following Tuesday, January 11. At the hearing it became evident that the British Government was determined to support Hutchinson. Alexander Wedderburn, an ambitious Scot who had recently become Solicitor General in the North Ministry, had been "hired" to defend Governor Hutchinson and Lieutenant Governor Oliver. Faced with such formidable opposition, Franklin asked for an adjournment to seek the advice of counsel. Then came news that fanned the already inflamed tempers of the British Ministry into an uncontrollable conflagration. On January 19, 1774, the British ship *Hayley* reached Dover from Boston, and three days later *The St. James's Chronicle* printed a complete description of the Boston Tea Party. The following day the ship *Polly* docked at Gravesend with its cargo of tea, rejected at Philadelphia, still in the hold. On Thursday, January 27, Governor Hutchinson's official report of the assault on British property arrived in London, and Lord North and his Cabinet met that evening to ponder the crisis. They decided, as a first step, to make an example of Benjamin Franklin. In this excerpt from his long letter to Thomas Cushing of Boston, Franklin narrated the experience in the Cockpit, the Privy Council's meeting place, that ended his love affair with England forever.

London, February 15, 1774

The transactions relating to the tea had increased and strengthened the torrent of clamour against us. No one had the least expectation of success to the petition; and, though I had asked leave to use counsel, I was half inclined to waive it, and save you the expense; but Mr. Bollan was now strongly for it, as they had refused to hear him. And, though fortified by his opinion, as he had long experience in your affairs, I would at first have ventured to deviate from the instructions you sent me in that particular, supposing you to allow some discretionary liberty to your agents; yet, now that he urged it as necessary, I employed a solicitor, and furnished him with what materials I could for framing a brief....

The briefs being prepared and perused by our counsel, we had a consultation at Mr. Dunning's chambers in Lincoln's Inn. I introduced Mr. Arthur Lee, as my friend and successor in the agency. The brief, as you will see by a copy I send you, pointed out the passages of the letters, which were applicable in support of the particular charges contained in the resolutions and petition. But the counsel observed, we wanted evidence to prove those passages false; the counsel on the other side would say, they were true representations of the state of the country; and, as to the political reflections of the writers, and their sentiments of government, their aims to extend and enforce the power of Parliament and diminish the privileges of their countrymen, though these might appear in the letters and need no other proof, yet they would never be considered here as offences, but as virtues and merits. The counsel therefore thought it would answer no good end to insist on those particulars; and that it was more advisable to state as facts the general discontent of the people, that the governors had lost all credit with them, and were become odious, &c.; facts of which the petition was itself full proof, because otherwise it could not have existed; and then show that

*The issue of* The St. James's Chronicle *that described the Boston Tea Party*

it must in such a situation be necessary for his Majesty's service, as well as the peace of the province, to remove them. By this opinion, great part of the brief became unnecessary.

Notwithstanding the intimations I had received, I could not believe that the solicitor-general would be permitted to wander from the question before their Lordships into a new case, the accusation of another person for another matter, not cognizable before them, who could not expect to be there so accused, and therefore could not be prepared for his defence. And yet all this happened, and in all probability was preconcerted; for all the courtiers were invited, as to an entertainment, and there never was such an appearance of privy counsellors on any occasion, not less than thirty-five, besides an immense crowd of other auditors.

The hearing began by reading my letter to Lord Dartmouth, enclosing the petition, then the petition itself, the resolves, and lastly the letters, the solicitor-general making no objections, nor asking any of the questions he had talked of at the preceding board. Our counsel then opened the matter, upon their general plan, and acquitted themselves very handsomely; only Mr. Dunning, having disorder on his lungs that weakened his voice exceedingly, was not so perfectly heard as one could have wished. The solicitor-general then went into what he called a history of the province for the last ten years, and bestowed plenty of abuse upon it, mingled with encomium on the governors. But the favorite part of his discourse was levelled at your agent, who stood there the butt of his invective ribaldry for near an hour, not a single Lord adverting to the impropriety and indecency of treating a public messenger in so ignominious a manner, who was present only as the person delivering your petition, with the consideration of which no part of *his* conduct had any concern. If he had done a wrong, in obtaining and transmitting the letters, that was not the tribunal where he was to be accused and tried. The cause was already before the Chancellor. Not one of their Lordships checked and recalled the orator to the business before them, but, on the contrary, a very few excepted, they seemed to enjoy highly the entertainment, and frequently burst out in loud applauses. This part of his speech was thought so good, that they have since printed

*A nineteenth-century engraving depicting Franklin's ordeal before the Lords in Council in Whitehall*

it, in order to defame me everywhere, and particularly to destroy my reputation on your side of the water; but the grosser parts of the abuse are omitted, appearing, I suppose, in their own eyes, too foul to be seen on paper....

The reply of Mr. Dunning concluded. Being very ill, and much incommoded by standing so long, his voice was so feeble, as to be scarce audible. What little I heard was very well said, but appeared to have little effect.

Their Lordship's Report, which I send you, is dated the same day. It contains a severe censure, as you will see, on the petition and the petitioners; and, as I think, a very unfair conclusion from my silence, that the charge of surreptitiously obtaining the letters was a true one; though the solicitor, as appears in the printed speech, had acquainted them that the matter was before the Chancellor; and my counsel had stated the impropriety of my answering there to charges then trying in another court. In truth I came by them honourably, and my intention in sending them was virtuous, if an endeavour to lessen the breach between two states of the same empire be such, by showing that the injuries complained of by one of them did not proceed from the other, but from traitors among themselves.

It may be supposed, that I am very angry on this occasion, and therefore I did purpose to add no reflections of mine on the treatment the Assembly and their agent have received, lest they should be thought the effects of resentment and a desire of exasperating. But, indeed, what I feel on my own account is half lost in what I feel for the public. When I see, that all petitions and complaints of grievances are so odious to government, that even the mere pipe which conveys them becomes obnoxious, I am at a loss to know how peace and union are to be maintained or restored between the different parts of the empire. Grievances cannot be redressed unless they are known; and they cannot be known but through complaints and petitions. If these are deemed affronts, and the messengers punished as offenders, who will henceforth send petitions? And who will deliver them? It has been thought a dangerous thing in any state to stop up the vent of griefs. Wise governments have therefore generally received petitions with some indulgence, even when but slightly founded. Those, who think themselves injured by their rulers, are sometimes, by a mild and prudent answer, convinced of their error. But where complaining is a crime, hope becomes despair.

The day following I received a written notice from the secretary of the general postoffice, that his Majesty's postmaster-general *found it necessary* to dismiss me from my office of deputy postmaster-general in North America.

In these same tense weeks, Franklin wrote two sharply contrasting letters to his son. The first, on February 2, only three days after his ordeal in the Cockpit, reflected the anger he was still feeling. The second displayed a cooler, more dispassionate view of the affair.

London, February 2, 1774.

This Line is just to acquaint you that I am well, and that my Office of Deputy-Postmaster is taken from me. As there is no Prospect of your being ever promoted to a better Government, and that you hold has never defray'd its Expenses, I wish you were well settled in your farm. 'Tis an honester and a more honourable, because a more independent Employment. You will hear from others the Treatment I have receiv'd. I leave you to your own Reflections and Determinations upon it....

February 18, 1774

Some tell me that it is determined to displace you likewise, but I do not know it as certain. I only give you the hint, as an Inducement to you to delay awhile your removal to Amboy, which in that Case would be an Expense and Trouble to no purpose. Perhaps they may expect that your Resentment of their Treatment of me may induce you to resign, and save them the shame of depriving you when they ought to promote. But this I would not advise you to do. Let them take your place if they want it, though in truth I think it is scarce worth your Keeping, since it has not afforded you sufficient to prevent your running every year behindhand with me. But one may make something of an Injury, nothing of a Resignation.

COLLECTION OF MRS. JAMES MANDERSON CASTLE, JR.

*William Franklin by Mather Brown*

Meanwhile, the British Ministry proceeded to espouse the policy of repression recommended by Governor Thomas Hutchinson. In a letter to Thomas Cushing, Franklin described and discussed some of the bills—the so-called Punitive, or Coercive, Acts; in America called the Intolerable Acts—being proposed to punish Boston for the Tea Party.

London, April 16, 1774.

The Torrent is still violent against America. A Bill is brought in to alter the Charter appointing the Council by the Crown, giving Power to the Governors to nominate and commission Magistrates without Consent of Council, and Forbidding any Town Meeting to be held in the Province...without the Permission of the Governor, and for that Business only for which such Permission shall be requested. The Manner of appointing Jurors is likewise to be altered. And another Bill is to provide for the Security of Persons who may be concern'd in executing or enforcing Acts of Parliament there, by directing their Trials for any thing done by them to be in some neighbouring Province or in Great Britain at the Discretion of the Governor. I hope to get the Breviates of these Bills in time to send by this Ship. They will meet with Opposition in both Houses; but there is little Hope that they will not pass, we having very few Friends in Parliament at present. The House will probably sit 'till some time in June, perhaps longer, and till they hear the Effect of these Measures in America. I think to stay here as long as they sit.... General Gage has been hastily commission'd and sent away to be your Governor. It is given out that Copies of several Letters of mine to you are sent over here to the Ministers, and that their Contents are treasonable, for which I should be prosecuted if Copies could be made Evidence. I am not conscious of any treasonable Intention, and I know that much Violence must be us'd with my Letters before they can be construed into Treason, yet having lately seen two of my Actions, one my Endeavour to lessen the Differences between the two Countries, the other to stop a dangerous Quarrel between Individuals, and which I should have thought and still think to be good Actions, condemn'd as bad ones by high Authority, I am not to wonder if less than a small Lump in my Forehead is voted a Horn. And you will not wonder if my future Letters contain mere Relations of Facts, without any of my Sentiments upon them, which perhaps I have been too forward in offering. With the greatest Respect I have the honour to be, Sir....

In the midst of this political turmoil came a personal blow that Franklin felt almost as keenly as the Stevensons did. He told about it in a letter to Deborah.

London, May 5, 1774

Our Family here is in great Distress. Poor Mrs Hewson has lost her Husband, and Mrs Stevenson her Son-in-law. He died last Sunday Morning of a Fever which baffled the Skill of our best Physicians. He was an excellent young Man, ingenious, industrious, useful, and beloved by all that knew him. She is left with two young Children, and a third soon expected. He was just established in a profitable growing Business, with the best Prospects of bringing up his young Family advantageously. They were a happy Couple!

In America the First Continental Congress met on September 5, 1774, in Philadelphia to discuss the political crisis. In a letter to Thomas Cushing, Franklin reported on the impact that the calling of this assembly, as a demonstration of American unity, had in England.

London, Sept. 3. 1774

It is a long time since I have been favoured by a Line from you. I suppose you thought me on my return to America, & that your Letters would probably not reach me here: But I have been advised by our Friends to stay till the Result of your Congress should arrive. The Coolness, Temper, & Firmness of the American Proceedings; the Unanimity of all the Colonies, in the same Sentiments of their Rights, & of the Injustice offered to Boston; and the Patience with which those Injuries are at Present borne, without the least Appearance of Submission; have a good deal surprized and disappointed our Enemies, and the Tone of Publick Conversation, which has been violently against us, begins evidently to turne; so that I make no doubt that before the meeting of Parliament it will be as general in our Favour. All who know well the State of things here, agree, that if the Non Consumption Agreement should become general, and be firmly adhered to, this Ministry must be ruined, and our Friends succeed them, from whom we may hope a great Constitutional Charter to be confirmed by King, Lords, & Commons, whereby our Liberties shall be recognized and established, as the only sure Foundation of that Union so necessary for our Common welfare. You will see a stronger Opposition in our Favour at the next Meeting of Parliament than appear'd in the last: But as I have said in former Letters, we should depend chiefly upon ourselves.

A few days later, Franklin wrote his last letter—although he did not realize it at the time—to his wife Deborah. Some six months earlier she had suffered a stroke, which had considerably impaired her physically and mentally. Apparently Franklin's son and daughter decided not to tell him about her condition, hoping no doubt that he would soon return, as he had assured William he planned to do. But she died in December, 1774, without seeing her husband again. For some fifteen of their forty-four-year married life, they had been separated.

*Deborah Franklin*

London, September 10, 1774

It is now nine long Months since I received a Line from my dear Debby. I have supposed it owing to your continual Expectation of my Return; I have feared that some Indisposition had rendered you unable to write; I have imagined any thing rather than admit a Supposition that your kind Attention towards me was abated. And yet when so many other old Friends have dropt a Line to me now and then at a Venture, taking the Chance of its finding me here or not as it might happen, why might I not have expected the same Comfort from you, who used to be so diligent and faithful a Correspondent, as to omit scarce any Opportunity?

The Continental Congress was an extralegal gathering, upon which no royal official could look with favor. It inevitably put a strain on the relationship between Franklin and his son. In the following letter, he was more than a little curt in his discussion of Governor Franklin's alternative suggestion, a congress of royal governors who would mediate the quarrel.

London, Sept. 7, 1774

You say my Presence is wish'd for at the Congress, but no Person besides in America has given me the least Intimation of such a Desire; and it is thought by the great Friends of the Colonies here, that I ought to stay till the Result of the Congress arrives, when my Presence here may be of Use. In my Opinion all depends on the Americans themselves. If they make, & keep firm Resolutions not to consume British Manufactures till their Grievances are redress'd and their Rights acknowledged, this Ministry must fall, and the aggrieving Laws be repeal'd. This is the Opinion of all wise men here.

I hear nothing of the Proposal you have made for a Congress of Governors etc. I do not so much as you do wonder that the Massachusetts have not offered Payment for the Tea: 1. Because of the uncertainty of the Act, which gives them no surety that the Port shall be opened on their making that Payment. 2, no specific Sum is demanded. 3, no one knows what will satisfy the Custom-house Officers, nor who the "others" are, that must be satisfied; nor what will satisfy them. And 4, after all they are in the King's Power, how much of the Port shall be opened. As to "doing Justice before they ask it," that should have been thought of by the Legislature here, before they demanded it of the Bostonians. They have extorted many Thousand Pounds from America unconstitutionally, under Colour of Acts of Parliament, and with an armed Force. Of this Money they ought to make Restitution. They might first have taken out Payment for the Tea, &c. and return'd the Rest. But you, who are a thorough Courtier, see every thing with Government Eyes.

It has become almost a historical cliché to picture Franklin as a voice of moderation and compromise. But in these months before the outbreak of the Revolution, he spoke with a voice that was far from temperate. What he had seen and experienced in England enraged him. Most of the time, he was able to mask this rage, but sometimes in letters to intimate correspondents it blazed out. No better example of his fury and his essential toughness exists than this letter to his Boston cousin, Jonathan Williams, Sr.

London, September 28, 1774

Cousin Jonathan showed me last night the Letters he had just received from you and his Mother. The Firmness they express, under your present Difficulties, gave me great Pleasure. The Unanimity and Resolution of the Colonies, astonishes their Enemies here, being totally unexpected. By its Continuance, you will undoubtedly carry all your Points: by giving way you will lose every thing. Strong Chains will be forged for you, and you will be made to pay for both the Iron and the Workmanship. I rejoice to see the Zeal with which your Cause is taken up by the other Colonies. But were they all to desert New England, she ought in my Opinion to hold the same Determination of defending her Rights, even if all Europe were to league with Britain in attempting to enslave her. And I think she would finally succeed; for it is inconceivable what a small, virtuous, determined People may affect, with the Blessing of God, in defence of their Liberty, against Millions of Adversaries. History gives us many Instances of this kind.

I did once wish the destroyed Tea to be voluntarily paid for, before this or any compulsory Act should be formed. But now my Opinion is, that you should state an Account, charge Government here with all the Tea Duties, and other unconstitutional Revenue Duties that have been extorted from you by an armed Force under colour of Acts of Parliament, from the Commencement of those Acts; then give Credit for the Tea, and strike a Ballance. If it be against you, offer to pay it. If for you, demand it....

The Cry against America here is greatly abated; new Advocates for her are daily arising. The Manufacturers and Merchants begin to have their Apprehensions, and will soon begin to feel what they apprehend; they will then bestir themselves in Opposition to these absurd Measures. You have only to be firm, united, and persevering.

Hutchinson, I hear, flatters the Ministry with Assurances that you will soon be tired of the Contest and submit, and he is supposed to be well acquainted with your Temper and Meanness of Spirit....

If you should ever tamely submit to the Yoke prepared for you, you cannot conceive how much you will be despised here, even by those who are endeavoring to impose it on you: your very Children and Grandchildren will curse your Memories for entailing Disgrace upon them and theirs; and making them ashamed to own their Country. If you continue on the contrary to make a virtuous, firm and steady Resistance, your very Enemies will honour you, endeavour to reconcile themselves with you, and court your Friendship: and your Friends will almost adore you. Poltroons are neither regarded by Friends or Foes. They are fit only to bear Burthens, and be paid with Contempt. They deserve no better Treatment.

This brief note, written to Edmund Burke, who was not only a leader of the opposition in Parliament but also agent for New York, succinctly described Franklin's final role in England—ambassador without portfolio for the yet-unformed American nation.

Craven Street, Monday, Dec. 19, 1774
Having just received a Petition from the American Congress to the King, with a Letter directed to the North-American Agents among whom you are named;

*Franklin's London calling card*

this is to request you would be pleased to meet the other Agents to-morrow Noon, at Waghom's Coffeehouse, Westminster, in order to consider the said Letter, and agree upon the time and manner of presenting the Petition.

A letter to Jonathan Shipley revealed Franklin's deep commitment to America. "The Speech" to which he referred was a denunciation of British policy and an unequivocal statement of support for the American cause, which Shipley had made in mid-1774. Franklin had had it printed and widely distributed in both England and America.

London, January 7, 1775

I find it impossible to visit my dear Friend at Twyford.... My Time is totally engrossed by Business.

The Petition from the Congress has been presented to the King by Lord Dartmouth to whom we delivered it for that purpose. The Answer we received was, that his Majesty had been pleased to receive it very graciously, and had commanded him to tell us, "it contained Matters of such Importance that he should as soon as they met lay it before his two Houses of Parliament." We have been advised not to let it be printed till it has been communicated to Parliament as an immediate Publication might be deemed disrespectful to the King. But I inclose a Copy for your Perusal. It will fall short of what you wish in the Manner, not equalling the admirable Remonstrances of the French Parliaments or the *Cour des Aides;* but having made some Allowances for unpolished America, you will not I hope think it much amiss. When I consider that Congress, as consisting of Men, the free, unbiased, unsollicited Choice of the Freeholders of a great Country, selected from no other Motives than the general Opinion of their Wisdom and Integrity, to transact Affairs of the greatest Importance to their Constituents, and indeed of as great Consequence as any that have come under Consideration in any great Council for Ages past; and that they have gone through them with so much Coolness, though under great Provocations to Resentment; so much Firmness, under Cause to apprehend Danger; and so much Unanimity, under every Endeavour to divide and sow Dissensions among them; I cannot but look upon them with great Veneration. And I question whether I should be so proud of any Honour any King could confer upon me, as I am of that

*Jonathan Shipley*

I received by only having my Health drank by that Assembly.

In America, some of Franklin's friends were moving in the opposite political direction. Joseph Galloway had presented a plan of union to the Continental Congress, calling for an American Parliament that would be subordinate to England's Parliament. It was narrowly defeated, six Colonies to five. Deeply offended by this rejection, and by personal attacks on his loyalty, Galloway withdrew from Congress and sent the plan to Franklin, who replied in two letters. The first, on February 5, 1775, was moderate in tone. "I cannot but lament with you the impending calamities Britain and her colonies are about to suffer from great imprudencies on both sides," he said. "Those arising there, are more in your view; these here, which I assure you are very great, in mine." His second letter, written three weeks later, was more critical. It reflected the downward spiral of his last-ditch negotiations with the British Ministry to prevent war.

London, Feb. 25, 1775.

In my last per Falconer I mention'd to you my showing your Plan of Union to Lords Chatham and Camden. I now hear, that you had sent it to Lord Dartmouth. Lord Gower I believe alluded to it, when in the House he censur'd the Congress severely, as first resolving to receive a Plan for uniting the Colonies to the Mother Country, and afterwards rejecting it, and ordering their first Resolution to be eras'd out of their Minutes. Permit me to hint to you, that it is whisper'd here by ministerial People, that yourself and Mr. Jay of New York are Friends to their Measures, and give them private Intelligence of the Views of the Popular or Country Party in America. I do not believe this; but I thought it a Duty of Friendship to acquaint you with the Report.

I have not heard what Objections were made to the Plan in the Congress, nor would I make more than this one, that, when I consider the extream Corruption prevalent among all Orders of Men in this old rotten State, and the glorious publick Virtue so predominant in our rising Country, I cannot but apprehend more Mischief than Benefit from a closer Union. I fear they will drag us after them in all the plundering Wars, which their desperate Circumstances, Injustice, and Rapacity, may prompt them to undertake; and their wide-wasting Prodigality and Profusion is a Gulph that will swallow up every Aid we may distress ourselves to afford them.

Here Numberless and needless Places, enormous

Salaries, Pensions, Perquisites, Bribes, groundless Quarrels, foolish Expeditions, false Accounts or no Accounts, Contracts and Jobbs, devour all Revenue, and produce continual Necessity in the Midst of natural Plenty. I apprehend, therefore, that to unite us intimately will only be to corrupt and poison us also. . . . However, I would try any thing, and bear any thing that can be borne with Safety to our just Liberties, rather than engage in a War with such near relations, unless compelled to it by dire Necessity in our own Defence.

But, should that Plan be again brought forward, I imagine, that, before establishing the Union, it would be necessary to agree on the following preliminary Articles.

1.   The Declaratory Act of Parliament to be repeal'd.

2.   All Acts of Parlt, or Parts of Acts, laying Duties on the Colonies to be repeal'd.

3.   All Acts of Parlt altering the Charters, or Constitutions, or Laws of any Colony, to be repeal'd.

4.   All Acts of Parlt restraining Manufacturers to be repeal'd.

5.   Those Parts of the Navigation Acts, which are for the Good of the whole Empire, such as require that Ships in the Trade should be British or Plantation built, and navigated by 3/4 British Subjects, with the Duties necessary for regulating Commerce, to be reënacted by both Parliaments.

6.   Then, to induce the Americans to see the regulating Acts faithfully executed, it would be well to give the Duties collected in each Colony to the Treasury of the Colony, and let the Govr and Assembly appoint the Officers to collect them, and proportion their Salaries. Thus the Business will be cheaper and better done, and the Misunderstandings between the two Countries, now created and fomented by the unprincipled Wretches, generally appointed from England, be entirely prevented.

These are hasty Thoughts submitted to your Consideration.

You will see the new Proposal of Lord North, made on Monday last, which I have sent to the Committee. Those in Administration, who are for violent Measures, are said to dislike it. The others rely upon it as a means of *dividing,* and by that means subduing us. But I cannot

*Franklin's staunch friend, Edmund Burke, conferred with him about a speech on conciliating the Colonies just before Franklin sailed for home.*

conceive that any Colony will undertake to grant a Revenue to a Government, that holds a Sword over their Heads with a Threat to strike the moment they cease to give, or do not give so much as it is pleas'd to expect. In such a Situation, where is the Right of giving our own Property freely, or the Right to judge of our own Ability to give? It seems to me the Language of a Highwayman, who, with a Pistol in your Face, says, "Give me your Purse, and then I will not put my Hand into your Pocket. But give me all your Money, or I will shoot you through the Head."

In clubs and in private homes during his last weeks in England, Franklin heard almost incredible contempt and scorn heaped on America. William Strahan came to him with a story about a Scottish sergeant in Boston who had captured forty American militiamen singlehanded. In a debate in the House of Lords, Franklin heard the spokesman for the Ministry make "base reflections on American courage, religion, understanding &c." Americans were condemned as "the lowest of mankind, and almost of a different species from the English of Britain." Franklin became so angry that he drew up a blazing memorial, which he considered presenting to Lord Dartmouth. It was a fiery attack on the Punitive Acts, in which he demanded "satisfaction" for damage the laws had done to Massachusetts and New England. Friends, such as Thomas Walpole, warned him that it might be considered "a national affront" and persuaded him not to submit it. By this time Franklin had reserved a cabin aboard the Pennsylvania packet and was within a few days of departing. On one of his last days in London, Franklin conferred with Edmund Burke, who was planning to make a major speech on conciliating the Colonies and wanted to take as realistic a position as possible from an American point of view. Throughout these last weeks, Franklin had been negotiating with the Ministry through intermediaries such as his Quaker friend, Dr. John Fothergill. Not long after Burke left Craven Street, Franklin received a letter from the honest doctor urging him to warn Americans—and particularly well-meaning Philadelphia Quakers—"that whatever specious pretenses are offered, (by the Ministry) they are all hollow; and that to get a larger field on which to fatten a herd of worthless parasites is all that is regarded." War was very close and Franklin knew it. On his last day in London he spent several hours with his scientist friend Joseph Priestley, going over newspapers recently arrived from America. Franklin selected articles that might win sympathy for the American cause if they were reprinted in English papers. This last attempt to play the propagandist on America's behalf, a role in which he had tragically failed, overwhelmed him. "He was frequently not able to proceed for the tears literally running down his cheeks," Priestley later said.

# Chapter 9

# The Oldest Revolutionary

At sea, en route to Philadelphia, Franklin wrote the longest letter of his life—a ninety-seven-page report detailing his futile attempt to negotiate a reconciliation between England and America. It began with two very significant words: "Dear Son." Nothing underscores more clearly Franklin's growing fear that he and William were on a collision course. When he reached Philadelphia on May 5, 1775, war had already begun. On April 19, fighting had broken out at Lexington and Concord, and the British army was now besieged inside Boston by an impromptu gathering of New England militiamen. The first letter Franklin wrote upon his arrival was also to William. While there is no evidence that they had met by this time, the letter seems to carry on an argument that had already begun. William refused to resign as Royal Governor of New Jersey, claiming that he felt obligated to the Ministry because they had not dismissed him. One thing is evident, Franklin believed that William should have resigned the moment he heard the news about Lexington.

> May 7, 1775.
>
> I don't understand it as any favour to me or to you, the being continued in an office by which, with all your prudence, you cannot void running behind-hand, if you live suitably to your Station. While you are in it I know you will execute it with fidelity to your master, but I think independence more honourable than any service, and that in the state of American Affairs which, from the present arbitrary measures is likely soon to take place, you will find yourself in no comfortable Situation, and perhaps wish you had soon disengaged yourself.

The next letter Franklin wrote was to Joseph Galloway, probably the person—after his son—he most cared about in America. Galloway had been elected to the Second Continental Congress, which was gathering in Philadelphia at this time. But he had declined to serve.

Monday, May 8, 1775

I am much obliged by your kind Congratulations. I am concerned at your Resolution of quitting public Life at a time when your Abilities are so much wanted. I hope you will change that Resolution. I hear my Son is to be at Burlington this day Week to meet his Assembly. I had purposed (if he could not conveniently come hither) to meet him there, and in my Return to visit you at Trevose. I shall know in a Day or two, how that will be. But being impatient to see you, I believe I shall accept the kind Offer of your Carriage, and come to you directly. If I conclude upon that, I shall let you know. At present I am so taken up with People coming in continually, that I cannot stir, and can scarce think what is proper or practicable.

Franklin promptly began communicating with influential friends in England, a practice he continued throughout the war. This letter to Edmund Burke made sarcastic use of the anti-American propaganda that Franklin—and Burke—had heard so often in Parliament.

Philadelphia, May 15, 1775

You will see by the Papers that Gen. Gage call'd his Assembly to propose Lord North's pacific Plan, but before they could meet drew the Sword, and began the War. His Troops made a vigorous Retreat, 20 Miles in 3 Hours, scarce to be parallell'd in History: The feeble Americans, who pelted them all the Way, could scarce keep up with them.

All People here feel themselves much oblig'd by your Endeavours to serve them. I hear your propos'd Resolves were negativ'd by a great Majority; which was denying the most notorious Truths; and a kind of rational Lying, of which they may be convicted by their own Records.

The Congress is met here, pretty full. I had not been here a Day before I was return'd a Member. We din'd together on Saturday, when your Health was among the foremost.

William Temple Franklin had come to America with his grandfather. Meeting his father and stepmother for the first time, the handsome sixteen-year-old charmed and delighted the childless William Franklins. He was soon spending most of his time at the opulent new mansion that the province of New Jersey had had built for Governor Franklin in Perth Amboy. Franklin, busy in the Continental Congress, tried to keep in touch with his grandson by mail. The "young Gentlemen" referred to were Benjamin Franklin Bache and William Bache, Sally's oldest sons.

Philada, June 13, 1775.

My dear Billy,

I wonder'd it was so long before I heard from you. The Packet it seems was brought down to Philadelphia, and carry'd back to Burlington before it came hither. I am glad to learn by your Letters that you are happy in your new Situation, and that tho' you ride out sometimes, you do not neglect your Studies. You are now in that time of Life which is the properest to store your Mind with such Knowledge as is hereafter to be ornamental and useful to you. I confide that you have too much Sense to let the Season slip. The Ancients painted *Opportunity* as an old Man with Wings to his Feet & Shoulders, a great Lock of Hair on the forepart of his Head, but bald behind; whence comes our old Saying, *Take Time by the Forelock*; as much as to say, when it is past, there is no means of pulling it back again; as there is no Lock behind to take hold of for that purpose. —

I am sorry your Things have suffered so much Damage in their Way to you; and I fear if I send the Glass you write for, it may likewise be hurt in the Carriage, as I have no Convenience at present of packing it safely, and the Boatmen and Waggoners are very careless People. If you want to use a Glass, your Father has a better, which he will lend you. But a Perspective Glass is not so good as the Eye for Prospects, because it takes in too small a Field. It is only useful to discern better some particular Objects. So, as I expect you here after the Vacation, to go to the College, I think it best to keep the Glass for you till you come, when you will find it in your Desk and Book Case with your little Beginning of a Library; and I hope about the same time your Books and Things from London will be arrived.

I have received a long Letter from Mrs. Stevenson. It is a kind of Journal for a Month after our Departure, written on different Days, & of different Dates, acquainting me who has call'd, and what is done, with all the small News. In four or five Places, she sends her Love to her dear Boy, hopes he was not very sick at Sea, &c., &c. Mrs. Hewson and the Children were well. She was

*Contemporary German engraving of the Battle of Lexington, April 19, 1775.*

*Greene homestead in Warwick, R.I.,
where Jane Mecom was sheltered*

afraid, she says, to see some of your Friends, not knowing how to excuse your not taking leave of them.

Your shirts will go by to-morrow's Stage. They are in a little Trunk, and I hope will get safe to hand. Mr & Mrs Bache send their Love to you. The young Gentlemen are well and pleas'd with your remembring them. Will has got a little Gun, marches with it, and whistles at the same time by way of Fife. I am ever, Your affectionate Grandfather

B FRANKLIN

The situation in Boston deeply concerned Franklin, from a personal as well as a political point of view. Many of his friends and relatives had been forced to flee into the country as refugees. Of particular concern was the fate of his sister Jane, who was sixty-four and in ill health. He received a letter from her early in June, telling in plaintive terms how she left town with only a few bits of furniture and clothing piled on a wagon. Franklin's old friend Catherine Ray Greene had taken Jane into her Warwick, Rhode Island, home, in spite of the fact that the house was already crowded with other refugee relatives. In the following letter Franklin replied to Jane.

Philada June 17, 1775

I wrote to you some time since, having heard from one of the Delegates that you were at Warwick, and I supposed it must be with that good Family, so I directed my Letter to you there; I hope you receiv'd it. I have since received your kind Letter of May 14. with one from dear Mrs Green. I sympathise most sincerely with you and the People of my native Town & Country. Your Account of the Distresses attending their Removal affects me greatly. I desired you to let me know if you wanted any thing, but have not since heard from you. I think so many People must be a great Burthen to that hospitable House; and I wish you to be other wise provided for as soon as possible, and I wish for the Pleasure of your Company, but I know not how long we may be allowed to continue in Quiet here if I stay here, nor how soon I may be ordered from hence; nor how convenient or inconvenient it may be for you to come hither, leaving your Goods as I suppose you have in Boston. My son tells me he has invited you to Amboy: Perhaps that may be a Retreat less liable to Disturbance than this: God only knows, but you must judge. Let me know however if I can render you any Service; and in what way. You know it will give me Pleasure.

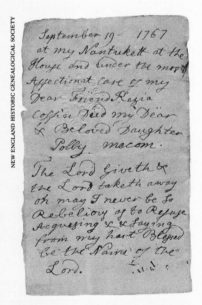

*No portrait of Jane is known to exist; reproduced here is the last page of her manuscript "Book of Ages."*

On the day Franklin wrote to Jane, the Battle of Bunker Hill was fought on Charlestown Heights outside of Boston. In the course of the battle, the town of Charlestown, a handsome village of about three hundred houses opposite Boston, was almost totally destroyed by hot shot fired from British warships. Bunker Hill aroused new rage in Franklin, and he vented it on his old friend William Strahan, who was bombarding him with letters urging him to play a conciliatory role. In this short, pungent paragraph Franklin summed up — and, perhaps, released — much of his anger. On reflection, he decided not to send the letter. But he later made use of it as a propaganda piece in the newspapers.

Philada July 5, 1775

Mr. Strahan,

You are a Member of Parliament, and one of that Majority which has doomed my Country to Destruction. — You have begun to burn our Towns, and murder our People. — Look upon your Hands! They are stained with the Blood of your Relations! — You and I were long Friends: — You are now my Enemy, — and I am

Yours,

B Franklin

Early in October, Franklin paid his last visit to Massachusetts. But it was not on the peaceful business of postmaster nor to see old friends and relations. The Continental Congress appointed him, Benjamin Harrison of Virginia, and Thomas Lynch of South Carolina to confer with George Washington on reorganizing and supplying the American army. From Washington's headquarters in Cambridge, Franklin wrote to Richard Bache.

Cambridge Headquarters, October 19, 1775

Dear Son

We hear you have had an Alarm at Philadelphia. I hope no ill consequences have attended it. I wonder I had no Line from you. I make no doubt of our People's defending their City and Country bravely, on the most trying Occasions.

I hear nothing yet of Mr Goddard, but suppose he is on the Road. I suppose we shall leave this Place next Week. I shall not return in Company with the other Delegates, as I call for my Sister, and we shall hardly be able to travel so fast, but I expect to be at Philadelphia within a few Days of them.

There has been a plentiful Year here as well as with us: And there are as many chearful Countenances among those who are driven from House and Home at Boston or lost their All at Charlestown, as among other People.

*Cartoon of the Battle of Bunker Hill*

Not a Murmer has yet been heard, that if they had been less zealous in the Cause of Liberty they might still have enjoyed their Possessions. For my own Part though I am for the most prudent Parsimony of the publick Treasure, I am not terrified by the Expence of this War, should it continue ever so long. A little more Frugality, or a little more Industry in Individuals will with Ease defray it. Suppose it 100,000 £ a Month or 1,200,000 £ a Year: If 500,000 Families will each spend a Shilling a Week less, or earn a Shilling a Week more; or if they will spend 6 pence a Week less and earn 6 pence a Week more, they may pay the whole Sum without otherwise feeling it. Forbearing to drink Tea saves three fourths of the Money; and 500,000 Women doing each threepence Worth of Spinning or Knitting in a Week will pay the rest.* I wish nevertheless most earnestly for Peace, this War being a truly unnatural and mischievous one: but we have nothing to expect from Submission but Slavery, and Contempt. I am ever Your affectionate Father

B. F.

[*Postscript:*] Love to dear Sally and the Children.

PS. Oct. 24.    We purpose setting out homewards tomorrow. Here is a fine healthy Army, wanting nothing but some Improvement in its Officers, which is daily making.

*How much more then may be done by the superior Frugality and Industry of the Men?

Franklin was not the man to remain passive in the face of British attempts to prevent the Americans from getting European aid. Congress appointed him to the Secret Committee of Foreign Correspondence, and since he had more contacts abroad than any other American, he was soon acting as the chairman. In this role, he wrote the instructions for Silas Deane, the first American agent to be sent to Europe.

Philadelphia, March 2, 1776

On your arrival in France you will for some little Time be engaged in the Business of providing goods for the Indian Trade. This will give good Countenance to your appearing in the Character of a Merchant, which we wish you continually to retain among the French in general, it being probable that the Court of France may not like it should be known publickly, that any Agent from the Colonies is in that Country.

When you come to Paris, by delivering Doctor Franklin's

Letters to Monsr Le Roy—and Monsr Dubourg, you will be introduced to a Set of acquaintance, all friends to the American cause. By conversing with them, you will have a good Opportunity of learning the Parisian French and you will find in Monsr. Dubourgh, a Man prudent, faithful, secret, intelligent in Affairs, and capable of giving you very sage advice. It is scarce necessary to pretend any other business at Paris, than the gratifying of that Curiosity which draws Numbers thither yearly, merely to see so famous a City.

With the assistance of Monsr Dubourg, who understands English, you will be able to make immediate Application to Monsr de Vergennes, Minister &c. either personally or by a Letter, if Monsr Dubourg advises that method, acquainting him, that you are in France upon Business for the American Congress in the Character of a Merchant. That having something to communicate to him that may be mutually beneficial to France and the Colonies, you request an Audience of him, and that he would be pleased to appoint the Time and place.

At this Audience, if agreed to, it may be well to show him first your Letter of Credence, and then acquaint him, that the Congress finding that in the common course of Commerce, it was not practicable to furnish the Continent of America with the Quantities of Arms and Ammunition necessary for its defence (the Ministry of Great Britain having been extremely industrious to prevent it) you have been dispatched by their Authority to apply to some European power for a supply.

That France had been pitched on for the first Application, from an Opinion that if we should, (as there is great Appearance we shall) come to a total Separation from Great Britain, France would be looked upon as the Power, whose Friendship it would be fittest for us to obtain and cultivate. That the Commercial Advantages, Britain had enjoyed with the Colonies had contributed greatly to her late Wealth and Importance.

That it is likely great part of our Commerce will naturally fall to the Share of France, especially if she favors us in this Application, as that will be a means of gaining and securing the friendship of the Colonies. And, that as our Trade rapidly increasing with our Increase of People and in a greater proportion, her part of it will be extremely valuable.

*First American agent sent to Europe*

That the Supply we at present want is Cloathing and Arms for 25,000 Men, with a suitable Quantity of Ammunition, and 100 field pieces. That we mean to pay for the same by Remittances to France, Spain, Portugal and the French Islands, as soon as our Navigation can be protected by ourselves or Friends and that we shall besides want great Quantities of Linens and Woolens, with other Articles for the Indian Trade, which you are now actually purchasing, and for which you ask no Credit; and that the whole (if France should grant the other supplies) would make a Cargoe, which it might be well to secure by a Convoy of two or three Ships of War.

If you should find Monsr. De Vergennes reserved and not inclined to enter into free conversation with you, it may be well to shorten your Visit, request him to consider what you have proposed, acquaint him with your place of lodging; that you may yet stay some time at Paris and that knowing how precious his Time is, you do not presume to ask another Audience.

But that if he should have any Commands for you, you will upon the least Notice, immediately wait upon him.

If at a future Conference, he should be more free and you find a Disposition to favor the Colonies, it may be proper to acquaint him, that they must necessarily in your Opinion be anxious to know the disposition of France on certain points, which with his Permission, you would mention. Such as, whether, if the Colonies should form themselves into an Independent State, France would probably acknowledge them as such, receive their Ambassadors, enter into any Treaty or Alliance with them, for Commerce, or defence, or both? If so, on what principal Conditions? Intimating, that you shall speedily have an Opportunity of sending to America, if you do not immediately return.

And that he may be assured of your fidelity and Secrecy in transmitting carefully any thing he would wish to convey to the Congress on that Subject.

In subsequent Conversations, you may as you find it convenient, enlarge on these Topics that have been the Subject of our Conferences with you, to which you may add occasionally, the well known substantial Answers; we usually give to the several Calumnies thrown out against us.

If these Supplies on the Credit of the Congress should

be refused, you are to endeavor the obtaining a permission of purchasing those Articles, or as much of them, as you can find credit for.

You will keep a daily Journal of all your material Transactions and particularly of what passes in your conversation with great personages; and you will by every safe Opportunity furnish us with such Information, as may be important. . . .

> B. FRANKLIN.
> B. HARRISON.
> JOHN DICKINSON.
> ROBT MORRIS.
> JOHN JAY.

Congress next sought Franklin's help in a crisis on another front. The American war effort in Canada was faltering. Congress appointed Franklin, Charles Carroll, and Samuel Chase of Maryland to investigate the situation and if possible persuade the French Canadians to support the American cause. En route, Franklin paused to mail an angry letter to another Englishman he knew was sympathetic to the American cause, Anthony Todd, Secretary of the Post Office. The sentence about "Allen and his People, with Lovell," referred to the fate of Ethan Allen, captured with several of his men while assaulting Montreal and shipped to England in chains, and James Lovell, who was imprisoned by the British and taken with them to Halifax when they evacuated Boston.

New York, March 29, 1776

Dear Sir. . . .

How long will the *Insanity* on your side the Water continue? Every day's plundering of our Property and Burning our Habitations, serves but to exasperate and unite us the more: The Breach between you and us grows daily wider and more difficult to heal. Britain without us can grow no stronger; without her we shall become a tenfold greater and mightier people. Do you choose to have so increasing a Nation of Enemies? Do you think it prudent by your Barbarities to fix us in a rooted hatred of your Nation, and make all our innumerable Posterity detest you? Yet this is the way in which you are now proceeding. Our Primers begin to be printed with Cutts of the Burning of Charlestown, of Falmouth, of James-Town, of Norfolk, with the Flight of Women and Children from these defenceless Places, some falling by Shot in their Flight. Allen and his People, with Lovell an amiable Character and a Man of Letters all in CHAINS on board your Ships;* while we treat your People that are our Prisoners with the utmost Kindness and Humanity. Your Ministers may imagine that we shall soon be tired of this, and submit, but they are mistaken, as you may recollect they have been hitherto in every Instance, in which I told you at the time that they were mistaken. And I now venture to tell you, that though this War may be a long one (and I think it will probably last beyond my Time) we shall with God's Help finally get the better of you; the Consequences I leave to your Imagination....

P.S.    Since writing the above I have been riding round the Skirts of this Town to view the Works, they are but lately begun but prodigiously forward, all Ranks of People working at them as Volunteers with the greatest Alacrity and without pay, to have them ready for the Reception of Genl. Howe, who having finished his Visit to Boston is daily expected here.

What will you do with this Spirit? You can have no Conception of Merchants and Gentlemen working with Spades and Wheelbarrows among Porters and Negroes. I suppose you will scarce believe it.

[*In the margin:*] *Is any body among you weak enough to imagine that these *Mischiefs* are neither to be paid for nor be revenged?

The trip to Canada proved to be an exhausting experience for a man of seventy. Only the hospitality of Philip Schuyler and his family, first at Albany and then at their country home in Saratoga, enabled Franklin to survive. For a few days he was so weak that he felt death was imminent, and he wrote farewell letters, such as this one to Josiah Quincy of Boston. His son Josiah Quincy, Jr., had visited Franklin in London in late 1774, and had died on the voyage home. The letter is perhaps most interesting because of Franklin's comments on the steady progress toward a declaration of independence in the Continental Congress—progress to which he lent all his influence, from the day he landed in Philadelphia. "Troublesome neighbors" was a reference to the British army, which had evacuated Boston on March 17, 1776.

Saratoga, April 15, 1776.

I am here on my way to Canada, detained by the present state of the Lakes, in which the unthawed ice obstructs navigation. I begin to apprehend that I have undertaken a fatigue, that, at my time of life, may prove too much for me; so I sit down to write to a few friends by way of farewell.

I congratulate you on the departure of your late troublesome neighbours. I hope your country will now for some time have rest, and that care will be taken so to fortify Boston, as that no force shall be able again to get footing there. Your very kind letter of November 13th, enclosing Lord Chatham's and Lord Camden's speeches, I duly received. I think no one can be more sensible than I am of the favours of corresponding friends, but I find it impossible to answer as I ought. At present I think you will deem me inexcusable, and therefore I will not attempt an apology. But if you should ever happen to be at the same time oppressed with years and business, you may then extenuate a little for your old friend.

The notes of the speeches taken by your son, whose loss I shall ever deplore with you, are exceedingly valuable, as being by much the best account preserved of that day's debate.

You ask, "When is the Continental Congress by *general consent* to be formed into a supreme legislature; alliances, defensive and offensive, formed; our ports opened; and a formidable naval force established at the public charge?" I can only answer at present, that nothing seems wanting but that "general consent." The novelty of the thing deters some, the doubt of success, others, the vain hope of reconciliation, many. But our enemies take continually every proper measure to remove these obstacles, and their endeavours are attended with success, since every day furnishes us with new causes of increasing enmity, and new reasons for wishing an eternal separation; so that there is a rapid increase of the formerly small party, who were for an independent government.

*Philip Schuyler's home in Saratoga*

LOSSING, *Pictorial Fieldbook of the Revolution*

Canada was brutally cold and unpleasant, and it was evident to Franklin and his fellow commissioners that the situation was hopeless. The French Canadians had no interest in siding with the Protestant Americans, the British had reinforced Quebec, and the American army was on the brink of disintegration. Franklin left his fellow commissioners to do what they could, and went home. Exhausted and ill, Franklin took little part in the feverish politicking in the Continental Congress that preceded the Declaration of Independence. Gout may not have been the only reason for his nonattendance. On June 17, Governor William Franklin of New Jersey was arrested and arraigned before a committee of the New Jersey

Assembly as "a virulent enemy of this country." Refusing to sign a parole, which would have permitted him to live unmolested on his farm near Burlington, New Jersey, William was sent to jail in Connecticut. Franklin did not, of course, mention his personal embarrassment in this letter to George Washington.

> Philadelphia, June 21. 76
>
> I am much obliged by your kind Care of my unfortunate Letter, which at last came safe to Hand. — I see in it a Detail of the Mighty Force we are threatened with; which however I think is not certain will ever arrive; and I see more certainly the Ruin of Britain if she persists in such expensive distant Expeditions, which will probably prove more disastrous to her than anciently her Wars in the Holy Land. —
>
> I return Gen. Sulivan's Letter enclos'd: Am glad to find him in such Spirits. — and that the Canadians are returning to their regard for us. — I am just recovering from a severe Fit of the Gout, which has kept me from Congress & Company almost ever since you left us, so that I know little of what has pass'd there, except that a Declaration of Independence is preparing.

Although Franklin was a member of the committee directed to prepare a declaration of independence, he changed only a few minor words in Jefferson's draft. There is no clear historical evidence that he said, as he signed it, "We must all hang together, or we will all hang separately." But the tradition is a strong one, and the expression was current in Congress at the time. Not many days after the Declaration was voted, Franklin received a letter from Richard Lord Howe, who had come to America in the dual role of peace commissioner and commander in chief of the British navy. His brother, General Sir William Howe, was in command of the British army. Lord Howe had been one of the unofficial spokesmen for the Government in the fruitless negotiations Franklin conducted in London to prevent the war. In America, Howe declared the purpose of his mission was the "establishment of lasting peace and union with the colonies." He hoped the "deep-rooted prejudices of America, and the necessity of preventing her trade from passing into foreign channels" would not "keep us still a divided people." Franklin's tough reply was not calculated to raise his Lordship's hopes.

> Philadelphia, July 30th, 1776.
>
> My Lord,
>
> I receiv'd safe the Letters your Lordship so kindly forwarded to me, and beg you to accept my thanks.
>
> The official dispatches, to which you refer me, contain

nothing more than what we had seen in the Act of Parliament, viz. Offers of Pardon upon Submission, which I was sorry to find, as it must give your Lordship Pain to be sent upon so fruitless a Business.

Directing Pardons to be offered to the Colonies, who are the very Parties injured, expresses indeed that Opinion of our Ignorance, Baseness, and Insensibility, which your uninform'd and proud Nation has long been pleased to entertain of us; but it can have no other effect than that of increasing our Resentments. It is impossible we should think of Submission to a Government, that has with the most wanton Barbarity and Cruelty burnt our defenceless Towns in the midst of Winter, excited the Savages to massacre our Peacefull Farmers, and our Slaves to murder their Masters, and is even now bringing foreign Mercenaries to deluge our Settlements with Blood. These atrocious Injuries have extinguished every remaining Spark of Affection for that Parent Country we once held so dear; but, were it possible for *us* to forget and forgive them, it is not possible for *you* (I mean the British Nation) to forgive the People you have so heavily injured. You can never confide again in those as Fellow Subjects, and permit them to enjoy equal Freedom, to whom you know you have given such just Cause of lasting Enmity. And this must impel you, were we again under your Government, to endeavour the breaking our Spirit by the severest Tyranny, and obstructing, by every Means in your Power, our growing Strength and Prosperity.

But your Lordship mentions "the King's paternal solicitude of promoting the Establishment of lasting *Peace* and Union with the Colonies." If by Peace is here meant a Peace to be entered into between Britain and America, as distinct States now at War, and his Majesty has given your Lordship Powers to treat with us of such a Peace, I may venture to say, though without Authority, that I think a Treaty for that purpose not yet quite impracticable, before we enter into foreign Alliances. But I am persuaded you have no such Powers. Your nation, though, by punishing those American Governors, who have fomented the Discord, rebuilding our burnt Towns, and repairing as far as possible the mischiefs done us, might yet recover a great Share of our Regard, and the greatest Part of

*Lord Howe by H. Singleton*

our growing Commerce, with all the Advantage of that additional Strength to be derived from a Friendship with us; but I know too well her abounding Pride and deficient Wisdom, to believe she will ever take such salutary Measures. Her Fondness for Conquest, as a warlike Nation, her lust of Dominion, as an ambitious one, and her wish for a gainful Monopoly, as a commercial One, (none of them legitimate Causes of war,) will all join to hide from her Eyes every view of her true Interests, and continually goad her on in those ruinous distant Expeditions, so destructive both of Lives and Treasure, that must prove as pernicious to her in the End, as the Crusades formerly were to most of the Nations in Europe.

I have not the Vanity, my Lord, to think of intimidating by thus predicting the Effects of this War; for I know it will in England have the Fate of all my former Predictions, not to be believed till the Event shall verify it.

Long did I endeavour, with unfeigned and unwearied Zeal, to preserve from breaking that fine and noble China Vase, the British Empire; for I knew, that, being once broken, the separate Parts could not retain even their Shares of the Strength and Value that existed in the Whole, and that a perfect Reunion of those Parts could scarce ever be hoped for. Your Lordship may possibly remember the tears of Joy that wet my Cheek, when, at your good Sister's in London, you once gave me Expectations that a Reconciliation might soon take Place. I had the Misfortune to find those Expectations disappointed, and to be treated as the Cause of the Mischief I was laboring to prevent. My Consolation under that groundless and malevolent Treatment was, that I retained the Friendship of many wise and good Men in that country, and, among the rest, some Share in the Regard of Lord Howe.

The well-founded Esteem, and, permit me to say, Affection, which I shall always have for your Lordship, makes it Painful to me to see you engaged in conducting a War, the great Ground of which, as expressed in your Letter, is "the necessity of preventing the American trade from passing into foreign Channels." To me it seems, that neither the Obtaining or Retaining of any trade, how valuable soever, is an Object for which men

*Center section of the State House in Philadelphia, as it looked when Congress was in session during 1776*

may justly spill each other's Blood; that the true and sure Means of extending and securing Commerce is the goodness and Cheapness of Commodities; and that the profit of no trade can ever be equal to the Expence of compelling it, and holding it, by Fleets and Armies.

I consider this War against us, therefore, as both unjust and unwise; and I am persuaded, that cool, dispassionate Posterity will condemn to Infamy those who advised it; and that even Success will not save from some Degree of Dishonor those, who voluntarily engaged to Conduct it. I know your great motive in coming hither was the hope of being Instrumental in a Reconciliation; and I believe, when you find *that* to be impossible on any Terms given you to propose, you will relinquish so odious a Command, and return to a more honourable private Station.

With her husband in jail, Elizabeth Franklin wrote tearful letters to Temple, in Philadelphia, telling how the local American troops were abusing her and plundering the Governor's property. Temple received permission from his grandfather to visit his stepmother. Meanwhile the British army, in their campaign to seize New York, was moving toward a clash with George Washington's Americans. A battle began on Long Island at dawn on the day that Franklin wrote this letter. The "dear little Girl" Franklin mentions was Sally Bache's short-lived fourth child, born December 1, 1775.

Philadelphia, August 27, 1776

Dear Grandson

Your Letter acquainting us with your safe Arrival was very agreable to us all. But as you are near the Scene of Action, we wish to hear from you by every Post, and to have all the News. It will cost you but little Trouble to write, and will give us much Satisfaction.

The Family has been in great Grief, from the Loss of our dear little Girl. She suffer'd much: but is now at Rest. Will is to come home to-morrow; he will help to comfort us.

Give my Love to your Mother, and let me know what you hear from your Father.

I am, Your affectionate Grand Father

B FRANKLIN

[*Postscript:*] Say how you spend your time; I hope in some Improvement.

All sorts of requests and calls for help from soldiers and citizens rained in upon Franklin. In Congress, meanwhile, he struggled in vain to persuade his fellow Americans to make the compromises necessary to create a confederacy. Yet he remained optimistic. As he wrote this letter to Anthony Wayne, replying to his request for aid for the Pennsylvania troops stationed at Ticonderoga, Franklin did not know that by this time the American army on Long Island had been badly beaten and driven into its entrenchments on Brooklyn Heights.

Philadelphia, August 28, 1776

I have received two of your Favours, which were immediately communicated to the Board of War, who are in Committee of Congress appointed to take Care of every thing in that Department, and who will I make no doubt take the necessary Measures for supplying your Wants. But as America is new in the Business of Providing for Armies, there must be for a time Deficiencies that are very inconvenient to the Troops, and which Experience only can bring us into the Mode of Preventing. I am pleas'd to find your People bear them with a Soldierly Spirit, and I hope they will soon be remedied.

A general Action is every day expected at New York. If the Enemy is beaten, it will probably be decisive as to them; for they can hardly produce such another Armament for another Campaign: But our growing Country can bear considerable Losses, and recover them, so that a Defeat on our part will not by any means occasion our giving up the Cause. Much depends on the Bravery of you who are posted at Ticonderoga. If you prevent the Junction of the two Armies, their Project for this Year will be broken, the Credit of the British Arms thro'out Europe and of the Ministry in England will be demolish'd, and the Nation grow sick of the Contest.

I am much oblig'd by your Draft of the Situation of our Troops, and of the Defences. I pray heartily for your Success, not doubting you will deserve it.

The greatest Unanimity continues in the Congress. The Convention of this Province is sitting, engag'd in framing a new Government. The greatest Part of our Militia are in New Jersey. Arms and Ammunition are daily arriving, the French Government having resolv'd to wink at the Supplying of us: So that in another Year our People throughout the Continent will be both better

arm'd and better disciplin'd, as most of them will have some Experience of a Camp Life and actual Service.

Meanwhile, Franklin had to cope with a loyalist uprising in his own family. William Temple Franklin asked for permission to visit his father, to carry a letter from his stepmother to him. This did not justify the trip in Franklin's opinion. Temple apparently wrote a rather angry reply to his grandfather, defending his projected trip and showing the strong influence of his loyalist stepmother. In his reply, Franklin tried to avoid a quarrel. Jonathan Trumbull was chief executive of Connecticut.

Philada Sept. 22. 1776

Dear Grandson,

You are mistaken in imagining that I am apprehensive of your carrying dangerous Intelligence to your Father; for while he remains where he is, he could make no use of it were you to know and acquaint him with all that passes. You would have been more in the right if you would have suspected me of a little tender Concern for your Welfare, on Acct of the Length of the Journey, your Youth and Inexperience, the Number of Sick returning on that Road with the Infectious Camp Distemper, which makes the Beds unsafe, together with the Loss of Time in your Studies, of which I fear you begin to grow tired. To send you on such a Journey merely to avoid the being oblig'd to Govr Trumbull for so small a Favour as the forwarding a Letter, seems to me inconsistent with your Mothers usual Prudence. I rather think the Project takes its rise from your own Inclination to a Ramble, & Disinclination for Returning to College, join'd with a Desire I do not blame of seeing a Father you have so much Reason to love, — They send to me from the Office for my Letter, so I cannot add more than to acquaint you, I shall by next post if desired send several Frank'd Covers directed to Govr Trumbull, for Mrs. F. to use as she has occasion. I write to him in the first now sent, to introduce her Request. She may desire her Husband to send his Letters to her under Cover to me. It will make but 2 Days odds. The Family is well & join in Love to her & you,

Your affectionate Grandfather
B FRANKLIN

*Franklin's friend Josiah Wedgwood, an American sympathizer, made these three medallions of Franklin (left, above), his son William, and his grandson William Temple (above).*

Six days later, Franklin wrote a cryptic note to Temple, which settled the unspoken argument about the young man's political destiny. The "something offering" was the opportunity to accompany Franklin to France as his secretary. The Congress had appointed Franklin, Silas Deane, and Thomas Jefferson (later replaced by Arthur Lee) commissioners to negotiate a treaty of alliance with France.

Philadelphia, September 28, 1776

Dear Temple,

I hope you will return hither immediately, and that your Mother will make no Objection to it, something offering here that will be much to your Advantage if you are not out of the Way. I am so hurried that I can only add Ever your affectionate Grandfather.

B FRANKLIN

[Postscript:] My Love to her.

On the eve of Franklin's departure for France, the prospects for America's future seemed grim. Washington's army had suffered two serious defeats at New York and had abandoned the city. Congress was in disarray, unable to agree on articles of confederation, because the small states feared the power of the large states. Yet Franklin remained undaunted. As a last gesture of defiance and determination, he pledged his property in Philadelphia and raised four thousand pounds, which he lent to Congress. On the day before he sailed, he wrote the following letter to an unknown correspondent, probably in Boston. The fragment of the letter was later communicated to the Massachusetts Council.

Philadelphia, October 25, 1776

BEING once more ordered to Europe, and to embark this day, I write this line, etc.

As to our public affairs, I hope our people will keep up their courage. I have no doubt of their finally succeeding by the blessing of God, nor have I any doubt that so good a cause will fail of that blessing. It is computed that we have already taken a million sterling from the enemy. They must soon be sick of their piratical project. No time should be lost in fortifying three or four posts on our extended coast as strong as art and expense can make them. Nothing will give us greater weight and importance in the eyes of the commercial states than a conviction that we can annoy, on occasion, their trade and carry our prizes into safe harbours; and whatever expense we are at in such fortifying will be soon repaid by the encouragement and success of privateering.

# Chapter 10

# Bonhomme Richard

In spite of the optimistic reports that Franklin had received while he was in America, the mood of the French Government was far from the whole-hearted support that the American Revolution so desperately needed. The French people instinctively sympathized with the Americans, but King Louis XVI and many of his advisers feared that France lacked the financial resources to fight a war with England. They espoused a wait-and-see policy. If the Americans successfully resisted the English, and made it clear they were an ally worth having in a war, France would consider joining them. Franklin had barely landed in the little fishing village of Auray, than he went to work to convince the French that the Americans were more than holding their own. This letter was written to Barbeu Dubourg, translator of many of Franklin's writings.

Auray in Brittany, December 4, 1776.
My dear good friend will be much surprised to receive a letter from me dated in France, when neither of us had been expecting such a thing. I left Philadelphia the 26th of October, on a vessel of war, belonging to Congress, and in thirty days dropped anchor in Quiberon Bay. On our voyage we captured two British vessels and brought them with us. Our ship is destined for Nantes, but the wind being unfavourable to entering the Loire, we waited some days in Quiberon Bay, until becoming impatient to put my feet on land, I availed myself of a boat to get here, whence I shall go by land to Nantes, where I shall probably rest for a few days. Learning that the post leaves here this evening, I seize the opportunity to salute you, as well as my dear Madame Dubourg and Mesdlles. Prehesson and Basseport, whom I hope soon to have the pleasure of finding in good health.

*The port of Auray, where Franklin landed on his arrival in France*

I suppose that Messrs. Deane and Morris have the honour of being known to you, and as I do not know their address, I take the liberty of addressing each of them a word under your cover, and beg you to transmit it to them. I shall see to the reimbursement of your expenses.

I see that you have had bad news of our affairs in America, but they are not true. The British, with the assistance of their ships, have gained a footing in two islands, but they have not extended their foothold on the continent, where we hold them at a respectful distance. Our armies were one or two miles apart when I left, and both entrenched. In different skirmishes which had occurred lately between parties of five hundred and a thousand men on each side, we have always had the advantage, and have driven them from the field with loss, our fire being more destructive than theirs. On the sea we have seriously molested their commerce, taking large numbers of their ships in the West Indies, which are daily brought to our ports. But I do not care to dwell upon these subjects until I shall have the pleasure of seeing you.

Franklin had brought with him not only William Temple Franklin, but also Sally's son, seven-year-old Benjamin Franklin Bache. In a journal Franklin kept of their trip, most of which has been lost, he recorded the journey from Auray to Nantes in the following words: "The carriage was a miserable one, with tired horses, the evening dark, scarce a traveler but ourselves on the road; and to make it more *comfortable,* the driver stopped near a wood we were to pass through, to tell us that a gang of eighteen robbers infested that wood, who but two weeks ago had robbed and murdered some travelers on that very spot." In Nantes Franklin wrote to Silas Deane, who had been in Paris more than six months, working for the American Government.

Nantes, December 7, 1776
I wrote a Line to you on Wednesday last, from Auray (where I landed out of the Ship of War that brought me over) acquainting you with my Arrival and with our Appointment (jointly with Mr Arthur Lee) to negotiate a Treaty of Commerce and Friendship with the Court of France, for which I have with me ample Instructions. I have acquainted no one here with this Commission, continuing incog. as to my publick Character; because not being sufficiently acquainted with the Disposition and present Circumstances of this Court, relative to our

Contest with GB. I cannot judge whether it would be agreable to her at this time to receive publickly Ministers from the Congress as such, and I think we should not embarras her unnecessarily on the one hand, nor subject ourselves to the Hazard of a disgraceful Refusal on the other. I therefore send you herewith a Copy of our Commission, that you may have time to consider and advise upon it before my Arrival at Paris, for which Place I shall set out as soon as I can, being oblig'd to wait here a little for my Baggage, which continues on board the Ship, and the Wind has not yet been favourable to bring her from Quiberon Bay into this River. We are impowered by a Vote of Congress, to live in such a Stile at Paris, as we shall find proper. A Cargo, suppos'd to the Value of 3000£ Sterling brought in the Ship with me is to be sold by our Merchants here, and the Produce is to be subject to the Drafts of the Commissioners towards their Expences. And the Committee have Orders to add to the Fund, till they make it up 10,000 £. *I requested you to provide me a Lodging. If in the same Hotel with you, it will be the more agreable.* I have with me two Grandsons; one about 16, who will serve me as a private Secretary; the other a Child of 7, whom I purpose to place in some Boarding School, that he may early learn the French Language. One Bed in the meantime may serve them both; but I must have them in the same Lodging with me till I can place the young one. M. Penet talks of accompanying me to Paris. I suppose we may set out about the Middle of next Week, but cannot be certain, because it depends on my receiving my Baggage, and that depends on the Winds. In the mean time it would be a vast Satisfaction to me to hear from you, or meet you, but I do not see how it can be manag'd.

*The Count de Vergennes*

Soon settled in the Hôtel de Hambourg with Silas Deane Franklin lost no time going to work on his diplomatic business. The first letter was to the French Foreign Minister, the Count de Vergennes, the second to the Committee of Secret Correspondence.

Paris, December 23, 1776.

I beg leave to acquaint your Excellency that we are appointed and fully empowered by the Congress of the United States of America to propose and negotiate a treaty of amity and commerce between France and the United States. The just and generous treatment their trading ships have received by a free admission into the ports of this kingdom, with other considerations of respect, has induced the Congress to make this offer first to France. We request an audience of your Excellency, wherein we may have an opportunity of presenting our credentials, and we flatter ourselves that the propositions we are authorized to make are such as will not be found unacceptable.

With the greatest regard, we have the honour to be,
Your Excellency's most obedient
and most humble servants,
B FRANKLIN,
SILAS DEANE,
ARTHUR LEE.

Paris, January 4, 1777

I arrived here about two weeks since, where I found Mr. Deane. Mr. Lee has since joined us from London. We have had an Audience of the Minister Count De Vergennes, and were respectfully received. We left for his consideration a sketch of the proposed treaty. We are to wait upon him to-morrow with a strong memorial, requesting the aids mentioned in our instructions. By his advice, we had an Interview with the Spanish ambassador, Count d'Aranda, who seems well disposed towards us, and will forward copies of our memorials to his court, which will act, he says, in perfect concert with this. Their fleets are said to be in fine order, manned and fit for the sea. The cry of this nation is for us, but the court, it is thought, views an approaching war with reluctance. The press continues in England. As soon as we can receive a positive answer from these courts we shall despatch an express with it.

*Arthur Lee by John Trumbull*

At the same time, Franklin did not forget his friends. One of the first letters he wrote to England went to Polly Stevenson Hewson. The marten fur cap was an item that Franklin had picked up on his trip to Canada. He wore it in Paris, partly because a scalp irritation made wearing a wig uncomfortable. Another, stronger reason was the striking effect it had on the Parisians, who regarded it as an example of American simplicity and boldness. For a Frenchman, defiance of fashion was the height of courage. It was for such shrewd propaganda strokes—and the popularity of his book, *The Way to Wealth*—that Franklin became known throughout France as Bonhomme Richard.

Paris, Jan. 12, 1777

My dear, dear Polly,

Figure to yourself an old Man, with grey Hair Appearing under a Martin Fur Cap, among the Powder'd Heads of Paris. It is this odd Figure that salutes you, with handfuls of Blessings on you and your dear little ones.

On my Arrival here, Mlle. Biheron gave me great Pleasure in the Perusal of a Letter from you to her. It acquainted me that you and yours were well in August last. I have with me here my young Grandson, Benja. Franklin Bache, a special good Boy. I give him a little French Language and Address, and then send him over to pay his Respects to Miss Hewson. My Love to all that love you, particularly to dear Polly. I am ever, my dear Friend, your affectionate

B FRANKLIN

P.S.    Temple, who attends me here, presents his Respects. I must contrive to get you to America. I want all my Friends out of that wicked Country. I have just seen in the Papers 7 Paragraphs about me, of which 6 were Lies.

A few days later, Franklin said farewell to that English dream that had absorbed so much of his time and attention—the western colony. In this letter to Thomas Walpole, he also seized the opportunity to do a little propagandizing with that influential Englishman, who was in close touch with many leading politicians. Major Trent was William Trent, one of the American partners in the Grand Ohio Company.

Paris, January 12, 1777

I left Major Trent well. He had Thoughts of applying to Congress relating to the Lands of our Purchase, but was dissuaded by Mr Galloway. I had some Information that Virginia, which claims all the Crown Lands within its Boundary, will not dispute that Purchase with us, but expects the Purchase-Money to be paid into their Treasury. It may be long before these Matters can be adjusted; and longer still before we shall see Peace. Had Lord Chatham's first wise Motion for withdrawing the Troops, been attended to by your mad Ministry; or his Plan of Accommodation been accepted and carried into Execution, all this Mischief might have been prevented. If that great Man be yet living, I pray you to present my affectionate Respects to him, and also to Lord Camden.

As the Money I left with your good Brother cannot now be of any Use to me in England, I request a Letter of

Credit for the Amount on some Banker here: I mean the Money for my two Shares.

About this time Franklin wrote a less important but more interesting letter to Julianna Ritchie, wife of Philadelphia merchant William Ritchie. Writing from Cambrai, where she was living as a governess to five wealthy young Englishwomen who were studying in France, she had warned Franklin that he was surrounded by spies—which was nothing less than the truth. Franklin's reply reveals his keen insight into the nature of his mission. He had already seen that the more the British learned about the French Government's clandestine aid to America, the more likely they were to declare war on France.

> Paris, Jan. 19, 1777.
>
> I am much oblig'd to you for your kind Attention to my Welfare in the Information you give me. I have no doubt of its being well founded. But as it is impossible to discover in every case the Falsity of pretended Friends who would know our Affairs; and more so to prevent being watch'd by Spies, when interested People may think proper to place them for that Purpose; I have long observ'd one Rule which prevents any Inconvenience from such Practices. It is simply this, to be concern'd in no Affairs that I should blush to have made publick, and to do nothing but what Spies may see & welcome. When a Man's Actions are just & honourable, the more they are known, the more his Reputation is increas'd & establish'd. If I was sure therefore that my Valet de Place was a Spy, as probably he is, I think I should not discharge him for that, if in other Respects I lik'd him. The various Conjectures you mention concerning my Business here must have their Course. They amuse those that make them, & some of those that hear them; they do me no harm, and therefore it is not necessary that I should take the least Pains to rectify them.

A few days later, Franklin wrote in a far sterner tone to Joseph Priestley. The "Fix'd Air" to which he referred was oxygen, which Priestley had discovered in 1772.

> Paris, Jan. 27, 1777.
>
> I received your very kind Letter of Feby last, some time in September. Major Carleton, who was so kind as to forward it to me, had not an Opportunity of doing it sooner. I rejoice to hear of your continual Progress in those useful Discoveries; I find that you have set all the

Philosophers of Europe at Work upon Fix'd Air; and it is with great Pleasure I observe how high you stand in their Opinion; for I enjoy my Friends' fame as my own.

The Hint you gave me jocularly, that you did not quite despair of the Philosopher's Stone, draws from me a Request, that, when you have found it, you will take care to lose it again; for I believe in my conscience, that Mankind are wicked enough to continue slaughtering one another as long as they can find Money to pay the Butchers. But, of all the Wars in my time, this on the part of England appears to me the wickedest; having no Cause but Malice against Liberty, and the Jealousy of Commerce. And I think the Crime seems likely to meet with its proper Punishment; a total loss of her own Liberty, and the Destruction of her own Commerce.

I suppose you would like to know something of the state of Affairs in America. In all Probability we shall be much stronger the next campaign than we were in the last; better arm'd, better disciplin'd, and with more Ammunition. When I was at the camp before Boston, the Army had not 5 Rounds of Powder a Man. This was kept a Secret even from our People. The World wonder'd that we so seldom fir'd a Cannon; we could not afford it; but we now make Powder in Plenty.

To me it seems, as it has always done, that this War must end in our favour, and in the Ruin of Britain, if she does not speedily put an end to it. An English Gentleman here the other day, in Company with some French, remarked, that it was folly in France not to make War immediately; *And in England,* reply'd one of them, *not to make Peace.*

Do not believe the reports you hear of our internal Divisions. We are, I believe, as much united as any People ever were, and as firmly.

Meanwhile, Franklin kept the pressure on the French. This letter, signed by the three American commissioners, was aimed at forcing France to abandon its policy of watchful waiting. The promise of no separate peace exceeded the commissioners' instructions from Congress, but they had jointly decided it was worth the risk.

Paris, Feb. 2d. 1777.

It is considered that in the present situation of things at the Courts of France and Spain, we find no probability of obtaining any effectual aid, alliance or declaration of war against Great Britain, without the following stipulation; therefore

We the Commissioners plenipotentiary from the Congress of the United States of America, are unanimously of Opinion, that if France and Spain should conclude a Treaty of Amity and Commerce with our States, and enter into a War with Great Britain in consequence of that, or of open aid given to our States; it will be right and proper for us, or in absence of the others, for any one of us, to stipulate and agree that the United States shall not separately conclude a Peace, nor aid Great Britain against France or Spain, nor intermit their best exertions against Great Britain during the continuance of such War. Provided always that France and Spain, do on their part enter into a similar stipulation, with our States.

Good news from America—Washington's Christmas Day victory at Trenton—inspired Franklin to reach for his pen and write one of his best satires, directed at the British policy of hiring Hessians. It was addressed from the Count de Schaumbergh to the Baron Hohendorf, commanding the Hessian troops in America.

Rome, February 18, 1777.

On my return from Naples, I received at Rome your letter of the 27th December of last year. I have learned with unspeakable pleasure the courage our troops exhibited at Trenton, and you cannot imagine my joy on being told that of the 1950 Hessians engaged in the fight, but 345 escaped. There were just 1605 men killed, and I cannot sufficiently commend your prudence in sending an exact list of the dead to my minister in London. This precaution was the more necessary, as the report sent to the English ministry does not give but 1455 dead. This would make 483,450 florins instead of 643,500 which I am entitled to demand under our convention. You will comprehend the prejudice which such an error would work in my finances, and I do not doubt you will take the necessary pains to prove that Lord North's list is false and yours correct.

The court of London objects that there were a hundred wounded who ought not to be included in the list, nor paid for as dead; but I trust you will not overlook my instructions to you on quitting Cassel, and that you will not have tried by human succor to recall the life of the unfortunates whose days could not be lengthened but by the loss of a leg or an arm. That would be making them a

BOTH: ANNE S. K. BROWN MILITARY COLLECTION

*Above and opposite, groups of*
*Hessian soldiers in America*

pernicious present, and I am sure they would rather die than live in a condition no longer fit for any service. I do not mean by this that you should assassinate them; we should be humane, my dear Baron, but you may insinuate to the surgeons with entire propriety that a crippled man is a reproach to their profession, and that there is no wiser course than to let every one of them die when he ceases to be fit to fight.

I am about to send to you some new recruits. Don't economize them. Remember glory before all things. Glory is true wealth. There is nothing degrades the soldier like the love of money. He must care only for honour and reputation, but this reputation must be acquired in the midst of dangers. A battle gained without costing the conqueror any blood is an inglorious success, while the conquered cover themselves with glory by perishing with their arms in their hands. Do you remember that of the 300 Lacedaemonians who defended the defile of Thermopylae, not one returned? How happy should I be could I say the same of my brave Hessians!

It is true that their king, Leonidas, perished with them: but things have changed, and it is no longer the custom for princes of the empire to go and fight in America for a cause with which they have no concern. And besides, to whom should they pay the thirty guineas per man if I did not stay in Europe to receive them? Then, it is necessary also that I be ready to send recruits to replace the men you lose. For this purpose I must return to Hesse. It is true, grown men are becoming scarce there, but I will send you boys. Besides, the scarcer the commodity the higher the price.

Requests for letters of recommendation from Frenchmen eager to try their luck in America were a constant torment to Franklin. In a cooler moment, Franklin attacked the problem with humor and wrote one of his more famous compositions, "Model of a Letter of Recommendation of a Person You Are Unacquainted With." Temple Franklin says that his grandfather actually used it several times in France to shame persons who were making especially indiscreet applications.

Paris, April 2, 1777.

The bearer of this, who is going to America, presses me to give him a Letter of Recommendation, tho' I know nothing of him, not even his name. This may seem extraordinary, but I assure you it is not uncommon here.

Sometimes, indeed one unknown Person brings another equally unknown, to recommend him; and sometimes they recommend one another! As to this Gentleman, I must refer you to himself for his Character and Merits, with which he is certainly better acquainted than I can possibly be. I recommend him however to those Civilities, which every Stranger, of whom one knows no Harm, has a Right to; and I request you will do him all the good Offices, and show him all the Favour that, on further Acquaintance, you shall find him to deserve.

The British, in their vexation and frustration with the Americans, refused to treat captives—especially men captured at sea from American warships and privateers—as prisoners of war. Instead, they crowded them into wretched prisons, threatened them with transportation to British colonies in Asia and Africa, and then cynically offered them the opportunity of volunteering to fight aboard British ships. Franklin protested this treatment in a blazing letter to the British Ambassador Lord Stormont. Stormont returned the letter with a note: "The King's ambassador receives no letters from rebels but when they come to implore His Majesty's mercy."

Paris, April 2, 1777.

We did ourselves the Honour of writing some time since to your Lordship on the Subject of Exchanging Prisoners. You did not condescend to give us any Answer, and therefore we expect none to this. We however take the Liberty of sending you Copies of certain Depositions which we shall transmit to Congress whereby it will be known to your Court that the United States are not unacquainted with the barbarous Treatment their People receive when they have the Misfortune of being your Prisoners here in Europe. And that if your Conduct towards us is not altered it is not unlikely that severe Reprisals may be thought justifiable from the Necessity of putting some Check to such abominable Practices. For the sake of Humanity it is to be wish'd that Men would endeavour to alleviate as much as possible the unavoidable Misseries attending a State of War. It has been said that among the civilized Nations of Europe the ancient Horrors of that State are much diminished. But the Compelling Men by Chains, Stripes & Famine to fight against their Friends and Relations, is a new Mode of Barbarity which your Nation alone has the Honour of inventing. And the sending American Prisoners of War to Africa and Asia remote from all Probability of Exchange and where they can scarce hope ever to hear from their Families even if the Unwholesomeness of the Climate does not put a speedy End to their Lives, is a manner of treating Captives that you can justify by no Precedent or Custom except that of the black Savages of Guinea.

Benjamin Vaughan, a young Englishman who was a close friend of Lord Shelburne and other opposition politicians, became the first of many Englishmen to attempt to persuade Franklin to discuss peace terms. In this letter, Franklin suggested an inconspicuous place to meet.

[Paris] Thursday, September 18, 1777

I shall be very happy to see my dear Friend if it may be without Inconvenience to him; and the sooner the happier. The Duke de Chaulnes, who was with me last Night, has ask'd me to dine with him on Sunday, when he expected you: But that is a long time for me to wait; And I cannot think of another Place where a Meeting with me would not occasion Speculation. Yes: There is *les Bains de Poitevin* a large white wooden Building upon a Boat in the River opposite to the Tuilleries. You may go there in a Hackney Coach; and you will find me there at Six in the Evening precisely. The People know me only by Sight as I go there often to bathe. Ask for an old Englishman with grey Hair.

With all his problems and duties, Franklin did not forget his favorite correspondents, such as his sister Jane. This letter supplies us with a charming description of his new residence, the Hôtel de Valentinois in the village of Passy, outside Paris on the Seine, and of his life there.

Passy, near Paris, Oct. 5, 1777

I enjoy here an exceeding good State of Health. I live in a fine airy House upon a Hill, which has a large Garden with fine Walks in it, about ½ an hours Drive from the City of Paris. I walk a little every Day in the Garden, have a good Appetite & sleep well. I think the French Cookery agrees with me better than the English; I suppose because there is little or no Butter in their sauces: for I have never once had the Heartburn since my being here tho' I eat heartily, which shows that my Digestion is good. I have got into a good Neighborhood, of very agreable People who appear very fond of me; at least they are pleasingly civil: so that upon the whole I live as comfortably as a Man can well do so far from his Home and his Family.

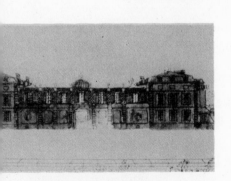

*Franklin's grandson Benjamin Franklin Bache made this drawing of the Hôtel de Valentinois.*

In the fall of 1777, the news from America was almost all bad. One British army, commanded by General John Burgoyne, was advancing down the lakes from Canada, and had captured the key fortress of Fort Ticonderoga. Another British army, commanded by Sir William Howe, after beating Washington at Brandywine Creek, had moved against Philadelphia. The city fell shortly thereafter—especially bitter news for Franklin. Not only was most of his property in the city, but his family, including his sister Jane Mecom, was there too. Then, on December 4, came the best possible news, brought by Jonathan Loring Austin of Boston. Burgoyne and his entire army had been captured at Saratoga. Franklin immediately prepared the following announcement, translated here from the French, to be circulated throughout Paris.

[Paris, December 4, 1777]

Mail arrived from Philadelphia at Dr. Franklin's home in Passy after 34 days.

On October 14th Burgoyne had to lay down his arms, 9200 men killed or taken prisoner.

The terms of surrender were brought with Gates.

Besides the General, 4 members of the English Parliament were among the prisoners.

They left Howe in Philadelphia, where he is imprisoned.

All communication with his fleet is cut off.

17 of his ships which wanted to approach were destroyed or captured.

Washington with his army, other generals with detached forces and militia are surrounding the city. General Gates and his victorious army are coming to join them.

*Contemporary German engraving of the surrender of General Burgoyne*

Franklin's next logical move was to increase the diplomatic pressure on France. The following letter to Vergennes, signed by the three commissioners, but written by Franklin, did that job very neatly.

Passy, December 8, 1777

The Commissioners from the Congress of the United States of America, beg leave to represent to your Excellency, that it is near a year since they had the Honour of putting into your Hands the Propositions of the Congress for a Treaty of Amity and Commerce with this Kingdom, to which, with sundry other Propositions contained in subsequent Memorials, requesting the Aid of Ships of War, and offering Engagements to unite the Forces of the said States with those of France and Spain in acting against the Dominions of Great Britain, and to make no Peace but in Conjunction with those Courts, if Britain should declare War with them; to all which they have yet received no determinate Answer; and apprehending that a Continuance of this State of Uncertainty with regard to those Propositions, together with the Reports that must soon be spread in America of rigorous Treatment met with by our Armed Ships in the Ports of these Kingdoms, may give Advantage to our Enemies in making ill Impressions on the Minds of our People, who, from the Secrecy enjoyn'd us, cannot be informed of the Friendly and essential Aids that have been so generously but privately afforded us; the Commissioners conceive, that, the present Circumstances considered, the compleating such a Treaty at this Time would have the most happy Effect, in raising the Credit of the United States abroad, and strengthening their Resolutions at Home; as well as discouraging their internal Enemies, and confirming their Friends that might otherwise waver: And the Commissioners are further of Opinion that the Aid of Ships desired might at this Juncture be employed to great Advantage in America; which when honour'd with a Conference they could more particularly explain. They therefore request your Excellency most earnestly to resume the Consideration of those Affairs, and appoint them some speedy Day of Audience thereupon.

They also pray that their grateful Acknowledgements may be presented to the King for the additional Aid of three Millions which he has been so graciously pleased to promise them; and that his Majesty may be assured whatever Engagements they may enter into in behalf of the United States, in pursuance of the full Powers they are vested with, will be executed with the most punctual Good Faith by the Congress, who believing their Interests to be the same, and that a secure Increase of the Commerce, Wealth and Strength of France and Spain will be one Consequence of their Success in this Contest, wish for nothing so much, after establishing their own Liberty, as a firm and everlasting Union with these Nations.

Simultaneously, Franklin was supplying his friends in England with information that would, he hoped, bring down the North Ministry and make a negotiated peace possible. The following letter to Thomas Walpole had such a political purpose, evident in the postscript. The medallion

*Franklin made this charming sketch of one of the neighboring gardens that he enjoyed while in Passy.*

Franklin mentioned was distributed by the thousands across France as part of the propaganda campaign to popularize the American cause. "Dr. B." is Edward Bancroft, the secretary to the American mission, a Connecticut-born physician who spent most of his life in London. He was at the same time on the British payroll as a spy. But as this letter makes clear, he also contributed in a modest way to the American cause.

> Paris, December 11, 1777
>
> I am sorry Lord Chatham's Motion for a Cessation of Arms, was not agreed to. Every thing seems to be rejected by your mad Politicians that would lead to Healing the Breach; and every thing done that can tend to make it everlasting. . . .
>
> From a Sketch Dr. B. had which was drawn by your ingenious and valuable Son, they have made here Medaillons in *terre cuit*. A Dozen have been presented to me, and I think he has a Right to one of them. Please deliver it to him with my Compliments.
>
> With the greatest Esteem and Respect I am ever Dear Sir, Your most obedient humble Servant
>
> B FRANKLIN
>
> [*Postscript:*] My sincere Respects if you please to your noble Friends, Lords Chatham and Cambden.
> Blessed are the Peacemakers.

The French responded positively to Franklin's pressure, and an enormous diplomatic victory seemed to be in sight. At the same time, ironically, Franklin was forced in this letter to Robert Morris to reveal for the first time the mounting acrimony within the American mission in Paris. The "five of us in this City" included the three commissioners—himself, Silas Deane, and Arthur Lee; Arthur's brother William Lee, who had been appointed the commercial agent for the Americans in France; and Ralph Izard, a wealthy South Carolinian who had been appointed Ambassador to Tuscany and was in Paris, awaiting permission to enter the country to which he was accredited. Izard tended to side with the two Lees against Franklin and Deane.

> Paris, December 21, 1777
>
> I remember that long before I was ordered here, you once did me the Honour to say, you should not dislike being sent to France with me. Since my being here, I have frequently wish'd that Appointment had taken place. I think I should have pass'd my time more comfortably. We are now five of us in this City, all honest and capable Men (if I may include myself in that Description) and all meaning well for the Public but our

*Medallion of Franklin made by Jean Baptiste Nini, after a sketch done by the son of Thomas Walpole*

Tempers do not suit, and we are got into Disputes and Contentions that are not to our Credit, and which I have sometimes feared would go to Extremes. You know the natural Disposition of some of us, how jealous, how captious, how suspicious even of real Friends, and how positive, after suspecting a while, that the Suspicions are certain Truths, *"Confirmations strong, as Proofs from holy Writ."* You will therefore, I am persuaded, if Complaints of one another should come to your hands, make due Allowance for such Tempers, and suffer no Man to be condemn'd unheard. I do not write thus on my own Account, as I am not apprehensive of your receiving any Complaints of me; for tho' it is difficult to live in peace with such Characters, how much soever one esteems them for the Virtues and Abilities they otherwise possess, I have however done it tolerably hitherto; but as I am not sure it can last, I wish most sincerely that we were separated; for our being together seems of no Use, and, as we hinted formerly in a joint Letter, is attended with many Inconveniencies. Such Inconveniencies being formerly experienced by other States, is, I suppose, the Reason, that no Power in Europe, for a Century past, has sent more than one Person to one Court. Possibly this desirable Event may soon take place; for if France and Spain acknowledge us as independent States, the other Courts will follow, and receive our Envoys.

I have the Pleasure to assure you, that all Europe is of our side except the King of England and his Placemen and Pensioners, Contractors and Expecters. There is however a furious Ferment in his Parliament about his Measures; and if you could be fortunate enough to treat Howe as you have done Burgoyne, he would be in danger of two *old Houses* falling on his Head.

The British Ministry, learning through spies such as Edward Bancroft that a treaty with France was imminent, launched a peace offensive of its own, sending Paul Wentworth, chief of the British Secret Service in France, to find out from Franklin if he would accept anything short of independence as peace terms. Franklin toyed with Wentworth, inviting him to dinner and letting him argue his case for more than two hours. Then he told the spy that America was prepared to fight fifty years for independence. Franklin had passed along previous British peace offers to the French Government. He said nothing about Wentworth's visit, although he knew that French spies would instantly report it to the Count de

Vergennes. The French had been hesitating about completing the negotiations for the treaty of alliance and commerce, because Spain declined to join them. Now, they reacted with alarmed alacrity. The French Undersecretary for Foreign Affairs, Conrad Alexandre Gérard, met with Franklin, Deane, and Lee at Deane's lodgings in Paris. Franklin wrote out the following response to Gérard's question. Gérard glanced at it and quietly informed them the King had given his word—the treaty would be signed.

January 8, 1778

Question,   What is necessary to be done to give such Satisfaction to the American Commissioners, as to engage them not to listen to any Propositions from England for a new Connection with that Country?

Answer,   The Commissioners have long since propos'd a Treaty of Amity and Commerce, which is not yet concluded: the immediate Conclusion of that Treaty will remove the Uncertainty they are under with regard to it, and give them such a Reliance on the Friendship of France, as to reject firmly all Propositions made to them of Peace from England, which have not for their Basis the entire Freedom and Independence of America, both in Matters of Government and Commerce.

British spy Edward Bancroft

While the details of the treaty were being worked out with the French, Franklin had to cope with the mounting personal feuds inside the American mission. Ralph Izard was particularly troublesome, feeling that Franklin should have consulted him about certain clauses in the treaty that concerned the trade of the southern states with the French West Indies. Franklin cut him down with the following letter.

Passy, Jan. 29, 1778

I received yours late last Evening. Present Circumstances which I will explain to you when I have the Honr of seeing you, prevent my giving it a full Answer now. The Reasons you offer had before been all under Consideration; but I must submit to remain some days under the Opinion you appear to have form'd not only of my poor Understanding in the general Interests of America, but of my Defects in Sincerity, Politeness & Attention to your Instructions. These offences I flatter myself will admit of fair Excuses [or rather will be found not to have existed]. You mention, that you *feel yourself hurt.* Permit me to offer you a Maxim, which has thro' Life been of Use to me & may be so to you in preventing such imaginary Hurts. It is, always to *suppose* one's Friends *may be right* till one *finds* them wrong; rather than *to suppose them wrong* till one *finds* them right. You have heard and imagined all that can be said or suppos'd on one side of the Question, but not on the other.

The British continued to attempt to stave off the Franco-American alliance. James Hutton, an old Craven Street neighbor of Franklin's ("My Lord Hutton" of *The Craven Street Gazette*) and a leading member of the Moravian Church, visited Franklin in France, no doubt at the instigation of British politicians, to see whether Franklin would discuss peace informally with him. In a letter to Hutton, Franklin opened a campaign to force the British to surrender, as the price of peace, considerably more than the territory ruled by the Thirteen Colonies in revolt.

Passy, February 1, 1778.

You desired, that if I had no Propositions to make, I would at least give my Advice. I think it is Ariosto who says, that all things lost on Earth are to be found in the Moon; on which somebody remarked, that there must be a great deal of good Advice in the Moon. If so, there is a good deal of mine, formerly given and lost in this Business. I will, however, at your Request give a little more, but without the least Expectation that it will be followed; for none but God can at the same time give good Counsel, and Wisdom to make use of it.

You have lost by this mad War, and the Barbarity with which it has been carried on, not only the Government and Commerce of America, and the public Revenues and private Wealth arising from that Commerce, but what is more, you have lost the Esteem, Respect, Friendship, and Affection of all that great and growing People, who consider you at present, and whose Posterity will consider you, as the worst and wickedest Nation upon Earth. A Peace you may undoubtedly obtain by dropping all your Pretensions to govern us; and, by your superior skill in huckstering negotiation, you may possibly make such an apparently advantageous Treaty as shall be applauded in your Parliament; but, if you do not, with the Peace, recover the Affections of that People, it will not be a lasting nor a profitable one, nor will it afford you any part of that Strength, which you once had by your Union with them, and might (if you had been wise enough to take Advice) have still retained.

To recover their Respect and Affection, you must tread back the Steps you have taken. Instead of honouring and rewarding the American Advisers and Pro-

*Conrad Alexandre Gérard, French Undersecretary for Foreign Affairs*

moters of this War, you should disgrace them; with all those who have inflamed the Nation against America by their malicious Writings; and all the Ministers and Generals who have prosecuted the War with such Inhumanity. This would show a national change of Disposition of what had passed.

In proposing terms, you should not only grant such as the Necessity of your Affairs may evidently oblige you to grant, but such additional ones as may show your Generosity, and thereby demonstrate your good Will. For instance, perhaps you might, by your Treaty, retain all Canada, Nova Scotia and the Floridas. But if you would have a real friendly as well as able Ally in America, and avoid all occasions of future Discord, which will otherwise be continually arising on your American Frontiers, you should throw in those Countries. And you may call it, if you please, an Indemnification for the needless and cruel burning of their Towns, which Indemnification will otherwise be some time or other demanded.

I know your People can not see the Utility of such Measures, and will never follow them, and even call it Insolence and Impudence in me to mention them. I have, however, complied with your Desire, and am, as ever, your affectionate friend,

B FRANKLIN

*Engraving of David Hartley, after a portrait by George Romney*

David Hartley was a member of Parliament who had acted on Franklin's plea and laid out money to relieve the distresses of American prisoners in England. Franklin opened this letter by thanking him; but then, in the second paragraph he went on to far more important matters. The day after he wrote this letter, Franklin signed the treaty of alliance and commerce with France. The "certain Person" to whom he referred may have been Lord North, or more probably Lord Chatham, the one man with prestige enough to organize significant opposition to the North Ministry. Insistence on complete control and a refusal to make any political arrangements with allies were Chatham's most notable traits—and they considerably lessened his effectiveness as an English politician.

[Paris,] February 5, 1778

I am exceedingly obliged by your interesting yourself so warmly in behalf of those unhappy people. I understand you advanc'd money: Your bills on that account will be punctually paid. As yet I have heard of none.

Understanding that a certain Person promised to make

proposals for healing a certain Breach, I postpon'd and delayed a material operation till I shou'd hear what those proposals were. I am now told that he will not make them till he finds it in his power to do what he pleases. Therefore Adieu my dear friend; and I bid you all *Good Night.*

On February 6, in the office of the Ministry of Foreign Affairs, Franklin, Deane, and Lee signed the treaty of alliance and commerce with France. The treaty was to have been signed on February 5, but it had been put off because Gérard, the French negotiator, had a cold. On both days, the Americans noticed that Franklin wore the same suit he had worn the day that Wedderburn had abused him at the Cockpit. They asked him why, and he smiled and said, "To give it a little revenge." Panicked, the North Ministry now pushed through Parliament two conciliatory bills that gave the Americans everything that Franklin had demanded in his peace negotiations in 1775. But they were hedged with provisos and qualifications to make them palatable to members of Parliament who wanted to fight to the finish. In this letter to Hartley, Franklin tore the peace proposals apart. Perhaps the most significant part of the letter, however, is the postscript. Once more, Franklin was making it clear that if the North Ministry were to be replaced, peace would be possible.

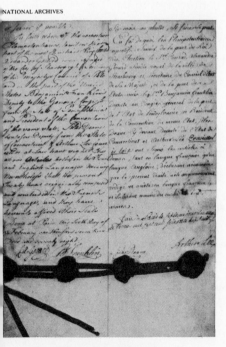

*The 1778 treaty with France, bearing the signatures of Franklin, Deane, and Lee*

Passy, Feb. 26, 1778.

I receiv'd yours of the 18th and 20th of this Month, with Lord North's proposed Bills. The more I see of the Ideas and Projects of your Ministry, and their little Arts and Schemes of amusing and dividing us, the more I admire the prudent, manly, and magnanimous Propositions contained in your intended Motion for an Address to the King. What Reliance can we have on an Act expressing itself to be only a Declaration of the *Intention* of Parliament concerning the *Exercise* of the Right of imposing Taxes in America, when, in the Bill itself, as well as in the Title, a Right is suppos'd and claimed, which never existed; and a *present Intention* only is declared not to use it, which may be changed by another Act next Session, with a Preamble, that this *Intention* being found inexpedient, it is thought proper to repeal this Act, and resume the Exercise of *the Right* in its full Extent? If any solid permanent Benefit was intended by this, why is it confin'd to the Colonies of North America, and not extended to the loyal ones in the Sugar Islands? But it is now needless to criticise, as all Acts that suppose your future Government of the Colonies can be no longer significant.

*Porcelain statuette of Louis XVI
and Franklin, commemorating the
signing of the treaty of alliance*

In the Act for appointing Commissioners, instead of full Powers to agree upon Terms of Peace and Friendship, with a Promise of ratifying such Treaty as they shall make in pursuance of those Powers, it is declared that their Agreements shall have no force nor Effect, nor be carried into Execution till approved of by Parliament, so that every thing of Importance will be uncertain. But they are allow'd to proclaim a Cessation of Arms, and revoke their Proclamation, as soon as in confidence of it, our Militia have been allowed to go home: They may suspend the Operation of Acts, prohibiting Trade; and take off the Suspension when our Merchants, in consequence of it have been induc'd to send their Ships to Sea; in short, they may do every thing that can have a Tendency to divide and distract us, but nothing that can afford us Security. Indeed, Sir, your Ministers do not yet know us. We may not be quite so cunning as they; but we have really more Sense as well as more Courage than they have ever been willing to give us Credit for: And I am persuaded that these Acts will rather obstruct Peace than promote it, and that they will not in America answer the mischievous and malevolent Ends for which they were intended. In England they may indeed amuse the Public Creditors, give Hopes and Expectations, that shall be of some present use, and continue the Mismanagers a little longer in their Places. *Voilà tout!*

In return for your repeated Advice to us, not to conclude any Treaty with the House of Bourbon, permit me to give (through you) a little Advice to the Whigs in England. Let nothing induce them to join with the Tories, in supporting and continuing this wicked War against the Whigs of America, whose Assistance they may hereafter want to secure their own Liberties, or whose Country they may be glad to retire to for the Enjoyment of them.

If Peace by a Treaty with America, upon equal Terms were really desired, your Commissioners need not go there for it; supposing that as they are impower'd by the Bill "to treat with such Person or Persons, as in their Wisdom and Discretion they shall think meet," they should happen to conceive, that the Commissioners at Paris might be included in that Description. I am ever, dear Sir, &c.

B FRANKLIN

P.S. Seriously, on further thoughts, I am of opinion, that, if wise and honest men, such as Sir George Saville, the Bishop of St. Asaph, and yourself, were to come over here immediately with powers to treat, you might not only obtain peace with America, but prevent a war with France.

To help English credit sink a little faster, Franklin, the previous year, had composed the following catechism relating to the British national debt.

[Paris, spring or summer, 1777?]

*Question* 1. Supposing this debt to be only one hundred and ninety-five millions of pounds sterling at present, although it is much more, and that was all to be counted in shillings, that a man could count at the rate of one hundred shillings per minute, for twelve hours each day, till he has counted the whole, how long would he take in doing it?

*Answer.* One hundred forty-eight years, one hundred nine days, and twenty-two hours.

*Q.* 2. The whole of this sum being three thousand nine hundred millions of shillings, and the coinage standard being sixty-two in the Troy pound, what is the whole weight of this sum?

*A.* Sixty-one millions, seven hundred fifty-two thousand, four hundred and seventy-six Troy pounds.

*Q.* 3. How many ships would carry this weight, suppose one hundred tons each?

*A.* Three hundred and fourteen ships.

*Q.* 4. How many carts would carry this weight, suppose a ton in each?

*A.* Thirty-one thousand, four hundred and fifty-two carts.

*Q.* 5. The breadth of a shilling being one inch, if all these shillings were laid in a straight line, close to one another's edges, how long would that line be that would contain them?

*A.* Sixty-one thousand, five hundred fifty-two miles; which is nine thousand, five hundred seventy-two miles more than twice round the whole circumference of the earth.

*Q.* 6. Suppose the interest of this debt to be three and a half per cent per annum, what does the whole annual interest amount to?

*A.* Six millions, seven hundred and seventy thousand pounds.

*Q.* 7. How doth government raise this interest annually?

*A.* By taxing those who lent the principal, and others.

*Q.* 8. When will government be able to pay the principal?

*A.* When there is more money in England's treasury than there is in all Europe.

*Q.* 9. And when will that be?

*A.* Never.

Franklin discussed the French alliance and other matters in more homely fashion in this charming letter to Catherine Ray Greene.

Paris, Feb. 28, 1778.

My dear old Friend

Don't be offended at the Word *old;* I don't mean to call you an *old Woman;* it relates only to the Age of our Friendship; which on my part has always been a sincerely affectionate one, and I flatter myself the same on yours.

I received your kind Letter from Boston of Oct. 28. which gave me great Pleasure, as it inform'd me of the Welfare of you and your Family. I continue hearty, as do my two Grandsons, who present their Respects to you & Mr. Greene, being pleas'd with your Remembrance of them. We are all glad to hear of Ray, for we all love him. —I have been often much concern'd for my Friends at Warwick, hearing that the Enemy was so near them. I hope your Troubles will not be of much longer Duration: For tho' the Wickedness of the English Court, & its Malice against us is as great as ever, its Horns are shortened; its Strength diminishes daily; and we have formed an Alliance here, & shall form others, that will help to keep the Bull quiet and make him orderly. —I chat, you see as usual, any how, with you, who are kind enough never to *criticise* Improprieties in my Compositions or anything else. —I see by yours that my Sisters granddaughter is married. I wish the young Folks joy and Lasting Happiness. I pity my poor old Sister, to be so harassed & driven about by the enemy. For I feel a little myself the Inconvenience of being driven about by my friends. —I live here in great Respect and dine every day with great folks; but I still long for home & for

Liberté des Etats-Unis reconnue par la France.
*janvier 1778.*

*Le Docteur Francklin & les Américains, recevant le Traité d'Alliance où leur liberté est reconnue.*

*In this French woodcut, the King gives Franklin and the Americans a paper on which is written "Liberty."*

Repose; and should be happy to eat Indian Pudding in your Company & under your hospitable Roof.

Silas Deane became a political problem. Unstable and contentious, he was almost too ready to quarrel with the Lees and Ralph Izard. Both sides sought supporters in the Continental Congress. Finally Congress, distressed by the feud and alarmed at its potential harm to the American cause, recalled Deane to answer charges made by William and Arthur Lee that he had stolen millions from the money advanced to the United States by France. Franklin sent Deane on his way with the following letter of almost unqualified support, addressed to the president of the Continental Congress, Henry Laurens.

Passy, near Paris, March 31, 1778.
My colleague, Mr. Deane, being recall'd by Congress, and no Reasons given that have yet appear'd here, it is apprehended to be the Effect of some Misrepresentations from an Enemy or two at Paris or at Nantes. I have no doubt, that he will be able clearly to justify himself; but, having lived intimately with him now fifteen months, the greatest part of the time in the same House, and been a constant Witness of his public Conduct, I cannot omit giving this Testimony, tho' unask'd, in his Behalf, that I esteem him a faithful, active, and able Minister, who, to my knowledge, has done in various ways great and important Service to his Country, whose Interests I wish may always, by every one in her employ, be as much and as effectually promoted.

Arthur Lee became incensed when he discovered that Conrad Alexander Gérard had been appointed an ambassador to America and was to be escorted to Philadelphia by Deane, who would thus be traveling in an atmosphere of triumph. Lee declared himself insulted and blamed Franklin. He got the following reply.

Passy, April 3, 1778
It is true I have omitted answering some of your Letters. I do not like to answer angry Letters. I hate Disputes. I am old, cannot have long to live, have much to do and no time for Altercation. If I have often receiv'd and borne your Magisterial Snubbings and Rebukes without Reply, ascribe it to the right Causes, my Concern for the Honour & Success of our Mission, which would be hurt by our Quarrelling, my Love of Peace, my Respect for your good Qualities, and my Pity of your Sick Mind, which is forever tormenting itself, with its Jealousies, Suspicions &

Fancies that others mean you ill, wrong you, or fail in Respect for you. — If you do not cure your self of this Temper it will end in Insanity, of which it is the Symptomatick Forerunner, as I have seen in several Instances. God preserve you from so terrible an Evil: and for his sake pray suffer me to live in quiet.

A few days later, Franklin sent the following letter to Deane, who was waiting at Toulon to sail to America. "The Negociator" was William Pulteney, a member of Parliament sent by George III and Lord North with secret proposals for peace.

> Passy, April 7, 1778
>
> I have had a long and very angry Letter from Mr Lee, about your going without acquainting him with it, in which his Disorder seems to encrease, for he raves not only against you and me, but seems to resent the Court's sending a Minister to Congress without advising with him. I bear all his Rebukes with Patience, for the Good of the Service: but it goes a little hard with me.
>
> The Negociator is gone back apparently much chagrin'd at his little Success. I have promis'd him faithfully that since his Propositions could not be accepted they should be buried in Oblivion. I therefore desire earnestly that you would put that Paper immediately in the Fire on the Receipt of this, without taking or suffering to be taken any Copy of it, or communicating its Contents.

At one point during these tense months, David Hartley warned Franklin that he was possibly in danger of being assassinated by British Government agents. "If tempestuous hours should come, take care of your own safety; events are uncertain, & men may be capricious," wrote Hartley. This was Franklin's reply.

> [Passy, April, 1778]
>
> I thank you for your kind caution, but having nearly finished a long life, I set but little value on what remains of it. Like a draper, when one chaffers with him for a remnant, I am ready to say, "As it is only the fag end, I will not differ with you about it; take it for what you please." Perhaps the best use such an old fellow can be put to, is to make a martyr of him.

While acting as America's chief spokesman in France, Franklin was also the unofficial admiral of the American navy in European waters. In this letter to John Paul Jones—following the thirty-year-old captain's sensationally successful twenty-eight-day foray in British home waters aboard the *Ranger* the previous April—the American minister discussed a variety of naval affairs.

Passy, June 10, 1778.

In consequence of the high Opinion the Minister of the Marine has of your Conduct and Bravery, it is now settled (observe, that this is to be a Secret between us, I being expressly enjoin'd not to communicate it to any other Person, not even to the other Gentlemen,) that you are to have the Frigate from Holland, which actually belongs to Government, and will be furnished with as many good French Seamen as you shall require. But you are to act under Congress' commission. As you may like to have a Number of Americans, and your own are homesick, it is proposed to give you as many as you can engage out of two hundred Prisoners, which the Ministry of Britain have at length agreed to give us in Exchange for those you have in your hands. They propose to make the exchange at Calais, where they are to bring the Americans. Nothing is wanting to this, but a List of yours, containing their Names and Rank; immediately on the Receipt of which, an equal Number are to be prepared and sent in a ship to that Port, where yours are to meet them. Pray send this List by the Return of the Post if possible. If by this means you can get a good new Crew, I think it will be best that you are quite free of the old, for a Mixture might introduce the Infection of that Sickness you complain of. But this may be left to your Discretion.

Perhaps we shall join you with the *Providence*, Captain Whipple, a new Continental Ship of 30 Guns, which in coming out of the river of Providence gave the two frigates that were posted to intercept her each of them so heavy a Dose of her 18 and 12 pounders, that they had not the courage, or were not able, to pursue her. The *Boston* is suppos'd to be gone from Bordeaux.

It seems to be desired by those concern'd in your future Ship that you should step up to Versailles, (where one will meet you,) in order to such a Settlement of Matters and Plans with those who have the Direction, as cannot well be done by Letter. I wish it may be convenient to you to do it directly. The project of giving you the Command of this Ship pleases me the more, as it is a probable Opening to the higher Preferment you so justly merit.

*Franklin helped plan John Paul Jone's expedition in 1779, leading to America's first major naval victory.*

305

John Adams replaced Silas Deane as American commissioner. From Franklin's point of view it was not the best possible change. Adams was temperamentally inclined to side with Arthur Lee, who had the backing in Congress of many New Englanders, in particular, Samuel Adams. But even Adams was appalled by Lee's manner and conduct. He was equally displeased by Franklin's easygoing style of running his side of the mission. Temple Franklin was not a very diligent private secretary. Many details, particularly on the accounting side, were left undone. Adams proposed to reorganize procedures. Franklin, eager to placate him, heartily concurred in this soothing letter.

> Passy, Saturday, Sept. 26, 1778
>
> I very much approve your Plan with regard to our future Accounts and wish it to be followed.
>
> The Accounts that have been shown you, are only those of the Person we had entrusted with the receiving and paying our Money; and intended merely to show how he was discharged of it. We are to separate from that Account the Articles for which Congress should be charged, and those for which we should give Credit.
>
> It has always been my Intention to pay for the Education of my Children, their Clothes &c. as well as for Books and other Things for my private Use; and whatever I spend in this Way, I shall give Congress Credit for, to be deducted out of the Allowance they have promis'd us. But as the Article of Clothes for ourselves here is necessarily much higher than if we were not in public Service, I submit it to your Consideration whether that Article ought not to be reckoned among Expences for the Publick. I know I had Clothes enough at home to have lasted me my Lifetime in a Country where I was under small Necessity of following new Fashions.

*John Adams by Charles Willson Peale*

American prisoners in England were never far from Franklin's mind. When several of them in Forton Prison charged in a bitter letter that American commissioners in France were guilty of neglect and indifference, Franklin immediately replied.

> Passy, October 20, 1778
>
> I have just received yours of the 2d. Instant. I beg that you will be assured that your long Detention, is not owing to any Neglect of you by the Commissioners. Our first Applications for exchanging you, were haughtily rejected. You were at that time consider'd as Rebels, committed for High Treason, who could only be delivered by course of Law. We then did every thing in our Power to make

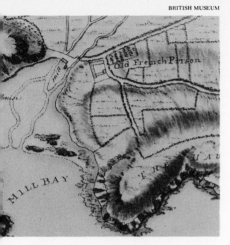

*Map of Plymouth showing the Old French Prison, where American captives were interned*

your situation as comfortable as possible. When Time and Circumstances produced a Disposition to consider you in a more favourable light, we proposed that on your being all discharg'd, we would give up all we had here, and an Order to receive the Ballance of the number in America; this was refused, but good Mr. Hartley has finally by long solicitation obtain'd an Agreement of the Lords of the Admiralty to an exchange of Man for Man, and the Pass required for a Cartel Ship to bring over as many of you as we have here to give in Return, was sent to England in September. The Execution has been delay'd 'till a precise List could be sent of our Number. Of this we have only been a few days informed. By this Post I have written a Letter to Mr. Hartley, which I hope will remove that difficulty, and that those who have been longest in confinement to the number of 250. at least from the two Prisons of Forton and Plymouth will now soon be at liberty. Nothing in the Power of the Commissioners will be wanting to liberate the rest as soon as possible, for the Sufferings of so many of our brave Countrymen, affect us very sensibly.

A good idea of how Franklin's fame attracted to him people from all walks of French life, from high-level diplomats to crackpot would-be scientists, is provided by this fragment from a lost journal that he kept during 1778.

Passy, Sunday, December 13, 1778. A.M. A man came to tell me he has invented a Machine, which would go of itself, without the help of a Spring, Weight, Air, Water, or any of the Elements, or the Labour of Man or Beast; and with force sufficient to work four Machines for cutting Tobacco; that he had experienc'd it, would shew it me if I would come to his House, and would sell the Secret of it for Two hundred Louis. I doubted it, but promis'd to go to him in order to see it.

A Monsieur Coder came with a Proposition in Writing, to levy 600 Men to be employ'd in landing on the Coast of England and Scotland, to burn and ransom Towns and Villages, in order to put a stop to the English proceeding in that Way in America. I thanked him, and told him I could not approve it, nor had I any Money at Command for such Purposes. Moreover that it would not be permitted by the Government here.

A Man came with a Request that I would patronize and

recommend to Government an Invention he had, whereby a Hussar might so conceal his arms and [habiliments], with Provision for 24 Hours, as to appear a common Traveller, by which Means a considerable Body might be admitted into a Town, one at a time unsuspected, and afterwards assembling, surprize it. I told him I was not a Military Man, of course no Judge of such Matters, and advised him to apply to the *Bureau de la Guerre.* He said he had no Friends and, so could procure no Attention. — The number of wild Schemes propos'd to me is so great, and they have heretofore taken so much of my time, that I begin to reject all, tho' possibly *some* of them may be worth Notice.

Received a parcel from an unknown Philosopher who submits to my Consideration a Memoir on the Subject of *Elementary fire,* containing Experiments in a dark Chamber. It seems to be well written, and is in English, with a little Tincture of French Idiom. I wish to see the Experiments, without which I cannot well judge of it.

The continuing acrimony in the American mission, and the angry debate that exploded in Congress over the charges against Silas Deane, convinced most Americans that there should be only one representative for the United States in France. The choice of Franklin was a foregone conclusion. In this letter, he informed the Count de Vergennes of his new title. The Count d'Estaing was the commander of the French fleet in American waters.

Passy, February 14, 1779.

I have the honour to acquaint your Excellency that I have received from the Congress their appointment to be their minister plenipotentiary at this Court, together with a letter of credence to be presented to his Majesty. I beg thereupon your Excellency's advice and direction.

I have need also of your counsel with regard to the trial and punishment of some conspirators on board our frigate, the *Alliance,* which is just arrived. I would have done myself the honour of waiting on your Excellency today, but am not quite well enough to go abroad in such weather.

I have received a number of letters from America, all expressing the highest esteem for the Count d'Estaing and the Marquis de la Fayette. As I think they will give you and M. de Sartine some pleasure, I send you the originals, praying only to have them returned.

As his comment on the *Alliance* suggests, Franklin's new title also meant that he now bore on his shoulders all the woes and worries of the American mission in France, from buying supplies to directing privateers and warships to maintaining good relations with the French. Nevertheless, he found time for the problems that had concerned him earlier, particularly the welfare of prisoners. In this letter, he replied to a group of British and Irish captives, notably one John Walsh, who had written to him complaining of harsh treatment.

Passy March 2d. 1779.

I am sorry to understand by your Memorial of the 16. Past, which came to hand but Yesterday, that you are still in that uncomfortable Situation on board the Brigantine in Brest Road, having understood that Orders had been long since given for taking you on Shore. I write again this Day to the Minister of the Marine, to obtain a Renewal of those Orders; and I hope in consequence that you will soon be better accommodated. I imagine the Delay has been in Part occasioned by the constant Expectations given us from England, of sending over a Cartel Ship with a Number of Americans to exchange for you. The Passport for that Ship was sent from hence in September last: And we have been told from time to time these 3 Months past, that a Ship was actually taken up and victual'd for that Service; but as yet she has not appear'd. I shall be glad to receive the Account you mention of the Provisions that have been afforded to you. It was always the Desire and Intention of the Commissioners here that you should be well treated.

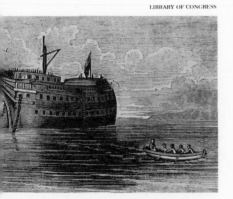

*Americans escaping from a British prison ship, nineteenth-century view*

As the war dragged on, American finances became more and more disorganized. The paper money that Congress had printed in vast quantities began to depreciate sharply. Obtaining additional financing from France became one of Franklin's primary concerns, as this letter to Vergennes demonstrated. Ferdinand Grand was the Americans' banker in France.

Passy, March 9, 1779

It is with great Reluctance that I give your Excy any farther Trouble on the Subject of a Loan of Money. But the Bearer, Mr. Grand, who is much better acquainted with the Nature & Manner of such Operations than I am, being of Opinion that the sum we want might with your Permission & Countenance be procur'd in France, I beg you would be so good as to hear him upon the Subject, both of the Necessity of obtaining such a Loan, & of the Means of accomplishing it.

Franklin always sought for ways to mitigate the harsher practices of eighteenth-century warfare. As a scientist, too, he responded favorably to a plea from English friends to grant a safe passage to Captain Cook, who had sailed to the South Seas before the war began. Ironically, by the time Franklin wrote this generous message, Cook was dead, killed in a skirmish with the natives of the Hawaiian Islands.

[Passy, March 10, 1779]

To all Captains and Commanders of arm'd Ships acting by Commission from the Congress of the United States of America, now in War with Great Britain.
Gentlemen,

A Ship having been fitted out from England before the Commencement of this War, to make Discoveries of new Countries, in Unknown Seas, under the Conduct of that most celebrated Navigator and Discoverer Captain Cook; an Undertaking truely laudable in itself, as the Increase of Geographical Knowledge, facilitates the Communication between distant Nations, in the Exchange of useful Products and Manufactures, and the Extension of Arts, whereby the common Enjoyments of human Life are multiplied and augmented, and Science of other kinds encreased to the Benefit of Mankind in general. This is therefore most earnestly to recommend to every one of you; that in case the said Ship which is now expected to be soon in the European Seas on her Return, should happen to fall into your Hands, you would not consider her as an Enemy, nor suffer any Plunder to be made of the Effects contain'd in her, nor obstruct her immediate Return to England, by detaining her or sending her into any other Part of Europe or to America; but that you would treat the said Captain Cook and his People with all Civility and Kindness, affording them, as common Friends to Mankind, all the Assistance in your Power, which they may happen to stand in need of. In so doing you will not only gratify the Generosity of your own Dispositions, but there is no doubt of your obtaining the Approbation of the Congress, and your other American Owners.

Franklin's hearty sense of humor made him a congenial correspondent for sailors such as John Paul Jones. He mixed business and pleasure in this lively letter. Lord Selkirk was the Scottish nobleman whose house Jones had raided in his first voyage, aboard the *Ranger,* in the hope of seizing him as a hostage for the better treatment of American prisoners. Selkirk was away from home, and Jones contented himself with stealing his silver plate—which led to a long and acrimonious correspondence between them.

*J. B. Nini made medallions of Franklin and his French hosts, Madame and Monsieur Leray de Chaumont, in 1778.*

Passy, March 14. 1779

I yesterday rec'd your favour of the 4th inst. I did not understand from M. Alexander that Lord Selkirk had any particular Objection to receiving the Plate from you. It was general, that tho' he might refuse it if offer'd him by a public Body, as the Congress, he cou'd not accept it from any private Person whatever. I know nothing of M. Alexander's having any Enmity to you, nor can I imagine any Reason for it. But on the whole it seems to me not worth your while to give yourself any farther Trouble about Lord Selkirk. You have now the Disposal of what belongs to the Congress; and may give it with your own Share, if you think fit, in little Encouragements to your men on particular Occasions....

I have look'd over the Copy of my Letter to you of Feby 24, not being able to imagine what Part of it could give you the Idea that I hinted at an Affair I never knew. Not finding anything in the Letter, I suppose it must have been the Postscript of which I have no Copy, and which I know now that you could not understand—tho' I did not when I wrote it. The story I alluded to is this: L'Abbé Rochon had just been telling me & Madame Chaumont that the old Gardiner & his Wife had complained to the Curate, of your having attack'd her in the Garden about 7 o'clock the evening before your Departure, and attempted to ravish her relating all the Circumstances, some of which are not fit for me to write. The serious Part of it was yt three of her Sons were determin'd to kill you, if you had not gone off; the Rest occasioned some Laughing; for the old Woman being one of the grossest, coarsest, dirtiest & ugliest that we may find in a thousand, Madame Chaumont said it gave a high Idea of the Strength of Appetite & Courage of the Americans. A Day or two after, I learnt yt it was the femme de Chambre of Mademoiselle Chaumont who had disguis'd herself in a Suit, I think, of your Cloaths, to divert herself under that Masquerade, as is customary the last evening of Carnival: and that meeting the old Woman in the Garden, she took it into her Head to try her Chastity, which it seems was found Proof.

Franklin was an ideal ambassador to France. In this letter to Josiah Quincy, his old Boston friend, he told how much he enjoyed the French people. He then developed a theme that was to dominate many of his letters: Americans should do more for themselves.

Passy, April 22, 1779.

It is with great Sincerity I join you in acknowledging and admiring the Dispensations of Providence in our Favour. America has only to be thankful, and to persevere. God will finish his Work, and establish their Freedom; and the Lovers of Liberty will flock from all Parts of Europe with their Fortunes to participate with us of that Freedom, as soon as Peace is restored.

I am exceedingly pleas'd with your Account of the French Politeness and Civility, as it appeared among the Officers and People of their Fleet. They have certainly advanced in those Respects many degrees beyond the English. I find them here a most amiable Nation to live with. The Spaniards are by common Opinion suppos'd to be cruel, the English proud, the Scotch insolent, the Dutch Avaricious, &c., but I think the French have no national Vice ascrib'd to them. They have some Frivolities, but they are harmless. To dress their Heads so that a Hat cannot be put on them, and then wear their Hats under their Arms, and to fill their Noses with Tobacco, may be called Follies, perhaps, but they are not Vices. They are only the effects of the tyranny of Custom. In short, there is nothing wanting in the Character of a Frenchman, that belongs to that of an agreable and worthy Man. There are only some Trifles surplus, or which might be spared.

Will you permit me, while I do them this Justice, to hint a little Censure on our own Country People, which I do in Good will, wishing the Cause removed. You know the Necessity we are under of Supplies from Europe, and the Difficulty we have at present in making Returns. The Interest Bills would do a good deal towards purchasing Arms, Ammunition, Clothing, Sailcloth, and other Necessaries for Defence. Upon Enquiry of those who present these Bills to me for Acceptance, what the Money is to be laid out in, I find that most

*Franklin was received cordially at the royal palace and found the French to be "a most amiable Nation."*

of it is for Superfluities, and more than half of it for Tea. How unhappily in this Instance the Folly of our People, and the Avidity of our Merchants, concur to weaken and impoverish our Country. I formerly computed, that we consum'd before the War, in that single Article, the value of £500,000 Sterling annually. Much of this was sav'd by stopping the Use of it. I honoured the virtuous Resolution of our Women in foregoing that little Gratification, and I lament that such Virtue should be of so short Duration. Five Hundred Thousand Pounds Sterling, annually laid out in defending ourselves, or annoying our Enemies, would have great Effects. With what Face can we ask Aids and Subsidies from our Friends, while we are wasting our own Wealth in such Prodigality?

The moment Arthur Lee and Ralph Izard returned to America, they began a propaganda campaign to smear Franklin's reputation and get him fired. In a letter to Richard Bache, Franklin commented on their motives and tactics, which included nasty rumors about William Temple Franklin's loyalty.

Passy, June 2, 1779.

I am very easy about the efforts Messrs. Lee and Izard are using, as you tell me, to injure me on that side of the water. I trust in the justice of the Congress, that they will listen to no accusations against me, that I have not first been acquainted with, and had an opportunity of answering. I know those gentlemen have plenty of ill will to me, though I have never done to either of them the smallest injury, or given the least just cause of offence. But my too great reputation, and the general good will this people have for me, and the respect they show me, and even the compliments they make me, all grieve those unhappy gentlemen; unhappy indeed in their tempers, and in the dark, uncomfortable passions of jealousy, anger, suspicion, envy, and malice. It is enough for good minds to be affected at other people's misfortunes; but they, that are vexed at everybody's good luck, can never be happy. I take no other revenge of such enemies, than to let them remain in the miserable situation in which their malignant natures have placed them, by endeavouring to support an estimable character; and thus, by continuing the reputation the world has hitherto indulged me with, I shall continue

*Mr. and Mrs. Ralph Izard by Copley*

*Imaginative French drawing of Franklin presenting his grandson Temple to Voltaire; the meeting actually took place in Voltaire's house and Temple was eighteen.*

them in their present state of damnation; and I am not disposed to reverse my conduct for the alleviation of their torments.

I am surprised to hear, that my grandson, Temple Franklin, being with me, should be an objection against me, and that there is a cabal for removing him. Methinks it is rather some merit, that I have rescued a valuable young man from the danger of being a Tory, and fixed him in honest republican Whig principles; as I think, from the integrity of his disposition, his industry, his early sagacity, and uncommon abilities for business, he may in time become of great service to his country. It is enough that I have lost my *son;* would they add my *grandson?* An old man of seventy, I undertook a winter voyage at the command of Congress, and for the public service, with no other attendant to take care of me. I am continued here in a foreign country, where, if I am sick, his filial attention comforts me, and, if I die, I have a child to close my eyes and take care of my remains. His dutiful behaviour towards me, and his diligence and fidelity in business, are both pleasing and useful to me. His conduct, as my private secretary, has been unexceptionable, and I am confident the Congress will never think of separating us.

I have had a great deal of pleasure in Ben [Benjamin Franklin Bache] too. He is a good, honest lad, and will make, I think, a valuable man. He had made as much proficiency in his learning as the boarding school he was at could well afford him; and, after some consideration where to find a better for him, I at length fixed on sending him to Geneva. I had a good opportunity by a gentleman of that city; who had a place for him in his chaise, and has a son about the same age at the same school. He promised to take care of him, and enclosed I send you the letters I have since received relating to him and from him. He went very cheerfully, and I understand is very happy. I miss his company on Sundays at dinner. But, if I live, and I can find a little leisure, I shall make the journey next spring to see him, and to see at the same time *the old thirteen United States* of Switzerland.

Thanks be to God, I continue well and hearty. Undoubtedly I grow older, but I think the last ten years have made no great difference. I have sometimes the gout, but they say that is not so much a disease as a remedy. God bless you.

To nine-year-old Benjamin Franklin Bache at school in Geneva, Franklin wrote a series of charming letters, of which the following is a good example.

Passy, Augt 19, 1779.

My dear Child,

Do not think that I have forgotten you, because I have been so long without writing to you. I think of you every day, and there is nothing I desire more than to see you furnish'd with good Learning, that I may return you to your Father and Mother so accomplish'd with such Knowledge & Virtue as to give them Pleasure, and enable you to become an honourable Man in your own Country. I am therefore very willing you should have a Dictionary, and all such other Books as M. de Marignac or M. Cramer shall judge proper for you. Those Gentlemen are very good to you and you are I hope very thankful to them, and do everything chearfully they advise you to do; by so doing you will recommend yourself to me, and all good People as well as we will love & esteem you for your dutiful Behaviour.

Your Friends Cochran and Deane are well, Cochran gave me a Letter for you a long time since, which I mislaid, but having now found it, I send it inclos'd. The Small Pox is in that Pension, and 4 of the Scholars are dead of it. I will speak to Cochran to send you their Names. He has not yet had it. How happy it is for you that your Parents took care to have you inoculated when you were an Infant! Which puts you out of that Danger. ...I continue very well, Thanks to God; and I shall always love you very much if you continue to be a good Boy; being ever

Your affectionate Grandfather
B. F.

Let me know what you are learning,}
    & whether you begin to draw. —}

Dr. FRANKLIN, prefents his Compliments to and defires the honour of    Company at Dinner, on Monday the 5th of *Ju'y*; in order to celebrate the ANNIVERSARY of the DECLARATION of AMERICAN INDErENDENCE.

Paffy,    1779.

*An Anfwer if you pleafe.*

*Franklin's invitation for the 5th of July, 1779, to celebrate Independence*

Franklin seldom missed an opportunity to trouble the English in their home waters. This letter to Captain George Blackwell neatly solved the problem of a shortage of commissions from Congress, a solution that enabled Captain Blackwell to cruise in international waters as a legally constituted privateer.

315

Passy. Sept 14. 1779

I am Sorry I cannot give you the Commission you desire having none left. — But I see nothing amiss in your taking what you can, and carrying it in tho' without a Commission, for since the Congress, in reprisal, have immitated the government of England, and encourage sailors employ'd in ships to seize and bring them in giving them the whole as a Reward for their breach of Trust, I should think there is stronger Reason for allowing an honest Man the Prize he has openly taken from the Enemy and that resolution of Congress seems to me to be of the Nature of a General Commission. However, the taking particular Commissions is certainly the best and most regular and ought not to be dispenc'd with, unless in such Cases as yours, where Circumstances have made it at Present impracticable.

The Marquis de Lafayette had returned to France, after a highly successful military career in America. He was soon busy organizing a raid on the English coast, for which he sought Franklin's advice. Franklin suggested that he might make ransom demands on various English towns. In this letter, Franklin discussed other possibilities, as well as the Franco-American alliance.

*Louis XVI and the Marquis de Lafayette painted on the top of a box*

Passy, Aug. 19, 1779.

I have just now received your favour of the 17th. I wrote to you a Day or two ago, and have little to add. You ask my Opinion, what Conduct the English will probably hold on this Occasion, and whether they will not rather propose a Negociation for a Peace. I have but one Rule to go by in devining of those people, which is, that whatever is prudent for them to do, they will omit; and what is most imprudent to be done, they will do it. This like other general Rules, may some times have its Exceptions; but I think it will hold good for the most part at least while the present Ministry continues, or rather while the present Madman has the Choice of Ministers. You desire to know whether I am satisfied with the Ministers here? It is impossible for anybody to be more so. I see they exert themselves greatly in the Common Cause and do everything for us that they can. We can wish for nothing more, unless our great Want of Money should make us wish for a Subsidy, to enable us to act more vigorously, in expelling the enemy from their remaining Posts, and reducing Canada. But their own Expences are so great, that I cannot press such an Addition to it. I hope however that we shall get some Supplies of Arms and Ammunition, and perhaps when they can be spar'd some Ships to aid in reducing New York and Rhodeisland. At present I know of no good Opportunity of Writing to America. There are Marchant Ships continually going, but they are very uncertain Conveyances. I long to hear of your safe Arrival in England: but the Winds are adverse, and we must have Patience.

Franklin did not forget science, in spite of all he had to do, running the European side of the war. This letter to Joseph Priestley contains some of his most famous speculations about the future.

Passy, Feb. 8, 1780

Your kind Letter of September 27 came to hand but very lately, the Bearer having staied long in Holland. I always rejoice to hear of your being still employ'd in experimental Researches into Nature, and of the Success you meet with. The rapid Progress *true* Science now makes, occasions my regretting sometimes that I was born so soon. It is impossible to imagine the Height to which may be carried, in a thousand years, the Power of Man over Matter. We may perhaps learn to deprive large Masses of their Gravity, and give them absolute Levity, for the sake of easy Transport. Agriculture may diminish its Labour and double its Produce; all Diseases may by sure means be prevented or cured, not excepting even that of Old Age, and our Lives lengthened at pleasure even beyond the antediluvian Standard. O that moral Science were in as fair a way of Improvement, that Men would cease to be Wolves to one another, and that human Beings would at length learn what they now improperly call Humanity!

With talk of peace in the air, Franklin sent this sunny letter to George Washington, containing perhaps the most moving words he ever wrote about America's future.

Passy, March 5 1780.

Should peace arrive after another Campaign or two, and afford us a little Leisure, I should be happy to see your Excellency in Europe, and to accompany you, if my Age and Strength would permit, in visiting some of its ancient and most famous Kingdoms. You would, on this side of the Sea, enjoy the great Reputation you have acquir'd, pure and free from those little Shades that the Jealousy and Envy of a Man's Countrymen and Co-temporaries are ever endeavouring to cast over living Merit. Here you would know, and enjoy, what Posterity will say of Washington. For 1000 Leagues have nearly the same Effect with 1000 Years. The feeble Voice of those grovelling Passions cannot extend so far either in Time or Distance. At present I enjoy that Pleasure for you, as I frequently hear the old Generals of this martial Country, (who study the Maps of America, and mark upon them all your Operations,) speak with sincere Approbation and great Applause of your conduct; and join in giving you the Character of one of the greatest Captains of the Age.

I must soon quit this Scene, but you may live to see our Country flourish, as it will amazingly and rapidly after the War is over. Like a Field of young Indian Corn, which long Fair weather and Sunshine had enfeebled and discolored, and which in that weak State, by a Thunder Gust, of violent Wind, Hail, and Rain, seem'd to be threaten'd with absolute Destruction; yet the Storm being past, it recovers fresh Verdure, shoots up with double Vigour, and delights the Eye, not of its Owner only, but of every observing Traveller.

Franklin's mission to France, by this date, had already been extremely successful. He had negotiated treaties of alliance and commerce between his fledgling nation and Continental Europe's leading power, and he had repeatedly won grants to continue financing the American war effort. But he had five more years abroad, years that were to be capped by his most dramatic diplomatic achievement—the securing of peace.

*A Picture Portfolio*

# An American Abroad

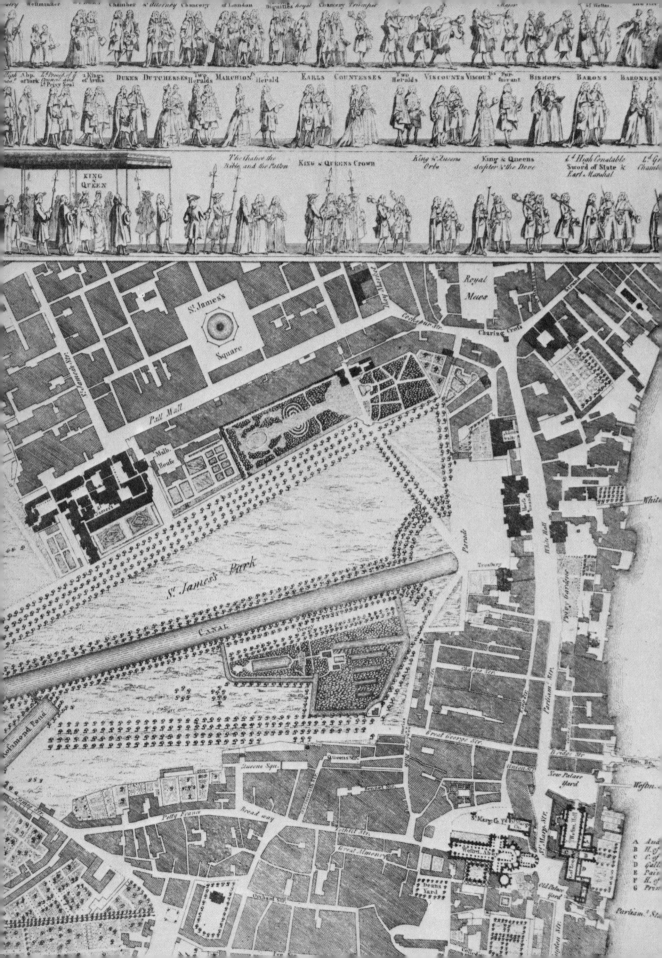

## THE LONDON YEARS

Franklin spent nearly thirty years abroad. Eighteen of these were passed in London, where he had been sent as a Colonial agent for Pennsylvania in 1757 and whence he departed on the eve of the Revolution, his country's leading spokesman. As the splendid portrait of him painted in 1766 by David Martin attests, he was then in the prime of life, and at first he and England conducted a happy love affair. In 1761 he watched the coronation of George III, for which the map at left was printed, and soon after called him "the best King any nation was ever blessed with." But over the years he became sadly yet firmly convinced that the America Colonies must sever all ties with the mother country.

322

*The Cravenstreet Gazette.* N° 113

Saturday, Sept. 22. 1770

This Morning Queen Margaret, accompanied by her first
Maid of Honour Miss Franklin, set out for Rochester.
Immediately on their Departure, the whole Street was in
Tears—from a heavy Shower of Rain.

It is whispered that the new Family Administration
which took place on her Majesty's Departure, promises,
like all other new Administrations, to govern much better
than the old one.

We hear that the great Person (so called from his enormous Size) of a certain Family in a certain Street, is
grievously affected at the late Changes, and would hardly be comforted this Morning, tho' the new Ministry promised him
a roasted Shoulder of Mutton & Potatoes, for his Dinner.

It is said, that the same great Person intended to pay his
Respects to another great Personage this Day, at St. James's, it being Coronation-Day; hoping thereby a little to amuse his Grief, but
was prevented by an Accident, Queen Margaret, or her Maid of
Honour having carried off the Key of the Drawers, so that the Lady
of the Bedchamber could not come at a laced Shirt for his Highness.
Great Clamours were made on this Occasion against her Majesty.

Other Accounts say, that the Shirts were afterwards found
tho' too late, in another Place. And some suspect, that the Wanting
a Shirt from those Drawers was only a ministerial Pretence
to excuse Picking the Locks, that the new Administration might have
every thing at Command.

## A SECOND HOME

For the long years Franklin lived in London away from his own family, he lodged in four rooms of the agreeable little house at left, No. 7 Craven Street, and later across the street at No. 36. His landlady was Mrs. Margaret Stevenson, whose daughter Polly (far left) named Franklin godfather of her first child and for whose delight and pleasure he wrote *The Craven Street Gazette*, a burlesque of contemporary British newspapers. Craven Street ran back from the Thames River, close to the tower in the painting above. It was wonderfully convenient for Franklin, within easy walking distance of the Government offices in Whitehall, seen at far left.

323

## LONDON HAUNTS

Even before Franklin reached London, the distinguished Royal Society had awarded him its Copley Medal for his electrical experiments (below, far left). The society's house in Crane Court (below, left), became one of his favorite spots and many of its members his closest friends. He joined the Society of Antiquaries, also a senior learned society; the reception of a new member into that dignified company is depicted at left. The Royal Society of Arts was another congenial place. When James Barry painted the murals for its new Adams brothers' building (above), he sketched Franklin in his fur hat (below) but never actually painted him in. A detail of the actual mural (below, right) shows Franklin's friend William Shipley, founder, with his "plan."

(!)

Dear Son,

Twyford at the Bishop
of St Asaph's,
1771.

and the Journey I took for that purpose.
7 Now imagining it may be equally
agreeable to you to know the Circumstances of my Life, many of which you
are yet unacquainted with; and
expecting a Weeks uninterrupted
Leisure in my present Country
Retirement, I set down to write
them for you. To
which I have besides some other
Inducements. Having emerg'd
from the Poverty & Obscurity in which
I was born & bred, to a State of
Affluence & some Degree of
Reputation in the World, and having gone so far thro'
Life with a considerable Share of Fe-
licity, the conducing Means
I made use of, with the Blessing of God,
which so well suc-
ceeded, my Posterity may like
to know, as they
may find some of them suitable to
their own Situations, & therefore
fit to be imitated. —That Felicity, when I reflected on it, has
induc'd me sometimes to say, that
were it offer'd to my Choice, I should
have no Objection to a Repetition
of the same Life from its Beginning, only asking the Advantages
Authors have in a second Edition
to correct some Faults of the first.
So would I change some sinister
Accidents & Events of it for others more favourable
but tho' this were deny'd,
I should still accept the Offer.
Since such a Repetition is not to be expected,
the next Thing most like living one's

I have ever had a Pleasure in
obtaining any little Anecdotes of my Ancestors. You
may remember the Enquiries I made
among the Remains of my Relations
when you were with me in England;
the Notes one of my Uncles
(who had the same kind of
Curiosity in collecting Family Anecdotes) one put into my Hands,
furnish'd me with several Particulars
relating to our Ancestors.
From those Notes I learnt that the Family had liv'd in the same Village,
Eton in Northamptonshire, for 300
Years, & how much longer he knew
not, on a Freehold of
about 30 Acres, aided by the Smith's
Business which had continued in
the Family till his Time, the eldest
Son being always bred
to that Business. —When I search'd
the Register at Eton I found an Account of their Births, Marriages
and Burials, from the year 1555 only, there
being no Register kept in that Parish
at any time preceding.
By that Register I perceiv'd that I was
the youngest Son of the youngest Son
for 5 Generations back. My Grandfather Thomas, who was born in 1598,
liv'd at Eton till he grew too old to
follow Business longer, when he went
to live with his Son John, a Dyer
at Banbury in Oxfordshire,
with whom my Father serv'd an Apprenticeship. There my Grandfather died

## "THE SWEET AIR OF TWYFORD"

It may have been William Shipley who introduced Franklin to his brother Jonathan, Bishop of St. Asaph (left). If so, it was a happy occurrence, for Franklin found the bishop a staunch friend of America and in his large and friendly home in the quiet village of Twyford (above) he found the time and inclination to write the first part of his renowned *Autobiography* (original manuscript page opposite). When Franklin returned to town he wrote his host: "I now breathe with reluctance the smoke of London, when I think of the sweet air of Twyford."

327

## COUNTRY LIFE

Franklin's circle of friends was wide, and he
wrote, not immodestly, to his son William that his
company was "so much desired that I...could
spend the whole summer in the country houses of
inviting friends, if I choose it." One such house,
whose "Gardens are a Paradise" (above, right),
belonged to Lord and Lady le Despencer. The lord,
better known as Sir Francis Dashwood, had had a
checkered career before Franklin knew him as
Postmaster General of England. He founded a
rake's club of "monks" who conducted "rites of a
nature subversive of all Decency." In the print
above he is shown at these mock devotions.
Franklin was also close to the young Earl of
Shelburne (right), who as Secretary of State for
the Colonies in 1767–68 was always a good friend
to America. He was host to Franklin at his beautiful country home, Bowood (far right).

328

*New-York, May 8, 1775.*

## Extract of a Letter From Philadelphia,

*To a Gentleman in this City, dated the 6th inst.*

YESTERDAY evening Dr. F R A N K L I N arrived here from London in six weeks, which he left the 20th of March, which has given great joy to this town, he says we have no favours to expect from the Ministry, nothing but submission will satisfy them, they expect little or no opposition will be made to their troops, those that are now coming are for New-York, where it is expected they will be received with cordiality. As near as we can learn there are about four thousand troops coming in this fleet, the men of war and transports are in a great measure loaded with dry goods, to supply New-York, and the country round it, agents are coming over with them. Dr. *Franklin* is highly pleased to find us arming and preparing for the worst events, he thinks nothing else can save us from the most abject slavery and destruction, at the same time encourages us to believe a spirited opposition, will be the means of our salvation. The Ministry are alarmed at every opposition, and lifted up again at every thing which appears the least in their favour, every letter and every paper from hence, are read by them.

*N E W - Y O R K:*
Printed by J O H N A N D E R S O N, at Beekman's-Slip.

## FRIENDS AND ENEMIES

In his professional life as agent for four Colonies (Pennsylvania, Georgia, New Jersey, Massachusetts), Franklin made many friends and many enemies. Two men sympathetic to America's cause during the Stamp Act crisis were Lord Rockingham and his secretary Edmund Burke, seen at left in Sir Joshua Reynolds's fine unfinished portrait. Rockingham was then Prime Minister, and it was Burke who arranged for Franklin to testify in Parliament, working out with him the questions and answers of the interrogation that resulted in the Stamp Act's repeal. To Burke, Franklin was "the friend of the human race." When the understanding Earl of Shelburne was eliminated in a cabinet shuffle, Lord Hillsborough (above, far left) became Secretary of State for the Colonies. He and Franklin had little use for each other, and after one of their unsatisfactory conferences, Franklin described his character as "Conceit, Wrongheadedness, Obstinacy and Passion." Another bitter enemy was Alexander Wedderburn (above, left), Solicitor General in the North Ministry. It was Wedderburn who subjected Franklin to a degrading ordeal before the Privy Council, while he was supposedly defending Governor Hutchinson in the case arising from Franklin's disclosure of the "Hutchinson letters." After the attack, during which he remained entirely silent, Franklin commented: "Spots of Dirt thrown upon my character, I suffered while fresh to remain; I . . . rely'd on the vulgar adage, that they would all rub off when they were dry." During the last sad days of his eighteen-year-long sojourn in London, when war between England and her American Colonies seemed imminent, Franklin received overtures from Richard Lord Howe. Invited to Howe's sister's home to play chess (above), he held several talks with Howe only to realize that no solution was possible. A broadside (above, right) announced Franklin's return to Philadelphia and declared him "highly pleased to find us arming and preparing for the worst events. . . ."

## ENVOY TO PARIS

Nine months after a bitter Franklin had returned to America from England, his country enlisted him to go abroad again, to persuade France to become an ally in the war against England. In his marten cap among the powdered heads of Paris, Franklin took the French by storm. He lived most comfortably in the mansion at left in the Parisian suburb of Passy—"about ½ an hours Drive from the City." From its terrace Franklin had a splendid view of the Seine and from here he was able to watch the balloon ascensions that later became all the rage (below, far left). Indeed, he was even satirized in an English cartoon of the period, which showed him in dark glasses (3) having cut the ropes of a balloon inscribed *America* with a knife inscribed *Sedition*, while George Washington goes aloft in the suspended basket.

## INDÉPENDANCE DES ÉTATS-UNIS.

Le 4 Juillet 1776, les Treize Colonies Confédérées (connues depuis sous le nom d'États-Unis) ont déclarées, par le Congrès, libres et indépendantes. N. Gerard, porteur des pouvoirs de LOUIS XVI, Roi de France, Benjamin Franklin, pour les États-Unis, signent à Paris, le 6 Février 1777, un Traité d'amitié et de commerce, et un Traité d'alliance éventuelle, mis en vigueur par la déclaration de guerre survenue entre la France et l'Angleterre.

Le Comte d'Estaing, le Marquis de la Fayette, le Comte de Rochambeau, &c. combattent pour la cause des Américains, soutenue avec tant de gloire par le Général Washington. Capitulation faite le 19 Octobre 1782 par le Lord Cornwalis, dont le désastre accélère la Paix. L'indépendance des États-Unis est reconnue par les Traités de Paix. Pénétrés de reconnaissance pour les services que LOUIS XVI leur a rendus, les États-Unis ont depuis fait élever à Philadelphie un monument qui en éternisera le souvenir. Cet exemple est d'autant plus mémorable, que les Siècles passés n'offrent aucun exemple de monumens élevés par des Républiques à la gloire d'un Souverain. Les Traités de Paix ont rendu aux Nations la liberté des mers ; bienfait dont l'Europe est redevable à la générosité de LOUIS XVI. Le Port de Cherbourg, ouvrage immortel du règne de ce grand Prince, doit affermir cette liberté si utile aux Peuples.

A Paris chez Blin, Imprimeur en Taille-Douce, Place Maubert, N.º 17, vis à vis la rue des 3 Portes. A.P.D.R.

334

## ROYAL ALLY

The painting above of Franklin's reception at the Court of France when Louis XVI (seated on the sofa with Marie Antoinette) avowed the treaties of alliance and commerce between France and America—although highly idealized—does reflect the esteem with which Franklin was regarded. When Franklin left France, the King gave him a miniature of himself (top left) in a frame studded with 408 diamonds (later sold by the family). At left, America pays homage to Louis, Franklin, and Washington, who worked together to secure her independence.

## THE PEACEMAKER

In Paris, on September 3, 1783, the treaty signaling peace with England and recognition of American sovereignty was at long last signed (below). For Franklin— shown at center in Benjamin West's unfinished painting (opposite), surrounded by his fellow American commissioners, John Jay, John Adams, Henry Laurens, and his grandson and secretary William Temple Franklin—it was the capstone of a long and illustrious career, and to him the lion's share of the credit belongs. Franklin remained in Paris for two more years negotiating commercial treaties. As he prepared to leave for home, a venerable figure well into his eightieth year, he wrote to his English friend David Hartley, whose signature also appears on the treaty below: "We were long fellow labourers in the best of all works, the work of peace. I leave you still in the field, but having finished my day's task, I am going home *to go to bed!*" Happily, he lived another five years.

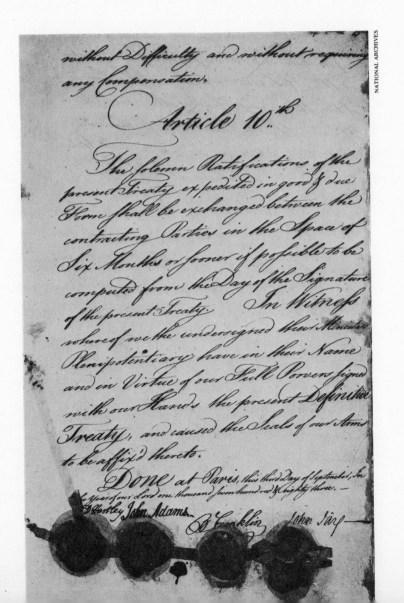

Chapter **11**

# Mr. Ambassador

There were times during his years in France when Benjamin Franklin almost gave up under the weight of his multiple harassments. In a letter to his nephew Jonathan Williams, Jr., who handled American business affairs at Nantes, the ambassador discussed another immense project that had fallen into his lap—buying and shipping to the American army fifteen thousand uniforms, fifteen thousand muskets, and two thousand barrels of powder. Some of it was supposed to go aboard the *Alliance* but was left onshore by the mutinous Captain Landais, who was supported and encouraged in this act of defiance by Arthur Lee.

Passy, June 27, 1780.

Dear Jonan:—

To get rid of all farther Projects and Propositions which I never understand relating to the Shiping of the Goods, I entrusted you with that Business and impower'd you to freight a Ship or Ships. But I have not succeeded, for in yours of the 23rd you send me new Schemes. No other Man-of-War to go under the Command of Comme Jones can at present be obtained: Assist him in getting out with the *Ariel;* after that you and M. de Chaumont may unite in finding some means of sending the rest of the Goods. You and he can agree and assist each other; but there never can be any Union of Counsels or Endeavors between the Commodore and him. I was told that if we would obtain the *Ariel,* she would do our Business; I join'd in the application and we obtained her. Now she is too Little and another is wanted. I will absolutely have nothing to do with any new Squadron Project. I have been too long in hot Water, plagu'd almost to Death with the Passions, Vagaries, and ill

Humours and Madnesses of other People. I must have a little Repose. This to yourself, and believe me ever,

Your affectionate Uncle,

B FRANKLIN

Franklin's relationship to his daughter was a strange mixture of affection and condescension. He seemed to find it difficult to recognize her many good qualities, perhaps identifying her too closely with his devoted though none too gifted wife, Deborah. The first letter below is a good example of the rather peremptory tone he often took with her, while the second has more of his natural sunshine in it.

Passy, March 16. 1780.

Dear Sally,

I received your kind Letters of Sept. 14. and 25th. You mention the Silk being in a Box with Squirrel Skins, but it is come to hand without them or the Box. Perhaps they were spoilt by the Salt Water and thrown away; for the Silk is much damag'd and not at all fit to be presented as you propose. Indeed I wonder how having yourself scarce Shoes to your Feet, it should come into your Head to give Cloathes to a Queen. I shall see if the Stains can be cover'd by Dyeing it, and make Summer Suits of it, for myself, Temple and Benny.

I send some of Ben's Letters inclosed to his Father. He is well taken Care of, and well contented. But I fancy you had rather he should be with me. Perhaps I may therefore recall him. Tho' I really think he is better at Geneva for his Learning. Many Persons of Quality here, send their Sons there, for the same Reason tho' the Religion is different.

I am glad to hear that Weaving Work is so hard to get done. Tis a Sign there is much Spinning. All the Things you Order will be sent, as you continue to be a good Girl, and spin and knit your Family Stockings.

My Health and Spirits continue and I am ever, Your affectionate Father

B FRANKLIN

*The* Alliance *returning to America in 1780, where her captain, Pierre Landais, was court-martialed.*

Passy, June 27. 1780.

Dear Sally

I received your pleasing Letters of Nov. 14. Mr. Aston whom you recommended to me has been here, and I treated him with the Civilities you desired. I was glad to hear that William, Betsy and Louis, tho' the two latter are yet Strangers to me, were all well and lively. Will was always lively. Tell me what Improvement he makes in his Learning. He ought to read and begin to write by this time. I hope to have a Letter from him soon. Ben writes to me often. He is very glorious at present, having obtained the Prize of his School for a best Translation from the Latin into French; which was presented to him in the Cathedral Church by the first Magistrate of the City. I send you his Letter and his Masters containing the News of this Important Event. He gives a Treat on the Occasion to the rest of the Scholars for which I shall pay with much Pleasure.... The Congress have kept me in constant Expectation of being assisted by a Secretary; but he has not yet appeared, and Temple and I are absolute Drudges. I am ever My dear Child, Your affectionate Father

B FRANKLIN

Temple presents his Duty.

To compound Franklin's problems, John Adams—who had returned to the United States in 1779 when he was relieved of his original commission—was now back in Europe. Although Adams had a new commission to negotiate peace, he had nothing to do. The British had renewed the war with vigor, capturing all of Georgia and most of South Carolina, including the key city of Charleston and its defending American army. Adams proceeded to pick a quarrel with the Count de Vergennes, which Franklin tried to smooth over in this letter.

Passy, August 3, 1780.

It was indeed with great Pleasure that I received the letter your Excellency did me the Honour of writing to me, communicating that of the President of Congress, and the Resolutions of that Body relative to the Succours then expected. For the Sentiments therein expressed are so different from the Language held by Mr. Adams in his late Letters to your Excellency as to make it clear that it was from his particular Indiscretion alone, and not from any Instructions received by him, that he has given such just Cause of Displeasure, and that it is impossible his Conduct therein should be approved by his Constituents. I am glad he has not admitted me to any Participation of those Writings, and that he has taken the Resolution he expresses, of not communicating with me, or making use of my Intervention in his future Correspondence; a Resolution that I believe he will keep, as he has never yet communicated to me more of his Business in Europe than I have seen in Newspapers. I live upon Terms of Civility with him, not of Intimacy. I shall as you desire lay before Congress the whole Correspondence which you have sent me for that purpose.

Franklin eventually found a fellow diplomat in whom he could confide, John Jay, who had been designated minister plenipotentiary to the Spanish court with instructions to negotiate a treaty with Spain and secure a loan. In this important letter, he advised Jay how to handle the Spaniards and discussed Jay's fear that the Spaniards were seeking to deprive Americans of the western territory along the Mississippi, as well as the right to use that river. But the overriding theme is the desperate condition of America's finances.

Passy, October. 2, 1780.

I received duly and in good Order the several Letters you have written to me of Augt. 16. 19. Sept. 8. and 22. The Papers that accompanied them of your writing, gave me the Pleasure of seeing the Affairs of our Country in such good Hands, and the Prospect from your Youth of its having the Service of so able a Minister for a great Number of Years: But the little Success that has attended your late Applications for Money mortified me exceedingly; and the Storm of Bills which I found coming upon us both, has terrified and vexed me to such a Degree that I have been deprived of Sleep, and so much indispos'd by continual Anxiety as to be render'd almost incapable of Writing.

At length I got over a Reluctance that was almost invincible, and made another Application to the Government here for more Money. I drew up and presented a State of Debts and newly expected Demands, and requested its Aid to extricate me. Judging from your Letters that you were not likely to obtain anything considerable from your Court, I put down in my Estimate the 25,000 Dollars drawn upon you with the same Sum drawn upon me, as what would probably come to me for Payment. I have now the Pleasure to acquaint you that my Memorial was received in the kindest and most friendly Manner; and tho' the Court here is not without its Embarrassments, on Account of Money, I was told to make myself easy, for that I should be assisted with what was necessary. Mr. Searle arriving about this Time, and assuring me there had been a plentiful Harvest, and

*John Jay*

*Franklin had his own small printing press in Passy. This is a specimen of stencils made for him by Bery; the notations are in Franklin's hand.*

great Crops of all Kinds; that the Congress had demanded of the several States, Contributions in Produce; which would be chearfully given; that they would therefore have Plenty of Provisions to dispose of; and I being much pleased with the generous Behavior just experienced, I presented another Paper, proposing in order to ease us, that the Congress might furnish their Army in America with Provisions in Part of Payment for the sums lent us. This Proposition I was told was well taken: But it being consider'd that the States having the Enemy in their Country and obliged to make great Expences for the present Campaign, the furnishing so much Provisions as the French Army would need might straiten and be inconvenient to the Congress; his Majesty did not at this time think it right to accept the Offer.

You will not wonder at my loving this good Prince: He will win the Hearts of all America:

If you are not so fortunate in Spain, continue however the even good Temper you have hitherto manifested. Spain owes us nothing, therefore whatever Friendship she shows us in lending Money or furnishing Cloathing, &ca. tho' not equal to our Wants and Wishes, is however *tant de gagné;* those who have begun to assist us are more likely to continue than to decline, and we are still so much obliged as their Aids amount to. But I hope and am confident that Court will be wiser, than to take Advantage of our Distress and insist on our making Sacrifices by an Agreement, which the Circumstances of such Distress would hereafter weaken, and the very Proposition can only give Disgust at present. Poor as we are, yet as I know we shall be rich, I would rather agree with them to buy at a great Price the whole of their Right on the Missisipi than sell a Drop of its Waters. A Neighbour might as well ask me to sell my Street Door.

I wish you could obtain an Account of what they have supplied us with already, in Money and Goods.

Mr. Grand informing me that one of the Bills drawn on you, having been sent from hence to Madrid, was come back unaccepted, I have directed him to pay it; and he has at my Request undertaken to write to the Marquis D'Yranda, to assist you with Money to answer such Bills as you are not otherwise enabled to pay, and to draw on him for the Amount, which Drafts I shall answer here, as far as the Sum above mentioned of twenty five thousand Dollars. If you expect more acquaint me. But pray write to Congress as I do to forbear this Practice, which is so extreamly hazardous and may some time or other prove very mischevous to their Credit and Affairs. I have undertaken too for all the Bills drawn on Mr. Laurens that have yet appear'd. He was to have sailed 3 Days after Mr. Searle, that is the 18th of July. Mr. Searle begins to be in pain for him, having no good Opinion of the little Vessel he was to embark in.

We have Letters from America to the 7th of August. The Spirit of our People was never higher. Vast Exertions making preparatory for some important Action. Great Harmony and Affection between the Troops of the two Nations. The New Money in good Credit &ca. &ca.

I will write to you again shortly and to Mr. Carmichael. I shall now be able to pay up your Salaries compleat for the Year. But as Demands unforeseen are continually coming upon me I still retain the Expectations you have given me of being reimbursed out of the first Remittances you receive.

If you find any Inclination to hug me for the good News of this Letter, I constitute and appoint Mrs. Jay my attorney to receive in my Behalf your Embraces.

Not even John Paul Jones gave Franklin any peace of mind at this time. The following letter chastised the commodore for spending money like a drunken sailor, which he seldom was.

Passy, Nov. 1. 1780.

I received duly yours of Oct. 13 and 20th. I am extreamly sorry for your Misfortune. The Storm was a terrible one, it was well you escaped with your Lives.

Since your Departure I have received the Acct. of Messrs. Gourlade and Moylan, and I am astonished to find that I am charged with so heavy a Sum as near 100,000 Livres for the Expences of the *Ariel*. After having twice entreated you for god Sake to consider my Circumstances, the Difficultyes I had to provide for so many Expences, and not take any thing but what was absolutely necessary, which you promised me fully you would attend to, I am surprised to find a charge of near 6000 Livres for Shot, which cannot be wanted in America where they are made in Plenty; 5566 Livres 16 for Drugs, an enormous Quantity, and more than 20000

Livres for Slops. &c. after all the officers and Sailors had had considerable Advances made them, without consulting me. Perhaps it will be said, that the Drugs and Slops may be wanted or useful in America. But you will easily conceive on Reflection that if every Person in office in a Ship of the States takes the Liberty of judging what is wanted in America, and in what Quantities, and to order those Quantities leaving me to pay for them, It may not only be involved in unexpected Debt and Demands as At Present, but very unnecessary and unproportioned Supplies may be sent over to the Damage of the Publick. I find myself therefore under the Necessity of putting Stop to this Proceeding: And I know no other way of doing it, than by absolutely refusing Payment of such Charges, made without my Orders or Consent first obtained. Some Medecins and some Slops may be necessary, but those Quantities appear to me enormous.

From America, with winter coming on, Lafayette frantically wrote, asking Franklin what had happened to the fifteen thousand uniforms supposed to have been purchased and shipped by then. Franklin replied to this question and discussed other matters, including a propaganda project on which he and Lafayette were collaborating.

Passy, Dec. 9. 1780.

There has been a kind of Fatality attending the affair of sending out the Cloathing. A Number of unforeseen and unaccountable Accidents have delay'd and prevented it from time to time. Part of it is however at length gone; and the Rest in a fair Way of going soon, with the Arms, Powder, &c. You may depend on my procuring and forwarding all I can, that is necessary for the Operations of our Army.

I congratulate you on the Escape from Arnold's Treachery. His Character is in the light of all Europe already on the Gibbet and will hang there in Chains for Ages.

I wish you had been more particular relating to the Plan you mention of the Eastern States; as I do not fully understand it.

You being now upon the Spot can easily obtain and send me all the authenticated Accounts of the Enemies Barbarity that are necessary for our little Book, or What is better get some body there to write it, and send me a Copy that I may adapt the Cuts to it. I have found an excellent Engraver for the Purpose.

In spite of the brave things Franklin said about the reviving American war effort, the opening of the year 1781 saw the American cause tottering. In desperation, Washington dispatched to France a special envoy of his own, Colonel John Laurens, to plead for more aid, and Congress asked Franklin to assist him. Before Laurens arrived, Franklin wrote this masterful letter to Vergennes, which obtained six million livres.

Passy, Feb. 13, 1781.

I have just received from Congress their Letter for the King, which I have the honour of putting herewith into the hands of your Excellency. I am charged, at the same time, to "represent, in the strongest Terms, the unalterable Resolution of the United States to maintain their Liberties and Independence; and inviolably to adhere to the Alliance at every hazard, and in every Event; and that the Misfortunes of the last Campaign, instead of repressing, have redoubled their Ardour; that Congress are resolved to employ every Resource in their Power to expel the Enemy from every Part of the United States, by the most vigorous and decisive Cooperation with Marine and other Forces of their illustrious Ally; that they have accordingly called on the several States for a powerful Army and ample Supplies of Provisions; and that the States are disposed effectually to comply with their Requisitions. That if, in Aid of their own Exertions, the Court of France can be prevailed on to assume a Naval Superiority in the American Seas, to furnish the Arms, Ammunition, and Clothing, specified in the Estimate heretofore transmitted, and to assist with the Loan mentioned in the Letter, they flatter themselves, that, under the divine Blessing, the War must speedily be terminated, with Glory and Advantage to both Nations."

By several Letters to me from intelligent Persons it appears, that the great and expensive Exertions of the last Year, by which a Force was assembled capable of facing the Enemy, and which accordingly drew towards New York, and lay long near that City, was rendred ineffectual by the Superiority of the Enemy at Sea; and that their Success in Carolina had been chiefly owing to that Superiority, and to the want of the necessary Means for furnishing, marching, and paying the Expence of Troops sufficient to defend that Province. The Marquis de la Fayette writes to me, that it is impossible to conceive, without seeing it, the Distress the Troops have

*Colonel John Laurens*

suffer'd for want of Cloathing; and the following is a Paragraph of a Letter from General Washington, which I ought not to keep back from your Excellency, viz. "I doubt not you are so fully informed by Congress of our political and military State, that it would be superfluous to trouble you with any thing relative to either. If I were to speak on Topicks of the kind, it would be to shew that our present Situation makes one of two Things essential to us; a Peace, or the most vigorous Aid of our Allies, particularly in the Article of *Money*. Of their Disposition to serve us, we cannot doubt; their Generosity will do every thing their Means will permit." They had in America great Expectations, I know not on what Foundation, that a considerable Supply of Money would be obtained from Spain; but that Expectation has failed: And the Force of that Nation in those Seas has been employ'd to reduce small Forts in Florida, without rendring any direct Assistance to the United States; and indeed the long Delay of that Court, in acceding to the Treaty of Commerce, begins to have the Appearance of its not inclining to have any Connection with us; so that, for effectual Friendship, and for the Aid so necessary in the present Conjuncture, we can rely on France alone, and in the Continuance of the King's Goodness towards us.

I am grown old. I feel myself much enfeebled by my late long illness, and it is probable I shall not long have any more Concern in these Affairs. I therefore take this Occasion to express my Opinion to your Excellency, that the present Conjuncture is critical; that there is some Danger lest the Congress should lose its Influence over the people, if it is found unable to procure the Aids that are wanted; and that the whole System of the new Govern't in America may thereby be shaken; that, if the English are suffer'd once to recover that Country, such an Opportunity of effectual Separation as the present may not occur again in the Course of Ages; and that the Possession of those fertile and extensive Regions, and that vast SeaCoast, will afford them so broad a Basis for future Greatness, by the rapid growth of their Commerce, and Breed of Seamen and Soldiers, as will enable them to become the *Terror of Europe*, and to exercise with impunity that Insolence, which is so natural to their Nation, and which will increase enormously with the Increase of their Power.

**LE ROI**

*Silhouette of Louis XVI, 1781*

Eager as he was to use his reputation in France to forward the American cause, Franklin knew when to draw the line. He did so in this letter to French author Felix Nogaret.

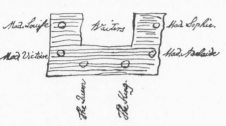

*In 1767 Franklin had visited France, where he was presented to Louis XV; he made this sketch of the royal family seated at their Sunday supper.*

Passy, March 8, 1781.

I received the Letter you have done me the honour of writing to me the 2d instant, wherein, after overwhelming me with a Flood of Compliments, which I can never hope to merit, you request my Opinion of your Translation of a Latin Verse, that has been apply'd to me. If I were, which I really am not, sufficiently skilled in your excellent Language, to be a proper Judge of its Poesy, the Supposition of my being the Subject, must restrain me from giving any Opinion on that Line, except that it ascribes too much to me, especially in what relates to the Tyrant; the Revolution having been the work of many able and brave Men, wherein it is sufficient Honour for me if I am allowed a small Share.

From England came more bad news. Thomas Digges, a Marylander to whom David Hartley had entrusted the task of distributing money to American prisoners in British jails, had turned out to be an embezzler. In this scorching letter to William Hodgson, an Englishman who represented the Americans in the negotiations to exchange prisoners, Franklin passed judgment on Digges.

Passy, April 1, 1781.

I received your respected Favour of the 20th past, and am shock'd exceedingly at the Account you give me of Digges. He that robbs the Rich even of a single Guinea is a Villain; but what is he who can break his sacred Trust, by robbing a poor Man and a Prisoner of Eighteen Pence given charitably for his Relief, and repeat that Crime as often as there are Weeks in a Winter, and multiply it by robbing as many poor Men every Week as make up the Number of near 600? We have no Name in our Language for such atrocious Wickedness. If such a Fellow is not damn'd, it is not worth while to keep a Devil.

From America came news that Lee and Izard were now both in Congress, making ferocious attacks on Franklin. Although he professed to scorn their criticisms, Franklin knew too much about the vagaries of legislative bodies to feel that he could ignore them with impunity. He therefore decided to outmaneuver them, by handing in his resignation. He was also depressed and weakened by a very severe attack of the gout, which had all but crippled him for several months. In this postscript to a letter he wrote to Sally and Richard Bache about their son Benjamin, he dwelt on his age and health, and carefully avoided the political aspects of the resignation.

Passy, May. 14, 1781

P.S.   I have written to Congress requesting they would send somebody to supply my Place, and permit me to retire, for that I find the Business too heavy for me, and too confining, being oblig'd to perform all the Functions of Consul, Judge of Admiralty, Merchant, Banker, &c. &c. besides that of Minister. I have borne the Burthen as long as I could; but I find that Age requires Rest. Yet it is not my purpose to return immediately home, unless ordered; chusing rather to remain here till the Peace, among a People that love me and whom I love, than to hazard an English Prison. My proper Situation indeed would be in my own House, with my Daughter to take care of me and nurse me in case of Illness, and with her Children who amuse me; but as this cannot well be at present, we must manage as we can.

In the same disenchanted mood, Franklin wrote to Robert Morris, discussing Morris's decision to become superintendent of America's chaotic finances.

Passy, July 26, 1781.

I have just received your very friendly Letter of the 6th of June past, announcing your Appointment to the Superintendence of our Finances. This gave me great Pleasure, as, from your Intelligence, Integrity, and Abilities, there is reason to hope every Advantage, that the Publick can possibly receive from such an Office. You are wise in estimating beforehand, as the principal Advantage you can expect, the consciousness of having done Service to your Country; for the Business you have undertaken is of so complex a Nature, and must engross so much of your Time and Attention, as necessarily to injure your private Interests; and the Publick is often niggardly, even of its Thanks, while you are sure of being censured by malevolent Criticks and Bug-writers, who will abuse you while you are serving them, and wound your Character in nameless Pamphlets; thereby resembling those little dirty stinking insects, that attack us only in the dark, disturb our Repose, molesting and wounding us, while our Sweat and Blood are contributing to their Subsistence. Every Assistance that my Situation here, as long as it continues, may enable me to afford you, shall certainly be given; for, besides my Affection for the glorious Cause we are both engaged in, I value myself upon your Friendship, and shall be happy if mine can be made of any Use to you.

Congress rejected Franklin's resignation. In this letter to William Carmichael, John Jay's secretary and later the American chargé d'affaires in Madrid, he showed little sign that the refusal distressed him.

Passy, Augt 24, 1781.

The Congress have done me the honour to refuse accepting my Resignation, and insist on my continuing in their Service till the Peace. I must therefore buckle again to Business, and thank God that my Health & Spirits are of late improved. I fancy it may have been a double Mortification to those Enemies you have mentioned to me, that I should ask as a Favour what they hop'd to vex me by taking from me; and that I should nevertheless be continued. But these sort of Considerations should never influence our Conduct. We ought always to do what appears best to be done, without much regarding what others may think of it. I call this Continuance an Honour, & I really esteem it to be a greater than my first Appointment, when I consider that all the Interest of my Enemies, united with my own Request, were not sufficient to prevent it. . . .

*A contemporary Dutch cartoon about armed neutrality shows an American (2, with B. Franklin written on his hat) stealing England's clothes.*

Mr Laurens's Business here was to solicit a large Aid in Money for the Army. It was thought that as he was a Witness of their Wants, he would be able to represent their Situation & Necessities more forcibly than I could do. He was indefatigable, while he staid, and took true Pains, but he *brusqu'd* the Ministers too much, and I found after he was gone that he had thereby given more Offence than I could have imagin'd. He obtain'd a Promise of a Loan of 10,000,000 to be borrowed in Holland: But as that Borrowing has not succeeded, he in fact obtained nothing. The Offence he gave will I hope have no durable Effects, tho' it produc'd me some Mortifications. Good humour and a kind Disposition towards us seems again to prevail. I had before his Arrival got the Grant of 6,000,000, and have since obtained more, or I could not have paid Mr Jay's Bills. . . .

I have accepted the Bill you last mentioned for 15,000 Dollars I had before accepted the Bill for 1700 Louis, being (with 50 left in my hands) the Amount of your half

Years Salaries, so that you are made easy on that head for the present;—but whether I shall have it in my Power to continue the Payments either to you or my self, is uncertain, and I would advise writing to Congress, as I shall do, for Remittances....

I have also just heard from Holland that the Affair of the Loan there is a good Train, & likely to succeed but this I do not depend on.

For a glimpse of history in the process of being made—or at least observed—by the leading participants, it is difficult to excel the following two letters that Franklin wrote to Vergennes.

*The surrender at Yorktown*

Passy Nov. 19. 1781.

I have the honour of sending to your Excellency some Advices I have just received. As the Letter from Virginia was received at New-Castle, a Town on the Delaware 40 Miles below Philadelphia, and probably after the Date of your Letters from thence, perhaps you may not have heard before, that M. DeBarras had joined M. deGrasse, and that the Northern Troops under the Generals Rochambeau and Washington, had joined the Marquis de la Fayette, and invested Cornwallis at York.

Passy. Novr. 20, 1781.

Your very obliging Letter communicating the News of the important Victory at York, gave me infinite Pleasure. The very powerful aid afforded by his Majesty to America this year, has rivetted the affections of that People, and the Success had made Millions happy. Indeed the King appears to me from this and another late Event, to be *le plus grand Faiseur d'heureux* that this World affords. May God prosper him, his Family and Nation to the End of Time!

As 1782 dawned, Yorktown seemed to have had no appreciable affect on Franklin's financial headaches. In fact, the French Government was almost bankrupt, and on January 28 Franklin wrote to Robert Morris, grimly informing him that there was no more money forthcoming from Louis XVI's treasury. Early in March, he sent Morris the following comments on hopeful signs of a peace movement in England.

Passy, March 7, 1782

You will see by the English Papers which I send to Mr. Secry. Livingston, that the Sense of the Nation is now fully against the Continuance of the America War. The Petitions of the Cities of London and Bristol were unanimous against it; Lord North muster'd all his Force, yet had a Majority against him of 19. It is said there were but two who voted with him, that are not Place men or Pensioners; and that even these in their private Conversations condemn the Prosecution of the War, and lay it all upon the King's Obstinacy. We must not however be lull'd by these Appearances. That Nation is changeable. And tho' some what humbled at Present, a little Success may make them as insolent as ever. I remember that when I was a boxing Boy, it was allow'd after an Adversary said he had enough, to give him a rising Blow. Let ours be a Douser.

A few months before Yorktown, Silas Deane, having returned to Europe full of bitterness over his cool reception from the Continental Congress, made a secret deal with the British Ministry and wrote a series of letters to America recommending a peace short of independence. He sent a copy of one of these letters to Franklin, and got the following reply.

Passy, April 19, 1782.

Sir,

I received the Letter you did me the honour to write to me the 30th. past, and will write to the purpose you desire respecting your Accounts. I hope the Method you propose for settling any disputable points in them will be approved and ordered. I received also your very long political Letter. The Multiplicity of Business on my Hands, on which Account you are so good as to excuse my not answering it, really makes it impossible for me to enter into the voluminous Discussions that would be necessary to do it fully. I can only say at present that I am not convinced; that perhaps my answer would not convince you; but that I think Time will. I am really sorry on your Account that you have written so much of the same kind to America. The Publication of those Letters has done great Prejudice to your Character there, and necessarily diminish'd much of the Regard your Friends had for you. You are now considered as having abandoned the Cause of your Country, and as having with Arnold espoused that of its Enemies. To me it appears that your Resentments and Passions have overcome your Reason and Judgment; and tho' my ancient Esteem and Affection for you induce me to make all the Allowances possible, in considering the Circumstances that have attended you since you first left France, yet the Lengths you have gone in endeavouring to discourage and diminish the Number of the Friends of our Country and Cause in Europe and America, and to encourage our Enemies, by those Letters, make it impossible for me to say with the same Truth & Cordiality as formerly that I am, Your affectionate Friend and humble Servant.

B FRANKLIN

Toward the end of March, 1782, Franklin heard that the North Ministry had at last fallen, and his old friend from the Stamp Act crisis, Lord Rockingham, was now the King's First Minister. Another good friend, Lord Shelburne, had come in as Secretary of State for American Affairs. Shelburne immediately dispatched a representative, Richard Oswald, to discuss peace terms with Franklin. The American ambassador kept a journal of the early months of the negotiation, which is too lengthy to be included here in its entirety. But the following excerpt gives us a graphic look at Franklin the diplomat in action, moving toward a goal that he had already suggested to David Hartley and other English friends—the British surrender of Canada.

[Franklin's record of a conversation with Richard Oswald, April 19, 1782]

I then remarked, that his Nation seem'd to desire Reconciliation with America; that I heartily wish'd the same thing, that a mere Peace would not produce half its Advantages if not attended with a sincere Reconciliation; that to obtain this the Party which had been the Aggressor and had cruelly treated the other, should show some Mark of Concern for what was past, and some Disposition to make Reparation; that perhaps there were things, which America might demand by way of Reparation, and which England might yield, and that the Effect would be vastly greater, if they appeared to be voluntary, and to spring from returning Good will; that I therefore wish'd England would think of offering something to relieve those who had suffer'd by its Scalping and Burning Parties. Lives indeed could not be restor'd nor compensated, but the Villages and Houses wantonly destroy'd might be rebuilt, &c. I then touch'd upon the Affair of Canada, and as in a former Conversation he had mention'd his Opinion, that the giving up of that Country to the English at the last Peace had been a politic Act in France, for that it had weaken'd the Ties between England and her Colonies, and that he himself had predicted from it the late Revolution, I spoke of the

Occasions of future Quarrel that might be produc'd by her continuing to hold it; hinting at the same time but not expressing too plainly that such a Situation, to us so dangerous, would necessarily oblige us to cultivate and strengthen our Union with France. He appear'd much struck with my Discourse.

In this letter to John Jay, written a few days after Franklin had seen Oswald, the ambassador announced the final triumph of his long struggle to free American sailors from British prisons.

Passy, April 24, 1782.

The Prince de Massaran being so good as to desire carrying a letter to you, I sit down to write you a few lines, though I hope soon to see you. . . .

In consequence of a proposition I sent over, the Parliament of Britain have just passed an act for exchanging American prisoners. They have near eleven hundred in the jails of England and Ireland, all committed as charged with high treason. The act is to empower the King, notwithstanding such commitments, to consider them as prisoners of war, according to the law of nations, and exchange them as such. This seems to be giving up their pretensions of considering us as rebellious subjects, and is a kind of acknowledgment of our independence. Transports are now taking up, to carry back to their country the poor, brave fellows, who have borne for years their cruel captivity, rather than serve our enemies, and an equal number of English are to be delivered in return. I have, upon desire, furnished passports for the vessels.

Our affairs in Holland are *en bon train*; we have some prospect of another loan there; and all goes well here.

The proposal to us of a separate peace with England has been rejected in the manner you wish, and I am pretty certain they will now enter into a general treaty.

Franklin was soon joined by Jay and John Adams. All had been appointed by Congress as commissioners to negotiate peace. A fourth commissioner, Henry Laurens, remained in England, ill from his long imprisonment in the Tower, where he had been put when he was captured en route to Europe. Negotiations did not progress as smoothly as Franklin hoped. Jay insisted that Britain recognize the independence of the United States before negotiations began. This delayed serious bargaining for almost two months. Franklin himself came down with a severe attack

*Victor Hugo made this drawing of Franklin's residence in Passy.*

353

of the gout and a bladder stone ailment, and in the meantime the English stiffened their stand considerably as a result of victories in the West Indies and at Gibraltar. Franklin's hope for a peace of reconciliation, which would have included the acquisition of Canada and Nova Scotia, vanished. In this letter to Robert R. Livingston, the American Secretary for Foreign Affairs, he discussed the situation.

Paris, October 14, 1782.

I have but just received information of this opportunity, and have only time allowed to write a few lines.

In my last of the 26th past, I mentioned that the negotiation for peace had been obstructed by the want of due form in the English commissions appointing their plenipotentiaries. In that for treating with us, the mentioning our States by their public name had been avoided, which we objected to; another is come, of which I send a copy enclosed. We have now made several preliminary propositions, which the English minister, Mr. Oswald, has approved, and sent to his court. He thinks they will be approved there, but I have some doubts. In a few days, however, the answer expected will determine. By the first of these articles, the King of Great Britain renounces, for himself and successors, all claim and pretension to dominion or territory within the Thirteen United States; and the boundaries are described as in our instructions, except that the line between Nova Scotia and New England is to be settled by commissioners after the peace. By another article, the fishery in the American seas is to be freely exercised by the Americans, wherever they might formerly exercise it while united with Great Britain. By another, the citizens and subjects of each nation are to enjoy the same protection and privileges in each others' ports and countries, respecting commerce, duties, &c., that are enjoyed by native subjects. The articles are drawn up very fully by Mr. Jay, who I suppose sends you a copy; if not, it will go by the next opportunity. If these articles are agreed to, I apprehend little difficulty in the rest. Something has been mentioned about the refugees and English debts, but not insisted on; as we declared at once, that, whatever confiscations had been made in America, being in virtue of the laws of particular States, the Congress had no authority to repeal those laws, and therefore could give us none to stipulate for such repeal....

The different accounts given of Lord Shelburne's

character, with respect to sincerity, induced the ministry here to send over M. de Rayneval, Secretary to the Council, to converse with him, and endeavour to form by that means a more perfect judgment of what was to be expected from the negotiations. He was five or six days in England, saw all the ministers, and returned quite satisfied, that they are sincerely desirous of peace, so that the negotiations now go on with some prospect of success. But the court and people of England are very changeable. A little turn of fortune in their favour sometimes turns their heads; and I shall not think a speedy peace to be depended on, till I see the treaties signed.

After more wrangling over the compensation for the loyalists, which Franklin fiercely opposed although his son William would have been one of the chief gainers, and some equally hot arguments over American fishing rights off Newfoundland, the Americans and British agreed to preliminary articles of peace. The Americans made this decision without consulting the French, who had only begun negotiating with the British. The Americans thus violated the strict letter of their instructions from Congress, which stipulated they were to consult their allies throughout the negotiations. Jay and Adams had urged this separate course on a reluctant Franklin, because they no longer trusted French intentions and feared that the French would join with the Spanish, in an attempt to deprive the United States of the lands between the Alleghenies and the Mississippi. Franklin now had the unpleasant task of informing the French Foreign Minister, the Count de Vergennes, that America had signed a separate treaty of peace. Vergennes was not happy with the news. Tartly, he accused Franklin of holding out "a certain hope of peace to America, without even informing yourself on the state of the negotiation on our part." He demanded to know how Franklin could do this with "propriety." Franklin replied in a letter that masterfully soothed the angry Frenchman, and simultaneously asked him for one more loan. He got it.

Passy, December 17, 1782

I received the letter your Excellency did me the honour of writing to me on the 15th instant. The proposal of having a passport from England was agreed to by me the more willingly, as I at that time had hopes of obtaining some money to send in the *Washington,* and the passport would have made its transportation safer, with that of our despatches, and of yours also, if you had thought fit to make use of the occasion. Your Excellency objected, as I understood it, that the English ministers, by their letters sent in the same ship, might

*A passport issued by Franklin in 1782
bears the Franklin coat of arms.*

convey inconvenient expectations into America. It was
therefore I proposed not to press for the passport till
your preliminaries were also agreed to. They have sent
the passport without being pressed to do it, and they
have sent no letters to go under it, and ours will prevent
the inconvenience apprehended. In a subsequent conversation, your Excellency mentioned your intention of
sending some of the King's cutters, whence I imagined,
that detaining the *Washington* was no longer necessary;
and it was certainly incumbent on us to give Congress as
early an account as possible of our proceedings, who
will think it extremely strange to hear of them by other
means, without a line from us. I acquainted your Excellency, however, with our intention of despatching
that ship, supposing you might possibly have something
to send by her.

Nothing has been agreed in the preliminaries contrary to the interests of France; and no peace is to take
place between us and England, till you have concluded
yours. Your observation is, however, apparently just,
that, in not consulting you before they were signed we
have been guilty of neglecting a point of *bienséance*.
But as this was not from want of respect for the King,
whom we all love and honour, we hope it will be ex-
cused, and that the great work, which has hitherto
been so happily conducted, is so nearly brought to perfection, and is so glorious to his reign, will not be ruined
by a single indiscretion of ours. And certainly the whole
edifice sinks to the ground immediately if you refuse on
that account to give us any further assistance.

We have not yet despatched the ship, and I beg leave
to wait upon you on Friday for your answer.

It is not possible for any one to be more sensible than
I am, of what I and every American owe to the King, for
the many and great benefits and favours he has bestowed
upon us. All my letters to America are proofs of this;
all tending to make the same impressions on the minds
of my countrymen, that I felt in my own. And I believe,
that no Prince was ever more beloved and respected by
his own subjects, than the King is by the people of the
United States. *The English, I just now learn, flatter
themselves they have already divided us.* I hope this
little misunderstanding will therefore be kept a secret,
and that they will find themselves totally mistaken.

A few weeks later, Franklin received sad news from England. Margaret Stevenson had died on January 1, 1783. In this moving letter to her daughter Polly, he wrote of his grief, and recalled his deep affection for Mrs. Stevenson, and for England.

Passy, Jan. 27. 1783.

—The Departure of my dearest Friend, which I learn from your last Letter, greatly affects me. To meet with her once more in this Life was one of the principal Motives of my proposing to visit England again, before my Return to America. The last Year carried off my Friends Dr. Pringle, and Dr. Fothergill, Lord Kaims, and Lord de Despencer. This has begun to take away the rest, and strikes the hardest. Thus the Ties I had to that Country, and indeed to the World in general, are loosened one by one, and I shall soon have no Attachment left to make me unwilling to follow.

I intended writing when I sent the 11 Books, but I lost the Time in looking for the 12th. I wrote with that; and hope it came to hand. I therein ask'd your Counsel about my coming to England. On Reflection, I think I can, from my Knowledge of your Prudence, foresee what it will be, viz. not to come too soon, lest it should seem braving and insulting some who ought to be respected. I shall, therefore, omit that Journey till I am near going to America, and then just step over to take Leave of my Friends, and spend a few days with you. I purpose bringing Ben with me, and perhaps may leave him under your Care.

At length we are in Peace, God be praised, and long, very long, may it continue. All Wars are Follies, very expensive, and very mischievous ones. When will Mankind be convinced of this, and agree to settle their Differences by Arbitration? Were they to do it, even by the Cast of a Dye, it would be better than by Fighting and destroying each other.

Spring is coming on, when Travelling will be delightful. Can you not, when your children are all at School, make a little Party, and take a Trip hither? I have now a large House, delightfully situated, in which I could accommodate you and two or three Friends, and I am but half an Hour's Drive from Paris.

In looking forward, Twenty-five Years seems a long Period, but, in looking back, how short! Could you imagine, that 'tis now full a Quarter of a Century since we were first acquainted? It was in 1757. During the greatest Part of the Time, I lived in the same House with my dear deceased Friend, your Mother; of course you and I saw and convers'd with each other much and often. It is to all our Honours, that in all that time we never had among us the smallest Misunderstanding. Our Friendship has been all clear Sunshine, without the least Cloud in its Hemisphere. Let me conclude by saying to you, what I have had too frequent Occasions to say to my other remaining old Friends, "The fewer we become, the more let us love one another."

Finally, France and Spain agreed to terms and signed preliminary peace treaties. In this letter to Robert R. Livingston, Franklin drew down the curtain on the great drama of the Revolution.

Passy, January 21, 1783.

I have just received your letters of November 9th and December 3d. This is to inform you, and to request you to inform the Congress that the preliminaries of peace between France, Spain, and England, were yesterday signed, and a cessation of arms agreed to by the ministers of those powers, and by us in behalf of the United States, of which act, so far as relates to us, I enclose a copy. I have not yet obtained a copy of the preliminaries agreed to by the three crowns, but hear, in general, that they are very advantageous to France and Spain. I shall be able, in a day or two, to write more fully and perfectly. Holland was not ready to sign preliminaries, but their principal points are settled. Mr. Laurens is absent at Bath, and Mr. Jay in Normandy, for their healths, but will both be here to assist in forming the definitive treaty. I congratulate you and our country on the happy prospects afforded us by the finishing so speedily this glorious revolution.

Thanks to Franklin's efforts, relations between France and the United States remained good. In this letter to Robert Morris, Franklin demonstrated, once more, the positive results of his approach. The "certain mischievous madman" referred to in the second paragraph was John Adams, who had become paranoid on the subject of France and French influence over the new American nation.

Passy, March 7, 1783.

With this I send you a copy of the last contract I made with this court, respecting the late loan of six millions, the terms of the loan, and the times of repayment. It

*From his first audience with King Louis, depicted above in a German engraving, until the signing of the peace treaty, Franklin worked diligently to maintain the "Kings Goodness towards us."*

was impossible for me to obtain more, and, indeed, considering the state of finances and expenses here, I wonder I have obtained so much. You will see by the enclosed Gazette, that the government is obliged to stop payment for a year of its own bills of exchange, drawn in America and the East Indies; yet it has advanced six millions to save the credit of ours. You will, I am sure, do all in your power to avoid drawing beyond your funds here; for I am absolutely assured, that no farther aid for this year is to be expected; and it will not be strange, that they should suffer your bills to take the same fate with their own.

You will also see in the contract fresh marks of the King's goodness towards us, in giving so long a term for payment, and forgiving the first year's interest. I hope the ravings of a certain mischievous madman here against France and its ministers, which I hear of every day, will not be regarded in America, so as to diminish in the least the happy union that has hitherto subsisted between the two nations, and which is indeed the solid foundation of our present importance in Europe.

Meanwhile, Franklin continued to write grandfatherly letters to Benjamin Franklin Bache. A few weeks after Franklin wrote this letter, he brought Benny back from Geneva, and kept him with him at Passy for the rest of his stay in France.

Passy, May 2. 1783

My dear Child,

I have receiv'd several Letters from you, and in the last a Specimen of your Drawing, which I was pleas'd with, as well as with your Letters. I am not going yet to England, as you supposed. When I do go there, I shall certainly take you with me. I send you the Medal you desire; but I cannot afford to give Gold Watches to Children. When you are more of a Man, perhaps, if you have behaved well, I may give you one or something that is better. You should remember that I am at a great Expence for your Education, to pay for your Board and Cloathing and Instruction in Learning that may be useful to you when you are grown up, and you should not tease me for expensive things that can be of little or no Service to you. Your Father and Mother and Brothers and Sisters were all well when I last heard from them: and I am ever Your affectionate Grandfather

B FRANKLIN

In September, 1783, the definitive treaty of peace was signed. It consisted of nothing more than the preliminary articles agreed to by the negotiators in the fall of 1782. But Franklin's enemies continued to harass him. In this letter to John Jay, he tried to defend himself against their latest slander. He wrote an identical letter to John Adams, on the same day. Both men responded with letters affirming their belief in Franklin's honesty and loyalty—but Jay wrote in far more friendly terms than did the often sour and cantankerous Adams.

Passy, September 10, 1783.

I have received a letter from a very respectable person in America, containing the following words, viz.

"It is confidently reported, propagated, and believed by some among us, that the Court of France was at the bottom against our obtaining the fishery and territory in that great extent, in which both are secured to us by the treaty; that our minister at that court favoured, or did not oppose, this design against us; and that it was entirely owing to the firmness, sagacity, and disinterestedness of Mr. Adams, with whom Mr. Jay united, that we have obtained these important advantages."

It is not my purpose to dispute any share of the honour of that treaty, which the friends of my colleagues may be disposed to give them; but, having now spent fifty years of my life in public offices and trusts, and having still one ambition left, that of carrying the character of fidelity at least to the grave with me, I cannot allow that I was behind any of them in zeal and faithfulness. I therefore think, that I ought not to suffer an accusation, which falls little short of treason to my country, to pass without notice, when the means of effectual vindication are at hand. You, Sir, were a witness of my conduct in that affair. To you and my other colleagues I appeal, by sending to each a similar letter with this, and I have no doubt of your readiness to do a brother Commissioner justice, by certificates that will entirely destroy the effect of that accusation.

In Paris, interest in war was soon replaced by a passion for ballooning. Although Franklin was still troubled by gout and a bladder stone, he roused himself from Passy and jouneyed to Paris to see one of these experiments. He then proceeded to write the following scientifically detailed report to Sir Joseph Banks, president of the Royal Society. On another occasion, questioned about the usefulness of balloons, Franklin replied to scoffers, "What good is a new-born baby?"

Passy, December 1. 1783.

In mine of yesterday I promised to give you an account of Messrs. Charles & Robert's experiment, which was to have been made this day, and at which I intended to be present. Being a little indisposed, and the air cool, and the ground damp, I declined going into the garden of the Tuileries, where the balloon was placed, not knowing how long I might be obliged to wait there before it was ready to depart, and chose to stay in my carriage near the statue of Louis XV., from whence I could well see it rise, and have an extensive view of the region of air through which, as the wind sat, it was likely to pass. The morning was foggy, but about one o'clock the air became tolerably clear, to the great satisfaction of the spectators, who were infinite, notice having been given of the intended experiment several days before in the papers, so that all Paris was out, either about the Tuileries, on the quays and bridges, in the fields, the streets, at windows, or on the tops of houses, besides the inhabitants of all the towns and villages of the environs. Never before was a philosophical experiment so magnificently attended. Some guns were fired to give notice that the departure of the balloon was near, and a small one was discharged, which went to an amazing height, there being but little wind to make it deviate from its perpendicular course, and at length the sight of it was lost. Means were used, I am told, to prevent the great balloon's rising so high as might endanger its bursting. Several bags of sand were taken on board before the cord that held it down was cut, and the whole weight being then too much to be lifted, such a quantity was discharged as to permit its rising slowly. Thus it would sooner arrive at that region where it would be in equilibrio with the surrounding air, and by discharging more sand afterwards, it might go higher if desired. Between one and two o'clock, all eyes were gratified with seeing it rise majestically from among the trees, and ascend gradually above the buildings, a most beautiful spectacle. When it was about two hundred feet high, the brave adventurers held out and waved a little white pennant, on both sides their car, to salute the spectators, who returned loud claps of applause. The wind was very little, so that the object though moving to the northward, continued long in view; and it was a great while before the admiring people began to dis-

*Franklin watched this balloon ascension with his pocket glass.*

361

*Franklin was too ill to attend the launching of this balloon from Versailles, but he nonetheless gathered data and wrote a report.*

perse. The persons embarked were Mr. Charles, professor of experimental philosophy, and a zealous promoter of that science; and one of the Messieurs Robert, the very ingenious constructors of the machine. When it arrived at its height, which I suppose might be three or four hundred toises, it appeared to have only horizontal motion. I had a pocket-glass, with which I followed it, till I lost sight first of the men, then of the car, and when I last saw the balloon, it appeared no bigger than a walnut. I write this at seven in the evening. What became of them is not yet known here. I hope they descended by daylight, so as to see and avoid falling among trees or on houses, and that the experiment was completed without any mischievous accident, which the novelty of it and the want of experience might well occasion. I am the more anxious for the event, because I am not well informed of the means provided for letting themselves down, and the loss of these very ingenious men would not only be a discouragement to the progress of the art, but be a sensible loss to science and society.

I shall enclose one of the tickets of admission, on which the globe was represented, as originally intended, but is altered by the pen to show its real state when it went off. When the tickets were engraved the car was to have been hung to the neck of the globe, as represented by a little drawing I have made in the corner.

I suppose it may have been an apprehension of danger in straining too much the balloon or tearing the silk, that induced the constructors to throw a net over it, fixed to a hoop which went round its middle, and to hang the car to that hoop.

Tuesday morning, December 2d. — I am relieved from my anxiety by hearing that the adventurers descended well near L'Isle Adam before sunset. This place is near seven leagues from Paris. Had the wind blown fresh they might have gone much farther....

P.S. Tuesday evening. — Since writing the above I have received the printed paper and the manuscript containing some particulars of the experiment, which I enclose. I hear further that the travellers had perfect command of their carriage, descending as they pleased by letting some of the inflammable air escape, and rising again by discharging some sand; that they descended over a field so low as to talk with the labourers in passing, and

mounted again to pass a hill. The little balloon falling
at Vincennes shows that mounting higher it met with a
current of air in a contrary direction, an observation
that may be of use to future aerial voyagers.

Although peace was a reality, Franklin was not inclined
to drop his guard against an obviously hostile England. In this excerpt from
his letter to Thomas Mifflin, the president of Congress, he explained why
he remained suspicious of the former mother country.

Passy, January 25. 1784.

With respect to the British Court we should I think be
constantly on our guard and impress strongly on our
minds that tho it has made peace with us it is not in
truth reconciled to us or to its loss of us but flatters itself with hopes that some change in the affairs of Europe
or some disunion among ourselves may afford them an
opportunity of recovering their dominion, punishing
those who have most offended and recuring our future
dependence. It is easy to see by the general turn of
y Ministerial news papers (light things indeed as straws
or feathers but like them they shew which way the wind
blows) and by the malignant improvement their ministers
make in all the foreign courts of every little accident or
dissention among us, the rise of a few Soldiers in Philadelphia, the resolves of some town meetings, the reluctance to pay taxes &c. all which are exaggerated to
represent our governments as so many anarchies of
which the people themselves are weary, the Congress as
having lost its influence being no longer respected. I say
that is easy to see by this conduct that they bear us no
good will and that they wish the reality of what they are
pleased to imagine. They have too numerous a royal
progeny to provide for some of whom are educated in
the military line. In these circumstances we cannot be
too carefull to preserve the friendships we have acquired
abroad & the union we have established at home, to
secure our credit by a punctual discharge of our obligations of every kind & our reputation by the wisdom of
our councils since we know not how soon we may have
a fresh occasion for friends for credit and for reputation.

Among his English friends, Franklin easily forgave and
forgot. This cheerful letter to William Strahan demonstrates how easily he
picked up the mood and the tone of their old friendship.

Passy, Feb. 16, 1784.

I receiv'd and read with Pleasure your kind Letter of the first Inst, as it inform'd me of the Welfare of you and yours. I am glad the Accounts you have from your Kinswoman at Philadelphia are agreable, and I shall be happy if any Recommendations from me can be serviceable to Dr. Ross, or any other friend of yours, going to America.

Your arguments, persuading me to come once more to England, are very powerful. To be sure, I long to see again my Friends there, whom I love abundantly; but there are difficulties and Objections of several kinds, which at present I do not see how to get over.

I lament with you the political Disorders England at present labours under. Your Papers are full of strange Accounts of Anarchy and Confusion in America, of which we know nothing, while your own Affairs are really in a Situation deplorable. In my humble Opinion, the Root of the Evil lies not so much in too long, or too unequally chosen Parliaments, as in the enormous Salaries, Emoluments, and Patronage of your great Offices; and that you will never be at rest till they are all abolish'd, and every place of Honour made at the same time, instead of a Place of Profit, a place of Expence and burthen.

Ambition and avarice are each of them strong Passions, and when they are united in the same Persons, and have the same Objects in view for their Gratification, they are too strong for Public Spirit and Love of Country, and are apt to produce the most violent Factions and Contentions. They should therefore be separated, and made to act one against the other. Those Places, to speak in our old stile (Brother Type), may be for the good of the *Chapel*, but they are bad for the Master, as they create constant Quarrels that hinder the Business. For example, here are near two Months that your Government has been employed in *getting its form to press*; which is not yet fit to *work on*, every Page of it being *squabbled*, and the whole ready to fall into *pye*. The Founts too must be very scanty, or stangely *out of sorts*, since your *Compositors* cannot find either *upper* or *lower case Letters* sufficient to set the word ADMINISTRATION, but are forc'd to be continually *turning for them*. However, to return to common (tho' perhaps too saucy) Language, don't despair; you have still one resource left, and that

*Frederick Mesmer had exploited his cult of animal magnetism successfully for several years before Franklin (at left in this cartoon) and a board of eminent French scientists exposed him as a fraud in 1784.*

not a bad one, since it may reunite the Empire. We have some Remains of Affection for you, and shall always be ready to receive and take care of you in Case of Distress. So if you have not Sense and Virtue enough to govern yourselves, e'en dissolve your present old crazy Constitution, and *send members to Congress.*

You will say my *Advice* "smells of *Madeira."* You are right. This foolish Letter is mere chitchat *between ourselves* over the *second bottle.*

In his final summer in Europe, Franklin received a letter from his son, who had retreated to England with a very ugly moral cloud over his head. He was wanted for murder. As head of the Board of Associated Loyalists, a guerrilla organization, William had ordered the hanging of a captive American. Congress ordered Washington to hang a British officer in retaliation, and only the intervention of Louis XVI prevented it. William expressed no repentance in his letter for this or any other aspect of the course he had chosen. Franklin struggled to meet his plea for reconciliation, but even in this guarded letter, it is obvious how difficult it was for him. The letter also contains a reference to the papers that helped form the present—and earlier—editions of Franklin's writings.

Passy, Aug. 16, 1784.

Dear Son,

I received your Letter of the 22d past, and am glad to find that you desire to revive the affectionate Intercourse, that formerly existed between us. It will be very agreable to me; indeed nothing has ever hurt me so much and affected me with such keen Sensations, as to find myself deserted in my old Age by my only Son; and not only deserted, but to find him taking up Arms against me, in a Cause, wherein my good Fame, Fortune and Life were all at Stake. You conceived, you say, that your Duty to your King and Regard for your Country requir'd this. I ought not to blame you for differing in Sentiment with me in Public Affairs. We are Men, all subject to Errors. Our Opinions are not in our own Power; they are form'd and govern'd much by Circumstances, that are often as inexplicable as they are irresistible. Your Situation was such that few would have censured your remaining Neuter, *tho' there are Natural Duties which precede political ones, and cannot be extinguish'd by them.*

This is a disagreable Subject. I drop it. And we will endeavour, as you propose mutually to forget what has

*A drawing of the reception of the American Loyalists in Great Britain included William Franklin (center, behind man with long wig).*

happened relating to it, as well as we can. I send your Son over to pay his Duty to you. You will find him much improv'd. He is greatly esteem'd and belov'd in this Country, and will make his Way anywhere. It is my Desire, that he should study the Law, as a necessary Part of Knowledge for a public Man, and profitable if he should have occasion to practise it. I would have you therefore put into his hands those Law-books you have, viz. Blackstone, Coke, Bacon, Viner, &c. He will inform you, that he received the Letter sent him by Mr. Galloway, and the Paper it enclosed, safe.

On my leaving America, I deposited with that Friend for you, a Chest of Papers, among which was a Manuscript of nine or ten Volumes, relating to Manufactures, Agriculture, Commerce, Finance, etc., which cost me in England about 70 Guineas; eight Quire Books, containing the Rough Drafts of all my Letters while I liv'd in London. These are missing. I hope you have got them, if not, they are lost. Mr. Vaughan has publish'd in London a Volume of what he calls my Political Works. He proposes a second Edition; but, as the first was very incompleat, and you had many Things that were omitted, (for I used to send you sometimes the Rough Drafts, and sometimes the printed Pieces I wrote in London,) I have directed him to apply to you for what may be in your Power to furnish him with, or to delay his Publication till I can be at home again, if that may ever happen.

I did intend returning this year; but the Congress, instead of giving me Leave to do so, have sent me another Commission, which will keep me here at least a Year longer; and perhaps I may then be too old and feeble to bear the Voyage. I am here among a People that love and respect me, a most amiable Nation to live with; and perhaps I may conclude to die among them; for my Friends in America are dying off, one after another, and I have been so long abroad, that I should now be almost a Stranger in my own Country.

I shall be glad to see you when convenient, but would not have you come here at present. You may confide to your son the Family Affairs you wished to confer upon with me, for he is discreet. And I trust, that you will prudently avoid introducing him to Company, that it may be improper for him to be seen with. I shall hear from you by him and any letters to me afterwards, will come safe under Cover directed to Mr. Ferdinand Grand, Banker at Paris. Wishing you Health, and more Happiness than it seems you have lately experienced, I remain your affectionate father,

B FRANKLIN

Temple went to England equipped with letters of introduction to many Franklin friends. In this one to Bishop Shipley, Franklin revealed the failure of William's attempt to become reconciled.

Passy, Augt. 22. 1784

When I am long without hearing from you I please my self with re-perusing some of your former Letters. In your last of April 24. 83. you mention the Departure of Anna Maria with her Husband for Bengal. I hope you have since heard often of their Welfare there. When you next favour me with a Line, please to be particular in letting me know how they do. My Grandson, a good Young Man, (who as a Son makes up to me my Loss by the Estrangement of his Father) will have the Honour of delivering you this Line, and will bring me I trust good Accounts of your Health and that of the rest of the Family. I beg leave to recommend him to your Civilities and Counsels. As to my self I am at present well and hearty, the Stone excepted, which however gives me but little Pain and not often, its chief Inconvenience being that it prevents my using a Carriage on the Pavement; but I can take some Exercise in Walking, am chearful & enjoy my Friends as usual. God be thanked!

Your kind Invitation to spend some time at Twyford with the Family I love, affects me sensibly. Nothing would make me happier. I have solicited the Congress to discharge me, but they have sent me another Commission, that will employ me another Year at least; and it seems my Fate, constantly to wish for Repose, and never to obtain it.

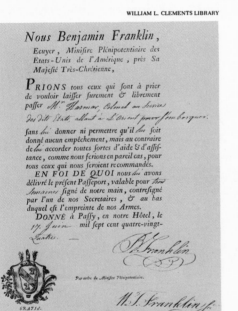

*A passport issued to Colonel Josiah Harmar of the American army carries signatures of Franklin and Temple.*

Franklin finally enticed Polly Stevenson Hewson to join him in Paris for the winter of 1784–85. Not content with that triumph, he immediately began attempting to persuade her to join him in America. In this letter he continued his campaign, which was eventually successful.

Passy, May 5, 1785.

My dear, dear Friend,

I receiv'd your little Letter from Dover, which gave me great Pleasure, as it inform'd me of your happy Progress so far in your way home. I hope the rest of your Journey was as prosperous.

You talk of Obligations to me, when in fact I am the Person oblig'd. I pass'd a long Winter, in a manner that made it appear the shortest of any I ever past. Such is the Effect of pleasing Society, with Friends one loves.

I have now receiv'd my Permission to return, and am making my Preparations. I hope to get away in June. I promise myself, or rather flatter myself, that I shall be happy when at home. But, however happy that Circumstance may make me, your joining me there will surely make me happier, provided your Change of Country may be for the advantage of your dear little Family. When you have made up your Mind on the Subject, let me know by a Line, that I may prepare a House for you as near me, and otherwise as convenient for you, as possible.

My neighbours begin to come out from Paris, and replace themselves in their Passy Houses. They enquire after you, and are sorry you are gone before they could make themselves known to you. For those who did know you speak well of you. M. le Veillard, in particular, has told me at different times, what indeed I knew long since, *C'est une bien digne Femme, cette Madame Hewson, une très aimable Femme.* I would not tell you this if I thought it would make you vain—er than you are; but that is impossible; you have too much good Sense.

So wish me a good Voyage, and, when you pray at Church for all that travel by Land or Sea, think of your ever affectionate Friend,

B. FRANKLIN

*Before Franklin left Paris he was invited to dine with Lafayette.*

F ranklin's departure from France was like a royal progress. Because his bladder stone made riding in a jouncing carriage impossible, he traveled in a litter drawn by the King's mules. The person from whom he parted with keenest regret was Mme. Helvétius, who will be introduced in Chapter 12. This letter is translated from the French.

Le Havre, July 19, '85

We arrived here, my very dear friend, safely yesterday evening. I was not at all tired. I felt even better than before my departure. We will stay here for a few days to wait for our baggage and our traveling companion, Mr. Houdon. When they come, we will leave France, the country *I love most in the world*; and I will leave *my dear Helvetius* there. She can be happy there. I am *not sure I will be happy* in America; but I must return. It seems to me that things are arranged badly in this world, when I see beings so very much made to be happy *to-gether forced* to separate.

I encountered so many difficulties with my plan to come here from Rouen through Eau, that I was very pleased to receive permission from the good Duc de Coigny to continue via litter. Tell the Fathers, the good Fathers, (nice) things for me, things full of friendship. I am not telling you that I love you. I would be told that there is nothing extraordinary and no merit at all in that, because everyone loves you. I only hope that you will always love me a little.

At Southampton, Franklin had brief reunions with several English friends. In these excerpts from his journal, he cryptically recounted this happy gathering of Franklinophiles, and also the cold formal meeting with his son, William. All hope of reconciliation had vanished on both sides by now, and nothing was discussed except outstanding business matters, such as the purchase of William's farm in New Jersey for Temple's benefit.

[1785]

[Sunday,] *July 24th.* We had a fair wind all night, and this morning at seven o'clock, being off Cowes, the captain represented to me the difficulty of getting in there against the flood; and proposing that we should rather run up to Southampton, which we did, and landed there between eight and nine. Met my son, who had arrived from London the evening before, with Mr. Williams and Mr. J. Alexander. Wrote a letter to the bishop of St. Asaph, acquainting him with my arrival, and he came with his lady and daughter, Miss Kitty, after dinner to see us; they talk of staying here as long as we do. Our meeting was very affectionate....

[Monday,] *July 25th.* The Bishop and family lodging in the same inn, the Star, we all breakfast and dine together. I went at noon to bathe in Martin's salt-water hot-bath, and, floating on my back, fell asleep, and slept near an hour by my watch without sinking or turning! a thing I never did before, and should hardly have thought possible. Water is the easiest bed that can be. Read over the writings of conveyance, &c., of my son's lands in New Jersey and New York to my grandson. Write to M. Ruellan, M. Limosin, M. Holker, and M.

Grand. Southampton a very neat, pretty place. The two French gentlemen, our friends, much pleased with it. The Bishop gives me a book in 4to, written by Dean Paley, and the family dine with us. Sundry friends came to see me from London.... Mr. Williams brought a letter from Mr. Nepean, secretary to Lord Townshend, addressed to Mr. Vaughan, expressing that orders would be sent to the customhouse at Cowes not to trouble our baggage, &c. It is still here on board the packet that brought it over....

[Tuesday,] *July 26th.* Deeds signed between W. Franklin and W. T. Franklin.

Mr. Williams, having brought sundry necessaries for me, goes down with them to Cowes, to be ready for embarking. Captain Jennings carries down our baggage that he brought from Havre. My dear friend, M. Le Veillard, takes leave to go with him. Mr. Vaughan arrives from London, to see me.

[Wednesday,] *July 27th.* Give a power to my son to recover what may be due to me from the British government. Hear from J. Williams that the ship is come.

We all dine once more with the Bishop and family, who kindly accept our invitation to go on board with us. We go down in a shallop to the ship. The captain entertains us at supper. The company stay all night.

[Thursday,] *July 28th.* When I waked in the morning found the company gone, and the ship under sail.

From France, as one of his last letters, Franklin had sent the following note to his fellow peacemaker, David Hartley. It is a near-perfect curtain line for his career in Europe.

Passy, July 5, 1785.

I cannot quit the coasts of Europe without taking leave of my ever dear Friend Mr. Hartley. We were long fellow labourers in the best of all works, the work of peace. I leave you still in the field, but having finished my day's task, I am going home *to go to bed!* Wish me a good night's rest, as I do you a pleasant evening. Adieu! and believe me ever yours most affectionately,

B FRANKLIN,

in his 80th year

# Chapter 12

# The Ladies of France

As he had done at Craven Street, and almost everywhere else he had lived, Franklin swiftly converted those around him at Passy into a kind of family—over which he presided as a combination father, lover, brother, and sage. He was also friendly with Frenchwomen outside the small Passy circle, such as the Countess d'Houdetot, once the beloved of Rousseau and heroine of his novel, *La nouvelle Héloïse,* and mistress of the highly touted poet of the day, Jean François de Saint-Lambert; and the Duchess d'Anville, mother of the Duke de la Rochefoucauld. But these were more formal relationships. Far more interesting were his friendships with two of his Passy neighbors, Mme. Brillon de Jouy and Anne-Catherine de Ligniville Helvétius, widow of a well-known philosopher. Many of the letters Franklin wrote to and received from these charming friends were undated. It therefore seems best to tell their story in this separate chapter. Most of the following letters have been newly translated from the French in which they were written. This letter to his niece Elizabeth Partridge gives us a cheerful picture of Franklin's reaction to the ladies of France—and a sad note on the vision of a man nearly seventy-four.

Passy, Oct. 11. 1779.

Your kind Letter, my dear Friend, was long in coming; but it gave me the Pleasure of knowing that you had been well in October and January last. The Difficulty, Delay & Interruption of Correspondence with those I love, is one of the great Inconveniencies I find in living so far from home: but we must bear these & more, with Patience, if we can; if not, we must bear them as I do with Impatience.

You mention the Kindness of the French Ladies to me. I must explain that matter. This is the civilest nation upon Earth. Your first Acquaintances endeavour

*Countess d'Houdetot*

to find out what you are like, and they tell others. If 'tis understood that you like Mutton, dine where you will you find Mutton. Somebody, it seems, gave it out that I lov'd Ladies; and then every body presented me their Ladies (or the Ladies presented themselves) to be *embrac'd*, that is to have their Necks kiss'd. For as to kissing the Lips or Cheeks it is not the Mode here, the first, is reckon'd rude, & the other may rub off the Paint. The French Ladies have however 1000 other ways of rendering themselves agreable; by their various Attentions and Civilities, & their sensible Conversation. 'Tis a delightful People to live with.

I thank you for the Boston Newspapers, tho' I see nothing so clearly in them as that your Printers do indeed want new Letters. They perfectly blind me in endeavouring to read them. If you should ever have any Secrets that you wish to be well kept, get them printed in those Papers.

Far deeper than this playful gamesmanship was Franklin's relationship to Mme. Brillon. She was a talented musician, considered one of the finest harpsichordists in Europe, and equally esteemed for her talent on the piano. She was also a composer, and numerous famous composers of the era dedicated works to her. But she had no desire for a public career. She was married to a man twenty-four years older than she, and was the mother of two daughters. She had a sensitive, very artistic temperament, and had been deeply devoted to her father, recently dead. Instinctively, she came to regard Franklin as a foster father on whom she could depend. But Mme. Brillon was also very French. She loved to sit on Franklin's lap and hug and kiss him, and responded wittily to the erotic badinage he loved. At first there was very little of the father in the role Franklin espoused. In this letter he discussed a bargain that he had just made with Mme. Brillon — she was to be his spiritual guide and assist him to save his soul.

Passy, Mar. 10

I am charm'd with the Goodness of my Spiritual Guide, and resign myself implicitly to her Conduct, as she promises to lead me to Heaven on so delicious a Road, when I could be content to travel thither even in the roughest of all ways with the Pleasure of her Company. How kindly partial to her Penitent in finding him, on examining his conscience, guilty of only one capital Sin, and to call that by the gentle Name of a *Foible!*

I lay fast hold of your promise to absolve me of all Sins past, present, & future, on the easy & pleasing

Condition of loving God, America and my Guide above all things. I am in Rapture when I think of being absolv'd of the *future*.

People commonly speak of *Ten* Commandments. — I have been taught that there are *twelve*. The first was *Increase & multiply* & replenish the Earth. The *Twelfth* is, A new Commandment I give unto you, *That ye love one another*. It seems to me they are a little misplac'd, And that the last should have been the first. However I never made any Difficulty about that, but was always willing to obey them both whenever I had an opportunity.

Pray tell me my dear Casuist, whether my keeping religiously these two Commandments tho' not in the Decalogue, may not be accepted in Compensation for my breaking so often one of the Ten I mean that which forbids Coveting my Neighbour's Wife, and which I *confess* I break constantly God forgive me, as often as I see or think of my lovely Confessor. And I am afraid I should never be able to repent of the Sin even if I had the full Posession of her.

And now I am consulting you upon a Case of Conscience I will mention the Opinion of a certain Father of the Church which I find myself willing to adopt, tho' I am not sure it is orthodox. It is this, that the most effectual Way to get rid of a certain Temptation is, as often as it returns, to comply with and satisfy it. Pray instruct me how far I may venture to practice upon this Principle?

*Manuscript page for the second violin part of Mme. Brillon's composition "Marche des Insurgents," which was to be played "vivement et fièrement"*

Mme. Brillon replied that she would not advise him without "consulting that neighbor whose wife you covet, because he is a far better casuist than I am. And then, too, as Poor Richard would say, in weighty matters two heads are better than one." Though she declined to yield, Mme. Brillon was as covetous as Franklin. She was extremely jealous of the time and attention he gave other French ladies and scolded him for it. He replied by donning his diplomat's role to propose a treaty of peace.

What a difference, my dear friend, between you and me: you find innumerable faults in me, while I see only one in you (but that might be the fault of my glasses) — I mean this kind of avarice which leads you to seek a monopoly of all my affections; and does not allow me any for the lovely ladies of your country. You suppose that it is impossible for my Affection (or my tenderness) to be divided without being diminished. You are wrong; and you forget the playful manner in which you have stopped me. You renounce and totally exclude all the sensuality that our love could have by only allowing me a few civil and honest Kisses, like the kind you would give to some little cousins: then, what am I getting that is so special, so that I can't give a little of it to others without a lessening of what belongs to you? The Workings of the Spirit, Esteem, Admiration, Respect and even Affection! (for an object) can multiply in so far as worthy objects present themselves; and nevertheless have the same thoughts for the first Object which has, as a result, no grounds to complain of an injury. They are by nature just as divisible as the sweet sounds of the piano produced by your skilful hands, twenty people can derive pleasure from them at the same time, without diminishing that which you kindly mean for me and (with as little reason) I can claim from your friendship, that these sweet sounds can neither reach or charm ears other than mine.

You see, then, how unjust you are in your demands, and in the open war you are declaring on me, if I do not capitulate; in fact, it is I who have the most Grounds to complain! My poor little love, that you, it seems to me, should have cherished, instead of being fat and pretty (like those of your elegant paintings) is thin and ready to die of hunger! from a lack of substantial food, which its mother inhumanely refuses. And now she wants to clip its little wings so that it won't be able to go look elsewhere! I think that neither of us can gain a single thing in this war; since I feel I am the weaker, I will offer a plan for peace (even though it should be done by the wisest).

For a peace to be durable the articles of the treaty must be governed by the most perfect principles of equity and equality: with this point of view in mind I have drawn up the following articles.

Article 1. That there ought to be peace, friendship, eternal love between Madame B. and Mr. Franklin.

Article 2. In order to maintain this inviolable peace, Madame B. on her side Stipulates and agrees that Mr. F. comes to her house every time she asks him to.

Article 3. That he stay at her house as much and as long as she wishes.

Article 4. That when he is at her house, he is obliged

*This charming aquatint was painted by Mme. Brillon and shows the view from Franklin's terrace in Passy.*

to drink tea, play chess, listen to music or do anything she may wish to ask.[1]

Article 5.    And that he love no woman other than her.

Article 6.    And the said Mr. F. on his side stipulates and agrees to go to Madame B.'s house as often as she wishes.

Article 7.    That he will stay there as long as she wishes.

Article 8.    That as long as he is with her, he will do everything he wants to.

Article 9.    And that he will love no other woman, as long as he finds her lovable.[2]

What do you think of those preliminaries? It seems to me they express the true manner of thinking and the real intention of each party more clearly than in many treaties.

I rest strongly, first, on the 8th Article, even though I am without much hope for your consent in the execution; and on the 9th also even though I despair of ever finding any other woman I could love with a tenderness equal to that I always feel for my dear, dear Friend.

[1] What he will be able to do is well understood.

[2] The women can go drown themselves.

When Mme. Brillon declined to sign the treaty, an undaunted Franklin returned with this impromptu parable.

A Beggar asked for a Louis from a wealthy Bishop. "You are foolish. One doesn't give Louis to Beggars." "How about a sou?" "No. That's too much." "A Liard then or your Blessing." "My Blessing! Yes. I will give you that." "I shall not accept it because you don't want to give its value in Liards." That was how much this Bishop loved his Neighbour. That was his Charity! And if I look at your charity, I don't find it much more admirable. I was very hungry and you didn't feed me; I was a Foreigner and almost as sick as Colin of your Song and you neither received me nor cured me, nor even helped me.

You who are as rich as an Archbishop in all the moral and Christian Virtues, and who could share a little portion of some of them with me without noticeable loss; you tell me that such a sacrifice is too much and that you don't want to make it. This is the kind of Charity you display toward a poor, miserable fellow who used to be affluent and who is now reduced to begging from you!

You say, however, that you love him but you would not give him your Friendship if it required spending the smallest little Piece of the Worth of a Liard, of your Virtues.

Franklin's deepening friendship with Mme. Brillon inspired him to write one of his most charming light essays — or bagatelles as they came to be called. It was prompted by a visit to the Moulin Joli, a small island in the Seine where mutual friends had a country house. Part of Franklin's purpose was to please Mme. Brillon, of course. The ostensible reason for the essay was to practice his French. He wrote it first in English, then translated it into French and allowed Mme. Brillon to correct it. But Franklin being Franklin, he transformed this practice session into a fascinating discussion of contemporary artistic and philosophical concerns in France. Paris at the time was torn by a dispute about the music of Gluck and Piccini. The scientists and philosophers, not yet in possession of the great principles of the conservation of energy, were locked in argument about how and when the world would end.

"The Ephemera," 1778

You may remember, my dear friend, that when we lately spent that happy day in the delightful garden and sweet society of the Moulin Joli. I stopped a little in one of our walks, and stayed some time behind the company. We had been shown numberless skeletons of a kind of little fly, called an ephemera, whose successive generations, we were told, were bred and expired within the day. I happened to see a living company of them on a leaf, who appeared to be engaged in conversation. You know I understand all the inferior animal tongues: my too great application to the study of them is the best excuse I can give for the little progress I have made in your charming language. I listened through curiosity to the discourse of these little creatures; but as they, in their national vivacity, spoke three or four together, I could make but little of their conversation. I found, however, by some broken expressions that I heard now and then, they were disputing warmly on the merit of two foreign musicians, one a *cousin*, the other a *moscheto*; in which dispute they spent their time, seemingly as regardless of the shortness of life as if they had been sure of living a month. Happy people! thought I; you are certainly under a wise, just, and mild government, since you have no public grievances to complain of, nor any subject of contention but the perfections and imperfections of foreign music. I turned my head from them to an old grey-headed one, who was single on another leaf, and talking to himself. Being amused with his soliloquy, I put it down in writing, in hopes it will likewise amuse her to whom I am so much indebted for the most pleasing of all amusements, her delicious company and heavenly harmony.

"It was," said he, "the opinion of learned philosophers of our race, who lived and flourished long before my time, that this vast world, the Moulin Joli, could not itself subsist more than eighteen hours; and I think there was some foundation for that opinion, since, by the apparent motion of the great luminary that gives life to all nature, and which in my time has evidently declined considerably towards the ocean at the end of the earth, it must then finish its course, be extinguished in the waters that surround us, and leave the world in cold and darkness, necessarily producing universal death and destruction. I have lived seven of those hours, a great age, being no less than four hundred and twenty minutes of time. How very few of us continue so long! I have seen generations born, flourish, and expire. My present friends are the children and grandchildren of the friends of my youth, who are now, alas, no more! And I must soon follow them; for, by the course of nature, though still in health, I cannot expect to live above seven or eight minutes longer. What now avails all my toil and labor, in amassing honey-dew on this leaf, which I cannot live to enjoy! What the political struggles I have been engaged in for the good of my compatriot inhabitants of this bush, or my philosophical studies for the benefit of our race in general! for, in politics, what can laws do without morals? Our present race of ephemerae will in a course of minutes become corrupt, like those of other and older bushes, and consequently as wretched. And in philosophy how small our progress! Alas! art is long, and life is short! My friends would comfort me with the idea of a name, they say, I shall leave behind me; and they tell me I have lived long enough to nature and to glory. But what will fame be to an ephemera who no longer exists? And what will become of all history in the eighteenth hour, when the world itself, even the whole Moulin Joli, shall come to its end and be buried in universal ruin?"

To me, after all my eager pursuits, no solid pleasures

*Engraving of an English garden on the island of Moulin Joli, which Franklin visited with Mme. Brillon*

now remain but the reflection of a long life spent in meaning well, the sensible conversation of a few good lady ephemerae, and now and then a kind smile and a tune from the ever amiable *Brillante.*

During this weekend at Moulin Joli, Mme. Brillon asked Franklin in all seriousness to become her adopted father. She told him, "You have taken in my heart the place of that father whom I loved and respected so much." Franklin, though declining to abandon completely the role of suitor, accepted the paternal role in this tender letter. Mme. Brillon had remained in the country, and Franklin was writing to her from Passy.

I accept with infinite pleasure, my dear friend, your very kind offer to adopt me as your father. I would be most happy to be the parent of such a good child; and since in coming and establishing myself here, I have lost the sweet Company and respectful Attention of an affectionate Daughter, this Loss will be made up, and I will have the Satisfaction of confidently reflecting that, if I spend my few remaining days here, another affectionate daughter will care for me during my lifetime, and will tenderly close my eyes when I must take my final Repose. Yes, my very dear child, I love you as a Father, with all my Heart. It's true that I sometime suspect this Heart of wanting to go further, but I try to hide this from myself.

I cannot stop recalling the memory of that hospitality where I was so often happy in your Company, and your friendship, without experiencing painful Regrets because of your Absence here. Your good Neighbours are very obliging, and they try to make Wednesday and Saturday evenings without you as nice as possible for me: But the Sight of those people that I was accustomed to seeing with you, constantly makes me aware that you are not there: this draws Sighs from me, for which I do not reproach myself, because even though at my age it is not becoming to say that I am in love with a young woman, there is nothing which prevents me from confessing that I admire and love a Collection of all feminine virtues and all admirable Talents; I love my Daughter because she is truly lovable, and because she loves me.

When Franklin came down with an attack of the gout, Mme. Brillon composed a poem in which M. Gout and the Sage, whom he was tormenting, discussed the Sage's many faults. Franklin was inspired to reply with one of his wittiest essays, "The Dialogue with the Gout."

*A French cartoon of 1778 depicts a headdress saluting the ideal of American independence and the "Triumph of Liberty."*

Midnight, October 22, 1780.

FRANKLIN.    Eh! Oh! Eh! What have I done to merit these cruel sufferings?

GOUT.    Many things; you have ate and drank too freely, and too much indulged those legs of yours in their indolence.

FRANKLIN.    Who is it that accuses me?

GOUT.    It is I, even I, the Gout.

FRANKLIN.    What! my enemy in person?

GOUT.    No, not your enemy.

FRANKLIN.    I repeat it; my enemy; for you would not only torment my body to death, but ruin my good name; you reproach me as a glutton and a tippler; now all the world, that knows me, will allow that I am neither the one nor the other.

GOUT.    The world may think as it pleases; it is always very complaisant to itself, and sometimes to its friends; but I very well know that the quantity of meat and drink proper for a man, who takes a reasonable degree of exercise, would be too much for another, who never takes any.

FRANKLIN.    I take—Eh! Oh!—as much exercise—Eh!—as I can, Madam Gout. You know my sedentary state, and on that account, it would seem, Madam Gout, as if you might spare me a little, seeing it is not altogether my own fault.

GOUT.    Not a jot; your rhetoric and your politeness are thrown away; your apology avails nothing. If your situation in life is a sedentary one, your amusements, your recreations, at least, should be active. You ought to walk or ride; or, if the weather prevents that, play at billiards. But let us examine your course of life. While the mornings are long, and you have leisure to go abroad, what do you do? Why, instead of gaining an appetite for breakfast, by salutary exercise, you amuse yourself, with books, pamphlets, or newspapers, which commonly are not worth the reading. Yet you eat an inordinate breakfast, four dishes of tea, with cream, and one or two buttered toasts, with slices of hung beef, which I fancy are not things the most easily digested. Immediately afterward you sit down to write at your desk, or converse with persons who apply to you on business. Thus the time passes till one, without any kind of bodily exercise. But all this I could pardon, in regard, as you say, to your sedentary condition. But what is your practice after dinner? Walking in the beautiful gardens of those friends, with whom you have dined, would be the choice of men of sense; yours is to be fixed down to chess, where you are found engaged for two or three hours! This is your perpetual recreation, which is the least eligible of any for a sedentary man, because, instead of accelerating the motion of the fluids, the rigid attention it requires helps to retard the circulation and obstruct internal secretions. Wrapt in the speculations of this wretched game, you destroy your constitution. What can be expected from such a course of living, but a body replete with stagnant humours, ready to fall a prey to all kinds of dangerous maladies, if I, the Gout, did not occasionally bring you relief by agitating those humours, and so purifying or dissipating them? If it was in some nook or alley in Paris, deprived of walks, that you played awhile at chess after dinner, this might be excusable; but the same taste prevails with you in Passy, Auteuil, Montmartre, or Sanoy, places where there are the finest gardens and walks, a pure air, beautiful women, and most agreeable and instructive conversation; all which you might enjoy by frequenting the walks. But these are rejected for this abominable game of chess. Fie, then Mr. Franklin! But amidst my instructions, I had almost forgot to administer my wholesome corrections; so take that twinge,—and that....

FRANKLIN.   Oh! Ehhh!—It is not fair to say I take no exercise, when I do very often, going out to dine and returning in my carriage.

GOUT.   That, of all imaginable exercises, is the most slight and insignificant, if you allude to the motion of a carriage suspended on springs. By observing the degree of heat obtained by different kinds of motion, we may form an estimate of the quantity of exercise given by each. Thus, for example, if you turn out to walk in winter with cold feet, in an hour's time you will be in a glow all over; ride on horseback, the same effect will scarcely be perceived by four hours' round trotting; but if you loll in a carriage, such as you have mentioned, you may travel all day, and gladly enter the last inn to warm your feet by a fire. Flatter yourself then no longer, that half an hour's airing in your carriage deserves the name of exercise. Providence has appointed few to roll in carriages, while he has given to all a pair of legs....

FRANKLIN.  How can you so cruelly sport with my torments?

GOUT.  Sport! I am very serious. I have here a list of offences against your own health distinctly written, and can justify every stroke inflicted on you.

FRANKLIN.  Read it then.

GOUT.  It is too long a detail; but I will briefly mention some particulars.

FRANKLIN.  Proceed. I am all attention.

GOUT.  Do you remember how often you have promised yourself, the following morning, a walk in the grove of Boulogne, in the garden de la Muette, or in your own garden, and have violated your promise, alleging, at one time, it was too cold, at another too warm, too windy, too moist, or what else you pleased; when in truth it was too nothing, but your insuperable love of ease?

FRANKLIN.  That I confess may have happened occasionally, probably ten times in a year.

GOUT.  Your confession is very far short of the truth; the gross amount is one hundred and ninety-nine times.

FRANKLIN.  Is it possible?

GOUT.  So possible, that it is fact; you may rely on the accuracy of my statement. You know M. Brillon's gardens, and what fine walks they contain; you know the handsome flight of an hundred steps, which lead from the terrace above to the lawn below. You have been in the practice of visiting this amiable family twice a week, after dinner, and it is a maxim of your own, that "a man may take as much exercise in walking a mile, up and down stairs, as in ten on level ground." What an opportunity was here for you to have had exercise in both these ways! Did you embrace it, and how often?

FRANKLIN.  I cannot immediately answer that question.

GOUT.  I will do it for you; not once.

FRANKLIN.  Not once?

GOUT.  Even so. During the summer you went there at six o'clock. You found the charming lady, with her

*This small sketch of Franklin was enclosed in a letter received by Abbé de la Roche, a friend Franklin made at the home of Mme. Helvétius.*

lovely children and friends, eager to walk with you, and entertain you with their agreeable conversation; and what has been your choice? Why to sit on the terrace, satisfying yourself with the fine prospect, and passing your eye over the beauties of the garden below, without taking one step to descend and walk about in them. On the contrary, you call for tea and the chess-board; and lo! you are occupied in your seat till nine o'clock, and that besides two hours' play after dinner; and then, instead of walking home, which would have bestirred you a little, you step into your carriage....

FRANKLIN.   What then would you have me do with my carriage?

GOUT.   Burn it if you choose; you would at least get heat out of it once in this way; or, if you dislike that proposal, here's another for you; observe the poor peasants, who work in the vineyards and grounds about the villages of Passy, Auteuil, Chaillot, &c.; you may find every day, among these deserving creatures, four or five old men and women, bent and perhaps crippled by weight of years, and too long and too great labour. After a most fatiguing day, these people have to trudge a mile or two to their smoky huts. Order your coachman to set them down. This is an act that will be good for your soul; and, at the same time, after your visit to the Brillons, if you return on foot, that will be good for your body.

FRANKLIN.   Ah! how tiresome you are!

GOUT.   Well, then, to my office; it should not be forgotten that I am your physician. There.

FRANKLIN.   Ohhh! what a devil of a physician!

GOUT.   How ungrateful you are to say so! Is it not I who, in the character of your physician, have saved you from the palsy, dropsy, and apoplexy? one or other of which would have done for you long ago, but for me.

FRANKLIN.   I submit, and thank you for the past, but entreat the discontinuance of your visits for the future; for, in my mind, one had better die than be cured so dolefully.... Oh! oh!—for Heaven's sake leave me! and I promise faithfully never more to play at chess, but to exercise daily, and live temperately.

GOUT.   I know you too well. You promise fair; but, after a few months of good health, you will return to your

*French salons of the eighteenth century were lively and elegant.*

old habits; your fine promises will be forgotten like the forms of last year's clouds. Let us then finish the account, and I will go. But I leave you with an assurance of visiting you again at a proper time and place; for my object is your good, and you are sensible now that I am your *real friend.*

A few days later he returned the draft of Mme. Brillon's poem about the sage and the gout with the following wry note.

I am returning the rough draft of your pretty story to you, my very dear daughter, since you insist on getting it back. I thought that in offering you a more attractive edition, which your work certainly deserved, I could convince you to let me keep the original, something I wanted, because I love what comes from your hand so much....

One of the characters in your story, i.e. The Gout, strikes me as reasoning well enough, except for her assumption that mistresses played some part in causing this painful ailment. I, personally, think the contrary, and here is my reasoning. When I was a young man and enjoyed more favours of the [fair] Sex than at present, I had no gout at all. Thus if the Ladies of Passy had had more of the kind of Christian charity which I have so often vainly recommended to you, I would not have gout now. I think this is very logical.

I feel much better. I have little pain, but I am very weak. As you can see, I can joke a little, but I can't be really gay until I hear that your precious health is restored.

Franklin soon found himself playing a father's role with Mme. Brillon in an unexpected way. She discovered that her husband was having an affair with the governess of her children. In a frenzy of emotion, she fled to Franklin for advice. After listening to her tearful story, he sent her this wise letter.

[May 10, 1782?]

You told me, my dear daughter, that your heart is too sensitive. I see clearly in your letters that this is too true. To be very sensitive to our faults is good because that leads us to avoid them in the future; but to be very sensitive to and afflicted by the faults of others is not good. It is up to them to be sensitive and to be afflicted by what they did badly; for us, we must preserve the tranquility which is the just portion of innocence and virtue. But you say: "Ingratitude is a frightful evil." It is true for the

*Engraving after Rosalie Filleul's*
*portrait of Franklin made in 1778*

ungrateful—but not for their benefactors. You have conferred acts of kindness on those people you have thought worthy of them; you have thus done your duty, since it is our duty to do good and you should be satisfied by it and happy in the thought. If they are ungrateful it is their crime and not yours; and it is up to them to be unhappy when they reflect on the baseness of their conduct toward you. If they insult you, think that although they could formerly have been your equals, they have, in this manner, placed themselves below you; if you take revenge by punishing them, you thereby restore them to their state of equality which they lost. But if you forgive them with no punishment, you keep them fixed in that low state into which they have fallen and from which they can never escape without repentance and full reparation. Then follow, my very dear daughter, the good resolution which you so wisely made, to continue to fulfill all your duties as a good mother, good wife, good friend, good neighbour, good Christian, etc. and ignore and forget, if possible, the insults you receive at present; and be assured that in time, the rectitude of your conduct will prevail upon the minds of even the worst people and even more on the minds of the individuals who are basically good and who also have common sense, even though for the present they are led astray by the artifices of other people. Then, everyone will quickly ask you for the return of your friendship and will become in the future, some of your most loyal friends.

I am sensitive to the fact that I have just written some very bad French; that could disgust you, you who write this charming language with so much purity and elegance. But, if you can, finally, decipher my awkward and improper expressions, you will have, at least the kind of pleasure derived from explaining riddles or discovering secrets.

Finally Franklin abandoned all hope of winning Mme. Brillon in this world. He accepted—or at least pretended to accept—her assurance that they would be happy together in heaven. But he had his own wry comments to make on their sojourn in Paradise, in this letter. Mme. d'Hardancourt was Mme. Brillon's mother. Father Pagin was Mme. Brillon's music teacher. The others were members of the Passy circle.

Since you assured me that we shall meet and recognize each other in Heaven, I have been thinking continually about the settlement of our Affairs in that land: because I have great confidence in your assurances and I believe implicitly in what you believe.

Probably more than forty years will elapse after my arrival there, before you follow me: I am a little afraid that during such a long period of time, you may forget me—I have therefore considered asking you to give me your word of honour not to renew your contract with Mr. B. I shall then give you mine to wait for you. But this gentleman is so kind and so generous toward us—he loves you—and we him—so much—that I cannot contemplate this idea without some scruples of conscience. Yet, the thought of an Eternity in which I would not be favoured with more than occasional permission to kiss your hands or your cheeks, or to spend more than two or three hours on Wednesday and Saturday evenings in your sweet company, is frightful. Finally, I cannot make this proposal, but since (along with everyone who knows you) I wish to see you happy in every way, we can agree not to talk about it anymore now and to leave it up to you, when we all meet: there to determine what you will judge best for your happiness and ours. Decide as you wish, I feel that I will love you eternally. If you reject me, maybe I will address myself to Madame D'Hardancourt, and maybe she will want to keep house with me; then I will spend my domestic hours agreeably with her; and I will be more within reach of seeing you, I will have enough time during those 40 years, to practice the Harmonica, and maybe I will be able to play well enough to be worthy to accompany your piano(forte), and from time to time we will have little concerts: the good Father Pagin will be one of the party, your neighbour and his dear family (Mr. Jupin), Mr. de Chaumont, Mr. B., Mr. Jourdon, Mr. Grammont, Madame du Tartre, the little mother and other chosen friends will be our audience, and the dear good girls, accompanied by some other young angels of whom you have already given me portraits, will sing Alleluia with us, all together we will eat roasted apples of paradise with butter and nutmeg; and we will have pity on those who are not dead.

*Self-portrait of Mme. Filleul,*
*another member of the Passy circle*

With Mme. Helvétius, Franklin had an entirely different relationship. She was the opposite of Mme. Brillon in almost every way. An aristocrat, she lived at Auteuil, the village next to Passy, in a highly uncon-

ventional ménage that consisted of herself, two free-thinking former priests
— Abbé Martin Lefebre de la Roche and Abbé André Morellet — and a young
physician, Pierre Georges Cabanis. Although at fifty-seven she was no longer
beautiful — her enemies called her the Ruins of Palmyra — Mme. Helvétius
fascinated Franklin and he plunged cheerfully into the hectic life of Auteuil.
He saw that Madame was a kind of goddess in her special world, and quickly
gave her a slightly sacrilegious nickname, Notre Dame d'Auteuil. In this
letter he tried to analyze the fascination she held for him and other men.

*Louis-Michel Van Loo's elegant
portrait of the fascinating,
still attractive Mme. Helvétius.*

I have in my way been trying to form some hypothesis to
account for your having so many friends and of such
various kinds. I see that statesmen, philosophers, historians, poets, and men of learning attach themselves to
you as straws to a fine piece of amber.

It is not that you make pretensions to any of their
sciences, and, if you did, similarity of studies does not
always make people love one another. It is not that you
take pains to engage them: artless simplicity is a striking
part of your character. I would not attempt to explain it
by the story of the ancient, who, being asked why
philosphers sought the acquaintance of kings, and kings
not that of philosophers, replied that philosophers knew
what they wanted, which was not always the case with
kings.

Yet thus far the comparison may go, that we find in
your sweet society that charming benevolence, that
amiable attention to oblige, that disposition to please
and be pleased, which we do not always find in the society
of one another. It springs from you; it has its influence on
us all; and in your company we are not only pleased with
you, but better pleased with one another and with
ourselves.

The cheerful disorder that reigned at Auteuil was
admirably described by Franklin in this letter to another French lady friend,
Mme. de la Frete.

My goodness, Madame, you did the right thing not to
come so far, in such a bad season for such a sad lunch. My
son and I were not so wise. I'll give you an account of it.

Since the invitation was for eleven o'clock, and since
you were among the group, I thought to find a breakfast in
the manner of a dinner; that there would be many people;
that we would have not only tea, but also coffee, chocolate,
maybe ham and several other good things. I decided to
go on foot; my shoes were a little too tight; I arrived

almost lame. Entering the courtyard, I was a little surprised to find it so empty of carriages, and to see that we [Franklin and Temple] were the first to arrive. We went upstairs. No noise at all. We went into the dining room. No one except M. l'Abbé and Mr. C—breakfast finished and eaten! Nothing on the table except some scraps of bread and a little butter. They exclaim; they run to tell Madame H. that we had come for breakfast. She leaves her toilette, and comes with her hair half-combed. They are surprised that I came since you wrote me that you weren't coming....

Finally another breakfast is ordered. One of them runs for fresh water, another for coal. They blow vigorously to make a fire. I was very hungry; it was so late; "A watched pot never boils," as Poor Richard says. Madame leaves for Paris and abandons us. We begin to eat. The butter is soon finished. M. l'Abbé asks if we want some more. Yes, certainly. He rings. No one comes. We talk, he forgets the butter. I scrape the plate; he understood why and ran to the kitchen to look for some. After a time he slowly returns, saying sadly, there is no more in the house. For my amusement, M. l'Abbé suggests a walk; my feet refuse to do it. As a result, we leave the breakfast there; and go upstairs to his room to find books with which to finish our meal.

Franklin was soon quite candidly in love with Mme. Helvétius. He used the abbés to carry notes for him, and wooed her with ingenious essays, such as this one.

The Flies of the Apartments of M. F. request Permission to present their Respects to Madame H., and to express in their best language their Gratitude for the Protection she has been kind enough to give them,

Bizz, izzz ouizz a ouizzz izzzzzzzzz, etc.
We have long lived under the hospitable Roof of the said bonhomme F. He has given us free Lodgings; we have also eaten and drunk the whole Year at his Expense without its having cost us anything. Often, when his Friends and himself have used up a Bowl of Punch, he has left a sufficient Quantity to intoxicate a hundred of us Flies.

We have drunk freely from it, and after that we have made our Sallies, our Circles and our Cotillions very prettily in the Air of his Bedroom, and have gaily consummated our little Loves under his Nose.

Finally, we would have been the happiest People in the World, if he had not permitted to remain over the top of his Wainscoting a Number of our declared Enemies, who stretched their Nets to capture us, and who tore us pitilessly to pieces. People of a Disposition both subtle and fierce, abominable Combination!

You, very excellent Lady, had the goodness to order that all these Assassins with their Habitations and their Snares be swept; and your Orders, as they always ought to be, were carried out immediately. Since that Time we have lived happily, and have enjoyed the Beneficence of the said bonhomme F. without fear.

There only remains one Thing for us to wish in order to assure the Stability of our Fortune; permit us to say it,

Bizz izzz ouizz a ouizzzz izzzzzz etc.,

It is to see both of you forming at last but one Ménage.

Finally, Franklin proposed to Mme. Helvétius. When she refused him, he went back to Passy and composed one of his most famous bagatelles, "The Elysian Fields."

Saddened by your barbarous resolution, stated so positively last night, to remain single the rest of your life, in honor of your dear husband, I went home, fell on my bed, believing myself dead, and found myself in the Elysian Fields.

I was asked if I had a wish to see some Important Persons—Take me to the Philosophers.—There are two who reside quite near here, in this Garden: they are very good neighbors and very good friends of each other.—Who are they?—Socrates and H——. I have prodigious esteem for both of them; but let me see H—— first, for I understand some French and not a word of Greek.

He received me with great courtesy, having known me by reputation, he said, for some time. He asked me a thousand questions on War, and on the present state of Religion, of Liberty, and of the Government in France.—But you are not enquiring at all about your dear Friend Madame H——; yet, she is excessively in love with you, and I was with her but an hour ago.

Ah! said he, you are reminding me of my former felicity. But one must forget, in order to be happy in this place. For several of the first years, I thought of nobody but her. Well, now I am consoled. I have taken another

*With a letter in praise of wine that Franklin sent to his friend Abbé Morellet, he included this drawing by Temple, proving that God —since He gave man elbows— intended him to drink.*

Wife. One as similar to her as I could find. She is not, to be sure, quite as beautiful, but she has just as much common sense, a little more wisdom, and she loves me infinitely. Her continuous endeavor is to please me; and she has gone out right now to search for the best Nectar and Ambrosia to regale me with tonight; Stay with me and you shall see her.

I notice, said I, that your former Friend is more faithful than you: For several good Matches have been offered her, and she has turned them all down. I confess that I, for one, loved her madly; but she was harsh toward me and rejected me absolutely for love of you.

I pity you, said he, for your misfortune; for she is truly a good and lovely woman, and most amiable....

As he was saying this, the new Madame H. came in with the Nectar. I recognized her instantly as Madame F., my former American Friend. I claimed her. But she said coldly, I have been a good Wife to you for forty-nine years and four months, almost half a century; be content with that. I have formed a new Connection here, that will last for Eternity.

Grieved by this Rebuke from my Euridyce, I resolved there and then to abandon those ungrateful Shadows, and to come back to this good World, to see the Sun again, and you. Here I am! Let's take our revenge.

The deep affection that existed between Franklin and his French ladies is nowhere better summed up than in this brief note, which he wrote to Mme. Brillon toward the close of his stay in France. It could have been written just as readily to Mme. Helvétius.

Saturday in Passy

Since one day, my dear friend, I will have to leave for America, with no hope of ever seeing you again, I have sometimes had the thought that it would be wise to cut myself off from you by degrees, first to see you just once a week, after that, only once every two weeks, once a month, etc., etc. so as to lessen little by little the inordinate desire that I always feel for your enchanting company, and in this way to avoid the great hurt that I must otherwise suffer at the final separation. But, in testing the experience, I find that instead of diminishing this desire, absence augments it. The hurt that I fear is, thus, incurable, and I will come to visit you this evening.

Chapter *13*

# The Nation's Patriarch

Although Franklin vowed that he was through with politics, he permitted himself to be elected President of Pennsylvania's Executive Council almost as soon as he reached America. He knew it was a mistake. When his sister Jane reproached him, he replied. "We have all of us wisdom enough to judge what others ought to do, or not to do in the management of their affairs; and 'tis possible that I might blame you as much if you were to accept the offer of a young husband." In this letter to Jonathan Shipley, he discussed his decision to take on a new duty at the age of eighty, and went on to tell the good bishop a little about affairs in America and the present state of the Franklin family.

Philadelphia, Feb. 24th, 1786.

I received lately your kind letter of Nov. 27th. My Reception here was, as you have heard, very honourable indeed; but I was betray'd by it, and by some Remains of Ambition, from which I had imagined myself free, to accept of the Chair of Government for the State of Pennsylvania, when the proper thing for me was Repose and a private Life. I hope, however, to be able to bear the Fatigue for one Year, and then to retire.

I have much regretted our having so little Opportunity for Conversation when we last met. You could have given me Informations and Counsels that I wanted, but we were scarce a Minute together without being broke in upon. I am to thank you, however, for the Pleasure I had after our Parting, in reading the new Book you gave me, which I think generally well written and likely to do good; tho' the Reading Time of most People is of late so taken up with News Papers and little periodical Pamphlets, that few now-a-days venture to attempt reading a

Quarto Volume. I have admir'd to see, that, in the last Century, a Folio, *Burton on Melancholly,* went through Six Editions in about Twenty Years. We have, I believe, more Readers now, but not of such large Books.

You seem desirous of knowing what Progress we make here in improving our Governments. We are, I think, In the right Road of Improvement, for we are making Experiments. I do not oppose all that seem wrong, for the Multitude are more effectually set right by Experience, than kept from going wrong by Reasoning with them. And I think we are daily more and more enlightened; so that I have no doubt of our obtaining in a few Years as much public Felicity, as good Government is capable of affording.

Your NewsPapers are fill'd with fictitious Accounts of Anarchy, Confusion, Distrsses, and Miseries, we are suppos'd to be involv'd in, as Consequences of the Revolution; and the few remaining Friends of the old Government among us take pains to magnify every little Inconvenience a Change in the Course of Commerce may have occasion'd. To obviate the Complaints they endeavour to excite, was written the enclos'd little Piece, from which you may form a truer Idea of our Situation, than your own public Prints would give you. And I can assure you, that the great Body of our Nation find themselves happy in the Change, and have not the smallest Inclination to return to the Domination of Britain. There could not be a stronger Proof of the general Approbation of the Measures, that promoted the Change, and of the Change itself, than has been given by the Assembly and Council of this State, in the nearly unanimous Choice for their Governor, of one who had been so much concern'd in those Measures; the Assembly being themselves the unbrib'd Choice of the People, and therefore may be truly suppos'd of the same Sentiments. I say nearly unanimous, because, of between 70 and 80 Votes, there were only my own and one other in the negative.

As to my Domestic Circumstances, of which you kindly desire to hear something, they are at present as happy as I could wish them. I am surrounded by my Offspring, a Dutiful and Affectionate Daughter in my House, with Six Grandchildren, the eldest of which you have seen, who is now at a College in the next Street, finishing the learned Part of his Education; the others promising, both

*Armorial bearings of the State of Pennsylvania, from a 1787 magazine*

391

*The Franklin coat of arms, embossed on one of Temple Franklin's books*

for Parts and good Dispositions. What their Conduct may be, when they grow up and enter the important Scenes of Life, I shall not live to *see,* and I cannot *foresee.* I therefore enjoy among them the present Hour, and leave the future to Providence.

He that raises a large Family does, indeed, while he lives to observe them, *stand,* as Watts says, *a broader Mark for Sorrow;* but then he stands a broader Mark for Pleasure too. When we launch our little Fleet of Barques into the Ocean, bound to different Ports, we hope for each a prosperous Voyage; but contrary Winds, hidden Shoals, Storms, and Enemies come in for a Share in the Disposition of Events; and though these occasion a Mixture of Disappointment, yet, considering the Risque where we can make no Insurance, we should think ourselves happy if some return with Success. My Son's Son, Temple Franklin, whom you have also seen, having had a fine Farm of 600 Acres convey'd to him by his Father when we were at Southampton, had drop'd for the present his Views of acting in the political Line, and applies himself ardently to the Study and Practice of Agriculture. This is much more agreable to me, who esteem it the most useful, the most independent, and therefore the noblest of Employments. His Lands are on navigable water, communicating with the Delaware, and but about 16 Miles from this City. He has associated to himself a very skillful English Farmer lately arrived here, who is to instruct him in the Business, and partakes for a Term of the Profits; so that there is a great apparent Probability of their Success.

You will kindly expect a Word or two concerning myself. My Health and Spirits continue, Thanks to God, as when you saw me. The only complaint I then had, does not grow worse, and is tolerable. I still have Enjoyment in the Company of my Friends; and, being easy in my Circumstances, have many Reasons to like Living. But the Course of Nature must soon put a period to my present Mode of Existence. This I shall submit to with less Regret, as, having seen during a long Life a good deal of this World, I feel a growing Curiosity to be acquainted with some other; and can chearfully, with filial Confidence, resign my Spirit to the conduct of that great and good Parent of Mankind, who created it, and who has so graciously protected and prospered me from my Birth to the present Hour. Wherever I am, I hope always to retain the pleasing remembrance of your Friendship, being with sincere and great Esteem, my dear Friend, yours most affectionately,

B FRANKLIN

P.S.  We all join in Respects to Mrs. Shipley, and best wishes for the whole amiable Family.

The separation from Mme. Helvétius was something Franklin felt most keenly in America. In this tender letter, he carried himself in his imagination back to Auteuil. "The Stars" was a nickname Franklin invented for Mme. Helvétius's daughters.

Philadelphia, 20 Oct. 1785

Yesterday was Wednesday. At 10 in the Morning, I thought of you, of your House, of your Table, of your Friends, etc. At this hour, I said, they are all at dinner, M. le Roy, M. Hennin, Abbés de la Roche & Morellet, M. Cabbanis, perhaps one of the little Stars. Madame is serving the whole Company, with as much Ease as Pleasure. But, alas, I was not there, to share in the gay conversation marked by good Sense, Wit, & Friendship, which season all her Meals.

You will be Pleased to Know that I am here in good Health and happy in the Bosom of my Family. But I failed to find the Rest I had hoped for; I have been asked to become Governor, & I have had the weakness to agree; so there I am busier than ever. — If I can do some good for my People, that will console me. Otherwise, I would wish that I had accepted your friendly Invitation to spend the rest of my days at your home.

Good-by, my good Friend, love me always, as I love you. Embrace for me all my Friends of your Circle, and always remember that I am bound to you with Feelings of greatest affection.

In this chatty letter to Jane Mecom, Franklin not only continued to demonstrate the affection he felt for his favorite sister, but also provided a good glimpse of himself, late in 1786. "That Soap" was the soap Franklin's father used to make, according to his private formula, which the family had preserved.

Philada, Sept. 21, 1786.

My dear Sister:

I received your kind Letter of the 25th past, by our Cousin Williams, who, besides, informs me of your Welfare, which gives me great Pleasure.

Your Grandson having finished all the Business I had to employ him in, set out for Boston a few Days before Cousin Williams arrived. I suppose he may be with you before this time.

I had begun to build two good Houses next the Street, instead of three old Ones which I pull'd down, but my Neighbour disputing my Bounds, I have been obliged to postpone till that Dispute is settled by Law. In the meantime, the Workmen, and Materials being ready, I have ordered an Addition to the House I live in, it being too small for our growing Family. There are a good many Hands employ'd, and I hope to see it cover'd in before Winter. I propose to have in it a long Room for my Library and Instruments, with two good Bedchambers and two Garrets. The Library is to be even with the Floor of my best old Chamber; and the Story under it will for the present be employ'd only to hold Wood, but may be made into Rooms hereafter. This Addition is on the Side next the River. I hardly know how to justify building a library at an Age that will so soon oblige me to quit it; but we are apt to forget that we are grown old, and Building is an Amusement.

I think you will do well to instruct your Grandson in the Art of making that Soap. It may be of use to him, and 'tis pity it should be lost.

Some knowing Ones here in Matters of Weather predict a hard Winter. Permit me to have the Pleasure of helping to keep you warm. Lay in a good Stock of Firewood, and draw upon me for the Amount. Your Bill shall be paid upon Sight by your affectionate Brother,

B FRANKLIN

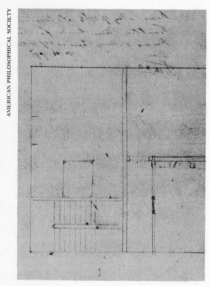

*Franklin's sketch of the second floor of his house in Philadelphia, with his double bed drawn in*

Although Franklin continued to assure his friends in Europe that all was well in the United States, he reacted like most Americans to Shays' Rebellion, the revolt of a group of destitute farmers in western Massachusetts. His old friend James Bowdoin was Governor of Massachusetts, and this sharpened Franklin's hostility to the violence. In this letter to Bowdoin, he stated his sentiments clearly. The proclamation offered a reward of 150 pounds for the capture of the four ringleaders.

Philada. March 6, 1787

I received the Letter you did me the honour lately to write me respecting the Proclamation for apprehending several Promoters of the Rebellion in your State. The

*James Bowdoin*

Proclamation was immediately printed in our Newspapers; and the Matter being laid before the Council and Assembly, it was thought fit to make an Addition to the Rewards your Government had offered, which will be done, tho' the usual Forms of Proceeding have occasioned some Delay. I congratulate your Excellency most cordially on the happy Success attending the wise and vigorous Measures taken for the Suppression of that dangerous Insurrection, and I pray most heartily for the future Tranquility of the State which you so worthily and happily govern. Its Constitution is I think one of the best in the Union, perhaps I might say in the World. And I persuade my self that the good Sense and sound Understanding predominant among the great Majority of your People, will always secure it from the mad Attempts to overthrow it, which can only proceed chiefly from the Wickedness, or from the Ignorance of a few who while they enjoy it are insensible of its Excellence.

Shays' Rebellion played a part, perhaps exaggerated by some historians, in awakening Americans to the defects of their Federal Government. The decision to reform it soon gathered momentum, and the Constitutional Convention met in Philadelphia on May 14, 1787. Franklin was an inevitable choice as one of Pennsylvania's delegates. Recognizing the crucial importance of the occasion, Franklin attended the Convention almost daily. It was his last outpouring of energy, a final expression of commitment to the American nation he had done so much to create. During the often bitter debates, he played his favorite role of conciliator and compromiser. Many of the compromises were achieved by very thin margins, and when the document was ready for a final vote, there was strong concern among many of the delegates that a substantial minority of those who had lost the arguments would vote against the final document. This would almost certainly guarantee its rejection by the states. The leaders of the Convention turned to Franklin and asked him to make a final plea for unanimity. He responded with this famous speech—which because of his growing infirmity he had to ask James Wilson to read for him—on the final day of the Convention. He next agreed to make a motion—actually drafted by the unpopular Gouverneur Morris—recommending members to sign as witnesses of the "unanimous consent of the states."

[September 17, 1787]

Mr. President,

I confess, that I do not entirely approve of this Constitution at present; but, Sir, I am not sure I shall never approve it; for, having lived long, I have experienced many

*A land grant and a commission appointing justices of the peace, both signed by Franklin in 1787 as the President of Pennsylvania's Supreme Executive Council, an office equivalent to Governor*

instances of being obliged, by better information or fuller consideration, to change my opinions even on important subjects, which I once thought right, but found to be otherwise. It is therefore that, the older I grow, the more apt I am to doubt my own judgment of others. Most men, indeed, as well as most sects in religion, think themselves in possession of all truth, and that wherever others differ from them, it is so far error. Steele, a Protestant, in a dedication, tells the Pope, that the only difference between our two churches in their opinions of the certainty of their doctrine, is, the Romish Church is *infallible,* and the Church of England is *never in the wrong.* But, though many private Persons think almost as highly of their own infallibility as that of their Sect, few express it so naturally as a certain French Lady, who, in a little dispute with her sister, said, "But I meet with nobody but myself that is *always* in the right." *"Je ne trouve que moi qui aie toujours raison."*

In these sentiments, Sir, I agree to this Constitution, with all its faults,—if they are such; because I think a general Government necessary for us, and there is no *form* of government but what may be a blessing to the people, if well administered; and I believe, farther, that this is likely to be well administered for a course of years, and can only end in despotism, as other forms have done before it, when the people shall become so corrupted as to need despotic government, being incapable of any other. I doubt, too, whether any other Convention we can obtain, may be able to make a better constitution; for, when you assemble a number of men, to have the advantage of their joint wisdom, you inevitably assemble with those men all their prejudices, their passions, their errors of opinion, their local interest, and their selfish views. From such an assembly can a *perfect* production be expected? It therefore astonishes me, Sir, to find this system approaching so near to perfection as it does; and I think it will astonish our enemies, who are waiting with confidence to hear, that our councils are confounded like those of the builders of Babel, and that our States are on the point of separation, only to meet hereafter for the purpose of cutting one another's throats. Thus I consent, Sir, to this Constitution, because I expect no better, and because I am not sure that it is not the best. The opinions I have had of its *errors* I sacrifice to the public good. I have never whispered a syllable of them abroad. Within these walls they were born, and here they shall die. If every one of us, in returning to our Constituents, were to report the objections he has had to it, and endeavour to gain Partisans in support of them, we might prevent its being generally received, and thereby lose all the salutary effects and great advantages resulting naturally in our favour among foreign nations, as well as among ourselves, from our real or apparent unanimity. Much of the strength and efficiency of any government, in procuring and securing happiness to the people, depends on *opinion,* on the general opinion of the goodness of that government, as well as of the wisdom and integrity of its governors. I hope, therefore, for our own sakes, as a part of the people, and for the sake of our posterity, that we shall act heartily and unanimously in recommending this Constitution, wherever our Influence may extend, and turn our future thoughts and endeavours to the means of having it *well administered.*

On the whole, Sir, I cannot help expressing a wish, that every member of the Convention who may still have objections to it, would with me on this occasion doubt a little of his own infallibility, and, to make *manifest* our *unanimity,* put his name to this Instrument.

In another letter to his sister Jane, written three days after the Convention adjourned, Franklin discussed the conclave, and then turned to an interesting disquisition on war and its alternatives.

Philadelphia, Sept. 20, 1787.

INDEPENDENCE NATIONAL HISTORICAL PARK

*View of the public buildings in Philadelphia during Franklin's time*

Dear Sister,

I received your kind Letter of the 16th past, which gave me the great Pleasure of learning that you were well. I thought I had before acknowledged the Receipt of yours per Colonel Sergeant.

The Convention finish'd the 17th Instant. I attended the Business of it 5 Hours in every Day from the Beginning, which is something more than four Months. You may judge from thence, that my Health continues; some tell me I look better, and they suppose the daily Exercise of going and returning from the Statehouse has done me good. You will see the Constitution we have propos'd in the Papers. The Forming of it so as to accommodate all the different Interests and Views was a difficult

Task; and perhaps, after all, it may not be received with the same Unanimity in the different States, that the Convention have given the Example of in delivering it out for their Consideration. We have, however, done our best, and it must take its chance.

I agree with you perfectly in your disapprobation of war. Abstracted from the inhumanity of it, I think it wrong in point of human prudence; for, whatever advantage one nation would obtain from another, whether it be part of their territory, the liberty of commerce with them, free passage on their rivers, &c. &c., it would be much cheaper to purchase such advantage with ready money than to pay the expense of acquiring it by war. An army is a devouring monster, and, when you have raised it, you have, in order to subsist it, not only the fair charges of pay, clothing, provisions, army, and ammunition, with numberless other contingent and just charges to answer and satisfy, but you have all the additional knavish charges of the numerous tribe of contractors to defray, with those of every other dealer who furnishes the articles wanted for your army, and takes advantage of that want to demand exorbitant prices. It seems to me, that, if statesmen had a little more arithmetic, or were more accustomed to calculation, wars would be much less frequent. I am confident, that Canada might have been purchased from France for a tenth part of the money England spent in the conquest of it. And if, instead of fighting with us for the power of taxing us, she had kept us in good humour by allowing us to dispose of our own money, and now and then giving us a little of hers, by way of donation to colleges, or hospitals, or for cutting canals, or fortifying ports, she might have easily drawn from us much more by our occasional voluntary grants and contributions, than ever she could by taxes. Sensible people will give a bucket or two of water to a dry pump, that they may afterwards, get from it all they have occasion for. Her ministry were deficient in that little point of common sense. And so they spent one hundred millions of her money, and after all lost what they contended for.

I lament the loss your town has suffered this year by fire. I sometimes think men do not act like reasonable creatures when they build for themselves combustible dwellings, in which they are every day obliged to use

*In this detail of a 1787 cartoon, the Pennsylvania Constitution is symbolically pictured as a rocky citadel whose defenders brandish a banner inscribed with the words "Franklin & Liberty."*

fire. In my new buildings, I have taken a few precautions, not generally used; to wit, none of the wooden work of one room communicates with the wooden work of any other room; and all the floors, and even the steps of the stairs, are plastered close to the boards, besides the plastering on the laths under the joists. There are also trap-doors to go out upon the roofs, that one may go out and wet the shingles in case of a neighbouring fire. But, indeed, I think the staircases should be stone, and the floors tiled as in Paris, and the roofs either tiled or slated....

I sent you lately a Barrel of Flour, and I blame myself for not sooner desiring you to lay in your Winter's Wood, and drawing upon me for it as last Year. But I have been so busy. To avoid such Neglect in Future, I now make the Direction general, that you draw on me every Year for the same purpose.

Adieu, my dear Sister, and believe me ever your affectionate brother,

B FRANKLIN

Franklin accepted a third one-year term as President of Pennsylvania. "This universal and unbounded confidence of a whole people flatters my vanity much more than a peerage could do," he told his sister Jane. At the same time, he gave much of his dwindling strength and energy to another presidency—that of the Pennsylvania Society for Promoting the Abolition of Slavery and the Relief of Free Negroes. In this fascinating letter, Franklin neatly needled the Governor of Rhode Island for the part his fellow citizens played in the continuation of the slave trade. Similar letters went to the governors of other northern states.

Philda Jany 12th, 1788

The Pennsylvania Society for promoting the abolition of Slavery, and the relief of free negroes unlawfully held in bondage have taken the liberty to request your Excellencys acceptance of a few Copies of their Constitution, and of the Laws of Pennsylvania which relate to one of the objects of their Institution, also of a Copy of Thomas Clarksons excellent essay upon the Commerce and Slavery of the Africans.

The Society have heard with great distress that a considerable part of the Slaves who have been sold in the Southern States since the establishment of the Peace have been imported in vessels fitted out in the State over which your Excellency presides. From your Excellencys Station they hope your influence will be exerted hereafter to prevent a practice which is so evidently repugnant to the political principles and forms of Government lately adopted by the Citizens of the United States, and which cannot fail of delaying the enjoyment of the blessings of peace and liberty by drawing down the displeasure of the great and impartial ruler of the Universe upon our Country.

Numerous friends urged Franklin to finish his *Autobiography.* He had added a few pages while he was in France. One of the most importunate pleaders was his Passy neighbor, Louis-Guillaume Le Veillard. In this friendly letter, Franklin responded to him, and mentioned, among other things, the heartening progress of the Constitution.

Philadelphia, June 8, 1788.

I received a few days ago your kind letter of the 3d of January. The *arrêt* in favour of the *non-catholiques* gives pleasure here, not only from its present advantages, but as it is a good step towards general toleration, and to the abolishing in time all party spirit among Christians, and the mischiefs that have so long attended it. Thank God, the world is growing wiser and wiser; and as by degrees men are convinced of the folly of wars for religion, for dominion, or for commerce, they will be happier and happier.

Eight States have now agreed to the proposed new constitution; there remain five who have not yet discussed it; their appointed times of meeting not being yet arrived. Two are to meet this month, the rest later. One more agreeing, it will be carried into execution. Probably some will not agree at present, but time may bring them in; so that we have little doubt of it becoming general, perhaps with some corrections. As to your friend's taking a share in the management of it, his age and infirmities render him unfit for the business, as the business would be for him. After the expiration of his presidentship, which will now be in a few months, he is *determined* to engage no more in public affairs, even if required; but his countrymen will be too reasonable to require it. You are not so considerate; you are a hard taskmaster. You insist on his writing *his life,* already a long work, and at the same time would have him continually employed in augmenting the subject, while the time shortens in which the work is to be executed. Gen-

*A slave cameo Wedgwood sent to Franklin when he was the President of the Pennsylvania Abolition Society*

eral Washington is the man that all our eyes are fixed on for *President,* and what little influence I may have, is devoted to him.

Unfortunately, Franklin's health broke down almost completely not long after he wrote the following letter. The bladder stone was giving him so much pain that he had had to take opium, which made it difficult for him to write. Sensing that death was near, he began to write farewells to close friends. One of the most tender letters went to Catherine Ray Greene.

Philadelphia, March 2, 1789.

Dear Friend,

Having now done with public affairs, which have hitherto taken up so much of my time, I shall endeavour to enjoy, during the small remainder of life that is left to me, some of the pleasures of conversing with my old friends by writing, since their distance prevents my hope of seeing them again.

I received one of the bags of sweet corn you were so good as to send me a long time since, but the other never came to hand. Even the letter mentioning it, though dated December 10th, 1787, has been above a year on its way; for I received it but about two weeks since from Baltimore in Maryland. The corn I did receive was excellent, and gave me great pleasure. Accept my hearty thanks.

I am, as you suppose in the abovementioned old letter, much pleased to hear, that my young friend Ray is "smart in the farming way," and makes such substantial fences. I think agriculture the most honourable of all employments, being the most independent. The farmer has no need of popular favour, nor the favour of the great; the success of his crops depending only on the blessing of God upon his honest industry. I congratulate your good spouse, that he, as well as myself, is now free from public cares, and that he can bend his whole attention to his farming, which will afford him both profit and pleasure; a business which nobody knows better how to manage with advantage.

I am too old to follow printing again myself, but, loving the business, I have brought up my grandson Benjamin to it, and have built and furnished a printing-house for him, which he now manages under my eye. I have great pleasure in the rest of my grandchildren, who are now in number eight, and all promising, the youngest only six months old, but shows signs of great good nature. My friends here are numerous, and I enjoy as much of their conversation as I can reasonably wish; and I have as much health and cheerfulness, as can well be expected at my age, now eighty-three. Hitherto this long life has been tolerably happy; so that, if I were allowed to live it over again, I should make no objection, only wishing for leave to do, what authors do in a second edition of their works, correct some of my *errata.* Among the felicities of my life I reckon your friendship, which I shall remember with pleasure as long as that life lasts, being ever, my dear friend yours most affectionately,

B FRANKLIN

In September, Franklin wrote sadly to Le Veillard that he had abandoned all hope of finishing his *Autobiography.* Opium had, he said, "taken away my Appetite and so impeded my Digestion that I am become totally emaciated, and little remains of me but a Skeleton covered with a Skin." A few days later, he wrote the following letter of farewell to George Washington, who had been inaugurated first President of the United States the previous April 30.

Philada, Sept. 16, 1789.

My Malady renders my Sitting up to write rather painful to me; but I cannot let my Son-in-law Mr. Bache part for New York, without congratulating you by him on the Recovery of your Health, so precious to us all, and on the growing Strength of our New Government under your Administration. For my own personal Ease, I should have died two Years ago; but, tho' those Years have been spent in excruciating Pain, I am pleas'd that I have lived with them, since they have brought me to see our present Situation. I am now finishing my 84th [year], and probably with it my Career in this Life; but in whatever State of Existence I am plac'd hereafter, if I retain any Memory of what has pass'd here, I shall with it retain the Esteem, Respect, and Affection, with which I have long been, my dear Friend, yours most sincerely,

B FRANKLIN

In France, another revolution was brewing. Franklin followed it as well as he could, but he was more concerned about the fate of his individual friends than anything else. In this letter to another Passy neighbor, Jean Baptiste Le Roy, he reflected this concern, and passed on the mournful news of his decline.

*French print showing the "terrible night" of October 5, 1789, when angry women marched on the royal palace at Versailles*

Philadelphia, November 13, 1789

It is now more than a year, since I have heard from my dear friend Le Roy. What can be the reason? Are you still living? Or have the mob of Paris mistaken the head of a monopolizer of knowledge, for a monopolizer of corn, and paraded it about the streets upon a pole.

Great part of the news we have had from Paris, for near a year past, has been very afflicting. I sincerely wish and pray it may all end well and happy, both for the King and the nation. The voice of *Philosophy* I apprehend can hardly be heard among those tumults. If any thing material in that way had occurred, I am persuaded you would have acquainted me with it. However, pray let me hear from you a little oftener; for, though the distance is great, and the means of conveying letters not very regular, a year's silence between friends must needs give uneasiness.

Our new Constitution is now established, and has an appearance that promises permanency; but in this world nothing can be said to be certain, except death and taxes.

My health continues much as it has been for some time, except that I grow thinner and weaker, so that I cannot expect to hold out much longer.

My respects to your good brother, and to our friends of the Academy, which always has my best wishes for its prosperity and glory. Adieu, my dear friend, and believe me ever yours most affectionately,

B FRANKLIN

In this letter to David Hartley, Franklin commented on the French Revolution and tossed off one of his most memorable lines.

Philada, Decr 4, 1789.

I received your Favor of August last. Your kind Condolences on the painful State of my Health are very obliging. I am thankful to God, however, that, among the numerous Ills human Life is subject to, one only of any Importance is fallen to my Lot; and that so late as almost to insure that it can be but of short Duration.

The Convulsions in France are attended with some disagreable Circumstances; but if by the Struggle she obtains and secures for the Nation its future Liberty, and a good Constitution, a few Years' Enjoyment of those Blessings will amply repair all the Damages their Acquisition may have occasioned. God grant, that not only the Love of Liberty, but a thorough Knowledge of the Rights of Man, may pervade all the Nations of the Earth, so that a Philosopher may set his Foot anywhere on its Surface, and say, "This is my Country."

Ezra Stiles, the president of Yale and an old friend, wrote to the philosopher, asking for a confidential statement of his religious beliefs. Franklin's reply contained an interesting combination of candor and caution.

Philada, March 9, 1790.

Reverend and dear Sir,

You desire to know something of my Religion. It is the first time I have been questioned upon it. But I cannot take your Curiosity amiss, and shall endeavour in a few Words to gratify it. Here is my Creed. I believe in one God, Creator of the Universe. That he governs it by his Providence. That he ought to be worshipped. That the most acceptable Service we render to him is doing good to his other Children. That the soul of Man is immortal, and will be treated with Justice in another Life respecting its Conduct in this. These I take to be the fundamental Principles of all sound Religion, and I regard them as you do in whatever Sect I meet with them.

As to Jesus of Nazareth, my Opinion of whom you particularly desire, I think the System of Morals and his Religion, as he left them to us, the best the World ever saw or is likely to see; but I apprehend it has received various corrupting Changes, and I have, with most of the present Dissenters in England, some Doubts as to his Divinity; tho' it is a question I do not dogmatize upon, having never studied it, and think it needless to busy myself with it now, when I expect soon an Opportunity of knowing the Truth with less Trouble. I see no harm, however, in its being believed, if that Belief has the good Consequence, as probably it has, of making his Doctrines more respected and better observed; especially as I do not perceive, that the Supreme takes it amiss, by distinguishing the Unbelievers in his Government of the World with any peculiar Marks of his Displeasure.

I shall only add, respecting myself, that, having experienced the Goodness of that Being in conducting me prosperously thro' a long life, I have no doubt of its Continuance in the next, though without the smallest Conceit of meriting such Goodness. My Sentiments on this Head you will see in the Copy of an old Letter enclosed, which I wrote in answer to one from a zealous Religionist, whom I had relieved in a paralytic case by electricity, and who, being afraid I should grow proud upon it, sent me his serious though rather impertinent Caution. I send you also the Copy of another Letter, which will shew something of my Disposition relating to Religion. With great and sincere Esteem and Affection, I am, Your obliged old Friend and most obedient humble Servant

B FRANKLIN

P.S. Had not your College some Present of Books from the King of France? Please to let me know, if you had an Expectation given you of more, and the Nature of that Expectation? I have a Reason for the Enquiry.

I confide, that you will not expose me to Criticism and censure by publishing any part of this Communication to you. I have ever let others enjoy their religious Sentiments, without reflecting on them for those that appeared to me unsupportable and even absurd. All Sects here, and we have a great Variety, have experienced my good will in assisting them with Subscriptions for building their new Places of Worship; and, as I have never opposed any of their Doctrines, I hope to go out of the World in Peace with them all.

A last letter went to Jane Mecom.

Philadelphia, 24 March, 1790

My dear Sister,

I received your kind letter by your ever good neighbor, Captain Rich. The information it contained, that you continue well, gave me, as usual, great pleasure. As to myself, I have been quite free from pain for near three weeks past, and therefore not being obliged to take any laudanum, my appetite has returned, and I have recovered some part of my strength. Thus I continue to live on, while all the friends of my youth have left me, and gone to join the majority. I have, however, the pleasure of continued friendship and conversation

*Ezra Stiles by Nathaniel Smibert*

405

B. J. FRANKLIN
EST
MORT

*French print announcing Franklin's
death to the country he loved*

with their children and grandchildren. I do not repine at my malady, though a severe one, when I consider how well I am provided with every convenience to palliate it, and to make me comfortable under it; and how many more horrible evils that human body is subject to; and what a long life of health I have been blessed with, free from them all.

You have done well not to send me any more fish at present. These continue good, and give me pleasure.

Do you know anything of our sister Scott's daughter; whether she is still living, and where? This family join in love to you and yours, and to cousins Williams, with your affectionate brother,

B. Franklin

P.S.   It is early in the morning, and I write in bed. The awkward position has occasioned the crooked lines.

Finally, there was one more joust with the British Government. The new Secretary of State, Thomas Jefferson, asked Franklin to help him settle the Maine boundary.

Philadelphia, April 8, 1790.

I received your letter of the 31st of last past, relating to encroachments made on the eastern limits of the United States by settlers under the British Government, pretending that it is the *western,* and not the *eastern* river of the Bay of Passamaquoddy which was designated by the name of St. Croix in the treaty of peace with that nation; and requesting of me to communicate any facts which my memory or papers may enable me to recollect, and which may indicate the true river, which the commissioners on both sides had in their view, to establish as the boundary between the two nations.

Your letter found me under a severe fit of my malady, which prevented my answering it sooner, or attending, indeed, to any kind of business. I now can assure you that I am perfectly clear in the remembrance that the map we used in tracing the boundary, was brought to the treaty by the commissioners from England, and that it was the same that was published by Mitchell above twenty years before. Having a copy of that map by me in loose sheets, I send you that sheet which contains the Bay of Passamaquoddy, where you will see that part of the boundary traced. I remember, too, that in that part of the boundary we relied much on the opinion of Mr. Adams, who had been concerned in some former disputes concerning those territories. I think, therefore, that you may obtain still further light from him.

That the map we used was Mitchell's map, Congress were acquainted at the time by a letter to their Secretary for Foreign Affairs, which I suppose may be found upon their files.

A few days later Franklin suffered an attack of pleurisy. After several days of agonizing pain, he seemed, momentarily, to recover. He rose from his bed. But he explained to his daughter Sally that he simply wanted the bed made, so that he might "die in a decent manner." Sally replied that she was praying that he would get well and live many more years. "I hope not," Franklin replied. A few hours later, an abscess in his lungs burst. He died at eleven o'clock at night on April 17, 1790. In Paris, the French Chamber of Deputies, at the suggestion of the Comte de Mirabeau, seconded by Lafayette and La Rochefoucauld, went into mourning for three days. Eulogies poured from French and American presses. Perhaps the most touching comment was made by Jane Mecom, when she heard the sad news. To her niece Sally Franklin Bache, she wrote, "He while living was to me every enjoyment. Whatever other pleasures were, as they mostly took their rise from him, they passed like little streams from a beautiful fountain. They remind me of two lines of a song Mr. Peters used to sing at your house: 'But now they are withered and waned all away.'"

*French drawing inscribed "Au Génie de Franklin," with a motto composed by Turgot: "Eripuit caelo fulmen, sceptrumque tyrannis." (He snatched the lightning from heaven, and the scepter from tyrants.)*

# Selected Bibliography

Aldridge, Alfred O. *Benjamin Franklin, Philosopher and Man.* Philadelphia: Lippincott, 1965.

———. *Franklin and his French Contemporaries,* New York: New York University Press, 1957.

Bowen, Catherine D. *Miracle at Philadelphia: The Story of the Constitutional Convention, May to September 1787,* Boston: Atlantic Monthly Press, Little Brown, 1966.

Bridenbaugh, Carl and Bridenbaugh, Jessica B. *Rebels and Gentlemen: Philadelphia in the Age of Franklin.* New York: Oxford University Press, 1965.

Burnett, Edmund C. *The Continental Congress.* New York: Norton, 1964.

Cohen, I. Bernard, *Benjamin Franklin: His Contribution to the American Tradition.* Indianapolis: Bobbs-Merrill, 1953.

Conner, Paul W. *Poor Richard's Politicks: Benjamin Franklin and His New American Order.* New York: Oxford University Press, 1965.

Fleming, Thomas. *The Man who Dared the Lightning: A New Look at Benjamin Franklin.* New York: Morrow, 1971.

Franklin, Benjamin. *The Autobiography of Benjamin Franklin.* Edited by Leonard W. Labaree *et al.* New Haven: Yale University Press, 1964.

———. *Benjamin Franklin's Autobiographical Writings.* Edited by Carl Van Doren. New York: Viking, 1945.

———. *The Complete Works of Benjamin Franklin.* Edited by John Bigelow, 10 vols. New York: Putnam, 1887-89.

———. *The Papers of Benjamin Franklin.* Vols. 1-14, Edited by Leonard W. Labaree *et al.* Vol. 15 —, Edited by William B. Willcox *et al.* New Haven: Yale University Press, 1959-

———. *The Works of Benjamin Franklin.* Edited by Jared Sparks. 10 vols. Boston: Hilliard, Gray: 1836-40.

———. *The Writings of Benjamin Franklin.* Edited by Albert H. Smyth. 10 vols. New York: Macmillan, 1905-7.

Granger, Bruce I. *Benjamin Franklin, an American Man of Letters.* Ithaca: Cornell University Press, 1964.

Hall, Max. *Benjamin Franklin & Polly Baker: The History of a Literary Deception.* Chapel Hill: University of North Carolina Press, 1960.

Hanna, William S. *Benjamin Franklin and Pennsylvania Politics,* Stanford: Stanford University Press, 1964.

Hays, I. Minis, ed. *Calendar of the Papers of Benjamin Franklin in the Library of the American Philosophical Society,* 5 vols. Philadelphia: American Philosophical Society, 1908.

Lopez, Claude-Anne. *Mon Cher Papa: Franklin and the Ladies of Paris.* New Haven: Yale University Press, 1966.

Morris, Richard B. *The Peacemakers: The Great Powers and American Independence.* New York: Harper & Row, 1965.

Nolan, James Bennett, *Benjamin Franklin in Scotland and Ireland: 1759 and 1771.* Philadelphia: University of Pennsylvania Press, 1956.

———. *General Benjamin Franklin: The Military Career of a Philosopher.* Philadelphia: University of Pennsylvania Press, 1956.

Rossiter, Clinton, *1787: The Grand Convention.* New York: Macmillan, 1966.

Roelker, William G., ed. *Benjamin Franklin and Catharine Ray Greene: Their Correspondence 1755-1790.* Philadelphia: American Philosophical Society, 1949.

Stourzh, Gerald. *Benjamin Franklin and American Foreign Policy.* Chicago: University of Chicago Press, 1954.

Van Doren, Carl, *Benjamin Franklin.* New York: Viking, 1938.

Van Doren, Carl, ed. *Letters and Papers of Benjamin Franklin and Richard Jackson 1753 — 1785,* Philadelphia: American Philosophical Society, 1947.

Van Doren, Carl, ed. *The Letters of Benjamin Franklin and Jane Mecom.* Princeton: Princeton University Press, 1950.

Wright, Esmond, ed. *Benjamin Franklin: A Profile.* New York: Hill & Wang. 1970.

# Acknowledgments

The Editors are particularly grateful to the American Philosophical Society in Philadelphia for permission to reprint documents in its possession, the greatest collection of Benjamin Franklin papers in existence. The selections from the *Autobiography* have been taken from *The Autobiography of Benjamin Franklin*, edited by Leonard W. Labaree, *et al.* (New Haven and London: Yale University Press, 1964); the original manuscript of the *Autobiography* is at the Henry E. Huntington Library and Art Gallery in San Marino, California. In addition the Editors would like to thank the following individuals and institutions for permission to reprint documents in their possession:

Adams Manuscript Trust, Massachusetts Historical Society, page 306 (top)
Archives des Affaires Etrangères, Paris, pages 296 (top) and 350 (center)
Archivo Historico Nacional, Madrid, pages 292-93
Blumhaven Library and Gallery, Philadelphia, page 304 (center)
Mugar Library, Boston University, pages 351-52
Bristol Historical Society, Rhode Island, pages 267-68
Cornell University Library, Ithaca, page 234 (top)
Mr. Albert F. Greenfield, Philadelphia, page 222 (top)
Haverford College Library, Haverford, Penna., page 277 (bottom)
Historical Society of Pennsylvania, pages 278-79
David C. Holland, Esq., London, pages 285-86 and 294 (top)
Indiana University Library, Bloomington, pages 257-58
Mrs. Martin H. Kendig, Chicago, pages 339-40
Manuscript Division, Library of Congress, Washington, D.C., pages 282-83, 298-99, 306-7, 307-8, 309 (top), 316 (top), 316-17, 343-45, 394-95
Mrs. Arthur Loeb, Philadelphia, page 264 (top)
Mr. Albert E. Lownes, Providence, pages 339-40
Manuscripts and History Division, New York State Library, Albany, page 221
Princeton University Library, Princeton, page 348 (top)
Sheffield Central Library, England, pages 258-59 and 264 (bottom)
The Collection of Edward Wanton Smith, Philadelphia, page 359 (bottom)
William L. Clements Library, University of Michigan, Ann Arbor, page 363
Benjamin Franklin Collection, Sterling Memorial Library, Yale University, New Haven, pages 259-60, 367 (center), 376-78, 387-88, and 388-89

The Editors also wish to express their appreciation to the many institutions and individuals who made available their pictorial materials for use in this volume. In particular the Editors are grateful to:

The American Philosophical Society, Philadelphia—Whitfield J. Bell, Jr., Librarian
*The Papers of Benjamin Franklin*, Yale University, New Haven—William B. Willcox, Editor; Dorothy W. Bridgwater, Mary L. Hart, Claude A. Lopez, G.B. Warden, Assistant Editors
Benjamin Franklin Collection, Sterling Memorial Library, Yale University (credited as Yale University Library)
Bibliothèque Nationale, Paris
British Museum, London
Historical Society of Pennsylvania, Philadelphia
Henry E. Huntington Library, San Marino, California
Library of Congress, Washington, D.C.
Library Company of Philadelphia
Musée de Blerancourt, France
National Portrait Gallery, London
New York Public Library
Lewis Walpole Library, Farmington, Conn.

Finally, the Editors thank Susan Storer in New York and Russell Ash, John Harris, Peter Stockham, and Ben Weinreb in London for advice and assistance in obtaining pictorial material; Sylvia J. Abrams in Washington for copyediting and proofreading; and Mary-Jo Kline in New York for compiling the chronology and bibliography.

# Index

416

of the Sale of those

the general Taste i

worth Market. ——

worth your Accep

of that Mr Chandler

him either at New

desire a little of you

Respects to Mrs John

with the greatest